Documenting America
A Reader in United States History

Volume One

Colonial Times to 1877

Edited by
Leonard Pitt
California State University
Northridge, California

KENDALL/HUNT PUBLISHING COMPANY
2460 Kerper Boulevard P.O. Box 539 Dubuque, Iowa 52004-0539

To Dale, again

Library of Congress Catalog Card Number: 89–80478

ISBN 0–8403–5245–X

Printed in the United States of America
10 9 8 7 6 5 4 3 2 1

Contents

Chapter Four: Race

Chapter Five: Nationality and Religion

Chapter Eight: Environment

Preface

The historian Laurens Van Der Post faults "the popular habit of lifting history out of its proper context and bending it to the values of another age and day. In this way history is never allowed to be itself."

One way to let history be itself is to focus on original sources. This book, *Documenting America*, is designed to do just that—to help students think about the past as professional historians do—by analyzing evidence and forming their own judgments about what the evidence means. The documents presented here have a particular framework in that they grow out of important controversies that invite the reader to think about and pass judgment on the issues. Using them becomes a form of detective work, rather than a process of memorization.

Many students regard history as a vast mountain of facts waiting to be memorized (and repeated on examinations). But, to professionals, history is a process of asking questions about past events and sifting the evidence left over from those events in order to create coherent mental pictures of what happened. Many different interpretations are possible. In this sense, virtually anyone can be an historian.

There is a bonus in mastering this process. Most of the methods that historians employ to understand past events can also be used to make sense of the present.

The documents in this collection come from a variety of sources: public speeches, newspaper reports, essays, books, letters, song lyrics, congressional reports, journals, diaries, autobiographies, legal depositions, law codes, court decisions, etc. They contain the words of leaders, but also of ordinary people. In other words, they consist of the many types of sources that historians draw upon when reconstructing the past.

Of course in order to interpret documents, it is necessary to have as much background information as possible. To explain the meaning of documents one has to understand their context. *Documenting America* provides enough context in the headnotes to at least begin the analysis. A basic text book will contain valuable additional background and class lectures and discussions will bring to light other data. Additional information can be found in the *Dictionary of American Biography* and in the *Dictionary of American History*, and in books and articles available in many libraries.

Asking questions, as I have already suggested, is at the heart of the historical process. In the headnotes I have listed some questions you might want to explore. Other questions will occur to you that are at least as useful for understanding what was going on.

I have grouped related documents together to highlight recurrent patterns of change. The groupings themselves are important. *Documenting America* makes no attempt to cover all major events, as a basic textbook might. Instead, it provides sets of documents organized by major themes of American history. These themes are eight in number: wealth; power; war; race; nationality and religion; women and the family; community; and environment. Presenting the documents topically helps the reader to understand particular subjects in greater depth and to make more sense of them than if a simple chronological order were followed. Yet the time when things happened and the sequence of events are important, often vital, to historical interpretation, and the students should check the dates of various articles—and even create a chronological chart—to help reveal hidden relationships.

I hope you will enjoy the kind of detective work this book entails. To master the technique of interpretation may take time and patience, but the reactions of my own students suggest that students using this book will experience the satisfaction of making their own interpretations of history. You will be intrigued to discover that many people may read a document and come to different interpretations. And you will be amazed that your interpretation makes as much sense as anyone else's. You will realize also that an imaginative interpretation differs from wild guesswork.

Incidentally, this book has a companion volume that deals with the earlier part of our history. It is entitled *Documenting America: A Reader in United States History, Volume 2, from 1865 to the Present,* and is issued by the same publisher.

As editor, I am very much interested in how this book will be used. I expect to change it as I receive information from readers. Please let me know how it works for you.

I wish to give grateful acknowledgement to two people who helped me greatly in the preparation of this work. My colleague, Ronald Schaffer, offered invaluable counsel in the picking of documents and the shaping of questions. My wife, Dale Pitt, gave general advice and performed extensive editorial work. Both should be exonerated, though, for any errors of fact or judgment that may appear here.

Leonard Pitt
February 1989

DRIVE THY BUSINESS, LET NOT THAT DRIVE THEE. SLOTH MAKES ALL THINGS DIFFICULT, INDUSTRY ALL EASY.
EARLY TO BED AND EARLY TO RISE; MAKES A MAN HEALTHY, WEALTHY, AND WISE.

Chapter One: Wealth

- **1.1** The Lure of Abundance
  Richard Hakluyt the Elder, 1585
- **1.2** The Rules of Mercantilism
  Navigation Act of 1660
- **1.3** The Work Force in Early Virginia
  1607, 1609, 1622
- **1.4** A Puritan Oligarchy
  John Cotton, 1636
- **1.5** Terms of Indenture
  1659, 1713
- **1.6** Poor Richard's Work Ethic
  Benjamin Franklin, 1732
- **1.7** "God's Chosen People"
  Thomas Jefferson, 1785, 1787, 1804
- **1.8** Capitalism's Apostle
  Alexander Hamilton, 1791
- **1.9** The Invention of the Cotton Gin
  Eli Whitney, 1793
- **1.10** Homesteads for Workingmen
  George Henry Evans, 1844; Volney E. Howard and Orlando B. Ficklin, 1852
- **1.11** A Middle-Class Response to Labor Riots
  The Nation, *1877*

1.1 The Lure of Abundance

Before setting out on a trip that would take him completely around the globe, Sir Walter Raleigh sought out the latest information about world geography. He went to see a young clergyman named Richard Hakluyt, who had studied all manner of travel accounts in Spanish, Italian and French. So well informed was Hakluyt that a high government official would soon ask him for a written report on the possible advantages of English colonization in the New World. The burning issue was what material wealth might be found or created there. Hakluyt's report of 1585, A Particular Discourse concerning Western Discoveries, *was read by Queen Elizabeth. He, and a younger cousin with the same name, thus became among the first important promoters of English settlement in North America. Below are listed most of Hakluyt's reasons for encouraging settlement—there were over thirty of them. The main one he overlooked was the possibility of finding gold and silver.*

Questions

What did Hakluyt list as the most important advantages of colonization? Did he forecast any disadvantages? In his projected colonization, what role would the colonies have, and what role would be reserved for the crown?

What image of the new lands was he projecting and on what information was it based? Was this an honest assessment or an exaggerated one to attract backers? How many of the objectives were eventually realized?

The glory of God by planting of religion among those infidels.

The increase of the force of the Christians.

The possibility of the enlarging of the dominions of the Queen's Most Excellent Majesty, and consequently of her honour, revenues, and of her power by this enterprise.

SOURCE: Richard Hakluyt the Elder, in Elizabeth Taylor, ed., *Original Writings of the Two Richard Hakluyts* (1585), II, 327–38.

An ample vent in time to come of the woollen cloths of England, especially those of the coarsest sorts, to the maintenance of our poor, that else starve or become burdensome to the realm; and vent also of sundry our commodities upon the tract of that firm land, and possibly in other regions from the northern side of that main. . . .

By return thence, this realm shall receive . . . most or all the commodities that we receive from the best parts of Europe, and we shall receive the same better cheap than now we receive them, as we may use the matter.

Receiving the same thence, the navy, the human strength of this realm, our merchants and their goods, shall not be subject to arrest of ancient enemies and doubtful friends as of late years they have been.

If our nation do not make any conquest there but only use traffic and change of commodities, yet, by means the country is not very mighty but divided into petty kingdoms, they shall not dare to offer us any great annoy but such as we may easily revenge with sufficient chastisement to the unarmed people there. . . .

The great plenty of buff hides and of many other sundry kinds of hides there now presently to be had, the trade of whale and seal fishing and of divers other fishings in the great rivers, great bays, and seas there, shall presently defray the charge in good part or in all of the first enterprise. . . .

The great broad rivers of that main that we are to enter into, so many leagues navigable or portable into the mainland, lying so long a tract with so excellent and so fertile a soil on both sides, do seem to promise all things that the life of man doth require and whatsoever men may wish that are to plant upon the same or to traffic in the same. . . .

If we find the country populous and desirous to expel us and injuriously to offend us, that seek but just and lawful traffic, then, by reason that we are lords of navigation and they not so, we are the better able to defend ourselves by reason of those great rivers and to annoy them in many places. . . .

The known abundance of fresh fish in the rivers, and the known plenty of fish on the sea-coast there, may assure us of sufficient victual in spite of the people, if we will use salt and industry.

The known plenty and variety of flesh of divers kinds of beasts at land there may seem to say to us that we may cheaply victual our navies to England for our returns. . . .

The navigating of the seas in the voyage, and of the great rivers there, will breed many mariners for service and maintain much navigation. . . .

Since great waste woods be there of oak, cedar, pine, walnuts, and sundry other sorts, many of our waste people may be employed in making of ships, hoys, busses, and boats, and in making of rosin, pitch, and tar. . . .

If mines of white or grey marble, jet, or other rich stone be found there, our idle people may be employed in the mines of the same and in preparing the same to shape, and, so shaped, they may be carried into this realm as good ballast for our ships and after serve for noble buildings. . . .

. . . Moreover, we shall not only receive many precious commodities besides from thence, but also shall in time find ample vent of the labour of our poor people at home, by sale of hats, bonnets, knives, fish-hooks, copper kettles, beads, looking-glasses, bugles, and a thousand kinds of other wrought wares that in short time may be brought in use among the people of that country, to the great relief of the multitude of our poor people and to the wonderful enriching of this realm. And in time, such league and intercourse may arise between our stapling seats there, and other parts of our Northern America, and of the islands of the same, that incredible things, and by few as yet dreamed of, may speedily follow, tending to the impeachment of our mighty enemies and to the common good of this noble government.

1.2 The Rules of Mercantilism

From the sixteenth to the eighteenth centuries, Great Britain and other colonial powers regulated their economies through a policy called mercantilism. Mercantilism meant regulating the quality and quantity of manufactured items, imposing tariffs against foreign imports, and acquiring colonies as a source for raw materials and a market for goods made in the mother country. The theory was that through these restrictions the empire would avoid foreign competition and gain wealth and prosperity. The opposite of mercantilism was laissez faire, where the government gave free reign to private enterprise, a theory that received its classic statement in Adam Smith's The Wealth of Nations, *published in 1776, the year of the American revolution.*

The basic mercantilist regulations for the English colonies were the Navigation Acts. Most comprehensive of them was the Navigation Act of 1660, excerpted below. It tightened regulations issued during the previous fifteen years, barred non-English ships from colonial trade, and enumerated colonial products that could be shipped only to England or its colonies. These restrictions won little support in the American colonies. But as they were poorly enforced, they did not interfere too much with colonial shipping and sometimes even encouraged colonial growth. For many years the colonies managed to grow despite them. After 1763, though, they were the source of much irritation and contributed to the revolutionary upheaval.

Questions

To what extent does this law express Hakluyt's projections in Document 1.1? Which goods does the law enumerate (i.e, regulate), and how? Did the colonists benefit from these regulations in any way?

What happened when these rules went unenforced for many years? Why did the colonials in the 1760s seem to resent these restrictions?

An Act for the Encouraging and Increasing of Shipping and Navigation—

For the increase of shipping and encouragement of the navigation of this nation, wherein, under the good providence and protection of God, the wealth, safety and strength of this kingdom is so much concerned; be it enacted by the King's most excellent majesty, and by the lords and commons in this present parliament assembled, and by the authority thereof, That from and after the first day of *December* one thousand six hundred

SOURCE: D. Pickering, ed., *Statutes at Large*, VII, 452 ff.

and sixty, and from thenceforward, no goods or commodities whatsoever shall be imported into or exported out of any lands, islands, plantations or territories to his Majesty belonging or in his possession, or which may hereafter belong unto or be in the possession of his Majesty, his heirs and successors, in *Asia, Africa* or *America,* in any other ship or ships, vessel or vessels whatsoever, but in such ships or vessels as do truly and without fraud belong only to the people of *England* or *Ireland,* dominion of *Wales* or town of *Berwick* upon *Tweed,* or are of the built of and belonging to any the said lands, islands, plantations or territories, as the proprietors and right owners thereof, and whereof the master and three fourths of the mariners at least are *English.* . . .

II. And be it enacted, That no alien or person not born within the allegiance of our sovereign lord the King, his heirs and successors, or naturalized, or made a free denizen, shall from and after the first day of *February,* 1661, exercise the trade or occupation of a merchant or factor in any the said places; upon pain of the forfeiture and loss of all his goods and chattels, . . . and all governors of the said lands, islands, plantations or territories . . . shall before their entrance into their government take a solemn oath, to do their utmost, that every the aforementioned clauses, and all the matters and things therein contained, shall be punctually and *bona fide* observed according to the true intent and meaning thereof; and upon complaint and proof made before his Majesty, his heirs or successors, or such as shall be by him or them thereunto authorized and appointed, that any the said governors have been willingly and wittingly negligent in doing their duty accordingly, that the said governor so offending shall be removed from his government.

III. And it is further enacted . . . , That no goods or commodities whatsoever, of the growth, production or manufacture of *Africa, Asia,* or *America,* or of any part thereof, or which are described or laid down in the usual maps or cards of those places, be imported into *England, Ireland* or *Wales,* islands of *Guernsey* and *Jersey,* or town of *Berwick* upon *Tweed,* in any other ship or ships, vessel or vessels whatsoever, but in such as do truly and without fraud belong only to the people of *England* or *Ireland,* dominion of *Wales,* or town of *Berwick* upon *Tweed* or of the lands, islands, plantations or territories in *Asia, Africa* or *America,* to his Majesty belonging, as the proprietors and right owners thereof, and whereof the master, and three fourths at least of the mariners are *English;* (2) under the penalty of the forfeiture of all such goods and commodities, and of the ship or vessel in which they were imported. . . .

IV. And it is further enacted . . . , That no goods or commodities that are of foreign growth, production or manufacture, and which are to be brought into *England, Ireland, Wales,* the islands of *Guernsey* and *Jersey,* or town of *Berwick* upon *Tweed,* in *English*-built shipping, or other shipping belonging to some of the aforesaid places, and navigated by *English* mariners, as aforesaid, shall be shipped or brought from any other place or places, country or countries, but only from those of the said growth, production or manufacture, or from those ports where the said goods and commodities can only, or are, or usually have been, first shipped for transportation, and from none other places or countries; under the penalty of the forfeiture of all such of the aforesaid goods . . . as also of the ship in which they were imported, . . .

V. And it is further enacted . . . , That any sort of ling, stock-fish, pilchard, or any other kind of dried or salted fish, usually fished for and caught by the people of *England, Ireland, Wales,* or town of *Berwick* upon *Tweed;* or any sort of cod-fish or herring, or any oil or blubber made or that shall be made of any kind of fish whatsoever, or any whale-fins or whale-bones, which shall be imported into *England, Ireland, Wales,* or town of *Berwick* upon *Tweed,* not having been caught in vessels truly and properly belonging thereunto as proprietors and right owners thereof, and the said fish cured saved and dried, and the oil and blubber aforesaid (which shall be accounted and pay as oil) not made by the people thereof, and shall be imported into *England, Ireland* or *Wales,* or town of *Berwick* upon *Tweed,* shall pay double aliens custom.

VI. And be it further enacted, . . . That from henceforth it shall not be lawful to any person or persons whatsoever, to load or cause to be loaden and carried in any bottom or bottoms, ship or ships, vessel or vessels whatsoever, whereof any stranger or strangers-born (unless such as shall be denizens or naturalized) be owners, part-owners or master, and whereof three fourths of the mariners at last shall not be *English,* any fish, victual, wares, goods, commodities or things, of what kind or nature soever the fame shall be, from one port or creek of *England, Ireland, Wales,* islands of *Guernsey* or *Jersey,* or town of *Berwick* upon *Tweed,* to another port or creek of the fame, or of any of them; under penalty . . . to forfeit all such goods shall be loaden and carried in any such ship or vessel, together with the ship or vessel, . . .

VIII. And it is further enacted . . . That no goods or commodities of the growth, production or manufacture of *Muscovy,* or to any the countries, dominions or territories to the . . . emperor of *Muscovy* or *Russia* belonging, as also that no sort of masts, timber or boards, no foreign salt, pitch, tar, rosin, hemp or flax, raisins, figs, prunes, olive-oils, no sorts of corn or grain, sugar, potashes, wines, vinegar, or spirits called *aqua-vitae,* or brandy-wine, shall from after the first day of April, 1662, be imported into *England, Ireland, Wales,* or town of *Berwick* upon *Tweed,* in any ship or ships . . . but in such as do truly and without fraud belong to the people thereof . . . and whereof the master and three fourths of the mariners at least are *English.* . . .

XVIII. And it is further enacted . . . That from and after the first day of *April,* 1661, no sugars, tobacco, cotton-wool, indicoes, ginger, fustick, or other dying wood, of the growth, production or manufacture of any *English* plantations in *America, Asia* or *Africa,* shall be shipped, carried, conveyed or transported from any of the said *English* plantations to any land . . . other than to such other *English* plantations as do belong to his Majesty. . . .

1.3 The Work Force in Early Virginia

The earliest English adventurers in North America had trouble exploiting the economic potential of the new land. At first they expected merely to skim off the wealth. They were not intending to plant colonies in the true sense of the word. Rather, they preferred setting up forts staffed by soldiers and traders who would deal with the Indians and, if necessary, rely on the mother country to supply basic necessities. This was certainly the thinking of the Virginia Company leaders in 1607. By 1609, they began correcting this policy. Gradually they converted to a new concept of establishing permanent and self-supporting "plantations" with resident farmers and artisans who would create new wealth in the old-fashioned way, by hard labor.

A perennial problem faced by the early Virginia authorities was assembling a suitable work force. They tried to determine what was the right mix of skills, how to hire people and entice them overseas for hard labor and which tools and supplies they would need to bring with them. In the documents that follow, colonial officials grapple with some of these labor problems. Included are a list of the adventurers' names in 1607, a call for new recruits in 1609, and a list of supplies in 1622.

The supply list is from a recruitment poster introducing the headright system to induce settlement. It says (the spelling has been modernized), "Whosoever transports himself, or any other at his own charge unto Virginia, shall for each person so transported before midsummer 1625 have to him and his heirs for ever fifty acres of land upon a first, and fifty acres upon a second division." It explains that "The inconveniencies that have happened to some persons which have transported themselves from England to Virginia, without provisions necessary to sustain themselves, hath greatly hindered the progress of that noble Plantation. For prevention of the like disorders hereafter . . . it is thought requisite to publish this short declaration . . . of such necessaries, as either private families or single persons shall have cause to furnish themselves with, for their better support at their first landing in Virginia."

Questions

Historians often must draw conclusions from bare lists such as these. What can you tell from these sources about the makeup of the work force? For example, what does the sex of the colonists say about the type of community they hoped to establish? How much farming will they do, how much effort will they devote to settlement activities as opposed to trading? Which goods will they produce, and which will they send for? How is the colony moving toward self-sufficiency?

List of Adventurers, 1607

The names of them that were the first planters, were these following.*

Counselors

Mr. Edward Maria Wingfield
Capt. Bartholomew Gosnoll
Capt. John Smyth
Capt. John Rat[c]liffe
Capt. John Martin
Capt. George Kendall

Gentlemen

Thomas Sands
John Robinson
Ustis Clovill
Kellam Throgmorton
Nathaniel Powell
Robert Behethland
Jeremy Alicock
Thomas Studley
Richard Crofts
Nicholas Houlgrace
Thomas Webbe
John Waler
William Tankard
Francis Snarsbrough
Edward Brookes
Richard Dixon
John Martin
George Martin
Anthony Gosnold
Thomas Wotton
Thomas Gore
Francis Midwinter

Carpenters

William Laxon
Edward Pising
Tho. Emry
Rob. Small
Anas Todkill
John Capper

Gentlemen

Mr. Robert Hunt, *Preacher*
Mr. George Percie
Anthony Gosnoll
Capt. Gabriell Archer
Robert Ford
William Bruster
Dru Pickhouse
John Brookes
James Read, *Blacksmith*
Jonas Profit, *Sailor*
Tho. Couper, *Barber*
John Herd, *Bricklayer*
William Garret, *Bricklayer*
Edward Brinto, *Mason*
William Love, *Tailor*
Nic. Skot, *Drummer*

Laborers

John Laydon
William Cassen
George Cassen
Tho. Cassen
William Rods
William White
Ould Edward
Henry Tavin
George Golding
John Dods
William Johnson
Will. Unger
Will. Wilkinson, *Surgeon*

Boys

Samuell Collier
Nat. Pecock
James Brumfield
Rich. Mutton

SOURCES: The 1607 item is from Lyon Gardiner Tyler, ed., *Narrative of Early Virginia, 1606–1625,* (New York, 1907), 125–126. The 1609 item from Alexander Brown, ed., *The Genesis of the United States* (New York, 1890), I, 352–53. The 1622 item is from the John Carter Brown Library at Brown University.

*With diverse others to the number of 105.

THE INCONVENIENCIES THAT HAVE HAPPENED TO SOME PERSONS WHICH HAVE TRANSPORTED THEMSELVES

from *England* to *Virginia*, vvithout prouisions necessary to sustaine themselues, hath *greatly hindred the Progresse of that noble Plantation: For preuention of the like disorders* heereafter, that no man suffer, either through ignorance or misinformation; it is thought requisite to publish this short declaration: wherein is contained a particular of such necessaries, *as either priuate families or single persons shall haue cause to furnish themselues with, for their better support at their first landing in* Virginia; *whereby also greater numbers may receiue in part, directions how to prouide themselues.*

Apparrell.

Apparrell for one man, and so after the rate for more.

	li.	s.	d.
One Monmouth Cap	00	01	10
Three falling bands	—	01	03
Three shirts	—	07	06
One waste-coate	—	02	02
One suite of Canuase	—	07	06
One suite of Frize	—	10	00
One suite of Cloth	—	15	00
Three paire of Irish stockins	—	04	—
Foure paire of shooes	—	08	08
One paire of garters	—	00	10
One doozen of points	—	00	03
One paire of Canuase sheets	—	08	00
Seuen ells of Canuase, to make a bed and boulster, to be filled in *Virginia* 8.s. One Rug for a bed 8. s. which with the bed seruing for two men, halfe is	—	08	00
Fiue ells coorse Canuase, to make a bed at Sea for two men, to be filled with straw, iiij. s. One coorse Rug at Sea for two men, will cost vj. s. is for one	—	05	00
	—	—	—
	04	00	00

Victuall.

For a whole yeere for one man, and so for more after the rate.

	li.	s.	d.
Eight bushels of Meale	02	00	00
Two bushels of pease at 3.s.	—	06	00
Two bushels of Oatemeale 4.s. 6.d.	—	09	00
One gallon of *Aquauitæ*	—	02	06
One gallon of Oyle	—	03	06
Two gallons of Vineger 1.s.	—	02	00
	—	—	—
	03	03	00

Armes.

For one man, but if halfe of your men haue armour it is sufficient so that all haue Peeces and swords.

	li.	s.	d.
One Armour compleat, light	—	17	00
One long Peece, fiue foot or fiue and a halfe, neere Musket bore	01	02	—
One sword	—	05	—
One belt	—	01	—
One bandaleere	—	01	06
Twenty pound of powder	—	18	00
Sixty pound of shot or lead, Pistoll and Goose shot	—	05	00
	—	—	—
	03	09	06

Tooles.

For a family of 6. persons and so after the rate for more.

	li.	s.	d.
Fiue broad howes at 2.s. a piece	—	10	—
Fiue narrow howes at 16.d. a piece	—	06	08
Two broad Axes at 3.s. 8.d. a piece	—	07	04
Fiue felling Axes at 18.d. a piece	—	07	06
Two steele hand sawes at 16.d. a piece	—	02	08
Two two-hand-sawes at 5. s. a piece	—	10	—
One whip-saw, set and filed with box, file, and wrest	—	10	—
Two hammers 12.d. a piece	—	02	00
Three shouels 18.d. a piece	—	04	06
Two spades at 18.d. a piece	—	03	—
Two augers 6.d. a piece	—	01	00
Sixe chissels 6.d. a piece	—	03	00
Two percers stocked 4.d. a piece	—	00	08
Three gimlets 2.d. a piece	—	00	06
Two hatchets 21.d. a piece	—	03	06
Two froues to cleaue pale 18.d.	—	03	00
Two hand bills 20. a piece	—	03	04
One grindlestone 4 s.	—	04	00
Nailes of all sorts to the value of	02	00	—
Two Pickaxes	—	03	—
	06	02	08

Houshold Implements.

For a family of 6. persons, and so for more or lesse after the rate.

	li.	s.	d.
One Iron Pot	00	07	—
One kettle	—	06	—
One large frying-pan	—	02	06
One gridiron	—	01	06
Two skillets	—	05	—
One spit	—	02	—
Platters, dishes, spoones of wood	—	04	—
	01	08	00

	li.	s.	d.
For Suger, Spice, and fruit, and at Sea for 6 men	00	12	06
So the full charge of Apparrell, Victuall, Armes, Tooles, and houshold stuffe, and after this rate for each person, will amount vnto about the summe of	12	10	—
The passage of each man is	06	00	—
The fraight of these prouisions for a man, will bee about halfe a Tun, which is	01	10	—
So the whole charge will amount to about	20	00	00

Nets, hookes, lines, and a tent must be added, if the number of people be greater, as also some kine.

And this is the vsuall proportion that the Virginia *Company doe bestow vpon their Tenants which they send.*

Whosoeuer transports himselfe or any other at his owne charge vnto *Virginia*, shall for each person so transported before Midsummer 1625. haue to him and his heires for euer fifty Acres of Land vpon a first, and fifty Acres vpon a second diuision.

FELIX KYNGSTON. 1622.

Figure 1.3. The supply list from a 1622 recruitment poster (Courtesy of the John Carter Brown Library at Brown University).

A Call for Recruits, 1609 –

To render a more particular satisfaction and account of our care, in providing to attend the *Right Honourable the Lord de la Warr*, in this concluded and present supply, men of most use and necessity to the *Foundation* of a *Commonwealth;* and to avoid both the scandal and peril of accepting idle and wicked persons; such as shame or fear compels into this action; and such as are the weeds and rankness of this land; who being the surfeit of an able, healthy, and composed body must need be the poison of one so tender, feeble, and as yet unformed: and to divulge and declare to all men what kind of persons, as well for their religion and conversations, as faculties, arts, and trades, we propose to accept of—we have thought it convenient to pronounce that for the first provision, we will receive no man that cannot bring or render some good testimony of his religion to God, and civil manners and behavior to his neighbor, with whom he hath lived; and for the second, we have set down in a table annexed, the proportion and number we will entertain in every necessary art, upon proof and assurance, that every man shall be able to perform that which he doth undertake, whereby such as are requisite to us may have knowledge and preparation, to offer themselves, and we shall be ready to give honest entertainment and content, and to recompense with extraordinary reward every fit and industrious person, respectively to *his pains and quality.*

The Table of Such as are Required to this Plantation.

4. *Honest and learned Ministers*
2. *Surgeons*
2. *Druggists*
10. *Iron men for the Furnace and Hammer*
2. *Armorers*
2. *Gun-founders*
6. *Blacksmiths*
10. *Sawyers*
6. *Carpenters*
6. *Shipwrights*
6. *Gardeners*
4. *Turners*
2. *Joiners*
2. *Soap-ash men*
4. *Pitch Boilers*
2. *Mineral men*
2. *Planters of Sugarcane*
4. *Brickmakers*
2. *Tile-makers*
10. *Fishermen*
6. *Fowlers*
4. *Sturgeon dressers and preservers of Caviar*
2. *Salt-makers*
6. *Coopers*
2. *Collar-makers for draught*
2. *Plowwrights*
4. *Rope-makers*
6. *Vine-dressers*
2. *Press-makers*
2. *Silk-dressers*
2. *Pearl Drillers*
2. *Bakers*
2. *Brewers*
2. *Colliers*

1.4 A Puritan Oligarchy

In setting up the New England colonies, the Puritan elders hoped to recreate the familiar, rigidly structured society they knew in England. And yet it turned out differently. They created an oligarchy (i.e., a government of the few), with theocratic elements (an established church) and also some democratic features (an elective body).

This mixed social structure emerges in a letter written by the Rev. John Cotton in 1636. He was answering an inquiry from England. A group of wealthy Puritans was considering settling in Massachusetts—but only if the conditions of life in the new land met certain expectations. The prospective settlers raised ten specific demands. Cotton, pastor of the Boston Congregational church and an influential colonist, responded with ten answers, excerpted below, to help convince them that the new community would meet their expectations.

Questions

Look at each of the demands and answers. Precisely what sort of society did the Puritans hope to establish?

To what extent did the social objectives promised by Cotton come to pass in practice? Did New England society resemble this vision in the next few generations? If not, what had changed, and why?

How do these social objectives compare with the objectives set down by Gov. John Winthrop in his lecture on Christian charity (see Chapter 7, below)?

Certain Proposals made by Lord Say, Lord Brooke, and other Persons of Quality, as Conditions of Their Removing to New-England, With the Answers Thereto.

Demand 1. That the common-wealth should consist of two distinct ranks of men, whereof the one should be for them and their heirs, gentlemen of the country, the other for them and their heirs, freeholders.

SOURCE: From Thomas Hutchinson, *The History of the Colony of Massachusetts Bay* (London, 1765), I, 490–498, *passim*.

Answer. Two distinct ranks we willingly acknowledge, from the light of nature and scripture; the one of them called Princes, or Nobles, or Elders (amongst whom gentlemen have their place) the other the people. Hereditary dignity or honours we willingly allow to the former, unless by the scandalous and base conversation of any of them, they become degenerate. Hereditary liberty, or estate of freemen, we willingly allow to the other, unless they also, by some unworthy and slavish carriage, do disfranchize themselves.

Dem. 2. That in these gentlemen and freeholders, assembled together, the chief power of the common-wealth shall be placed, both for making and repealing laws.

Ans. So it is with us.

Dem. 3. That each of these two ranks should, in all public assemblies, have a negative voice, so as without a mutual consent nothing should be established.

Ans. So it is agreed among us.

Dem. 4. That the first rank, consisting of gentlemen, should have power, for them and their heirs, to come to the parliaments or public assemblies, and there to give their free votes personally; the second rank of freeholders should have the same power for them and their heirs of meeting and voting, but by their deputies.

Ans. Thus far this demand is practised among us. The freemen meet and vote by their deputies; the other rank give their votes personally, only with this difference, there be no more of the gentlemen that give their votes personally, but such as are chosen to places of office, either governors, deputy governors, councellors, or assistants. All gentlemen in England have not that honour to meet and vote personally in Parliament, much less all their heirs. . . .

Dem. 5. That for facilitating and dispatch of business, and other reasons, the gentlemen and freeholders should sit and hold their meetings in two distinct houses.

Ans. We willingly approve the motion, only as yet it is not so practised among us. . . .

Dem. 6. That there shall be set times for these meetings, annually or half yearly, or as shall be thought fit by common consent. . . .

Ans. Public meetings, in general courts, are by charter appointed to be quarterly, which, in this infancy of the colony, wherein many things frequently occur which need settling, hath been of good use, but when things are more fully settled in due order, it is likely that yearly or half yearly meetings will be sufficient. For the continuance or breaking up of these courts, nothing is done but with the joint consent of both branches.

Dem. 7. That it shall be in the power of this parliament, thus constituted and assembled, to call the governor and all publick officers to acount, to create new officers, and to determine them already set up: and, the better to stop the way to insolence and ambition, it may be ordered that all offices and fees of office shall, every parliament, determine, unless they be new confirmed the last day of every session.

Ans. This power to call governors and all officers to account, and to create new and determine the old, is settled already in the general court or parliament, only it is not put forth but once in the year, viz. at the great and general court in May, when the governor is chosen.

Dem. 8. That the governor shall ever be chosen out of the rank of gentlemen.

Ans. We never practice otherwise, chusing the governor either out of the assistants, which is our ordinary course, or out of approved known gentlemen, as this year Mr. Vane. . . .

Dem. 10. That the rank of freeholders shall be made up of such, as shall have so much personal estate there, as shall be thought fit for men of that condition, and have contributed, some fit proportion, to the public charge of the country, either by their disbursements or labors.

Ans. We must confess our ordinary practice to be otherwise. For, excepting the old planters, . . . none are admitted freemen of this commonwealth but such as are first admitted members of some church or other in this country, and, of such, none are excluded from the liberty of freemen. And out of such only, I mean the more eminent sort of such, it is that our magistrates are chosen. Both which points we should willingly persuade our people to change, if we could make it appear to them, that such a change might be made according to God: for, . . . it seemeth to them, and also to us, to be a divine ordinance (and moral) that none should be appointed and chosen by the people of God, magistrates over them, but men fearing God. . . .

Obj. If it be said, there may be many carnal men whom God hath invested with sundry eminent gifts of wisdom, courage, justice, fit for government

Ans. Such may be fit to be consulted with and employed by governors, according to the quality and use of their gifts and parts, but yet are men not fit to be trusted with place of standing power or settled authority. . . .

Obj. If it be said again, that then the church estate could not be compatible with any commonwealth under heaven.

Ans. It is one thing for the church or members of the church, loyally to submit unto any form of government, when it is above their calling to reform it, another thing to chuse a form of government and governors discrepant from the rule. Now, it if be a divine truth, that none are to be trusted with public permanent authority but godly men, who are fit materials for church fellowship, then from the same grounds it will appear, that none are so fit to be trusted with the liberties of the commonwealth as church members. For, the liberties of the freemen of this commonwealth are such, as require men of faithful integrity to God and the state, to preserve the same. Their liberties, among others, are chiefly these. 1. To chuse all magistrates, and to call them to account at their general courts. 2. To chuse such burgesses, every general court, as with the magistrates shall make or repeal all laws. . . .

1.5 Terms of Indenture

In the eighteenth-century, there were too many able-bodied people looking for work in England, and too few in America. New methods of organizing agriculture left many people without earning power in the mother country. In America, land and resources were waiting to be exploited. The result was a system of labor recruitment and transportation to the New World. It was based on the old notion of apprenticeship. The employer offered to pay for transportation, job training and room-and-board for a period of time—usually four or five years; the employee served the employer exclusively before setting off on his or her own. This sounded fine in theory. Yet the majority of servants who entered this service came out of the apprenticeship weary and defeated, or physically disabled. Often they failed to rise on the social ladder.

Indenture agreements got their name originally from the fact that two duplicate copies were often notched uniformly (indented) at the edges for identification. One went to the employer, the other to the servant. The following two examples are fairly typical. The first item establishes the terms of labor of a woman servant working for a Virginia planter in 1659. The second concerns a Massachusetts apprentice in 1713.

Questions

What terms of labor are being promised here? What service besides labor are these workers obliged to give? What is the employer providing besides room and board? Clearly, the terms are one-sided, but do the workers receive anything worthwhile in return?

Were there any alternative systems of labor recruitment at the time? Compare this document to Document 1.3, and estimate what impact it might have had in Virginia a century earlier.

Were there any alternative systems of labor recruitment at the time? Compare this document to Document 1.3, and estimate what impact it might have had in Virginia a century earlier.

1659 –

This Indenture, Made the first Day of September, RRae, Annae Nunc Magnae Brittaniae Duodecimo annoq Dom., 1713, Wittnesseth that Nicholas Bourguess, a youth of Guarnsey, of his own free and voluntary will, and by and with the Consent of his present Master, Capt, John Hardy, of Guarnsey, aforesaid, Marriner, hath put himselfe a Servant vnto Mr. William English, of Salem, in the County of Essex, within the Province of the Massachusetts Bay in New England, Marriner, for the space of four yeares from the Day of the Date hereof, vntill the aforesaid Terme of four yeares be fully Compleat & Ended, During all which time the said Servant his said Master his heires, Executors, administrators or assignees Dwelling within the province aforesaid, shall well and faithfully serve, their lawful commands obey; he shall not absent himselfe from his or their service without Leave or Lycense first had from him or them; his Master's Money, goods or other Estate he shall not Purloine, embezzle or wast; at unlawfull Games he shall not Play; Tavernes or Alehouses he shall not Frequent; . . . [evil] he shall not Committ, nor Matrimony Contract; but in all things shall Demean himselfe as a faithfull Servant During the Terme aforesaid, and the aforesaid Master, on his part, doth for himselfe, his heires and assignees,

SOURCES: This 1713 item is from *Historical Collections of the Essex Institute* (Salem, Mass.: Henry Whipple and Son, 1859), I, 14–15. The 1659 item is from Maryland State Hall of Records, Annapolis, Maryland.

Covenant, promise and agree to and with the said Servant; that he or they shall and will provide & find him with sufficient Meat, Drink, Cloathing, washing & Lodging, & in Case of Sickness, with Phisick, and attendance During the Terme aforesaid, and to Learn him to read a Chapter well in the bible, if he may be capable of Learning it, & to Dismiss him with two suits of Apparell for all parts of his Body—the one for Lord's Days, the other for working Days.

In Testimony & for Confirmation whereof the parties aforenamed have Interchangeably set their hands and Seales the Day & Yeare first above written.

NICOLLAS BOURGAIZE,
SIGNED, SEALED & DELIVERED IN PRESENCE OF US,— JOHN HARDY.
MARG'T SEWALL, JUN'R, SUSANNAH SEWALL,
STEPHEN SEWALL, NOT. PUB. & JUSTICE PEACE.

1713 –

This Indenture made the 24th day of August in the Yeare of our Lord 1659 betweene Richard Smyth of Virginia Planter of the one parte And Margarett Williams of Bristoll Spinster of the other parte, Wittnesseth that the said Margarett doth hereby Covenant promise and grant to and with the said Richard his Executors & Assignes from the day of the date hereof, vntill her first and next arrivall at Virginea, and after for and during the tearme of ffower yeares to serue in such service, and imployment as the said Richard or his Assignes shall there imploy her, according to the Custome of the Countrey in the like kind. In consideration whereof the said Master doth hereby covenant and grant to and with the said Servant to pay for her passing, and to find and allow her meate, drinke, apparrell and lodging with other Necessaries during the said tearme, And at the end of the said tearme to pay vnto her One Ax one Howe, double Apparrell fifty acres of land one yeares provision according to the custome of the Countrey In wittnes whereof the parties abouenamed to these Indentures haue interchangeably sett their hands and Seales the day and yeare aboue written

SEALED & DD IN P^{E}SENCE OF GEO. HAWKINS
MD WORTH
THE MARKE OF MARGARETT WILLIAMS

1.6 Poor Richard's Work Ethic

Benjamin Franklin (1706-1790) did not invent the work ethic but, as America's original success story, he came to personify it, at least in the colonial period. His resumé is astonishing: although only self-educated, he became a printer and publisher, scientist and inventor (bifocals and lightning rods), postmaster general, delegate to the Second Continental Congress, coauthor of the Declaration of Independence, diplomat, and delegate to the Constitutional Convention of 1787. He was, in short, the most accomplished and popular American of his time, both here and abroad.

From 1723 to 1757 Franklin published an annual work known as Poor Richard's Almanack. *These books were laced with wise sayings and gave all sorts of practical advice to farmers, artisans and others. In 1758 he issued a compilation of his best sayings under the title,* The Way to Wealth *(excerpted below). The author speaks through an anonymous character, "Father Abraham," who preaches to a crowd. This essay, and Franklin's* Autobiography, *celebrates "the cult of success." It establishes a branch of popular literature that has since become typically American. His ideas, presented in homespun words easily understood by his contemporaries, had ancient roots. They stretched back to sixteenth and seventeenth century Lutheran and Calvinist ideals of labor and worldly enterprise, and to the ideas of Puritan elders like John Cotton. Interestingly, Franklin makes little or no reference to God's intervention.*

Questions

Which character virtues does Franklin celebrate? Why were they so popular in his time? What ideas could he have picked up from the Puritan fathers of New England? What does he consider the "greatest Prodigality"? Is he right that industrious people "shall never starve"? How does he—through Father Abraham—view leisure?

How do these virtues stand up today? Which of his maxims are still popular today? Do we still honor them, or merely give them lip-service? If it is the latter, which virtues do we actually value most in secular life? What has changed in American life to cause a change in values?

I have heard that nothing gives an Author so great Pleasure, as to find his Works respectfully quoted by other learned Authors. . . .

Judge, then, how much I must have been gratified by an Incident I am going to relate to you. I stopt my Horse lately where a great Number of People were collected at a Vendue of Merchant Goods. The House of Sale not being come, they were conversing on the Badness of the Times and one of the Company call'd to a plain clean old Man, with white Locks, "Pray, Father Abraham, what think you of the Times? Won't these heavy Taxes quite ruin the Country? How shall we be ever able to pay them? What would you advise us to?" Father *Abraham* stood up, and reply'd, . . .

"Friends," says he, "and Neighbours, the Taxes are indeed very heavy. *Poor Richard* says, *the greatest Prodigality*; since as he elsewhere tells us, and if those laid on by the Government were the only Ones we had to pay, we might more easily discharge them; but we have many others, and much more grievous to some of us. We are taxed twice as much by our Idleness, three times as much by our *Folly*; and from these

SOURCE: Albert Henry Smith, ed., *The Writings of Benjamin Franklin* (9 vols.; New York: Haskell House, 1907), III, 407–418.

Taxes the Commissioners cannot ease or deliver us by allowing an Abatement. However let us hearken to good Advice, and something may be done for us; *God helps them that help themselves,* as *Poor Richard says,* in his Almanack of 1733.

It would be thought a hard Government that should tax its People one-tenth Part of their *Time,* to be employed in its Service, But *Idleness* taxes many of us much more, if we reckon all that is spent in absolute *Sloth,* or doing of nothing, with that which is spent in idle Employment or Amusements that amount to nothing. *Sloth,* by bringing on Diseases, absolutely shortens life. *Sloth, like Rust, consumes faster than Labour wears; while the used key is always bright,* as *Poor Richard* says. *But dost thou love Life, then do not squander Time, for that's the stuff Life is made of,* as Poor Richard says. How much more than is necessary do we spend in sleep, forgetting that *The sleeping Fox catches no Poultry,* and that *There will be sleeping enough in the Grave,* as *Poor Richard* says. . . . If we are industrious, we shall never starve; for, as *Poor Richard* says, *At the working Man's House Hunger looks in, but dares not enter.* Nor will the Bailiff or the Constable enter, for *Industry pays Debts, while Despair encreaseth them,* says *Poor Richard.* What though you have found no Treasure, nor has any rich Relation left you a Legacy, *Diligence is the Mother of Good-luck* as *Poor Richard* says *and God gives all Things to Industry. Then plough deep, while sluggards sleep, and you shall have Corn to sell and to keep,* says *Poor Dick.* Work while it is called To-day, for you know not how much you may be hindered To-morrow, which makes *Poor Richard* say, *One to-day is worth two To-morrows,* and farther *Have you somewhat to do To-morrow, do it To-day.* If you were a Servant, would you not be ashamed that a good Master should catch you idle? Are you then your own Master, *be ashamed to catch yourself idle,* as *Poor Dick* says. When there is so much to be done for yourself, your Family, your Country, and your gracious King, be up by Peep of Day. . . .

So much for Industry, my Friends, and Attention to one's own Business; but to these we must add *Frugality,* if we would make our *Industry* more certainly successful. A Man may, if he knows not how to save as he gets, *keep his Nose all his Life to the Grindstone,* and die not worth a *Groat* at last. *A fat Kitchen makes a lean Will,* as *Poor Richard* says; and

> Many Estates are spent in the Getting,
> Since Women for Tea forsook Spinning and Knitting,
> And Men for Punch forsook Hewing and Splitting.

If you would be weathy, says he, in another Almanack, *think of Saving as well as of Getting: The Indies have not made Spain rich, because her Outgoes are greater than her Incomes.*

Away then with your expensive Follies, and you will not then have so much Cause to complain of hard Times, heavy Taxes, and chargeable Families. . . .

Here you are all got together at this Vendue of *Fineries* and *Knicknacks.* You call them *Goods;* but if you do not take Care, they will prove *Evils* to some of you. You expect they will be sold *cheap,* and perhaps they may for less than they cost; but if you have no Occasion for them, they must be *dear* to you. Remember what *Poor Richard* says: *Buy what thou hast no Need of, and ere long thou shalt sell thy Necessaries.* . . . Many a one, for the Sake of Finery on the Back, have gone with a hungry Belly, and half-starved their Families. *Silks and Satins, Scarlet and Velvets,* as *Poor Richard* says, *put out the Kitchen Fire.* . . .

And again, *Pride is as loud a Beggar as Want, and a great deal more saucy.* When you have bought one fine Thing, you must buy ten more, that your Appearance may be all of a Piece; but *Poor Dick* says, *'Tis easier to suppress the first Desire, than to satisfy all that follow it.* And 'tis as truly Folly for the Poor to ape the Rich, as for the Frog to swell in order to equal the ox.

> Great Estates may venture more,
> But little Boats should keep near shore. . . .

But what Madness must it be to *run in Debt* for these Super-Fluities! We are offered, by the Terms of this Vendue, *Six Months' Credit;* and that perhaps has induced some of us to attend it, because we cannot spare the ready Money, and hope now to be fine without it. But, ah, think what you do when you run in Debt; *you give to another Power over your Liberty.* If you cannot pay at the Time, you will be ashamed to see your Creditor; you will be in Fear when you speak to him; you will make poor pitiful sneaking Excuses, and by Degrees come to lose your Veracity, and sink into base downright lying; for, as *Poor Richard* says, *The second Vice is Lying, the first is running in Debt.* And again, to the same Purpose, *Lying rides upon Debt's Back.* Whereas a free-born *Englishman* ought not be be ashamed or afraid to see or speak to any Man living. But Poverty often deprives a Man of all Spirit and Virtue: *'Tis hard for an empty Bag to stand upright,* as *Poor Richard* truly says."

1.7 "God's Chosen People"

Thomas Jefferson (1743–1826) is America's apostle of agriculture. In the 1780s he envisioned an America as a nation not of artisans or factory operatives or city dwellers, but of self-sufficient farmers. He put his faith not in just any sort of agriculture, but agriculture based on family farms. This is a paradox, of course, since he was a planter and slave owner. While serving in the Washington administration, he would oppose Alexander Hamilton's schemes on centralization and fiscal policies (see Document 1.8, below) that represented a different vision of the future. This clash caused him to resign in protest in 1793. Farmers saw Jefferson as their champion and rallied around him politically.

His ideas on agriculture seemed to crystalize while he was in Europe. Having served as wartime governor of Virginia (1779–1781) and delegate to the Continental Congress (1783–1784), he went to France as minister to the American government during the era of the Articles of Confederation (1785–1789). There he viewed the degraded conditions of the lower classes and experienced the first rumblings of the French Revolution. His sentiments on farming are reflected in eloquent selections from Notes on Virginia *(1785) and from his correspondence.*

Questions

Why does Jefferson think farmers are more virtuous than other people? Is he reflecting true conditions, or merely creating a mythology? How self-sufficient were American farmers and how dependent were they on world market conditions? How does Jefferson's vision of the future compare with that of Hamilton's (see next document)?

Today farms are going on the auction block and farm families are turning to other enterprises in record numbers. What is happening to the Jeffersonian values that are so closely tied to agriculture as that way of life declines?

To John Jay, 1785—

WE HAVE now lands enough to employ an infinite number of people in their cultivation. Cultivators of the earth are the most valuable citizens. They are the most vigorous, the most independent, the most virtuous, and they are tied to their country, and wedded to its liberty and interests, by the most lasting bonds. As long, therefore, as they can find employment in this line, I would not convert them into mariners, artisans, or anything else. But our citizens will find employment in this line, till their numbers, and of course their productions, become too great for the demand, both internal and foreign. This is not the case as yet, and probably will not be for a considerable time. As soon as it is, the surplus of hands must be turned to something else. I should then, perhaps, wish to turn them to the sea in preference to manufactures; because, comparing the characters of the two classes, I find the former the most valuable citizens. I consider the class of artificers as the panders of vice, and the instruments by which the liberties of a country are generally overturned. . . .

To Hogendorp, 1785—

You ask what I think on the expediency of encouraging our States to be commercial? Were I to indulge my own theory, I should wish them to practise neither commerce nor navigation, but to stand, with respect to Europe, precisely on the footing of China. We should thus avoid wars, and all our citizens would be husbandmen. Whenever, indeed, our numbers should so increase so that our produce would overstock the markets of those nations who should come to seek it, the farmers must employ the surplus of their time in manufactures, or the surplus of our hands must be employed in manufactures or in navigation. But that day would, I think, be distant, and we should long keep our workmen in Europe, while Europe should be drawing rough materials, and even subsistence from America.

From Notes on the State of Virginia—

Those who labor in the earth are the chosen people of God, if ever He had a chosen people, whose breasts He has made His peculiar deposit for substantial and genuine virtue. It is the focus in which he keeps alive that sacred fire, which otherwise might escape from the face of the earth. Corruption of morals in the mass of cultivators is a phenomenon of which no age nor nation has furnished an example. It is the mark set on those, who, not looking up to heaven, to their own soil and industry, as does the husbandman, for their subsistence, depend for it on casualties and caprice of customers. Dependence begets subservience and venality, suffocates the germ of virtue, and prepares fit tools for the designs of ambition. . . .

Generally speaking, the proportion which the aggregate of the other classes of citizens bears in any State to that of its husbandmen, is the proportion of its unsound to its healthy parts, and is a good enough barometer whereby to measure its degree of corruption. While we have land to labor then, let us never wish to see our citizens occupied at a work-bench, or twirling a distaff. Carpenters, masons, smiths, are wanting in husbandry; but, for the general operations of manufacture, let our workshops remain in Europe. It is better to carry provisions and materials to workmen there, than bring them to the provisions and materials, and with them their manners and principles. The loss by the transportation of commodities across the Atlantic will be made up in happiness and permanence of government. The mobs of great cities add just so much to the support of pure government, as sores do to the strength of the human body.

To James Madison, 1787 –

This reliance cannot deceive us, as long as we remain virtuous; and I think we shall be so, as long as agriculture is our principal object, which will be the case, while there remain vacant lands in any part of America. When we get piled upon one another in large cities, as in Europe, we shall become corrupt as in Europe, and go to eating one another as they do there.

To Jean Baptiste Say, 1804 –

The differences of circumstance between this and the old countries of Europe, furnish differences of fact whereon to reason in questions of political economy. . . . There, for instance, the quantity of food is fixed, or increasing in a slow and only arithmetical ratio. . . . Here the immense extent of uncultivated and fertile lands enables every one who will labor to marry young, and to raise a family of any size. Our food, then, may increase geometrically with our laborers, and our births, however multiplied, become effective.

Again, there the best distribution of labor is supposed to be that which places the manufacturing hands alongside the agricultural; so that the one part shall feed both, and the other part furnish both with clothes and other comforts. Would that be best here? Egoism and first appearances say yes. Or would it be better that all our laborers should be employed in agriculture? In this case a double or treble portion of fertile lands would be brought into culture; a double or treble creation of food be produced, and its surplus go to nourish the now perishing births of Europe, who in return would manufacture and send us in exchange our clothes and other comforts. Morality listens to this, and so invariably do the laws of nature create our duties and interests. . . . In solving this question, too, we should allow its just weight to the moral and physical preference of the agricultural, over the manufacturing, man. My occupations permit me only to ask questions. They deny me the time, if I had the information, to answer them.

1.8 Capitalism's Apostle

Alexander Hamilton (1755–1804) was an apostle of capitalism. In the 1780s he developed a plan to make the United States economically independent of Europe through economic nationalism and government centralism. He believed that a national bank should be established, that the central government should assume the debts of the states at face value, that excise taxes should be passed to make people know the force of the government, and, as explained below, that the Federal government should foster industry (as well as agriculture). As the first secretary of the treasury and a leading economic theorist, he wrote this Report on Manufactures *in 1791 to advance the latter objective. It is part of a series of writings in behalf of his overall plan.*

Raised in the West Indies, Hamilton came to the mainland colonies in 1773, where he became involved in revolutionary politics. He had a distinguished military career in the Revolutionary army, concluding his service as General Washington's aide-de-camp. He was not an entrepreneur or banker, but a lawyer with excellent social ties through marriage (the wealthy Schuyler family of New York) and influential friends and associates. As co-author of The Federalist, *he supported the federal Constitution of 1787 (see document in chapter on Power) and served in the administration of George Washington.*

Hamilton was also a politician, serving a term in Congress and helping to found the Federalist Party. He was killed in a pistol duel with Aaron Burr.

Questions

What was Hamilton's vision of the future for his nation? Contrast his vision with that of Jefferson's in Document 1.7, above. Hamilton is associated with conservatism, but are there also liberal and radical elements in his belief system? Explain, taking into account, among other things, his belief in government support for industry.

Was Hamilton a better prophet than Jefferson; how much of what he advocated came to pass later? Which recent presidential administrations seem to follow his ideas most closely?

The expediency of encouraging manufactures in the United States, which was not long since deemed very questionable, appears at this time to be pretty generally admitted. . . .

There still are, nevertheless, respectable partrons of opinions unfriendly to the encouragement of manufactures. . . .

It ought readily to be conceded that the cultivation of the earth, as the primary and most certain source of national supply, as the immediate chief source of subsistence to man, as the principal source of those materials which constitute the nutriment of other kinds of labor, as including a state most favorable to the freedom and independence of the human mind—one, perhaps, most conducive to the multiplication of the human species, has intrinsically a strong claim to pre-eminence over every other kind of industry. . . .

But, without contending for the superior productiveness of manufacturing industry, it may conduce to a better judgment of the policy which ought to be pursued respecting its encouragement, to contemplate the subject under some additional aspects, tending not only to confirm the idea that this kind of industry has been improperly represented as unproductive in itself, but to evince, in addition, that the establishment and diffusion of manufactures have the effect of rendering the total mass of useful and productive labor, in a community, greater than it would otherwise be. . . .

It is now proper to proceed a step further, and to enumerate the principal circumstances from which it may be inferred that manufacturing establishments not only occasion a positive augmentation of the produce and revenue of the society, but that they contribute essentially to rendering them greater than they could possibly be without such establishments. . . .

1. As to the division of labor.

It has justly been observed that there is scarcely anything of greater moment in the economy of a nation than the proper division of labor. The separation of occupations causes each to be carried to a much greater perfection than it could possibly acquire if they were blended. This arises principally from three circumstances:

1st. The greater skill and dexterity naturally resulting from a constant and undivided application to a single object. It is evident that these properties must increase in proportion to the separation and simplification of objects, and the steadiness of the attention devoted to each; and must be less in proportion to the complication of objects, and the number among which the attention is distracted.

2nd. The economy of time, by avoiding the loss of it, incident to a frequent transition from one operation to another of a different nature. This depends on various circumstances; the transition itself, the orderly disposition of the implements, machines, and materials employed in the operation to be relinquished, the preparatory steps to the commencement of a new one, the interruption of the impulse which the mind of a workman acquires from being engaged in a particular operation, the distractions, hesitations and reluctances which attend the passage from one kind of business to another.

3rd. An extension of the use of machinery. A man occupied on a single object will have it more in his power, and will be more naturally led to exert his imagination, in devising methods to facilitate and abridge labor, than if he were perplexed by a variety of independent and dissimilar operations. Besides this, the fabrication of machines, in numerous instances, be-

SOURCE: From *The Works of Alexander Hamilton,* Henry Cabot Lodge, ed., (12 vols.; New York, 1904).

coming itself a distinct trade, the artist who follows it has all the advantages which have been enumerated for improvement in his particular art; and, in both ways, the invention and application of machinery are extended.

And from these causes united, the mere separation of the occupation of the cultivator from that of the artificer, has the effect of augmenting the productive powers of labor, and with them, the total mass of the produce or revenue of a country. In this single view of the subject, therefore, the utility of artificers or manufacturers, towards promoting an increase of productive industry, is apparent.

2. *As to an extension of the use of machinery, a point which, though partly anticipated, requires to be placed in one or two additional lights.*

The employment of machinery forms an item of great importance in the general mass of national industry. It is an artificial force brought in aid of the natural force of man; and, to all the purposes of labor, is an increase of hands, an accession of strength, unencumbered too by the expense of maintaining the laborer. May it not, therefore, be fairly inferred that those occupations which give the greatest scope to the use of this auxiliary contribute most to the general stock of industrious effort, and, in consequence, to the general product of industry?

It shall be taken for granted, and the truth of the position referred to observation, that manufacturing pursuits are susceptible, in a greater degree, of the application of machinery, than those of agriculture. . . .

The cotton-mill, invented in England, within the last twenty years, is a signal illustration of the general proposition which has been just advanced. In consequence of it, all the different processes for spinning cotton are performed by means of machines, which are put in motion by water, and attended chiefly by women and children—and by a smaller number of persons, in the whole, than are requisite in the ordinary mode of spinning. And it is an advantage of great moment, that the operations of this mill continue with convenience during the night as well as through the day. The prodigious effect of such a machine is easily conceived. To this invention is to be attributed, essentially, the immense progress which has been so suddenly made in Great Britain in the various fabrics of cotton.

3. *As to the additional employment of classes of the community not originally engaged in the particular business.*

This is not among the least valuable of the names by which manufacturing institutions contribute to augment the general stock of industry and production. In places where these institutions prevail, besides the persons regularly engaged in them, they afford occasional and extra employment to industrious individuals and families, who are willing to devote the leisure resulting from the intermissions of their ordinary pursuits to collateral labors, as a resource for multiplying their acquisitions or their enjoyments. The husbandman himself experiences a new source of profit and support from the increased industry of his wife and daughters . . . the employment of persons who would otherwise be idle, and in many cases a burthen on the community. . . . It is worthy of particular remark that, in general, women and children are renderd more useful, and the latter more early useful, by manufacturing establishments, than they would otherwise be. Of the number of persons employed in the cotton manufactories of Great Britain, it is computed that four-sevenths, nearly, are women and children, of whom the greater proportion are children, and many of them of a tender age. . . .

4. As to the promoting of immigration from foreign countries. . . .

. . . Manufacturers who, listening to the powerful invitations of a better price for their fabrics or their labor, of greater cheapness of provisions, and raw materials, or an exemption from the chief part of the taxes, burthens and restraints which they endure in the Old World, or greater personal independence and consequence, under the operation of a more equal government, and of what is far more precious than mere religious toleration, a perfect equality of religious privileges, would probably flock from Europe to the United States, to pursue their own trades or professions, if they were once made sensible of the advantages they would enjoy, and were inspired with an assurance of encouragement and employment, will, with difficulty, be induced to transplant themselves, with a view to becoming cultivators of land. . . .

Here is perceived an important resource, not only for extending the population, and with it the useful and productive labor of the country, but likewise for the prosecution of manufactures, without deducting from the number of hands which might otherwise be drawn to tillage, and even for the indemnification of agriculture for such as might happen to be diverted from it. Many, whom manufacturing views would induce to emigrate, would afterwards, yield to the temptation which the particular situation of this country holds out to agricultural pursuits. . . .

5. As to the furnishing greater scope for the diversity of talents and dispositions, which discriminate men from each other.

This is a much more powerful means of augmenting the fund of national industry than may at first sight appear. It is a just observation, that minds of the strongest and most active powers for their proper objects fall below mediocrity, and labor without effect if confined to uncongenial pursuits. And it is thence to be inferred, that the results of human exertion may be immensely increased by diversifying its objects. When all the different kinds of industry obtain in a community, each individual can find his proper element, and can call into activity the whole vigor of his nature. And the community is benefited by the services of its respective members, in the manner in which each can serve it with most effect. . . .

6. As to the affording a more ample and various field for enterprise.

. . . To cherish and stimulate the activity of the human mind, by multiplying the objects of enterprise, is not among the least considerable of the expedients by which the wealth of a nation may be promoted. . . .

The spirit of enterprise, useful and prolific as it is, must necessarily be contracted or expanded in proportion to the simplicity or variety of the occupations and productions which are to be found in a society. . . .

7. As to the creating, in some instances, a new, and securing, in all, a more certain and steady demand for the surplus produce of the soil.

This is among the most important of the circumstances which have been indicated. . . .

It is evident that the exertions of the husbandman will be steady or fluctuating, vigorous or feeble, in proportion to the steadiness or fluctuation, adequateness or inadequateness of the markets on which he must depend for the vent of the surplus which may be produced by his labor; and that such surplus, in the ordinary course of things, will be greater or less in the same proportion. . . .

. . . And though it should be true that, in settled countries, the diversification of industry is conducive to an increase in the productive powers of labor, and to an augmentation of revenue and capital, yet it is scarcely conceivable that there can be anything of so solid and permanent advantage to an uncultivated and unpeopled country as to convert its wastes into cultivated and inhabited districts. If the revenue, in the meantime, should be less, the capital, in the event, must be greater.

To these observations the following appears to be a satisfactory answer:

1st. If the system of perfect liberty to industry and commerce were the prevailing system of nations, the arguments which dissuade a country, in the predicament of the United States, from the zealous pursuit of manufactures would doubtless have great force. . . .

But the system which has been mentioned is far from characterizing the general policy of nations. The prevalent one has been regulated by an opposite spirit. The consequence of it is that the United States are, to a certain extent, in the situation of a country precluded from foreign commerce. They can, indeed, without difficulty, obtain from abroad the manufactured supplies of which they are in want; but they experience numerous and very injurious impediments to the emission and vent of their own commodities. Nor is this the case in reference to a single foreign nation only. The regulations of several countries, with which we have the most extensive intercourse, throw serious obstructions in the way of the principal staples of the United States.

In such a position of things, the United States cannot exchange with Europe on equal terms; and the want of reciprocity would render them the victim of a system which would induce them to confine their views to agriculture and refrain from manufactures. A constant and increasing necessity, on their part, for the commodities of Europe, and only a partial and occasional demand for their own, in return, could not but expose them to a state of impoverishment, compared with the opulence to which their political and natural advantages authorize them to aspire. . . .

It is no small consolation that already the measures which have embarrassed our trade have accelerated internal improvements, which, upon the whole, have bettered our affairs. To diversify and extend these improvements is the surest and safest method of indemnifying ourselves for any inconveniencies which those or similar measures have a tendency to beget. If Europe will not take from us the products of our soil, upon terms consistent with our interest, the natural remedy is to contract, as fast as possible, our wants of her.

2nd. The conversion of their waste into cultivated lands is certainly a point of great moment in the political calculations of the United States. But the degree in which this may possibly be retarded by the encouragement of manufactories does not appear to countervail the powerful inducements to afford that encouragement.

An observation made in another place is of a nature to have great influence upon this question. If it cannot be denied that the interests, even of agriculture, may be advanced more by having such lands of a State as are occupied under a good cultivation, than by having a greater quantity occupied under a much inferior cultivation; and if manufactories, for the reasons assigned, must be admitted to have a tendency to promote a more steady and vigorous cultivation of the lands occupied than would happen without them, it will follow that they are capable of indemnifying a country for a diminution of the progress of new settlements, and may serve to increase both the capital value and the income of its lands, even though they should abridge the number of acres under tillage.

But it does by no means follow that the progress of new settlements would be retarded by the extension of manufactures. The desire of being an independent proprietor of land is founded on such strong principles in the human breast, that, where the opportunity of becoming so is as great as it is in the United States, the proportion will be small of those whose situations would otherwise lead to it, who would be diverted from it toward manufactures. . . .

The remaining objections to a particular encouragement of manufactures in the United States now require to be examined.

One of these turns on the proposition that industry, if left to itself, will naturally find its way to the most useful and profitable employment. Whence it is inferred that manufactures, without the aid of government, will grow up as soon and as fast as the natural state of things and the interest of the community may require.

Against the solidity of this hypothesis, in the full latitude of the terms, very cogent reasons may be offered. These have relation to the strong influence of habit and the spirit of imitation; the fear of want of success in untried enterprises; the intrinsic difficulties incident to first essays toward a competition with those who have previously attained to perfection in the business to be attempted; the bounties, premiums, and other artificial encouragements with which foreign nations second the exertions of their own citizens in the branches in which they are to be rivalled. . . .

When former occupations ceased to yield a profit adequate to the subsistence of their followers, or when there was an absolute deficiency of employment in them owing to the superabundance of hands, changes would ensue; but these changes would be likely to be more tardy than might consist with the interest either of individuals or of the society. In many cases they would not happen, while a bare support could be insured by an adherence to ancient courses, though a resort to a more profitable employment might be practicable. To produce the desirable changes as early as may be expedient may therefore require the incitement and patronage of government.

The apprehension of failing in new attempts is, perhaps, a more serious impediment. There are dispositions apt to be attracted by the mere novelty of an undertaking; but these are not always those best calculated to give it success. To this it is of importance that the confidence of cautious, sagacious capitalists, both citizens and foreigners, should be excited. And to inspire this description of persons with confidence, it is essential that they should be made to see in any project which is new—and for that reason alone, if for no other, precarious—the prospect of such a degree of countenance and support from government, as may be capable of overcoming the obstacles inseparable from first experiments.

The superiority antecedently enjoyed by nations who have preoccupied and perfected a branch of industry, constitutes a more formidable obstacle than either of those which have been mentioned, to the introduction of the same branch into a country in which it did not before exist. To maintain, between the recent establishments of one country and the long-matured establishments of another country, a competition upon equal terms, both as to quality and price, is, in most cases, impracticable. The disparity in the one, or in the other, or in both must necessarily be so considerable as to forbid a successful rivalship, without the extraordinary aid and protection of government.

But the greatest obstacle of all to the successful prosecution of a new branch of industry in a country in which it was before unknown consists, as far as the instances apply, in the bounties, premiums, and other aids which are granted, in a variety of cases, by the nations in which the establishments to be imitated are previously introduced. It is well known (and particular examples, in the course of this report, will be cited) that certain nations grant bounties on the exportation of particular commodities, to enable their own workmen to undersell and supplant all competitors in the countries to which those commodities are sent. Hence the undertakers of a new manufacture have to contend, not only with the natural disadvantages of a new undertaking, but with the gratuities and remunerations which other governments bestow. To be enabled to contend with success it is evident that the interference and aid of their own government are indispensable. . . .

1.9 The Invention of the Cotton Gin

The future of cotton production, of slavery and of plantation agriculture in the United States all changed radically with the invention of the cotton gin. This amazingly simple machine was invented by the Yale graduate, Eli Whitney (1761–1825).

After leaving school in 1793, Whitney studied law while living on the Savannah, Georgia plantation of Gen. Nathanael Greene's widow. In conversation with local planters he learned of the difficulty of separating the seed from the fibre of short-staple cotton. That plant was then not even a commercial crop. They described a machine, already widely used in India, that could handle long-staple cotton but not the short-staple variety. Whitney had learned mechanical skills in his father's metalworking shop. It took him about ten days to produce a hand-cranked wooden cylinder with wire teeth that revolved through slots in a bar. The cotton that was hand fed into it was torn loose from the seed. Brushes revolving in the opposite direction cleaned the teeth. The patent office, established in 1790, granted him a patent in March 1794.

Whitney also helped pioneer a valuable new production method. U.S. army muskets were then being hand crafted by artisans. He arranged to manufacture them using unskilled, low-wage labor. Thus he helped develop the process of interchangeable parts and assembly-line methods later perfected by Henry Ford.

The letter reprinted below was written by Whitney to his father on September 11, 1793. It catches the inventor at a moment when he has already perfected a working model of the cotton gin, before he has received a patent, and while he is still speculating on whether he will prosper from it. The gin was easily copied by others, and what little money it earned went to paying off lawyers.

Questions

Inventors often have wild fantasies—was this true of Whitney, or did he have realistic expectations?

What role did technology play in American history before the Civil War? What were the objectives and procedures of the patent office in encouraging invention and enterprise and in protecting inventors? What are the advantages and disadvantages in one person or corporation having a patent monopoly? Typically, how are important inventions created today? Is there still a role for the amateur?

I went to N. York with the family of the late Major General Greene to Georgia. I went immediately with the family to their Plantation about twelve miles from Savannah with an expectation of spending four or five days and then proceed into Carolina to take the school as I have mentioned in former letters. During this time I heard much said of the extreme difficulty of ginning Cotton, that is, separating it from its seeds. There were a number of very respectable Gentlemen at Mrs. Greene's who all agreed that if a machine could be invented which would clean the cotton with expedition, it would be a great thing both to the Country and to the inventor. I involuntarily happened to be thinking on the subject and struck out a plan of a Machine in my mind, which I communicated to Miller, (who is agent to the Executors of Genl. Greene and resides in the family, a man of respectability and property) he was pleased with the Plan and said if I would pursue it and try an experiment to see if it would answer, he would be at the whole expense, I should loose nothing but my time, and if I succeeded we would share the profits. Previous to this I found I was like to be disappointed in my school, that is, instead of a hundred, I found I could get only fifty Guineas a year. I however held the refusal of the school until I tried some experiments. In about ten Days I made a little model, for which I was offered, if I would give up all right and title to it, a Hundred Guineas. I concluded to relinquish my school and turn my attention to perfecting the Machine. I made one before I came away which required the labor of one man to turn it and with which one man will clean ten times as much cotton as he can in any other way before known and also clesnse it much better than in the usual

SOURCE: Whitney to his father, Sept. 11, 1793, in M. B. Hammond., ed., in *American Historical Review*, 3:90–127 (1897–98).

mode. This machine may be turned by water or with a horse, with the greatest ease, and one man and a horse will do more than fifty men with the old machines. It makes the labor fifty times less, without throwing any class of People out of business.

I returned to the Northward for the purpose of having a machine made on a large scale and obtaining a Patent for the invention. I went to Philadelphia soon after I arrived, made myself acquainted with the steps necessary to obtain a Patent, took several of the steps and the Secretary of State Mr. Jefferson agreed to send the Patent to me as soon it could be made out—so that I apprehended no difficulty in obtaining the Patent—Since I have been here I have employed several workmen in making machines and as soon as my business is such that I can leave it a few days, I shall come to Westboro'. I think it is probable I shall go to Philadelphia again before I come to Westboro', and when I do come I shall be able to stay but few days. I am certain I can obtain a patent in England. As soon as I have got a Patent in America I shall go with the machine which I am now making, to Georgia, where I shall stay a few weeks to see it at work. From thence I expect to go to England, where I shall probably continue two or three years. How advantageous this business will eventually prove to me, I cannot say. It is generally said by those who know anything about it, that I shall make a Fortune by it. I have no expectation that I shall make an independent fortune by it, but think I had better pursue it than any other business into which I can enter. Something which cannot be foreseen may frustrate my expectations and defeat my Plan; but I am now so sure of success that ten thousand dollars, if I saw the money counted out to me, would not tempt me to give up my right and relinquish the object. I wish you, sir, not to show this letter nor communicate anything of its contents to any body except My Brothers and Sister, *enjoining* it on them to keep the whole a *profound secret.*

1.10 Homesteads for Workingmen

Free homesteading was supposed to give poor workingmen access to public lands in the West. Early proposals also included giving them funds to get there and to buy the tools and seed they might need initially. The concept of a free-homestead act sprang not from a farmers' movement but from the labor movement, in the decade between 1835 and 1844.

Homesteading was supposed to allow the frontier to serve as a safety-valve for social pressures. It would relieve unemployment and other social ills. Such a proposal was strongly resisted by entrenched eastern interests who wanted to retain laborers for factory work. Eventually the free-homestead idea caught on, and was enacted into law in 1862.

But as enacted, homesteading had a serious flaw. It lacked any financial provision that would help poor laborers get started on the land. Even worse, when the homesteads were being distributed, Congress also gave away a huge portion of the public domain in the West to the railroads to finance their new trackage. This made a mockery of the original concept. A distinguished historian, Charles Beard, later called it "almost a fraud upon farmers and industrial workers."

Three statements about homesteading follow. One is from the labor journalist, George Henry Evans, in his Working Man's Advocate *in 1844. Two others are from Congressional representatives Volney E. Howard and Orlando B. Ficklin in 1852.*

Questions

To whom does Evans appeal? What are his objectives and what means would he use to reach them? What are Howard's objections?

How did the Homestead Act actually work in practice? How much land was given away and to whom?

The American frontier is said to have worked as a safety-valve for social distress, sparing this country some of the revolutionary upheaval seen among the lower classes of Europe. How would one measure whether it really worked this way?

George Henry Evans, March 16, 1844—

The leading measure that we shall propose in this paper is *the Equal Right* of every man to the free use of a sufficient portion of the Earth to till for his *subsistence.* If man has a right to LIVE, as all subsistence comes from the earth, he has a right, in a state of nature, to a portion of its spontaneous products; in a state of civilization, to a portion of the earth to till for his subsistence. This right is now, no matter why, in possession of a comparative few, many of whom possess not only a sufficiency, but a superfluity, of land: yet we propose not to divest them of that superfluity, against their consent. We simply propose that the inequality extend no further; that *Government* shall no longer traffic or permit traffic in that which is the property of no man or government; that the Land shall be left, as Nature dictates, free to the use of those who choose to bestow their labor upon it.

We propose that the Public Lands of the States and of the United States shall be *free to actual settlers,* and to actual settlers only; that townships of six miles square shall be laid out in Farms and Lots, of any vacant one of which a man, *not possessed of other land,* may take possession and keep same during his life or pleasure, and with the right to sell his *improvements,* at any time, to any one *not possessed of other land.* . . .

We shall be told, perhaps, as we have been told occasionally by persons who had not reflected on the subject, that the public lands are so cheap *now* as to be accessible to all industrious persons who desire to settle on them. It is not so. Though the nominal price of the lands is one dollar and twenty-five cents an acre, the real price to the actual settler is nearer *ten dollars* an acre,

SOURCES: *The Working Man's Advocate* (New York), March 16, 1844; and *Congressional Globe,* 32 Cong., 1 Sess., Appendix, pp. 523, 583–584.

unless he chooses to become a squatter and trust to Congress for the privilege of purchasing his land at the government price; for the speculator, under the present system, goes ahead of the settler, picks out the best and most eligibly situated tracts, pays for them with paper money (itself a *monstrous cheat*) or its profits, and when the actual settler comes, he must either pay the speculator's price or go further into the wilderness, where he must struggle for years under the disadvantage of conveying his surplus products over bad roads to a distant market.

But suppose that the settler could obtain lands near a market at the government price, they would still be as inaccessible to the *bulk* of our surplus laboring population as if they were in the hands of the speculators. Some few become settlers under the present system; a few more might become so if speculation in land was entirely prohibited; but it needs that the lands should be *free*, in order that the surplus laborers may be absorbed; for the expense of removal to the lands, and of the necessary stock and provisions to bring them into successful cultivation, is more than many could mean. Many of the employed laborers, however, who might be able to meet these expenses, would gladly exchange their life of servitude for one of independence, even at the risk of encountering some hardships; and these would leave vacancies that might be filled by those unable to emigrates. . . .

If we were to take a census of New York for the purpose, we should probably find ten thousand men who desire or are preparing to emigrate to the Public Lands. Our proposition is equivalent to giving all such the sum of *two hundred dollars* each, for they would have to pay that amount for one hundred and sixty acres. . . .

Two hundred dollars, then at the least, and probably much more, will be saved by every emigrant to the Public Lands, from New York or elsewhere, if the plan that we have proposed is adopted by the people.

Volney E. Howard of Texas—

April 21, 1852

But, sir, I deny the constitutional power of Congress to grant away the public property in donations to the poor. This Government is not a national almshouse. . . . There is no sound distinction between giving money by direct appropriations from the Treasury, and land, in the purchase of which that money has been invested. It is no more the property of the nation in one case than in the other, nor less an appropriation. What right have we to tax the property and industry of all classes of society to purchase homesteads, and enrich those who may not be the possessors of the soil? . . .

It is a great mistake to suppose that you will materially better the condition of the man in the old States, or the Atlantic cities, by giving them one hundred and sixty acres of land in the far West. The difficulty with him is not that of procuring the land, but to emigrate himself and family to the country where it is, and to obtain the means of cultivating it. Without this the grant is useless to the poor man. The gift, to make it efficient, should be followed up by a further donation to enable the beneficiary to stock and cultivate it. It would be a far greater boon to all our citizens, of native and foreign origin, to furnish them for a few dollars, a rapid means of reaching the land States in the West; and this, in my opinion, may be accomplished by exercising the legitimate powers of the Government, and without drawing upon the

Treasury, or diminishing the value of the public domain as a source of revenue.

Orlando B. Ficklin of Illinois –

April 24, 1852

We are told by some that they are apprehensive, if this bill should pass, that there will be a rush from the old States to the new States—a kind of general stampede in the direction of the western and north and southwestern portions of this country. That will not be the case, however. In the first place, there are a great many individuals who are attached to home, kindred, and the fireside of their youth. . . . Those who are able to purchase will not select a tract of land in this new wilderness country, but will prefer to buy a home of their choice, land that has been improved by the erection of comfortable houses, and other conveniences, rather than take one not of their choice, and remain on it five years before perfecting their title.

There is still another class that will not avail themselves of this bill; they are such as are too poor to find means to pay the expense of emigrating from the older to the new States, and of settling on these lands; therefore those persons cannot go. . . . The man who is too poor to purchase land, but who has means to defray traveling expenses, will go and select him a home under this bill, improve the land and obtain a patent for it at the end of five years; but the man who is too poor to reach the lands cannot, of course, enjoy their benefits.

1.11 A Middle-Class Response to Labor Riots

The Gilded Age produced a more violent relationship between labor and capital than was known before the Civil War. The first major outbreak of labor strife in American history began in the summer of 1877 with a rash of railroad strikes. Railroad workers had suffered four years of hard times beginning with the business depression of 1873. In Martinsburg, Maryland they had accepted one pay cut but refused to take a second that was being forced on them by management. Labor stoppages spread along the rail arteries to Baltimore, Philadelphia, Pittsburgh, Buffalo, Cleveland, Toledo, Columbus, Cincinnati, Louisville, Indianapolis, St. Louis, Chicago, Kansas City, Omaha and even distant San Francisco.

This conflict was exceptionally violent and it was nationwide in scope. Laborers burned rail cars and equipment and refused to disperse on orders. Beleaguered governors called up state militias, but as the men were reluctant to fire on their local brothers, regular troops had to be called up also. In Indiana the national guard killed 19 men and wounded 100 more. Thirteen were killed and 43 wounded in Reading, Pennsylvania. Two-thirds of the rail mileage was tied up for a time. President Hayes was called on to intervene.

The labor violence of 1877 seemed to threaten the entire industrial system. It was more reminiscent of proletarian uprisings in Europe than anything in recent American experience. It caused fear and loathing among the middle class. The Nation, *a magazine of liberal persuasion, ran the following editorial protesting labor's role in the tragedy.*

Questions

Why did this event shock the middle class? What were their expectations in such matters? What attitudes does the public feel today when labor strikes erupt?

It is impossible to deny that the events of the last fortnight constitute a great national disgrace, and have created a profound sensation throughout the civilized world. . . . There has for fifty years been throughout Christendom a growing faith that outside the area of slave-soil the United States had—of course with the help of great natural resources—solved the problem of enabling labor and capital to live together in political harmony, and that this was the one country in which there was no proletariat and no dangerous class, and in which the manners as well as legislation effectually prevented the formation of one. That the occurrences of the last fortnight will do, and have done, much to shake or destroy this faith, and that whatever weakens it weakens also the fondly-cherished hopes of many millions about the future of the race, there is unhappily little question. We have had what appears a widespread rising, not against political oppression or unpopular government, but against society itself. What is most curious about it is that it has probably taken people here nearly as much by surprise as people in Europe. The optimism in which most Americans are carefully trained, and which the experience of life justifies to the industrious, energetic, and provident, combined with the long-settled political habit of considering riotous poor as the products of a monarchy and aristocracy, and impossible in the absence of "down-trodden masses," has concealed from most of the well-to-do and intelligent classes of the population the profound changes which have during the last thirty years been wrought in the composition and character of the population, especially in the great cities. Vast additions have been made to it within that period, to whom American political and social ideals appeal but faintly, if at all, and who carry in their very blood traditions which give universal suffrage an air of menace to many of the things which civilized men hold most dear. So complete has this illusion been that up to the day of the outbreak at Martinsburg thousands, even of the most reflective class, were gradually ridding themselves of the belief that force would be much longer necessary, or, indeed, was now necessary in the work of government. . . .

Another illusion which the riots have dispelled is that the means provided by the several States for the protection of life and

SOURCE: "The Late Riots," *The Nation* (August 2, 1877), Vol. XXV, no. 631, pp. 68–69.

property, in the shape of police and militia, are at all adequate. . . . A lawful enemy forms an organization which keeps to itself in a defined position, and its attacks are controlled by rules with which men are more or less familiar, and dictated by motives which can be guessed, and the force of which can be weighed. A mob, on the other hand, is essentially irrational, and its conduct has all the fitfulness and incomprehensibleness of that of a wild beast, and is just as merciless and destructive. It requires, therefore, to be met by a coolness and cohesiveness, and a presence of mind, which are not often called for in actual campaigning. . . . This regular troops have; this even the best militia has not and cannot have. The consequence is that a militia regiment, no matter how well drilled, when it finds itself acting against a mob, and the temper of the men begins to be tried by missiles and insults, loses very rapidly its sense of organization. The company and the regiment and the officers fade from the private's view, and he becomes in his own eyes an individual man, at whom a fellow on the sidewalk is throwing brickbats, so he gratifies his rage and provides for his personal safety by taking a shot at him. . . . Killing by militia is apt to rouse a thirst for vengeance, like the killing in a street-fight, while a volley from regulars has the terrors of legal execution. Of course there are militia regiments which are exceptions to this rule, and several during the late troubles have rendered inestimable service; but they are not to be relied on for serious emergencies, such as we trust every sensible man now sees are among the contingencies of American life.

The kindest thing which can be done for the great multitudes of untaught men who have been received on these shores, and are daily arriving, and who are torn perhaps even more here than in Europe by wild desires and wilder dreams, is to show them promptly that society as here organized, on individual freedom of thought and action, is impregnable, and can be no more shaken than the order of nature. The most cruel thing is to let them suppose, even for one week, that if they had only chosen their time better, or had been better led or better armed, they would have succeeded in forcing it to capitulate. In what way better provision, in the shape of public force, should be made for its defence we have no space left to discuss, but . . . it would be fatal to private and public credit and security to allow a state of things to subsist in which 8,000 or 9,000 day-laborers of the lowest class can suspend, even for a whole day, the traffic and industry of a great nation, merely as a means of extorting ten or twenty cents a day more wages from their employers, we presume everybody now sees. Means of prompt and effectual prevention—so plainly effectual that it will never need to be resorted to—must be provided, either by an increase of the standing army or some change in the organization of the militia which will improve its discipline and increase its mobility. There are, of course, other means of protection against labor-risings than physical ones, which ought not to be neglected, though we doubt if they can be made to produce much effect on the present generation. The exercise of greater watchfulness over their tongues by philanthropists, in devising schemes of social improvement, and in affecting to treat all things as open to discussion, and every question as having two sides, for purposes of legislation as well as for purposes of speculation, is one of them. . . . Persons of humane tendencies ought to remember that we live in a world of stern realities, and that the blessings we enjoy have not been showered upon us like the rain from heaven. Our superiority to the Ashantees or the Kurds is not due to right thinking or right feeling only, but to the determined fight which the more enlightened part of the community has waged from generation to generation against the ignorance and brutality, now of one class and now of another. In trying to carry on the race to better things nobody is wholly right or wise. In all controversies there are wrongs on both sides, but most certainly the presumptions in the labor controversy have always been in favor of the sober, orderly, industrious, and prudent, who work and accumulate and bequeath. It is they who brought mankind out of the woods and caves, and keep them out; and all discussion which places them in a position of either moral or mental inferiority to those who contrive not only to own nothing, but to separate themselves from property-holders in feeling or interest, is michievous as well as foolish, for it strikes a blow at the features of human character which raise man above the beasts.

Chapter Two: Power

2.1 Freedom of the Press

In 1734, John Peter Zenger, publisher of the New-York Weekly Journal, *printed articles alleging that the royal governor of New York Colony was corrupt and arrogant. At that time, anyone openly criticizing an English public offical could be prosecuted for libel. Governor William Cosby jailed Zenger, charging him with seditious libel, and ordering copies of his paper publicly burned. Seditious libel was defined as anything likely to lower the esteem of the government in the eyes of the people. A year later Zenger was brought to trial in the first important struggle in America for freedom of the press. His attorney, Andrew Hamilton, a skillful Philadelphia trial lawyer, tried to introduce witnesses who would validate the* Journal's *reports. The judge refused to hear them. Hamilton argued that the jury should judge for itself whether or not Zenger had told the truth about Cosby. Under a free government, he declared in a stirring speech, people should not be prosecuted for telling the truth. Liberty is the "only bulwark against lawless power." The jury agreed, and found Zenger not guilty, amid the cheers of the courtroom spectators.*

Zenger was a German (Palatine) refugee who had arrived in the colonies with a large group of immigrants in 1710 at the age of twelve. He learned his trade as an indentured apprentice to a pioneer printer and went into business printing mostly religious tracts and pamphlets. He later issued an account of his trial (excerpted below) that found a wide and appreciative audience here and in the mother country.

Although Zenger did not testify at his own trial, he was prepared to tell the court that he had migrated from a country where "tyranny, and arbitrary power had ruined almost all the people." Afterward, other judges found the decision wanting, so that the case had little immediate impact. But it gained stature over the years on two major legal points: that truth is an adequate defense against libel, and that a jury on its own judgement should determine general guilt or innocence.

Questions

Why did lawyer Hamilton emphasize the word "false"? Why did he stress the efforts to suppress evidence?

What rights does the press now have, or not have, in exposing the wrongdoing of public officials? What rights should it have?

Mr. Attorney. . . . The case before the court is whether Mr. Zenger is guilty of libeling His Excellency the Governor of New York, and indeed the whole administration of the government. Mr. Hamilton has confessed the printing and publishing, and I think nothing is plainer than that the words in the information [indictment] are scandalous, and tend to sedition, and to disquiet the minds of the people of this province. And if such papers are not libels, I think it may be said there can be no such thing as a libel.

Mr. Hamilton. May it please Your Honor, I cannot agree with Mr. Attorney. For though I freely acknowledge that there are such things as libels, yet I must insist, at the same time, that what my client is charged with is not a libel. And I observed just now that Mr. Attorney, in defining a libel, made use of the words "scandalous, seditious, and tend to disquiet the people." But (whether with design or not I will not say) he omitted the word "false."

Mr. Attorney. I think I did not omit the word "false." But it has been said already that it may be a libel, notwithstanding it may be true.

Mr. Hamilton. In this I must still differ with Mr. Attorney; for I depend upon it, we are to be tried upon this information now before the court and jury, and to which we have pleaded not guilty, and by it we are charged with printing and publishing a certain false, malicious, seditious, and scandalous libel. This word "false" must have some meaning, or else how came it there? . . .

Mr. Chief Justice. You cannot be admitted, Mr. Hamilton, to give the truth of a libel in evidence. A libel is not to be justified; for it is nevertheless a libel that it is true . . .

Mr. Hamilton. I thank Your Honor. Then, gentlemen of the jury, it is to you we must now appeal, for witnesses, to the truth of the facts we have offered, and are denied the liberty to prove. And let it not seem strange that I apply myself to you in this manner. I am warranted so to do both by law and reason.

The law supposes you to be summoned out of the neighborhood where the fact [crime] is alleged to be committed; and the reason of your being taken out of the neighborhood is because you are supposed to have the best knowledge of the fact that is to be tried. And were you to find a verdict against my client, you must take upon you to say the papers referred to in the information, and which we acknowledge we printed and published, are false, scandalous, and seditious. But of this I have no apprehension. You are citizens of New York; you are really what the law supposes you to be, honest and lawful men. And, according to my brief, the facts which we offer to prove were not committed in a corner; they are notoriously known to be true; and therefore in your justice lies our safety. And as we are denied the liberty of giving evidence to prove the truth of what we have published, I will beg leave to lay it down, as a standing rule in such cases, that the suppressing of evidence ought always to be taken for the strongest evidence; and I hope it will have weight with you. . . .

I hope to be pardoned, sir, for my zeal upon this occasion. It is an old and wise caution that when our neighbor's house is on fire, we ought to take care of our own. For though, blessed be God, I live in a government [Pennsylvania] where liberty is well understood, and freely enjoyed, yet experience has shown us all (I'm sure it has

SOURCE: J. P. Zenger, *The Trial of J. P. Z. of New York* (London, 1738), 10–17.

to me) that a bad precedent in one government is soon set up for an authority in another. And therefore I cannot but think it mine, and every honest man's duty, that (while we pay all due obedience to men in authority) we ought at the same time to be upon our guard against power, wherever we apprehend that it may affect ourselves or our fellow subjects.

I am truly very unequal to such an undertaking on many accounts. And you see I labor under the weight of many years, and am borne down with great infirmities of body. Yet old and weak as I am, I should think it my duty, if required, to go to the utmost part of the land, where my service could be of any use, in assist—to quench the flame of prosecutions upon informations, set on foot by the government, to deprive a people of the right of remonstrating (and complaining too) of the arbitrary attempts of men in power. Men who injure and oppress the people under their administration provoke them to cry out and complain; and then make that very complaint the foundation for new oppressions and prosecutions. I wish I could say there were no instances of this kind.

2.2 The Boston Massacre

From 1763 to 1776, the street riots that rumbled through the colonies contributed greatly to the growing rift with Britain. The Stamp Act riots, the Tea Act riots and the Boston Massacre were the most prominent episodes, but other less celebrated disturbances included protests by backwoods farmers and rent strikes by tenant farmers. Sometimes it was hard to tell when the colonists were engaging in class warfare and when they were battling the mother country.

The items that follow are meant to shed light on the Boston Massacre of March 5, 1770, a major episode of crowd disturbance in the pre-Revolutionary period. Two regiments of hated redcoats had been stationed in Boston since 1768 to enforce special customs duties. This was the peacetime standing army that British subjects detested. A rowdy crowd threw insults and rock-filled snowballs at the "lobsterbacks." Someone cried "Fire!" Muskets were discharged and five people lay dead.

Did the crowd unfairly provoke the soldiers? Were the soldiers justified in suppressing the provocation? Was the gunfire willful or accidental? A court generally agreed with the defense attorneys (John Adams and Josiah Quincy, Jr.), when it mildly punished two soldiers and released the rest. But U.S. history favors the dead patriots who are considered early martyrs to British tyranny.

Below are three accounts of the disturbance—two verbal and one graphic. The first is from the testimony of the redcoat officer of the day, Capt. Thomas Preston, the second is from

Figure 2.2. Engraving after Henry Pelham: *Boston Massacre, 1770* (Courtesy, Museum of Fine Arts, Boston).

a document authored by the city government, while the third is a famous engraving by Paul Revere. Agitators printed this picture on fliers distributed to the crowd to stir up sentiment against the defendants.

Questions

Which of the two written accounts of the Boston Massacre seems most plausible and why? How does the artist use his imagination to favor the rebellious crowd? What does this episode tell you about crowd behavior on the eve of a revolution?

Captain Preston's Account—

It is [a] matter of too great notoriety to need any proofs that the arrival of his Majesty's troops in Boston was extremely obnoxious to its inhabitants. They have ever used all means in their power to weaken the regiments, and to bring them into contempt by promoting and aiding desertions. . . .

One of their justices, most thoroughly acquainted with the people and their intentions, openly and publicly in the hearing of great numbers of people and from the seat of justice, declared "that the soldiers must now take care of themselves, *nor trust too much their arms,* for they were but a handful; that the inhabitants carried weapons concealed under their clothes, and would destroy them in a moment, *if they pleased.*" This, considering the malicious temper of the people, was an alarming circumstance to the soldiery. . . .

On Monday night about 8 o'clock two soldiers were attacked and beaten. But the party of the townspeople in order to carry matters to the utmost length, broke into two meetinghouses and rang the alarm bells, which I supposed was for fire as usual, but was soon undeceived. About 9 some of the guard came to and informed me the town inhabitants were assembling to attack the troops, and that the bells were ringing as the signal for that purpose and not for fire, and the beacon intended to be fired to bring in the distant people of the country. This, as I was captain of the day, occasioned my repairing immediately to the main guard. In my way there I saw the people in great commotion, and heard them use the most cruel and horrid threats against the troops. In a few minutes after I reached the guard, about one hundred people passed it and went toward the customhouse were the King's money is lodged. They immediately surrounded the sentry posted there, and with clubs and other weapons threatened to execute their vengeance on him. I was soon informed by a townsman their intention was to carry off the soldier from his post and probably murder him.

This I feared might be a prelude to their plundering the King's chest. I immediately sent a noncommissioned officer and twelve men to protect the sentry and the

SOURCE: Preston's version is from British Public Record Office, Colonial Office, S/759. The second item is from *A Short Narrative of the Horrid Massacre in Boston* (Boston, 1770), reprint edition (New York, 1849), pp. 13–19, 21–22, 28–30. Revere engraving reprinted by permission of The Museum of Fine Arts, Boston.

King's money, and very soon followed myself to prevent, if possible, all disorder, fearing lest the officer and soldiers, by the insults and provocations of the rioters, should be thrown off their guard and commit some rash act. They soon rushed through the people, and by charging their bayonets in half-circles, kept them at a little distance. Nay, so far was I from intending the death of any person that I suffered the troops to go to the post where the unhappy affair took place without any loading in their pieces; nor did I ever give orders for loading them. This remiss conduct in me perhaps merits censure; yet it is evidence, resulting from the nature of things, which is the best and surest that can be offered, that my intention was not to act offensively, but the contrary part, and that not without compulsion. The mob still increased and were more outrageous, striking their clubs or bludgeons one against another, and calling out, come on you rascals, you bloody backs, you lobster scoundrels, fire if you dare, God damn you, fire and be damned, we know you dare not, and much more such language was used. At this time I was between the soldiers and the mob, parleying with, and endeavoring all in my power to persuade them to retire peaceably, but to no purpose. They advanced to the points of the bayonets, struck some of them. On which some well behaved persons asked me if the guns were charged. I replied yes. They then asked me if I intended to order the men to fire. I answered no, by no means, observing to them that I was advanced before the muzzles of the men's pieces, and must fall a sacrifice if they fired; that the soldiers were upon the half cock and charged bayonets, and my giving the word fire under those circumstances would prove me to be no officer. While I was thus speaking, one of the soldiers having received a severe blow with a stick, stepped a little on one side and instantly fired, on which turning to and asking him why he fired without orders, I was struck with a club on my arm, which for some time deprived me of the use of it, which blow had it been placed on my head, most probably would have destroyed me. On this a general attack was made on the men by a great number of heavy clubs and snowballs being thrown at them, by which all our lives were in imminent danger, some persons at the same time from behind calling out, damn your bloods—why don't you fire. Instantly three or four of the soldiers fired, one after another, and directly after three more in the same confusion and hurry. The mob then ran away, except three unhappy men who instantly expired, one more is since dead, three others are dangerously, and four slightly wounded. The whole of this melancholy affair was transacted in almost twenty minutes. On my asking the soldiers why they fired without orders, they said they heard the word fire and supposed it came from me. This might be the case as many of the mob called out fire, fire, but I assured the men that I gave no such order; that my words were, don't fire, stop your firing. In short, it was scarcely possible for the soldiers to know who said fire, or don't fire, or stop your firing.

A Council was immediately called, on the breaking up of which three justices met and issued a warrant to apprehend me and eight soldiers. On hearing of this procedure I instantly went to the sheriff and surrendered myself, though for the space of four hours I had it in my power to have made my escape, which I most undoubtedly should have attempted and could easily executed, had I been the least conscious of any guilt. . . . I am, though perfectly innocent under most unhappy circumstances, having nothing in reason to expect but the loss of life in a very ignominous manner, without the interposition of his Majesty's royal goodness.

The Horrid Massacre in Boston, 1770—

Perpetrated in the Evening of the Fifth Day of March 1770, by Soldiers of the Twenty-ninth Regiment, which with the Fourteenth Regiment were then Quartered there; with Some Observations on the State of Things Prior to that Catastrophe. Gathered and Printed by the Town of Boston,

At the end of the late war, in which this province bore so distinguished a part, a happy union subsisted between Great Britain and the colonies. This was unfortunately interrupted by the Stamp Act; but it was in some measure restored by the repeal of it. It was again interrupted by other acts of Parliament for taxing America; and by the appointment of a Board of Commissioners, . . . By the said act the said Commissioners were "to be resident in some convenient part of his Majesty's dominions in America." . . .

The residence of the Commissioners here has been detrimental . . . [Also] while the town was surrounded by a considerable number of his Majesty's ships of war, two regiments landed and took possession of it; and to support these, two other regiments arrived some time after from Ireland; one of which landed at Castle Island, and the other in the town.

Thus were we, in aggravation of our other embarrassments, embarrassed with troops, forced upon us contrary to our inclination . . . who were quartered in the town in direct violation of an act of Parliament for quartering troops in America.

As they were the procuring cause of troops being sent hither, they must therefore be the remote and blameable cause of all the disturbances and bloodshed that have taken place in consequence of that measure.

We shall next attend to the conduct of the troops, and to some circumstances relative to them.

The challenging [of] the inhabitants by sentinels posted in all parts of the town before the lodgings of officers, which (for about six months, while it lasted), occasioned many quarrels and uneasiness.

Captain Wilson, of the fifty-ninth, exciting the Negroes of the town to take away their masters' lives and property, and repair to the army for protection, which was fully proved against him. The attack of a party of soldiers on some of the magistrates of the town—the repeated rescues of soldiers from peace officers—the firing of a loaded musket in a public street, to the endangering a great number of peaceable inhabitants—the frequent wounding of persons by their bayonets and cutlasses, and the numerous instances of bad behavior in the soldiery, made us early sensible that the troops were not sent here for any benefit to the town or province, and that we had no good to expect from such conservators of the peace.

It was not expected, however, that such an outrage and massacre, as happened here on the evening of the fifth instant, would have been perpetrated. There were then killed and wounded, by a discharge of musketry, eleven of his Majesty's subjects, viz.:

> Mr. Samuel Gray, killed on the spot by a ball entering his head.
> Crispus Attucks, a mulatto, killed on the spot, two balls entering his breast.
> Mr. James Caldwell, killed on the spot, by two balls entering his back.
> Mr. Samuel Maverick, a youth of

> seventeen years of age, mortally wounded; he died the next morning.
> Mr. Patrick Carr mortally wounded; he died the fourteenth instant.
> Christopher Monk and John Clark, youths about seventeen years of age, dangerously wounded. It is apprehended that they will die.
> Mr. Edward Payne, merchant, standing at his door; wounded.
> Messrs. John Green, Robert Patterson, and David Parker; all dangerously wounded. . . .

Samuel Drowne [a witness] declares that, about nine o'clock of the evening of the fifth of March current, standing at his own door in Cornhill, he saw about fourteen or fifteen soldiers of the twenty-ninth regiment, who came from Murray's barracks, armed with naked cutlasses, swords, etc., and came upon the inhabitants of the town, then standing or walking in Cornhill, and abused some, and violently assaulted others as they met them; most of them were without so much as a stick in their hand to defend themselves, as he very clearly could discern, it being moonlight, and himself being one of the assaulted persons. All or most of the said soldiers he saw go into King Street (some of them through Royal Exchange Lane), and there followed them, and soon discovered them to be quarreling and fighting with the people whom they saw there, which he thinks were not more than a dozen, when the soldiers came first, armed as aforesaid. Of those dozen people, the most of them were gentlemen, standing together a little below the Town House, upon the Exchange. At the appearance of those soldiers so armed, the most of the twelve persons went off, some of them being first assulted.

The violent proceedings of this party, and their going into King Street "quarreling and fighting with the people whom they saw there" (mentioned in Mr. Drowne's deposition), was immediately introductory to the grand catastrophe.

These assailants, who issued from Murray's barracks (so-called), after attacking and wounding divers persons in Cornhill, as above-mentioned, being armed, proceeded (most of them) up the Royal Exchange Lane into King Street; where, making a short stop, and after assaulting and driving away the few they met there, they brandished their arms and cried out, "Where are the boogers! Where are the cowards!" At this time there were very few persons in the street beside themselves. This party in proceeding from Exchange Lane into King Street, must pass the sentry posed at the westerly corner of the Custom House, which butts on that lane and fronts on that street. This is needful to be mentioned, as near that spot and in that street the bloody tragedy was acted, and the street actors in it were stationed: their station being but a few feet from the front side of the said Custom House. The outrageous behavior and the threats of the said party occasioned the ringing of the meeting-house bell near the head of King Street, which bell ringing quick, as for fire, it presently brought out a number of the inhabitants, who being soon sensible of the occasion of it, were naturally led to King Street, where the said party had made a stop but a little while before, and where their stopping had drawn together a number of boys, round the sentry at the Custom House. Whether the boys mistook the sentry for one of the said party, and thence took occasion to differ with him, or whether he first affronted them, which is affirmed in several depositions—however that may be, there was much foul language between them, and some of them, in consequence of his pushing at them with his bayonet, threw snowballs at him, which occasioned him to knock hastily at the door of the Custom House. From hence two persons thereupon proceeded immediately to the mainguard which was posted opposite to the State House, at a small distance, near the head of the said street. The officer on guard was Captain Preston, who with seven or eight soldiers, with firearms and charged bayonets, issued from the guardhouse, and in great haste posted himself and his soldiers in front of the Custom House, near the corner aforesaid. In passing to this station the soldiers pushed several persons with their bayonets, driving through the people in so rough a manner that it appeared they intended to create a disturbance. This occasioned some snowballs to be thrown at them, which seems to have been the only provocation that was given. Mr. Knox (between whom and Captain Preston there was some conversation on the spot) declares that while he was talking with Captain Preston, the soldiers of his detachment had attacked the people with their bayonets; and that there was not the least provocation given to Captain Preston or his party; the backs of the people being toward them when the people were attacked. He also declares that Captain Preston seemed to be in great haste and much agitated, and that, according to his opinion, there were not then present in King Street above seventy or eighty persons at the extent.

The said party was formed into a half circle; and within a short time after they had been posted at the Custom House, began to fire upon the people.

Captain Preston is said to have ordered them to fire, and to have repeated that order. One gun was fired first; then others in succession, and with deliberation, till ten or a dozen guns were fired; or till that number of discharges were made from the guns that were fired. By which means eleven persons will killed or wounded, as above represented.

2.3 To Respect God's Laws

The young English minister and school teacher Jonathan Boucher kept a loaded pistol on the pulpit as he preached in a Virginia Anglican church. Although a personal friend of George Washington, he was a Tory and his loyalist sermons against the "rebellious mischief" aroused suspicion and anger. Irate Whigs threatened him physically. In 1775 he fled to England, where he continued to oppose the colonial uprising. In 1797 he issued a book containing his anti-Revolutionary sermons. The preachment "On Civil Liberty, Passive Obedience, and Non-Resistance" is excerpted next.

Boucher's argument ultimately rests on the theory of the divine right of kings, already an unpopular idea in the English-speaking world. He also cites Biblical arguments and criticizes the theories of the English philosopher John Locke, particularly the "social compact" theory and a belief in the consent of the governed. The social compact, he says, is based on a fictional concept of history, an event that never happened.

Question

What is the theory of the social compact and how does Boucher attack it?

Would Boucher accept any and all *personal abuses, or would he draw the line somewhere against injustice and finally take up forcible resistance? How would he fare in a democratic republic?*

Compare Boucher's position with that of Tom Paine. How do their views differ, not only on rebellion, but on government, religion, human nature, and social privilege?

Could Boucher speak for all people—kings and subjects, farmers and planters, sailors and admirals—or is his a class-based argument better suited to the interests of people with money, rank and privilege?

Compare his views on passive resistance with those of Henry David Thoreau (Document 2.9, below).

Obedience to government is every man's duty, because it is every man's interest; but it is particularly incumbent on Christians, because (in addition to its moral fitness) it is enjoined by the positive commands of God; and, therefore, when Christians are disobedient to human ordinances, they are also disobedient to God. If the form of government under which the good providence of God has been pleased to place us be mild and free, it is our duty to enjoy it with gratitude and with thankfulness and, in particular, to be careful not to abuse it by licentiousness. If it be less indulgent and less liberal than in reason it ought to be, still it is our duty not to disturb and destroy the peace of the community by becoming refractory and rebellious subjects and *resisting the ordinances of God*. However humiliating such acquiescence may seem to men of warm and eager minds, the wisdom of God in having made it our duty is manifest. . . . To respect the laws is to respect liberty in the only rational sense in which the term can be used, for the liberty consists in a subserviency to law. "Where there is no law," says Mr. Locke, "there is no freedom." The mere man of nature (if such an one there ever was) has no freedom: *all his lifetime he is subject to bondage*. It is by being included within the pale of civil polity and government that he takes his rank in society as a free man.

Hence it follows that we are free, or otherwise, as we are governed by law, or by the mere arbitrary will, or wills, of any individual, or any number of individuals. and liberty is not the setting at nought and despising established laws—much less the making of our own wills the rule of our own actions, or the actions of others—and not bearing (whilst yet we dictate to others) the being dictated to, even by laws of the land; but it is the being governed by law and by law only. . . . To pursue liberty, then, in a manner not warranted by law, whatever the pretense may be, is clearly to be hostile to liberty; and those persons who thus *promise you liberty* are themselves *the servants of corruption.*

"Civil liberty (says an excellent writer) is a severe and a restained thing; implies, in the notion of it authority, settled subordinations, subjection, and obedience. . . . therefore, the love of liberty which does not produce this effect, the love of liberty which is not a real principle of dutiful behavior toward authority, is as hypocritical as the religion which is not productive of a good life. Licentiousness is, in truth, such an excess of liberty as is of the same nature with tyranny. For, what is the difference betwixt them, but that one is lawless power exercised under pretense of authority, or by persons vested with it; the other, lawless power exercised under pretense of liberty, or without any pretense at all? A people, then, must always be less free in proportion as they are more licentious, licentiousness being not only different from liberty but directly contrary to it—a direct breach upon it."

True liberty, then, is liberty to do everything that is right, and the being restrained from doing anything that is wrong. So far from our having a right to do everything that we please, under a notion of liberty, liberty itself is limited and confined—but limited and confined only by laws which are at the same time both its foundation and its support. It can, however, hardly be necessary to inform you that ideas and notions respecting liberty, very different from these, are daily suggested in the speeches and the writings of the times; and also that some opinions on the subject of government at large, which appear to me to be particularly loose and dangerous, are advanced in the sermon now under consideration; and that, therefore, you will acknowledge the propriety of my bestowing some farther notice on them both.

It is laid down in this sermon, as a settled maxim, that the end of government is "the common good of mankind." I am not sure that the position itself is indisputable; but, if it were, it would by no means follow that "this common good being matter of common consent." There is an appearance of logical accuracy and precision in this statement; but it is only an appearance. . . . In no instance have mankind ever yet agreed as to what is, or is not, "the common good.". . . . What one people in one age have concurred in establishing as the "common good," another in another age have voted to be mischievous and big with ruin. The premises, therefore, that "the common good is matter of common feeling," being false, the consequence drawn from it, viz., that government was instituted by "common consent," is of course equally false.

This popular notion, that government was originally formed by the consent or by a compact of the people, rest on, and is supported by, another similar notion, not less popular, nor better founded. This other notion is that the whole human race is born equal; and that no man is naturally inferior, or, in any respect, subjected to another; and that he can be made subject to another only by his own consent. . . . Man differs from man in everything that can be supposed to lead to supremacy and subjection, *as one star differs from another star in glory*. It was the purpose of the Creator that man should be social; but, without government, there can be no society; nor, without some relative inferiority and superiority, can there be any government. . . . On the principle of equality, neither his parents, nor even the vote of a majority of the society (however virtuously and honorably that vote might be obtained), can have any such authority over any man. . . . The same principle of equality that exempts him from being governed without his own consent clearly entitles him to recall and resume that consent whenever he sees fit; and he alone has a right to judge when and for what reasons it may be resumed.

Any attempt, therefore, to introduce this fantastic system into practice would reduce the whole business of social life to the wearisome, confused, and useless task of mankind's first expressing, and then withdrawing, their consent to an endless succession of schemes of government. Governments, through always forming, would never be completely formed; for the majority today might be the minority tomorrow, and, of course, that which is now fixed might and would be soon unfixed. Mr. Locke indeed says that, "by consenting with others to make one body-politic under government, a man puts himself under an obligation to every one of that society to submit to the determination of the majority, and to be concluded by it." For the sake of the peace of society, it is undoubtedly reasonable and necessary that this should be the case; but, on the principles of the system now under consideration, before Mr. Locke or any of his followers can have authority to say that it actually is the case, it must be stated and proved that every individual man, on entering into the social compact, did first consent, and declare his consent, to be concluded and bound in all cases by the vote of the majority. In making such a declaration, he would certainly consult both his interest and his duty; but at the same time he would also completely relinquish the principle of equality, and eventually subject himself to the possibility of being governed by ignorant and corrupt tyrants. Mr. Locke himself afterward disproves his own position respecting this supposed obligation to submit to the "determination of the majority," when he argues that a right of resistance still exists in the governed; for, what is resistance but a recalling and resuming the consent heretofore supposed to have been given, and in fact refusing to submit to the "determination of the majority"? It does not clearly appear what Mr. Locke exactly meant by what he calls "the determination of the majority"; but the only rational and practical public manner of declaring "the determination of the majority" is by law: the laws, therefore, in all countries, even in those that are despotically governed, are to be regarded as the declared "determination of a majority" of the members of that community; because, in such cases, even acquiescence only must be looked upon as equivalent to a declaration. A right of resistance, therefore, for which Mr. Locke contends, is incompatible with the duty of submitting to the determination of "the majority," for which he also contends.

It is indeed impossible to carry into effect any government which, even by compact, might be framed with this reserved right of resistance. . . .

Such theories of government seem to give something like plausibility to the notions of those other modern theorists who regard all governments as invasions of the naural rights of men, usurpations, and tyranny. On this principle it would follow, and could not be denied, that government was indeed fundamentally, as our people are sedulously taught it still is, an evil. Yet it is to government that mankind owe their having, after their fall and corruption been again reclaimed, from a state of barbarity and war, to the conveniency and the safety of the social state; and it is by means of government that society is still preserved, the weak protected from the strong, and the artless and innocent from the wrongs of proud oppressors. . . .

. . . The glory of God is much concerned that there should be good government in the world; it is, therefore, the uniform doctrine of the Scriptures that it is under the deputation and authority of God alone that *kings reign and princes decree justice.* Kings and princes (which are only othe words for supreme magistrates) were doubtless created and appointed, not so much for their own sakes, as for the sake of the people committed to their charge; yet are they not, therefore, the creatures of the people. So far from deriving their authority from any supposed consent or suffrage of men, they received their commission from Heaven; they receive it from God, the source and original of all power. However obsolete, therefore, either the sentiment or the language may now be deemed, it is with the most perfect propriety that the supreme magistrate, whether consisting of one or of many, and whether denominated an emperor, a king, an archon, a dictator, a consul, or a senate, is to be regarded and venerated as the vice regent of God. . . .

Let it be supposed, however, that even the worst may happen, which can happen: that our remonstrances are disregarded, our petitions rejected, and our grievances unredressed: what, you will naturally ask—what, in such a case, would I advise you to do? . . . To your question, therefore, I hesitate not to answer that I wish and advise you to act the part of reasonable men and of Christians. . . .

. . . If you think the duty of three pence a pound upon tea laid on by the British Parliament a grievance, it is your duty to instruct your members to take all the constitutional means in their power to obtain redress; if those means fail of success, you cannot but be sorry and grieved, but you will better bear your disappointment by being able to reflect that is was not owing to any misconduct of your own. And, what is the whole history of human life, public or private, but a series of disappointments? It might be hoped that Christians would not think it grievous to be doomed to submit to disappointments and calamities, as their Master submitted, even if they were as innocent. . . .

This visionary idea of a government by compact was, as Filmer says, "first hatched in the schools; and hath, ever since, been fostered by Papists, for good divinity.". . . In an evil hour it gained admittance into the Church of England; being first patronized by her during the civil wars, by "a few miscreants, who were as far from being true Protestants, as true Subjects." Mankind have listened, and continue to listen to it with a predilection and partiality. . . . What we wish to be true, we easily persuade ourselves is true. On this principle it is not difficult to account for our thus eagerly following these *ignes fatui* of our own fancies or "feelings," rather than the sober steady light of the word of God. . . .

It was not to be expected from an all-wise and all-merciful Creator, that, having formed creatures capable of order and rule, he should turn them loose into the world under the guidance only of their own unruly wills; that, like so many wild beasts, they might tear and worry one another in their mad contests for preeminence. His purpose from the first, no doubt, was, that men should *live godly and sober lives.* But, such is the sad estate of our corrupted nature, that, ever since the Fall, we have been averse from good, and prone to evil. We are indeed, so disorderly and unmanageable, that, were it not for the restraints and the terrors of human laws, it would not be possible for us to dwell together. But as men were clearly formed for society, and to dwell together, which yet they cannot do without the restraints of law, or, in other words, without government, it is fair to infer that government was also the original intention of God, who never decrees the end, without also decreeing the means . . . we find, that, copying after the fair model of heaven itself, wherein there was government even among the angels, the families of the earth were subjected to rulers, at first set over them by God; *for, there is no power, but of God; the powers that be are ordained of God.* The first father was the first king: and if (according to the rule just laid down) the law may be inferred from the practice, it was thus that all government originated; and monarchy is it's most ancient form.

2.4 A Radical's Manifesto

The Englishman Thomas Paine had lived in the colonies for only two years when he wrote his best-selling pamphlet, Common Sense. *It appeared anonymously in January 1776 and became an instant success. In a short time 300,000 of the three million colonists had read and debated its merits. His theme was independence.*

When Common Sense *appeared, British soldiers and colonials had already clashed in bloody battles, but most people were still fearful of independence. Paine savagely attacked the monarchy and declared of the long-standing relationship with England, " 'Tis time to part." Written in stirring prose, the pamphlet issued a resounding cry for rebellion and republicanism. It paved the way for the Declaration on Independence six months later. Thus it must be considered among the most important political treatises in the English language. A selection follows.*

Though a personal favorite of George Washington and other founding fathers, Tom Paine was a radical who made moderates nervous. He later wrote Rights of Man, *supporting the French Revolution, and* Age of Reason, *attacking all organized religion. These books won him many enemies. He spend the last years of his life in poverty and died in obscurity in 1809.*

Questions

On what grounds does Paine justify rebellion? What literary images and arguments does he use to undermine respect for the monarchy and cut the ties with England?

Were the conditions of the English colonies in January 1776 really "intolerable," or was there much exaggeration on the part of the rebels?

Compare this pamphlet with the Declaration of Independence. Can you see the connections?

What attitudes do Americans display toward current-day rebels? Cite examples.

In the following pages I offer nothing more than simple facts, plain arguments, and common sense. . . .

Volumes have been written on the subject of the struggle between England and America. Men of all ranks have embarked in the controversy, from different motives, and with various designs; but all have been ineffectual, and the period of debate is closed. Arms as the last resource decide the contest; the appeal was the choice of the king, and the continent has accepted the challenge. . . .

The sun never shone on a cause of greater worth. 'Tis not the affair of a city, a county, a province, or a kingdom; but of a continent—of at least one eighth part of the habitable globe. 'Tis not the concern of a day, a year, or an age; posterity are virtually involved in the contest, and will be more or less affected even to the end of time, by the proceedings now. Now is the seed-time of continental union, faith and honor. The least fracture now will be like a name engraved with the point of a pin on the tender rind of a young oak; the wound would enlarge with the tree, and posterity read it in full grown characters.

By referring the matter from argument to arms, a new era for politics is struck—a new method of thinkings has arisen. All plans, proposals, &c. prior to the nineteenth of April, *i.e.* to the commencement of hostilities, are like the almanacks of the last year; which though proper then, are superceded and useless now. Whatever was advanced by the advocates on either side of the question then, terminated in one and the same point, *viz.* a union with Great Britain; the only difference between the parties was the method of effecting it; the one proposing force, the other friendship; but it has so far happened that the first has failed, and the second has withdrawn her influence.

As much has been said of the advantages of reconciliation, which, like an agreeable dream, has passed away and left us as we were, it is but right that we should examine the contrary side of the argument, and inquire into some of the many material injuries which these colonies sustain, and always will sustain, by being connected with and dependant on Great Britain. To examine that connection and dependance, on the principles of nature and common sense, to see what we have to trust to, if separated, and what we are to expect, if dependant.

I have heard it asserted by some, that as America has flourished under her former connection with Great Britain, the same connection is necessary towards her future happiness, and will always have the same effect. Nothing can be more fallacious than this kind of argument. We may as well assert that because a child has thrived upon milk, that it is never to have meat, or that

SOURCE: Moncure D. Conway, ed., *The Writings of Thomas Paine* (New York, 1894), I, 84-87, 90-91, 100-101.

the first twenty years of our lives is to become a precedent for the next twenty. But even this is admitting more than is true; for I answer roundly, that America would have flourished as much, and probably much more, had no European power taken any notice of her. The commerce by which she hath enriched herself are the necessaries of life, and will always have a market while eating is the custom of Europe.

But she has protected us, say some. That she hath engrossed us is true, and defended the continent at our expense as well as her own, is admitted; and she would have defended Turkey from the same motive, *viz.* for the sake of trade and dominion.

Alas! we have been long led away by ancient prejudices and made large sacrifices to superstition. We have boasted the protection of Great Britain, without considering, that her motive was *interest* not *attachment;* and that she did not protect us from *our enemies* on *our account;* but from *her enemies* on *her own account,* from those who had no quarrel with us on any *other account,* and who will always be our enemies on the *same account.* Let Britain waive her pretensions to the continent, or the continent throw off the dependance, and we should be at peace with France and Spain, were they at war with Britain. The miseries of Hanover's last war ought to warn us against connections. . . .

But Britain is the parent country, say some. Then the more shame upon her conduct. Even brutes do not devour their young, nor savages make war upon their families; wherefore, the assertion, if true, turns to her reproach; but it happens not to be true, or only partly so, and the phrase *parent* or *mother country* hath been jesuitically adopted by the king and his parasites, with a low papistical design of gaining an unfair bias on the credulous weakness of our minds. Europe, and not England, is the parent country of America. This new world hath been the asylum for the persecuted lovers of civil and religious liberty from *every part* of Europe. Hither have they fled, not from the tender embrances of the mother, but from the cruelty of the monster; and it is so far true of England, that the same tyranny which drove the first emigrants from home, pursues their descendants still. . . .

It is pleasant to observe by what regular gradations we surmount the force of local prejudices, as we enlarge our acquaintance with the world. A man born in any town in England divided into parishes, will naturally associate most with his fellow parishioners (because their interests in many cases will be common) and distinguish him by the name of *neighbor;* if he meet him but a few miles from home, he drops the narrow idea of a street, and salutes him by the name of *townsman;* if he travel out of the county and meet him in any other, he forgets the minor divisions of street and town, and calls him *countryman, i.e. countyman;* but if in their foreign excursions they should associate in France, or any other part of *Europe,* their local remembrance would be enlarged into that of *Englishman.* And by a just parity of reasoning, all Europeans meeting in America, or any other quarter of the globe, are *countrymen;* for England, Holland, Germany, or Sweden, when compared with the whole, stand in the same places on the larger scale, which the divisions of street, town, and county do on the smaller ones; distinctions too limited for continental minds. Not one third of the inhabitants, even of this province, [Pennsylvania], are of English descent. Wherefore, I reprobate the phrase of parent or mother country applied to England only, as being false, selfish, narrow and ungenerous.

But, admitting that we were all of English descent, what does it amount to? Nothing. Britain, being now an open enemy, extinguishes every other name and title: and to say that reconciliation is our duty, is truly farcical. The first king of England, of the present line (William the Conqueror) was a Frenchman, and half the peers of England are descendants from the same country; wherefore, by the same method of reasoning, England ought to be governed by France. . . .

Our plan is commerce, and that, well attended to, will secure us the peace and friendship of all Europe; because it is the interest of all Europe to have America a free port. Her trade will always be a protection, and her barrenness of gold and silver secure her from invaders.

I challenge the warmest advocate for reconciliation to show a single advantage that this continent can reap by being connected with Great Britain. . . .

But the injuries and disadvantages which we sustain by the connection, are without number; and our duty to mankind at large, as well as to ourselves, instruct us to renounce the alliance: because, any submission to, or dependence on, Great Britain, tends directly to involve this continent in European wars and quarrels, and set us at variance with nations who would otherwise seek our friendship, and against whom we have neither anger nor complaint. As Europe is our market for trade, we ought to form no partial connection with any part of it. It is the true interest of America to steer clear of European contentions, which she never can do, while, by her dependence on Britain, she is made the makeweight in the scale of British politics.

Europe is too thickly planted with kingdoms to be long at peace, and whenever a war breaks out between England and any foreign power, the trade of America goes to ruin, *because of her connection with Britain.* The next war may not turn out like the last, and should it not, the advocates for reconciliation now will be wishing for separation then, because neutrality in that case would be a safer convoy than a man of war. Every thing that is right or reasonable pleads for separation. The blood of the slain, the weeping voice of nature cries, 'TIS TIME TO PART. Even the distance at which the Almighty hath placed England and America is a strong and natural proof that the authority of the one over the other, was never the design of heaven. . . .

The authority of Great Britain over this continent, is a form of government, which sooner or later must have an end. And a serious mind can draw no true pleasure by looking forward, under the painful and positive conviction that what he calls "the present constitution" is merely temporary. As parents, we can have no joy, knowing that this government is not sufficiently lasting to insure any thing which we may bequeath to posterity. . . .

Men of passive tempers look somewhat lightly over the offences of Great Britain, and, still hoping for the best, are apt to call out, *Come, come, we shall be friends again for all this.* But examine the passions and feelings of mankind: bring the doctrine of reconciliation to the touchstone of nature, and then tell me whether you can hereafter love, honor, and faithfully serve the power that hath carried fire and sword into your land? . . . I ask, hath your house been burnt? Hath your property been destroyed before your face? Are your wife and children destitute of a bed to lie on, or bread to live on? Have you lost a parent or a child by their hands, and yourself the ruined and wretched survivor? If you have not, then are you not a judge of those who have. But if you have, and can still shake hands with the murderers, then are you unworthy the name of husband, father, friend, or lover, and whatever may be your rank or title in life, you have the heart of a coward, and the spirit of a sycophant.

'Tis repugnant to reason, to the universal order of things, to all examples from former ages, to suppose that this continent can long remain subject to any external power. The most sanguine in Britain doth not think so. . . .

As to government matters, 'tis not in the power of Britain to do this continent justice: the business of it will soon be too weighty and intricate to be managed with any tolerable degree of convenience, by a power so distant from us, and so very ignorant of us; for if they cannot conquer us, they cannot govern us. To be always running three or four thousand miles with a tale or a petition, waiting four or five months for an answer, which, when obtained, requires five or six more to explain it in, will in a few years be looked upon as folly and childishness. There was a time when it was proper, and there is a proper time for it to cease.

Small islands not capable of protecting themselves are the proper objects for government to take under their care; but there is something absurd, in supposing a Continent to be perpetually governed by an island. . . . No man was a warmer wisher for a reconciliation than myself, before the fatal nineteenth of April, 1775, but the moment the event of that day was made known, I rejected the hardened, sullen-tempered Pharaoh of England for ever; and disdain the wretch, that with the pretended title of FATHER OF HIS PEOPLE can unfeelingly hear of their slaughter, and composedly sleep with their blood upon his soul.

But admitting that matters were now made up, what would be the event? I answer, the ruin of the continent. And that for several reasons.

First. The powers of governing still remaining in the hands of the king, he will have a negative over the whole legislation of this continent. And as he hath shown himself such an inveterate enemy to liberty, and discovered such a thirst for arbitrary power, is he, or is he not, a proper person to say to these colonies, *You shall make no laws but what I please!?* And is there any inhabitant of America so ignorant as not to know, that according to what is called the *present Constitution,* this continent can make no laws but what the king gives leave to; and is there any man so unwise as not to see, that (considering what has happened) he will suffer no law to be made here but such as suits *his* purpose? . . . Is the power who is jealous of our prosperity, a proper power to govern us? Whoever says *No,* to this question, is an independent for independency means no more than this, whether we shall make our own laws, or whether the king, the greatest enemy this continent hath, or can have, shall tell us *there shall be no laws but such as I like.*

. . . The king's negative here is ten times more dangerous and fatal than it can be in England; for there he will scarcely refuse his consent to a bill for putting England into as strong a state of defense as possible, and in America he would never suffer such a bill to be passed.

Secondly. That as even the best terms which we can expect to obtain can amount to no more than a temporary expedient, or a kind of government by guardianship, which can last no longer than till the colonies come of age, so the general face and state of things in the interim will be unsettled and unpromising. Emigrants of property will not choose to come to a country whose form of government hangs but by a thread, and who is every day tottering on the brink of commotion and disturbance; and numbers of the present inhabitants would lay hold of the interval to dispose of their effects, and quit the continent.

But the most powerful of all arguments is, that nothing but independence, *i.e.* a continental form of government, can keep the peace of the continent and preserve it inviolate from civil wars. I dread the event of a reconciliation with Britain now, as it is more than probable that it will be followed by a revolt some where or other, the consequences of which may be far more fatal than all the malice of Britain. . . .

Where there are no distinctions there can be no superiority; perfect equality affords no temptation. The Republics of Europe are all (and we may say always) in peace. Holland and Switzerland are without wars, foreign or domestic: Morarchical governments, it is true, are never long at rest: the crown itself is a temptation to enterprising ruffians at home; and that degree of pride and insolence ever attendant on regal authority, swells into a rupture with foreign powers in instances where a republican government, by being formed on more natural principles, would negociate the mistake. . . .

But where, say some, is the king of America? . . . in America the law is king. For as in absolute governments the king is law, so in free countries the law ought to be king; and there ought to be no other. . . .

2.5 The Declaration of Independence

On June 7, 1776 Richard Henry Lee introduce a resolution before the Continental Congress meeting in Philadelphia that called for a declaration of independence. After two days of debate the delegates voted to establish a committee headed by Jefferson to draft it. Jefferson's committee came back with a proposal on June 28. It was not an especially original statement, since it drew upon previous documents issued in Congress and used ideas about government popularized by colonial pamphleteers for the past decade, but it was a momentous one. "This morning is assigned for the greatest debate of all," John Adams wrote on July 1. "May Heaven prosper the new-born republic, and make it more glorious than any former republics have been." That very day nine colonies voted to adopt, two said no, one delegation split and one abstained. The following day, twelve delegations voted yes, while New York remained a hold-out. Then came the final polishing and cutting, when a long argument blaming the king for slavery was trashed. On July 4 it was proclaimed amid loud cheers. A replica of the king's arms was pried from above the statehouse door and tossed into a bonfire, and the revolution had begun in earnest.

Questions

Examine the complaints of the rebellious Congress. Were they real, or were they puffed up to strengthen the case for independence?

The Declaration was an expression of natural rights philosophy. How did this manifest itself?

What has been the lasting impact of this document in this country and elsewhere in the world?

When in the course of human events, it becomes necessary for one people to dissolve the political bands which have connected them with another, and to assume among the powers of the earth, the separate and equal station to which the Laws of Nature and of Nature's God entitle them, a decent respect to the opinions of mankind requires that they should declare the causes which impel them to the separation.

We hold these truths to be self-evident, that all men are created equal, that they are endowed by their Creator with certain unalienable Rights, that among these are Life, Liberty and the pursuit of Happiness. That to secure these rights, Governments are instituted among Men, deriving their just powers from the consent of the governed, That whenever any Form of Government becomes destructive of these ends, it is the Right of the People to alter or to abolish it, and to institute new Government, laying its foundation on such principles and organizing its powers in such form, as to them shall seem most likely to effect their Safety and Happiness. Prudence, indeed, will dictate that Governments long established should not be changed for light and transient causes; and accordingly all experience hath shewn, that mankind are more disposed to suffer, while evils are sufferable, than to right themselves by abolishing the forms to which they are accustomed. But when a long train of abuses and usurpations, pursuing invariably the same Object evinces a design to reduce them under absolute Despotism, it is their right, it is their duty, to throw off such Government, and to provide new Guards for their future security. Such had been the patient sufferance of these Colonies; and such is now the necessity which constrains them to alter their former Systems of Government. The history of the present King of Great Britain is a history of repeated injuries and usurpations, all having in direct object the establishment of an absolute Tyranny over these States. To prove this, let Facts be submitted to a candid world.

He has refused his Assent to Laws, the most wholesome and necessary for the public good.

He has forbidden his Governors to pass Laws of immediate and pressing importance, unless suspended in their operation till his Assent should be obtained; and when so suspended, he has utterly neglected to attend to them.

He has refused to pass other Laws for the accommodation of large districts of People, unless those People would relinquish the right of Representation in the legislature; a right inestimable to them and formidable to tyrants only.

He has called together legislative bodies at places unusual, uncomfortable, and distant from the depository of their Public Records, for the sole Purpose of fatiguing them into compliance with his measures.

He has dissolved Representative Houses repeatedly, for opposing,with manly firmness, his invasions on the rights of the People.

He has refused for a long time, after such dissolutions, to cause others to be elected; whereby the Legislative Powers, incapable of Annihilation, have returned to the People at large for their exercise; the State remaining in the mean time exposed to all the dangers of invasion from without, and convulsions within.

He has endeavoured to prevent the Population of these States; for that purpose obstructing the Laws for Naturalization of Foreigners; refusing to pass others to encourage their migrations hither, and raising the conditions of new Appropriations of Lands.

He has obstructed the Administration of Justice, by refusing his Assent to Laws for establishing Judiciary Powers.

He has made Judges dependent on his Will alone, for the tenure of their offices, and the amount and payment of their salaries.

He has erected a multitude of New Offices, and sent hither swarms of Officers to harass our People, and eat out their substance.

He has kept among us, in times of Peace, Standing Armies, without the Consent of our legislatures.

He has affected to render the Military independent of and superior to the Civil Power.

He has combined with others to subject us to a jurisdiction foreign to our constitution, and unacknowledged by our laws; giving his assent to their Acts of pretended Legislation:

For quartering large bodies of armed troops among us:

For protecting them, by a mock Trial, from Punishment for any Murders which they should commit on the Inhabitants of these States:

For cutting off our Trade with all parts of the world:

For imposing Taxes on us without our Consent:

For depriving us, in many cases, of the benefits of Trial by Jury:

For transporting us beyond Seas to be tried for pretended offences:

For abolishing the free System of English Laws in a neighbouring province, establishing therein an Arbitrary government, and enlarging it Boundaries, so as to render it at once an example and fit instrument for introducing the same absolute rule into these Colonies:

For taking away our Charters, abolishing our most valuable Laws, and altering fundamentally the Forms of our Governments:

For suspending our own Legislatures, and declaring themselves invested with Power to legislate for us in all cases whatsoever.

He has abdicated Government here by declaring us out of his protection, and waging War against us.

He has plundered our seas, ravaged our Coasts, burnt our towns, and destroyed the Lives of our People.

He is at this time transporting large Armies of foreign Mercenaries to compleat the works of death, desolation and tyranny, already begun with circumstances of

Cruelty & perfidy scarcely paralleled in the most barbarous ages, and totally unworthy the Head of a civilized nation.

He has constrained our fellow Citizens taken Captive on the high Seas to bear Arms against their Country, to become the executioners of their friends and Brethren, or to fall themselves by their Hands.

He has excited domestic insurrections amongst us, and has endeavoured to bring on the inhabitants of our frontiers, the merciless Indian Savages, whose known rule of warfare, is an undistinguished destructionof all ages, sexes and conditions.

In every stage of these Oppressions We have Petitioned for Redress in the most humble terms: Our repeated Petitions have been answered only by repeated injury. A Prince, whose character is thus marked by every act which may define a Tyrant, is unfit to be the ruler of a free people.

Nor have We been wanting in attentions to our British brethren. We have warned them from time to time of attempts by their legislature to extend an unwarrantable jurisdiction over us. We have reminded them of the circumstances of our emigration and settlement here. We have appealed to their native justice and magnanimity, and we have conjured them by the ties of our common kindred to disavow these usurpations, which, would inevitably interrupt our connections and correspondence. They too have been deaf to the voice of justice and of consanguinity. We must, therefore, acquiesce in the necessity, which denounces our Separation, and hold them, as we hold the rest of mankind, Enemies in War, in Peace Friends.

We, therefore, the Representatives of the United States of America, in General Congress, Assembled, appealing to the Supreme Judge of the world for the rectitude of our intentions, do, in the Name, and by Authority of the good People of these Colonies, solemnly publish and declare, That these United Colonies are, and of Right ought to be Free and Independent States; that they are Absolved from all Allegiance to the British Crown, and that all political connection between them and the State of Great Britian, is and ought to be totally dissolved; and that as Free and Independent States, they have full Power to levy War, conclude Peace, contract Alliances, establish Commerce, and to do all other Acts and Things which Independent States may of right do. And for the support of this Declaration, with a firm reliance on the protection of divine Providence, we mutually pledge to each other our Lives, our Fortunes and our sacred Honor.

JOHN HANCOCK, *President*
[other signatures follow]
1776

2.6 The Federalist Papers

The debate over the Constitution in 1787 and 1788 produced what is now generally recognized as the most important political treatise ever written in America. This document took the form of a series of newspaper articles, later issued as The Federalist. *The articles were anonymously signed by "Publius." But the true authorship by James Madison, the most important individual associated with the writing of the new Constitution, Alexander Hamilton, a prominent New York lawyer, and John Jay, a diplomat and lawyer, was no secret. The essays first appeared in New York and Virginia, where the ratification debate was still under way.*

The 85 essays comprising The Federalist *have been studied intensively by lawyers, judges, political scientists and ordinary citizen, as if the debate were still an ongoing issue. The authors argue the need for more effective union, explain the powers needed to bring it about, analyze the defects in the Confederation, meet the major objections to the Constitution, discuss the system of checks and balances in the Constitution, and describe in detail the structure and powers of the three branches of federal government.*

Number 10 by Madison is perhaps the most famous of all the essays from The Federalist, *and deals with the problem of factions in a republic. In Number 51 he attempts to explain checks and balances. Excerpts of both follow.*

Questions

In Number 10, Madison addresses the issue of factionalism—divergence and conflict of interests. How does he define factionalism? He asserts there are two ways of dealing with factional differences—by destroying liberty or levelling all people and classes. Amplify this point. What dangers does Madison see in majority rule? What is the benefit of a large republic?

Number 10 argues that there is an economic basis for our governmental institutions—a point that Karl Marx might have agreed with. If so, how might this argument apply to the men who wrote the Constitution?

In Number 51, Madison argues for checks and balances. How will it work and what will be its advantages?

The Constitution was intended to "create a more perfect union"—that is, more perfect than the government established under the Articles of Confederation. How did it improve matters? Consider this, as well: as originally written, the Constitution lacked a bill of rights, failed to come to grips with slavery, omitted rights for blacks and women, made no provisions for political parties, and said nothing about the right of the states to secede? In this sense, how "perfect" was it?

Number 10 –

Among the numerous advantages promised by a well-constructed Union, none deserves to be more accurately developed than its tendency to break and control the violence of faction. The friend of popular governments never finds himself so much alarmed for their character and fate as when he contemplates their

SOURCE: *The Federalist*, nos. 10, 51.

propensity to this dangerous vice. He will not fail, therefore, to set a due value on any plan which, without violating the principles to which he is attached, provides a proper cure for it. The instability, injustice, and confusion introduced into the public councils have, in truth, been the mortal diseases under which popular governments have everywhere perished, as they continue to be the favorite and fruitful topics from which the adversaries to liberty derive their most specious declamations. The valuable improvements made by the American constitutions on the popular models both ancient and modern, cannot certainly be too much admired; but it would be an unwarrantable partiality to contend that they have as effectually obviated the danger on this side, as was wished and expected. Complaints are everywhere heard from our most considerate and virtuous citizens, equally the friends of public and private faith and of public and personal iberty, that our governments are too unstable, that the public good is disregarded in the conflicts of rival parties, and that measures are too often decided, not according to the rules of justice and the rights of the minor party, but by the superior force of an interested and overbearing majority. However anxiously we may wish that these complaints had no foundation, the evidence of known facts will not permit us to deny that they are in some degree true. It will be found, indeed, on a candid review of our situation, that some of the distresses under which we labor have been erroneously charged on the operation of our governments; but it will be found, at the same time, that other causes will not alone account for many of our heaviest misfortunes; and, particularly, for that prevailing and increasing distrust of public engagements and alarm for private rights which are echoed from one end of the continent to the other. These must be chiefly, if not wholly, effects of the unsteadiness and injustice with which a factious spirit has tainted our public adminstrations.

By a faction I understand a number of citizens, whether amounting to a majority or minority of the whole, who are united and actuated by some common impulse of passion, or of interest, adverse to the rights of other citizens, or to the permanent and aggregate interests of the community.

There are two methods of curing the mischiefs of faction; the one, by removing its causes; the other, by controlling its effects.

There are again two methods of removing the causes of faction: the one, by destroying the liberty which is essential to its existence; the other, by giving to every citizen the same opinions, the same passions, and the same interests.

It could never be more truly said than of the first remedy that it was worse than the disease. Liberty is to faction what air is to fire, an ailment without which it instantly expires. But it could not be a less folly to abolish liberty, which is essential to political life, because it nourishes faction than it would be to wish the annihilation of air, which is essential to animal life, because it imparts to fire its destructive agency.

The second expedient is as impracticable as the first would be unwise. As long as the reason of man continues fallible, and he is at liberty to exercise it, different opinions will be formed. As long as the connection subsists between his reason and his self-love, his opinions and his passions will have a reciprocal influence on each other;

and the former will be objects to which the latter will attach themselves. The diversity in the faculties of men, from which the rights of property originate, is not less an insuperable obstacle to a uniformity of interests. The protection of these faculties is the first object of government. From the protection of different and unequal faculties of acquiring property, the possession of different degrees and kinds of property immediately results; and from the influence of these on the sentiments and views of the respective proprietors ensues a division of the society into different interests and parties.

The latent causes of faction are thus sown in the nature of man; and we see them everywhere brought into different degrees of activity, according to the different circumstances of civil society. A zeal for different opinions concerning religion, concerning government, and many other points, as well of speculation as of practice; an attachment to different leaders ambitiously contending for pre-eminence and power; or to persons of other descriptions whose fortunes have been interesting to the human passions, have, in turn, divided mankind into parties, inflamed them with mutual animosity, and rendered them much more disposed to vex and oppress each other than to co-operate for their common good. So strong is this propensity of mankind to fall into mutual animosities that where no substantial occasion presents itself the most frivolous and fanciful distinctions have been sufficient to kindle their unfriendly passions and excite their most violent conflicts. But the most common and durable source of factions has been the various and unequal distribution of property. Those who hold and those who are without property have ever formed distinct interests in society. Those who are creditors, and those who are debtors, fall under a like discrimination. A landed interest, a manufacturing interest, a mercantile interest, a moneyed interest, with many lesser interests, grow up of necessity in civilized nations, and divide them into different classes, actuated by different sentiments and views. The regulation of these various and interfering interests forms the principal task of modern legislation and involves the spirit of party and faction in the necessary and ordinary operations of the government.

No man is allowed to be a judge in his own cause, because his interest would certainly bias his judgment, and, not improbably, corrupt his integrity. With equal, nay with greater reason, a body of men are unfit to be both judges and parties at the same time; yet what are many of the most important acts of legislation but so many judicial determinations, not indeed concerning the rights of single persons, but concerning the rights of large bodies of citizens? And what are the different classes of legislators but advocates and parties to the causes which they determine? Is a law proposed concerning private debts? It is a question to which the creditors are parties on one side and the debtors on the other. Justice ought to hold the balance between them. Yet the parties are, and must be, themselves the judges; and the most numerous party, or in other words, the most powerful faction must be expected to prevail. Shall domestic manufactures be encouraged, and in what degree, by restrictions on foreign manufactures? are questions which would be differently decided by the landed and the manufacturing classes, and probably by neither with a sole regard to justice and the public good. The apportionment of taxes on the various descriptions of property is an act which seems to require the most exact impartiality; yet there is, perhaps, no legislative act in which greater opportunity and temptation are given to a predominent party to trample on the rules of justice. Every shilling with which they overburden the inferior number is a shilling saved to their own pockets.

It is in vain to say that enlightened statesmen will be able to adjust these clashing interests and render them all subservient to the public good. Enlightened statesmen will not always be at the helm. Nor, in many cases, can such an adjustment be made at all without taking into view indirect and remote considerations, which will rarely prevail over the immediate interest which one party may find in disregarding the rights of another or the good of the whole.

The inference to which we are brought is that the *causes* of faction cannot be removed and that relief is only to be sought in the means of controlling its *effects*.

If a faction consists of less than a majority, relief is supplied by the republican principle, which enables the majority to defeat its sinister views by regular vote. It may clog the administration, it may convulse the society; but it will be unable to execute and mask its violence under the forms of the Constitution. When a majority is included in a faction, the form of popular government, on the other hand, enables it to sacrifice to its ruling passion or interest both the public good and the rights of other citizens. To secure the public good and private rights against the danger of such a faction, and at the same time to preserve the spirit and the form of populace government, is then the great object to which our inquiries are directed. Let me add that it is the great desideratum by which this form of government can be rescued from the opprobrium under which it has so long labored and be recommended to the esteem and adoption of mankind.

By what means is this object attainable? Evidently by one of two only. Either the existence of the same passion or interest in a majority at the same time must be prevented, or the majority, having such coexistent passion or interest, must be rendered, by their number and local situation, unable to concert and carry into effect schemes of oppression. If the impulse and the opportunity be suffered to coincide, we well know that neither moral nor religious motives can be relied on as an adequate control. They are not found to be such on the injustice and violence of individuals, and lost their efficacy in proportion to the number combined together, that is, in proportion as their efficacy becomes needful.

From this view of the subject it may be concluded that a pure democracy, by which I mean a society consisting of a small number of citizens, who assemble and administer the government in person, can admit of no cure for the mischiefs of faction. A common passion or interest will, in almost every case, be felt by a majority of the whole; a communication and concert result from the form of government itself; and there is nothing to check the inducements to sacrifice the weaker party or an obnoxious individual. Hence it is that such democracies have ever been spectacles of turbulence and contention; have ever been found incompatible with personal security or the rights of the property; and have in general been as short in their lives as they have been violent in their deaths. Theoretic politicians, who have patronized this species of government, have erroneously supposed that by reducing mankind to a perfect equality in their political rights, they would at the same time be perfectly equalized and assimilated in their possessions, their opinions, and their passions.

A republic, by which I mean a government in which the scheme of representation takes place, opens a different prospect and promises the cure for which we are seeking. Let us examine the points in which it varies from pure democracy, and we shall comprehend both the nature of the cure and the efficacy which it must derive from the Union.

The two great points of difference between a democracy and a republic are: first, the delegation of the government, in the latter, to a small number of citizens elected by the rest; secondly, the greater number of citizens and greater sphere of country over which the latter may be extended.

The effect of the first difference is, on the one hand, to refine and enlarge the public views by passing them through the medium of a chosen body of citizens, whose wisdom may best discern the true interest of their country and whose patriotism and love of justice will be at least likely to sacrifice it to temporary or partial considerations. Under such a regulation it may well happen that the public voice, pronounced by the representatives of the people, will be more consonant to the public good than if pronounced by the people themselves, convened for the purpose. On the other hand, the effect may be inverted. Men of facetious tempers, of local prejudices, or of sinister designs, may, by intrigue, by corruption, or by other means, first obtain the suffrages, and then betray the interests of the people. The question resulting is, whether small or extensive republics are most favorable to the election of proper guardians of the public weal; and it is clearly decided in favor of the latter by two obvious considerations.

In the first place it is to be remarked that however small the republic may be the representatives must be raised to a certain number in order to guard against the cabals of a few; and that however large it may be they must be limited to a certain number in order to guard against the confusion of a multitude. Hence, the number of representatives in the two cases not being in proportion to that of the two constituents, and being proportionally greatest in the small republic, it follows that if the proportion of fit characters be not less in the large than in the small republic, the former will present a greater option, and consequently a greater probability of a fit choice.

In the next place, as each representative will be chosen by a greater number of citizens in the large than in the small republic, it will be more difficult for unworthy candidates to practise with success the vicious arts by which elections are too often carried; and the suffrages of the people being more free, will be more likely to center on men who possess the most attractive merit and the most diffusive and established characters.

It must be confessed that in this, as in most of other cases, there is a mean, on both sides of which inconveniencies will be found to lie. By enlarging too much the number of electors, you render the representative too little acquainted with all their local circumstances and lesser interests; as by reducing it too much, you render him unduly attached to these, and too little fit to comprehend and pursue great and national objects. The federal Constitution forms a happy combination in this respect; the great and aggregate interests being referred to the national, the local and particularly to the State legislatures.

The other point of difference is the greater number of citizens and extent of territory which may be brought within the compass of republican than of democratic government; and it is this circumstance principally which renders factious combinations less to be dreaded in the former than in the latter. The smaller the society, the fewer probably will be the distinct parties and interests composing it; the fewer the distinct parties and interests, the more frequently will a majority be found of the same party; and the smaller the number of individuals composing a majority, and the smaller the compass within which they are placed, the more easily will they concert and execute their plans of oppression. Extend the sphere and you take in a greater variety of parties and interests; you make it less probable that a majority of the whole will have a common motive to invade the rights of other citizens; or if such a common motive exists, it will be more difficult for all who feel it to discover their own strength and to act in unison with each other. Besides other impediments, it may be remarked that, where there is a consciousness of unjust or dishonorable purposes, communication is always checked by distrust in proportion to the number whose concurrence is necessary.

Hence, it clearly appears that the same advantage which a republic has over a democracy in controlling the effects of faction is enjoyed by a large over a small republic—is enjoyed by the Union over the States composing it. Does the advantage consist in the sutstitution of representatives whose enlightened views and virtuous sentiments render them superior to local prejudices and to schemes of injustice? It will not be denied that the representation of the Union will be most likely to possess these requisite endowments. Does it consist in the greater security afforded by a greater variety of parties, against the event of any one party being able to outnumber and oppress the rest? In an equal degree does the increased variety of parties comprised within the Union increase this security? Does it, in fine, consist in the greater obstacles opposed to the concert and accomplishment of the secret wishes of an unjust and interested majority? Here again the extent of the Union gives it the most palpable advantage.

The influence of factious leaders may kindle a flame within their particular States but will be unable to spread a general conflagration through the other States. A religious sect may degenerate into a political faction in a part of the Confederacy; but the variety of sects dispersed over the entire face of it must secure the national councils against any danger from that source. A rage for paper money, for an abolition of debts. for an equal division of property, or for any other improper or wicked project, will be less apt to pervade the whole body of the Union than a particular member of it, in the same proportion as such a malady is more likely to taint a particular country or district than an entire State.

In the extent and proper structure of the Union, therefore, we behold a republican remedy for the diseases most incident to republican government. And according to the degree of pleasure and pride we feel in being republicans ought to be our zeal in cherishing the spirit and supporting the character of federalists.

Publius

Number 51—

To what expedient, then, shall we finally resort for maintaining in practice the necessary partition of power among the several departments, as laid down in the Constitution? The only answer that can be given is, that as all these exterior provisions are found to be inadequate, the defect must be supplied, by so contriving the interior structure of the government as that its several constituent parts may, by their mutual relations, be the means of keeping each other in their proper places. Without presuming to undertake a full development of this important idea, I will hazard a few general observations, which may perhaps place it in a clearer light, and enable us to form a more correct judgment of the principles and structure of the government planned by the convention.

In order to lay a due foundation for that separate and distinct exercise of the different powers of government, which to a certain extent is admitted on all hands to be essential to the preservation of liberty, it is evident that each department should have a will of its own; and consequently should be so constituted that the members of each should have as little agency as possible in the appointment of the members of the others. Were this principle rigorously adhered to, it would require that all the appointments for the supreme executive, legislative, and judiciary magistracies should be drawn from the same fountain of authority, the people, through channels having no communication whatever with one another. Perhaps such a plan of constructing the several departments would be less difficult in practice than it may in contemplation appear. Some difficulties, however, and some additional expense would attend the execution of it. Some deviations, therefore, from the principle must be admitted. In the constitution of the judiciary department in particular, it might be inexpedient to insist rigorously on the principle: first, because peculiar qualifications being essential in the members, the primary consideration ought to be to select that mode of choice which best secures these qualifications; secondly, because the permanent tenure by which the appointments are held in that department, must soon destroy all sense of dependence on the authority conferring them.

It is equally evident, that the members of each department should be as little dependent as possible on those of the others, for the emoluments annexed to their offices. Were the executive magistrate, or the judges, not independent of the legislature in this particular, their independence in every other would be merely nominal.

But the great security against a gradual concentration of the several powers in the same department, consists in giving to those who administer each department the necessary constitutional means and personal motives to resist encroachments of the others. The provision for defense must in this, as in all other cases, be made commensurate to the danger of attack. Ambition must be made to counteract ambition. The interest of the man must be connected with the constitutional rights of the place. It may be a reflection on human nature, that such devices should be necessary to control the abuses of government. But what is government itself, but the greatest of all reflections on human nature? If men were angels, no government would be necessary. If angels were to govern men, neither external nor internal controls on governmment would be necessary. In framing a government which is to be administered by men over men, the great difficulty lies in this: you must first enable the government to control the governed; and in the next place oblige it to control itself. A dependence on the people is, no doubt, the primary control on the government; but experience has taught mankind the necessity of auxiliary precautions.

This policy of supplying, by opposite and rival interests, the defect of better motives, might be traced through the whole system of human affairs, private as well as public. We see it particularly displayed in all the subordinate distributions of power, where the constant aim is to divide and arrange the several offices in such a manner as that each may be a check on the other—that the private interest of every individual may be a sentinel over the public rights. These inventions of prudence cannot be less requisite in the distribution of the supreme powers of the State.

But it is not possible to give to each department an equal power of self-defense. In republican government, the legislative authority necessarily predominates. The remedy for this inconveniency is to divide the legislature into different branches; and to render them by different modes of election and different principles of action, as little connected with each other as the nature of their common functions and their common dependence on the society will admit. . . .

If the principles on which these observations are founded be just, as I persuade myself they are, and they be applied as a criterion to the several State constitutions, and to the federal Constitution, it will be found that if the latter does not perfectly correspond with them, the former are infinitely less able to bear such a test.

There are, moreover, two considerations particularly applicable to the federal system of America, which place that system in a very interesting point of view.

First. In a single republic, all the power surrendered by the people, is submitted to the administration of a single government; and the usurpations are guarded against by a division of the government into distinct and separate departments. In the compound republic of America, the power surrendered by the people is first divided between two distinct governments, and then the portion alloted to each subdivided among distinct and separate departments. Hence a double security arises to the rights of the people. The different governments will control each other, at the same time that each will be controlled by itself.

Second. It is of great importance in a republic not only to guard the society against the oppression of its rulers, but to guard one part of the society against the injustice of the other part. Different interests necessarily exist in different classes of citizens. If a majority be united by a common interest, the rights of the minority will be insecure. There are but two methods of providing against this evil: the one by creating a will in the community independent of the majority—that is, of the society itself; the other, by comprehending in the society so many separate descriptions of citizens as will render an unjust combination of a majority of the whole very improbable, if not impracticable. The first method prevails in all governments possessing an hereditary or self-appointed authority. This, at best, is but a precarious security; because a power independent of the society may as well espouse the unjust views of the major, as the rightful interests of the minor party, and may possibly be turned against both parties. The second method will be exemplified in the federal republic of the United States. Whilst all authority in it will be derived from and dependent on the society, the society itself will be broken into so many parts, interests, and classes of citizens, that the rights of individuals, or of the minority, will be in little danger from interested combinations of the majority. In a free government the security for civil rights must be the same as that for religious rights. It consists in the one case in the multiplicity of interests, and in the other in the multiplicity of sects. The degree of security in both cases will depend on the number of interests and sects; and this may be presumed to depend on the extent of country and number of people comprehended under the same government. This view of the subject must particularly recommend a proper federal system to all the sincere and considerate friends of republican government, since it shows that in exact proportion as the territory of the Union may be formed into more circumscribed Confederacies, or States, oppressive combinations of a majority will be facilitated; the best security, under the republican forms, for the rights of every class of citizens, will be diminished; and consequently the stability and independence of some member of the government, the only other security, must be proportionately increased. Justice is the end of government. It is the end of civil society. It ever has been and ever will be pursued until it be obtained, or until liberty be lost in the pursuit. In a society under the forms of which the stronger faction can readily unite and oppress the weaker, anarchy may as truly be said to reign as in a state of nature, where the weaker individual is not secured against the violence of the stronger. . . . In the extended republic of the United States, and among the great variety of interests, parties, and sects which it embraces, a coalition of a majority of the whole society could seldom take place on any other principles than those of justice and the general good; whilst there being thus less danger to a minor from the will of a major party, there must be less pretext, also, to provide for the security of the former, by introducing into the government a will not dependent on the latter, or, in other words, a will independent of the society itself. It is no less certain than it is important, notwithstanding the contrary opinions which have been entertained, that the larger [the] society, provided it lie within a practical sphere, the more duly capable it will be of self-government. And happily for the *republican cause,* the practicable sphere may be carried to a very great extent by a judicious modification and mixture of the *federal principle.*

2.7 The Anti-Federalist Response

The opponents of the Constitution of 1787 never produced a document as powerful as The Federalist *and were politically disorganized. But they did not lack arguments or supporters. The Anti-Federalists, as they came to be known, represented a variety of social classes and regional groupings. They included the artistocratic Virginians, Richard Henry Lee and George Mason; the Revolutionary War leader George Clinton of New York; the back-country radical farmer Patrick Henry; the prominent Maryland lawyer Luther Martin, who had attended the Constitutional Convention and championed the cause of the debtor farmers; and*

James Winthrop, a member of the famous Massachusetts family and the librarian of Harvard College.

The Anti-Federalists simply favored keeping the Articles of Confederation. They argued that: the Constitution lacked a bill of rights, and therefore threatened civil liberties; included awesome powers of taxation and threatened a fearful consolidation of government; endangered states' rights; inflated the powers of the President; gave all officers oligarchical authority; and enlarged the threat of a standing army. They argued that the country was far too large to work under this type of regime, and that amending the document would be practically impossible. The following selections draw on typical arguments by Patrick Henry, Richard Henry Lee, Luther Martin, and an anonymous party named "Centinel."

By lobbying the Virginia and New York conventions, the Anti-Federalists nearly organized a majority big enough to reject the Constitution. But by June 1788, nine states had completed ratification, and the "anti" cause was lost.

Questions

Consider what each author fears about the federal Constitution? How is the Confederation defended? What do you make of Henry's charge: "Here is a revolution as radical as that which separated us from Great Britain?" Martin attacks Hamilton as one of the "favorers of monarchy" and Madison as one who wanted "the total abolition of state governments." What is his alternative?

In the end, the back country areas and farmers leaned against the Constitution, while coastal sections and city dwellers tended to support it. Why, then, did the colonists decide to set aside the Articles of Confederation and adopt the Constitution?

Time has vindicated the Constitution and relegated the Articles to the dust bin of history. But have any of the dire warnings and predictions of the Anti-Federalists come to pass?

Patrick Henry—

I ROSE yesterday to ask a question which arose in my own mind. When I asked that question, I thought the meaning of my interrogation was obvious: the fate of this question and of America may depend on this. Have they said, We, the States? Have they made a proposal of a compact between states? If they had, this would be a confederation. It is otherwise most clearly a consolidated government. The question turns, sir, on that poor little thing—the expression, We, the people, instead of the states, of America. I need not take much pains to show, that the principles of this system are extremely pernicious, impolitic, and dangerous. Is this a monarchy like

England—a compact between prince and people, with checks on the former to secure the latter? Is this a confederacy like Holland—an association of a number of independent states, each of which retains its individual sovereignty? It is not a democracy, wherein the people retain all their rights securely. Had these principles been adhered to, we should not have been brought to this alarming transition, from a confederacy to a consolidated government. We have no detail of these great considerations, which in my opinion, ought to have abounded before we should recur to a government of this kind. Here is a revolution as radical as that which separated us from Great Britain. It is radical in this transition, our rights and privileges are endangered, and the sovereignty of the states will be relinquished: and cannot we plainly see, that this is actually the case? The rights of conscience, trial by jury, liberty of the press, all your immunities and franchises, all pretensions to human rights and privileges, are rendered insecure, if not lost, by this change so loudly talked of by some, and inconsiderately by others. Is this tame relinquishment of rights worthy of freemen? Is it worthy of that manly fortitude that ought to characterize republicans? It is said eight states have adopted this plan. I declare that if twelve states and a half had adopted it, I would with manly firmness, and in spite of an erring world, reject it. You are not to inquire how your trade may be increased, nor how you are to become a great and powerful people, but how your liberties can be secured; for liberty ought to be the direct end of your government. . . .

Is it necessary for your liberty, that you should abandon those great rights by the adoption of this system? Will the abandonment of your most sacred rights tend to the security of your liberty? Liberty, the greatest of all earthly blessings—give us that precious jewel, and you may take everything else! . . . . The Confederation, this same despised government, merits, in my opinion, the higher encomium: it carried us through a long and dangerous war: it rendered us victorious in that blood conflict with a powerful nation, it has secured us a territory greater than any European monarch possesses: and shall a government which has been thus strong and vigorous, be accused of imbecility, and abandoned for want of energy? Consider what you are about to do before you part with the government. . . . We are cautioned by the honorable gentleman who presides against faction and turbulence: I acknowledge also the new form of government may effectually prevent it: yet, there is another thing it will as effectually do: it will oppress and ruin the people. . . . This Constitution is said to have beautiful features, but when I come to examine these features, sir, they appear to me horribly frightful: among other deformities, it has an awful squinting; it squints towards monarchy: and does not this raise indignation in the breast of every true American? Your President may easily become king; your senate is so imperfectly constructed that your dearest rights may be sacrificed by what may be a small minority; and a very small minority may continue forever unchangeably this government, although horribly defective: where are your checks in this government? Your strong holds will be in the hands of your enemies.

If your American chief, be a man of ambition, and abilities, how easy is it for him to render himself absolute? The army, is in his hands, and if he be a man of address, it will be attached to him, and it will be the subject of long meditation with him to seize the first suspicious moment to accomplish his design; and, sir, will the American spirit solely relieve you when this happens? . . .

Mr. Chairman, it is now confessed that this is a national government. There is not a single federal feature in it. It has been alleged within these walls, during the debates, to be national and federal, as it suited the arguments of gentlemen.

But now when we have heard the definition of it, it is purely national. The honorable member James Madison was pleased to say, that the sword and purse included every thing of consequence. And shall we trust them out of our hands without checks and barriers? The sword and purse are essentially necessary for government. Every essential requisite must be in congress. Where are the purse and sword of Virginia? They must go to congress. What is become of our country? The Virginian government is but a name. It clearly results from his last argument that we are to be consolidated. We should be thought unwise indeed to keep 200 legislators in Virginia, when the government is in fact gone to Philadelphia or New York. We are as a state to form no part of the government. Where are your checks? The most essential objects of government are to be administered by congress. How then can the state governments be any check upon them? If we are to be a republican government it will be consolidated, not confederated.

Richard Henry Lee–

The plan of government now proposed is calculated totally to change our condition as a people. Instead of being thirteen republics, under a federal head, it is clearly designed to make us one consolidated government.

We shall view the convention with proper respect—and at the same time, that we reflect there were men of ability and integrity in it, we must recollect how the aristocratic parts of the community dominated its proceedings.

Thus will stand the states and the general governments, should the constitution be adopted without any alterations; but as to powers, the general government will possess all essential ones, and those of the states a mere shadow of power. And therefore unless the people shall make some great exertions to restore to the state governments their powers in matters of internal police, as to the powers to lay and collect, exclusively, internal taxes, to govern the militia, and to hold the decisions of their own judicial courts upon their own laws final, the balance cannot possibly continue long; but the state governments must be annihilated or continue to exist for no purpose.

The general government, far removed from the people, and none of its members elected oftener than once in two years, will be forgot or neglected, and its laws disregarded, unless a multitude of officers and military force be continually employed to make the government feared and respected. In this country neglected laws, or a military execution of them, must lead to a revolution, and to the destruction of liberty.

Should the United States be taxed by a house of representatives of two hundred members, the middle and lower classes of people could have no great share, in fact, in taxation: To suppose that this branch is sufficiently numerous to guard the rights of the people in the administration of the government, in which the purse and sword is placed, seems to argue that we have forgot what the meaning of representation is.

The party backing the new system of government is composed of a few but dangerous men, with their servile dependents; these avariciously grasp at all power and property: you may discover in all the actions of these men, an evident dislike to free and equal government, and they will go systematically to work to change, essentially, the forms of government in this country; these are called aristocrats. This party has taken the political field, and with their fashionable dependents, and the tongue and the pen, is endeavoring to establish in a great haste a government as class selfish as the Shayites attempted to set up, but cast in a politer form.

Luther Martin

The favorers of monarchy, and those who wished the total abolition of state governments—well knowing that a government founded on truly federal principles . . . would be destructive of their views; and knowing they were too weak in numbers openly to bring forward their system; conscious also that the people of America would reject it if proposed to them—joined their interest with that party who wished a system giving particular states the power and influence over the others, procuring in return mutual sacrifices from them, in giving the government great and undefined powers as to its legislative and executive; well knowing that, by departing from a federal system they paved the way for their favorite object—the destruction of the state governments, and the introduction of monarchy. . . .

The thirteen states are thirteen distinct, political individual existences, as to each other; the federal government is, or ought to be, a government over these thirteen political, individual existences, which form the members of that government; and as the largest state is only a single individual of the government, it ought to have only one vote; the smallest state, being also an individual member of the government, ought also to have one vote. By giving one state, or one or two states, more votes than the others, the others thereby are enslaved to such state or states, having the greater number of votes.

In a federal government over states equally free, sovereign, and independent, every state ought to have an equal share in making the federal laws or regulations, and in carrying them into execution, neither of which is the case in this system, but the reverse, the states not having an equal voice in the legislature, nor in the appointment of the executive, the judges, and the officers of government. In this whole system there is but one federal feature—the appointment of the senators by the states, and the equality of suffrage in that branch; but this feature is only federal in appearance. For six years the senators are rendered totally and absolutely independent of their state. During that time they may join in measures ruinous and destructive to their states, even such as should totally annihilate their state governments; and their state cannot recall them, nor exercise any control over them.

Viewing it [the Constitution] as a national government, calculated and designed to abolish the state governments—it was opposed for the following reasons: It was said that this continent was too extensive for one national government, which should have sufficient power and energy to persuade and hold in obedience, all its parts, consistently with the enjoyment and preservation of liberty. It was insisted that governments of a republican nature are those best calculated to preserve the freedom and happiness of the citizen—that governments of this kind are only calculated for a territory but small in extent—that the only method by which an extensive continent like America could be united together, consistently with the principles of freedom, must be by having a number of strong and energetic state governments.

By the power to lay and collect taxes the government has the power to lay what indirect taxes they please; afterwards to impose on the people direct taxes to what amount they choose, and thus to sluice them at every vein as long as they have a drop of blood, without any control or restraint; while all the officers for collecting those taxes are to be appointed by the federal government, and are not accountable to the states.

I voted against the section putting it out of the power of a state to pass any law impairing the obligation of contracts. I considered that there might be times of such great public distress as should render it the duty of a government in some measure to interfere, by passing laws totally or partially stopping courts of justice; or authorizing the debtor to pay by installments, or by delivering up his property to his creditor at a reasonable valuation. The times have been such as to render regulations of this kind necessary to prevent the wealthy creditor and the moneyed man from totally destroying the poor and industrious debtor.

[From] the best judgment I could form while in Convention, I then was, and yet remained, decidedly of the opinion that ambition and interest had so far blinded the understanding of some of the principal framers of the Constitution that, while they were labouring to erect a fabrick by which they themselves might be exalted and benefited, they were rendered insensible to the sacrifice of the freedom and happiness of the states and their citizens, which must, inevitably be the consequence. . . .

I most sacredly believe their object is the total abolition and destruction of all state governments, and the erection on their ruins of one great and extensive empire, calculated to aggrandize and elevate its rulers and chief officers far above the common herd of mankind, to enrich them with wealth, and to encircle them with honours and glory, and which according to my judgment on the maturest reflection, must inevitably be attended with the most humiliating and abject slavery of their fellow citizens, by the sweat of whose brows, and by the toil of whose bodies, it can only be effected.

"Centinel"—

The wealthy and ambitious, who in every community think they have a right to lord it over their fellow creatures, have availed themselves very successfully of this favorable disposition; for the people, thus unsettled in their sentiments, have been prepared to accede to any extreme of government. All the distresses and difficulties they experience, proceeding from various causes, have been ascribed to the impotency of the present confederation, and thence they have been led to expect full relief from the adoption of the proposed system of government; and in the other event, immediate ruin and annihilation as a nation. These characters flatter themselves that they have lulled all distrust and jealousy of their new plan, by gaining the concurrence of the two men in whom

America has the highest confidence [George Washington and Benjamin Franklin], and now triumphantly exult in the completion of their long meditated schemes of power and aggrandizement, I would be very far from insinuating that the two illustrious personages alluded to, have not the welfare of their country at heart; but that the unsuspecting goodness and zeal of the one has been imposed on, in a subject in which he must necessarily be inexperienced, from his other arduous engagements; and that the weakness and indecision attendant on old age has been practiced on in the other. . . .

But our situation is represented to be so *critically* dreadful, that, however reprehensible and exceptionable the proposed plan of government may be, there is no alternative between the adoption of it and absolute ruin. My fellow citizens, things are not at that crisis; it is the argument of tyrants; the present distracted state of Europe secures us from injury on that quarter, and as to domestic dissensions, we have not so much to fear from them as to precipitate us into this form of government, without it is a safe and a proper one. For remember, of all *possible* evils, that of *despotism* is the *worst* and the most to be dreaded.

Such a body as the intended Congress, unless particularly inhibited and restrained, must grasp at omnipotence, and before long swallow up the legislative, the executive, and the judicial powers of the several States. . . .

This grand machine of power and oppression, may be made a fatal instrument to overturn the public liberties, especially as the funds to support the troops may be granted for two years, whereas in Britain, the grants ever since the revolution in 1688, have been from year to year. A standing army with regular provision of pay and contingencies, would afford a strong temptation to some ambitious man to step up into the throne, and to seize absolute power. The keeping on foot a hired military force in time of peace, ought not to be gone into, unless two-thirds of the members of the federal legislature agree to the necessity of the measure, and adjust the members employed. . . .

From the foregoing illustration of the powers proposed to be devolved to Congress, it is evident that the general government would necessarily annihilate the particular governments, and that the security of the personal rights of the people by the state constitutions is superseded and destroyed; hence results the necessity of such security being provided for by a bill of rights to be inserted in the new plan of federal government. What excuse can we then make for the omission of this grand palladium, this barrier necessity of the most express declarations and restrictions, to protect the rights and liberties of mankind from the silent, powerful and over-active conspiracy of those who govern. . . .

The new plan, it is true, does propose to secure the people of the benefit of personal liberty by the habeas corpus, and trial by jury for all crimes, except in the case of impeachment; but there is no declaration that all men have a natural and unalienable right to worship Almight God, according to the dictates of their own consciences and understanding; and that no man ought, or of right can be, compelled to attend any religious worship, or erect or support any place of worship, or maintain any ministry contrary to or against his own free will and consent; and that no authority can or ought to be vested in or assumed by any power whatever that shall in any case interfere with, or in any manner control, the right of religious worship: that the trial by jury in civil causes as well as criminal, and the modes prescribed by the common law for the safety of life in criminal prosecutions, shall be held sacred; that the requiring of excessive bail, imposing of excessive fines and cruel and unusual punishments be forbidden; that monopolies in trade or arts, other than to authors of books or inventors of useful arts for a reasonable time, ought not to be suffered; that the right of the people to assemble peaceably for the purpose of consulting about public matters, and petitioning or remonstrating to the federal legislature, ought not to be prevented; that *the liberty of the press be held sacred;* that the people have a right to hold themselves, their houses, papers and possessions free from search or seizure; and that therefore warrants without oaths or affirmations first made affording a sufficient foundation for them, and whereby any officer or messenger may be commanded or required to search suspected places, or to seize any person or his property, not particularly described, are contrary to that right and ought not be granted; and that standing armies in time of peace are dangerous to liberty, and ought not to be permitted but when absolutely necessary; all of which is omitted to be done in the proposed government.

2.8 Federal Versus States' Rights

The Constitution of 1787 attempted to preserve the rights of the states even as it strengthened the powers of the federal government, but the balance required repeated testing and readjustment before the Civil War. It was so tested in the Supreme Court in the case of M'Culloch *v.* Maryland. *This case arose when the (second) Bank of the United States, with a branch located in Baltimore, refused to pay an annual $15,000 tax levied by Maryland law. This direct attack on the federal bank came from people who resented the Bank as a monopoly and an interference in the operation of state-chartered banks. In 1818 the state of Maryland sued the Bank's local cashier, James M'Culloch, for refusing to comply with Maryland law. A county court ruled against the federal Bank and the case ended up in the Supreme Court of the United States.*

M'Culloch *v.* Maryland *was decided in 1819 by U.S. Chief Justice John Marshall (1755–1835), who for 35 years dominated the Court and more than any other person in history molded its character. The attorney for the Bank was Daniel Webster.*

No case has ever been more important for establishing the supremacy of the federal government. It hinged on the meaning of Article I enumerating the powers of Congress, and on the "supremacy clause" of Article VI spelling out the relationship between the federal and state govenments. It presented two principle issues to the Court. Did Congress have the power to charter a Bank? And, could a state tax a federal institution? That is, if a conflict did exist between a law passed by a state and one passed by the federal government, should federal or state law take precedence?

Marshall believed in national supremacy. The Supreme Court held that since the Bank was necessary for Congress to meet its constitutional responsibilities, Congress had the implied power to charter a national bank. The states did not have the power to tax the federal government's activities, and the Maryland law could not constitutionally be applied to the federal bank. This decision greatly restricted the powers of the states. It also inflamed those who favored states' rights.

Questions

Summarize the main issues and Marshall's decision in your own words. How did he justify it?

Review other states' rights issues in the pre-Civil War era, particularly those regarding tariffs and slavery. How did these play themselves out in the courts, in Congress and elsewhere?

What contemporary issues involve local versus national interest?

. . . In discussing this question, the counsel for the state of Maryland have deemed it of some importance, in the construction of the Constitution, to consider that instrument, not as emanating from the people, but as the act of sovereign and independent states. The powers of the general government, it has been said, are delegated by the states, who alone are truly sovereign; and must be exercised in subordination to the states, who alone possess supreme dominion. It would be difficult to sustain this proposition. The convention which framed the Constitution was indeed elected by the state legislatures. But the instrument when it came from their hands, was a mere proposal, without obligation, or pretensions to it. It was reported to the then existing Congress of the United States, with a request that it might "be submitted to a convention of delegates, chosen in each state by the people thereof, under the recommendation of its legislature, for their assent and ratification." This mode of proceeding was adopted; and by the convention, by congress, and by the state legislatures, the instrument was submitted to the *people*. They acted upon it in the only manner in which they can act safely, effectively and wisely, on such a subject, by assembling in convention. It is true, they assembled in their several states—and where else should they have assembled? No political dreamer was ever wild enough to think of breaking down the lines which separate the states, and of compounding the American people into one common mass. Of consequence, when they act, they act in their states. But the measures they adopt do not, on that account, cease to be

SOURCE: Henry Wheaton, ed., *A Digest of the Decisions of the Supreme Court of the United States from 1789 to February Term, 1820* (New York, 1821), IV, 316 ff.

the measures of the people themselves, or become the measures of the state governments.

From these conventions, the Constitution derives its whole authority. The government proceeds directly from the people; is "ordained and established," in the name of the people; and is declared to be ordained "in order to form a more perfect union, establish justice, insure domestic tranquility, and secure the blessings of liberty to themselves and to their posterity." The assent of the states, in their sovereign capacity, is implied in calling a convention, and thus submitting that instrument to the people. But the people were at perfect liberty to accept or reject it; and their act was final. It required not the affirmance, and could not be negatived, by the state governments. The Constitution, when thus adopted, was of complete obligation, and bound the state sovereignties. The government of the union, then, . . . is emphatically and truly a government of the people. In form, and in substance, it emanates from them. Its powers are granted by them, and for their benefit. . . .

Among the enumerated powers, we do not find that of establishing a bank or creating a corporation. But there is no phrase in the instrument which, like the articles of confederation, excludes incidental or implied powers. . . . A constitution, to contain an accurate detail of all the subdivisions of which its great powers will admit, and of all the means by which they may be carried into execution, would partake of the prolixity of a legal code, and could scarcely be embraced by the human mind. It would, probably, never be understood by the public. Its nature, therefore, requires, that only its great outlines should be marked, its important objects designated, and the minor ingredients which compose those objects, be deducted from the nature of the objects themselves. That this idea was entertained by the framers of the American Constitution is not only to be inferred from the nature of the instrument, but from the language. Why else were some of the limitations, found in the 9th section of the 1st article, introduced? It is also, in some degree, warranted, by their having omitted to use any restrictive term which might prevent its receiving a fair and just interpretation. In considering this question, then, we must never forget that it is a *constitution* we are expounding. . . .

We admit, as all must admit, that the powers of the government are limited, and that its limits are not to be transcended. But we think the sound construction of the Constitution must allow to the national legislature that discretion, with respect to the means by which the powers it confers are to be carried into execution, which will enable that body to perform the high duties assigned to it, in the manner most beneficial to the people. Let the end be legitimate, let it be within the scope of the Constitution, and all means which are appropriate, which are plainly adapted to that end, which are not prohibited, but consist with the letter and spirit of the Constitution, are constitutional. . . . After the most deliberate consideration, and all means which are appropriate, which are plainly adapted to incorporate the Bank of the United States is a law made in pursuance of the Constitution, and is a part of the supreme law of the land. . . .

The states have no power, by taxation or otherwise, to retard, impede, burden, or in any manner control, the operations of the constitutional laws enacted by congress to carry into execution the powers vested in the general government. This is, we think, the unavoidable consequence of that supremacy which the Constitution has declared. We are unanimously of opinion, that the law passed by the legislature of Maryland, imposing a tax on the Bank of the United States, is unconstitutional and void.

2.9 Civil Disobedience

"Breaking the law for the sake of the law" is a quick way to define civil disobedience or passive resistance. It is an American tradition going back at least to Henry David Thoreau during the Mexican War. Thoreau (1817–1862) was a life-long resident of Concord, Massachusetts, a Harvard graduate, a school teacher and a lover of nature. He also hated slavery. Rather than support the Mexican War, in his eyes a conspiracy of slaveowners brought about to extend the boundaries of black bondage, he refused to pay his poll tax and went to jail.

To explain his position, Thoreau delivered a speech in his home town that has since become the classic statement on civil disobedience (an excerpt appears below). In the twentieth century these sentiments would be felt around the world. They influenced Mahatma Gandhi in India in the 1940s and Martin Luther King, Jr. in Birmingham, Alabama in the 1960s. But there are perplexing problems with civil disobedience. If it "goes too far" it becomes anarchy; if it does not happen at all, a social evil may last forever. How far is too far, and how far is not far enough, can never be determined beforehand. Society has never quite decided what to do about those who practice passive resistance. The same person may get thrown in jail, or receive a Nobel Peace prize—or both, as in the case of Dr. King.

Questions

What is a poll tax, and why does Thoreau refuse to pay it? What are his principal arguments in defense of civil disobedience? What is he trying to accomplish, and was he successful?

On what general grounds can one justify passive resistance, since if taken to its logical extreme it could threaten law and order? On what general grounds can one oppose it, since if this happens, aren't we denying a basic democratic right?

In addition to Gandhi and King, where, when and how has civil disobedience been used in recent times?

I heartily accept the motto,—"That government is best which governs least;" and I should like to see it acted up to more rapidly and systematically. Carried out, it finally amounts to this, which also I believe,—"That government is best which governs not at all;" and when men are prepared for it, that will be the kind of government which they will have. Government is at best but an expedient; but most governments are usually, and all governments are sometimes, inexpedient. . . .

But, to speak practically and as a citizen unlike those who call themselves no-government men, I ask for, not at once no government, but *at once* a better government. Let every man make known what kind of government would command his respect, and that will be one step toward obtaining it.

After all, the practical reason why, when the power is once in the hands of the people, a majority are permitted, and for a long period continue, to rule, is not because they are most likely to be in the right, nor because this seems fairest to the minority, but because they are physically the strongest. But a government in which the majority rule in all cases cannot be based on justice, even as far as men understand it. Can there not be a government in which majorities do not virtually decide right and wrong, but conscience?—in which majorities decide only those questions to which the rule of expediency is applicable? Must the citizen ever for a moment, or in the least degree, resign his conscience to the legislator? Why has every man a conscience then? I think that we should be men first, and subjects afterward. It is not desirable to cultivate a respect for the law, so much as for the right. The only obligation which I have a right to assume, is to do at any time what I think right. It is truly enough said, that a corporation has no conscience; but a corporation of conscientious men is a corporation *with* a conscience. Law never made men a whit more just; and, by means of their respect for it, even the well-disposed are daily made the agents of injustice. A common and natural result of an undue respect for law is, that you may see a file of soldiers, colonel, captain, corporal, privates, powder-monkeys and all, marching in admirable order over hill and dale to the wars, against their wills, aye, against their common sense and consciences, which makes it very steep marching indeed, . . . at the service of some unscrupulous man in power? . . .

How does it become a man to behave towards this American government today? I answer that he cannot without disgrace be associated with it. I cannot for an instant recognize that political organization as *my* government which is the *slave's* government also.

All men recognize the right of revolution; that is, the right to refuse allegiance to and to resist the government, when its tyranny or its inefficiency are great and unendurable. But almost all say that such is not the case now. But such was the case, they think, in the Revolution of '75. If one were to tell me that this was a bad government because it taxed certain foreign commodities brought to its ports, it is most probably that I should not make an ado about it, for I can do without them: all machines have their friction; and possibly this does enough good to counterbalance the evil. At any rate, it is a great evil to make a stir about it. But when the friction comes to have its machine, and oppression and robbery are organized, I say, let us not have such a machine any longer. In other words, when a sixth of the population of a nation which has undertaken to be the refuge of

SOURCE: Henry David Thoreau, "On the Duty of Civil Disobedience," in Elizabeth Peabody, ed., *Aesthetic Papers* (1849), 189–313.

liberty are slaves, and a whole country is unjustly overrun and conquered by a foreign army, and subjected to military law, I think that it is not too soon for honest men to rebel and revolutionize. What makes this duty the more urgent is the fact that the country so overrun is not our own, but ours is the invading army. . . .

I do not hesitate to say, that those who call themselves abolitionists should at once effectually withdraw their support, both in person and property, from the government of Massachusetts, and not wait till they constitute a majority of one, before they suffer the right to prevail through them. I think that it is enough if they have God on their side, without waiting for that other one. Moreover, any man more right than his neighbors, constitutes a majority of one already.

I meet this American government, or its representative the State government, directly, and face to face, once a year, no more, in the person of its tax-gatherer; this is the only mode in which a man situated as I am necessarily meets it; and it then says distinctly, Recognize me; and the simplest, the most effectual, and, in the present posture of affairs, the indispensablest mode of treating with it on this head, of expressing your little satisfaction with and love for it, is to deny it then. My civil neighbor, the tax-gatherer, is the very man I have to deal with,—for it is, after all, with men and not with parchment that I quarrel,—and he has voluntarily chosen to be an agent of the government. How shall he ever know well what he is and does as an officer of the government or as a man, until he is obliged to consider whether he shall treat me, his neighbor, for whom he has respect, as a neighbor and well-disposed man, or as a maniac and disturber of the peace, and see if he can get over this obstruction to his neighborliness without a ruder and more impetuous thought or speech corresponding with his action? I know this well, that if one thousand, if one hundred, if ten men whom I could name,—if ten *honest* men only,—aye if *one* HONEST man, in this state of Massachusetts, *ceasing to hold slaves*, were actually to withdraw from this copartnership, and be locked up in the county jail therefor, it would be the abolition of slavery in America. For it matters not how small the beginning may seem to be: what is once well done is done for ever. . . .

Under a government which imprisons any injustly, the true place for a just man is also a prison. The proper place to-day, the only place which Massachusetts has provided for her freer and less desponding spirits, is in her prisons, to be put out and locked out of the State by her own act, as they have already put themselves out by their principles. It is there that the fugitive slave, and the Mexican prisoner on parole, and the Indian come to plead the wrongs of his race, should find them; on that separate, but more free and honorable ground, where the State places those who are not *with* her but *against* her,—the only house in a slave-state in which a free man can abide with honor. If any think that their influence would be lost there, and their voices no longer afflict the ear of the State, that they would not be as an enemy within its walls, they do not know by how much truth is stronger than error, nor how much more eloquently and effectively he can combat injustice who has experienced a little in his own person. Cast your whole vote, not a strip of paper merely, but your whole influence. A minority is powerless while it conforms to the majority; it is not even a minority then; but it is irresistible when it clogs by its whole weight. If the alternative is to keep all just men in prison, or give up war and slavery, the State will not hesitate which to choose. If a thousand men were not to pay their tax-bills this year, that would not be a violent and bloody measure, as it would be to pay them, and enable the State to commit violence and shed innocent blood. This is, in fact, the definition of a peaceable revolution, if any such is possible. If the tax-gatherer, or any other public officer, asks me, as one has done, "But what shall I do?" my answer is, "If you really wish to do anything, sign your office." . . .

I have paid no poll-tax for six years. I was put into a jail once on this account, for one night; and, as I stood considering the walls of solid stone, two or three feet thick, the door of wood and iron, a foot thick, and the iron grating which strained the light, I could not help being struck with the foolishness of that institution which treated me as if I were mere flesh and blood and bones, to be locked up. I wondered that it should have concluded at length that this was the best use it could put me to, and had never thought to avail itself of my services in some way. I saw that, if there was a wall of stone between me and my townsmen, there was a still more difficult one to climb or break through, before they could get to be as free as I was. I did not for a moment feel confined, and the walls seemed a great waste of stone and mortar. I felt as if I alone of all my townsmen had paid my tax. They plainly did not know how to treat me, but behaved like persons who are underbred. In every threat and in every compliment there was a blunder; for they thought that my chief desire was to stand the other side of that stone wall. I could not but smile to see how industriously they locked the door on my meditations, which followed them out again without let or hinderance, and *they* were really all that was dangerous. As they could not reach me, they had resolved to punish my body; just as boys, if they cannot come at some person against whom they have a spite, will abuse his dog. I saw that the State was half-witted, that it was timid as a lone woman with her silver spoons, and that it did not know its friends from its foes, and I lost all my remaining respect for it, and pitied it. . . .

I know that most men think differently from myself; but those whose lives are by profession devoted to the study of these or kindred subjects, content me as little as any. Statesmen and legislators, standing so completely within the institution, never distinctly and nakedly behold it. They speak of moving society, but have no resting-place without it. They may be men of a certain experience and discrimination, and have no doubt invented ingenious and even useful systems, for which we sincerely thank them; but all their wit and usefulness lie within certain not very wide limits. They are wont to forget that the world is not governed by policy and expediency. Webster never goes behind government, and so cannot speak with authority about it. His words are wisdom to those legislators who contemplate no essential reform in the existing government; but for thinkers, and those who legislate for all time, he never once glances at the subject. . . . Comparatively, he is always strong, original, and above all, practical. Still his quality is not wisdom, but prudence. The lawyer's truth is not Truth, but consistency, or a consistent expediency. Truth is always in harmony with herself, and is not concerned chiefly to reveal the justice that may consist with wrong-doing. He well deserves to be called, as he has been called, the Defender of the Constitution. There are really no blows to be given by him but defensive ones. He is not a leader, but a follower. His leaders are the men of '87. . . .

The authority of government, even such as I am willing to submit to,—for I will cheerfully obey those who know and can do better than I, and in many things even those who neither know nor can do so well,—is still an impure one; to be strictly just, it must have the sanction and consent of the governed. It can have no pure right over my person and property but what I concede to it. The progress from an absolute to a limited monarchy, from a limited monarchy to a democracy, is a progress toward a true respect for the individual. . . .

2.10 The Impeachment of a President

The most serious crisis imaginable under the American Constitution is the impeachment of a President. The impeachment clause (Article II, Section 4) gives the people the means of removing their chief executive for "Treason, Bribery, or other high Crimes and Misdemeanors." At such times, the House of Representatives is called upon to hand down formal charges, and the Senate then hears the evidence and issue a verdict. The Supreme Court has a relatively minor role in the crisis; the Chief Justice presides at the Senate trial.

The process holds such awesome political implications that it has only been invoked twice. The first time, in 1868, Andrew Johnson survived the attack. The second time, in 1973, Richard Nixon was forced to resign.

Andrew Johnson and the Congress dominated by the Radical Republicans clashed mightily over Reconstruction policies. Johnson called down the wrath of the gods when he tried to remove Secretary of War Stanton in violation of the newly passed Tenure-of-Office Act. After a trial, the Senate exonerated him by one vote. The man who cast the decisive vote, and saved Johnson from conviction, was Sen. Edmund G. Ross of Kansas, a critic of the President but one who opposed the Tenure-of-Office Act.

Sections of the articles of impeachment are included below, along with Senator Ross' description of the scene in the Senate chamber when the decisive vote was taken.

Questions

Is the process outlined in the Constitution a good one, or does it invite corruption and demagoguery? How well did it work in 1868?

What was going on in Ross's mind when he "looked down into my open grave"? Had Johnson been toppled, what might have happened to the balance of power between the President and Congress?

Were the impeachment proceedings against Nixon more satisfactory than the one against Johnson? How do they compare? Explain.

In the House of Representatives, United States—

March 2, 1868

ARTICLES EXHIBITED BY THE HOUSE OF REPRESENTATIVES OF THE UNITED STATES, IN THE NAME OF THEMSELVES AND ALL THE PEOPLE OF THE UNITED STATES, AGAINST ANDREW JOHNSON, PRESIDENT OF THE UNITED STATES, IN MAINTENANCE AND SUPPORT OF THEIR IMPEACHMENT AGAINST HIM FOR HIGH CRIMES AND MISDEMEANORS IN OFFICE.

ARTICLE I. That said Andrew Johnson, President of the United States, on the 21st day of February, A.D. 1868, at Washington, in the district of Columbia, unmindful of the high duties of his office, of his oath of office, and of the requirement of the Constitution that he should take care that the laws be faithfully executed, did unlawfully and in violation of the Constitution and laws of the United States issue an order in writing for the removal of Edwin M. Stanton from the office of Secretary for the Department of War, said Edwin M. Stanton having been theretofore duly appointed and commissioned, by and with the advice and consent of the Senate of the United States, as such Secretary; and said Andrew Johnson, President of the United States, on the 12th day of August, A.D. 1867, and during the recess of said Senate, having suspended by his order Edwin M. Stanton from said office, and within twenty days after the first day of the next meeting of said Senate—that is to say, on the 12th day of December, in the year last aforesaid—having reported to said Senate such suspension, with the evidence and reasons for his action in the case and the name of the person designated to perform the duties of such office temporarily until the next meeting of the Senate; and said Senate thereafterwards, on the 13th day of January, A.D. 1868, having duly considered the evidence and reasons reported by said Andrew Johnson for said suspension, and having refused to concur in said suspension, whereby and by force of the provisions of an act entitled "An act regulating the tenure of certain civil offices," passed March 2, 1867, said Edwin M. Stanton did forthwith resume the functions of his office, whereof the said Andrew Johnson had then and there due notice; and said Edwin M. Stanton, by reason of the premises, on said 21st day of February, being lawfully entitled to hold said office of Secretary for the Department of War; which said order for the removal of said Edwin M. Stanton is in substance as follows; that is to say:

SOURCES: Richardson, ed. *Messages and Papers of the President*, VI, 709 ff.; and, Edmund G. Ross, "Historic Moments: The Impeachment Trial," in *Forum* (July, 1895), 519–24.

EXECUTIVE MANSION,
Washington, D.C., February 21, 1868.
HON. EDWIN M. STANTON,
Washington, D.C.

SIR: By virtue of the power and authority vested in me as President by the Constitution and laws of the United States, you are hereby removed from office as Secretary for the Department of War, and your functions as such will terminate upon the receipt of this communication.

You will transfer to Brevet Major-General Lorenzo Thomas, Adjutant-General of the Army, who has this day been authorized and empowered to act as Secretary of War *ad interim,* all records, books, papers, and other public property now in your custody and charge.

Respectfully, yours,
ANDREW JOHNSON.

which order was unlawfully issued with intent then and there to violate the act entitled "An act regulating the tenure of certain civil offices," passed March 2, 1867 . . . whereby said Andrew Johnson, President of the United States, did then and there commit and was guilty of a high misdemeanor in office.

ART. II. That on said 21st day of February, A.D 1868, at Washington, in the District of Columbia, said Andrew Johnson, President of the United States, . . . did, with intent to violate the Constitution of the United States and the act aforesaid, issue and deliver to one Lorenzo Thomas a letter of authority in substance as follows; that is to say:

EXECUTIVE MANSION,
Washington, D.C., February 21, 1868.
Brevet Major-General Lorenzo Thomas,
Adjutant-General United States Army,
Washington, D.C.

SIR: The Hon. Edwin M. Stanton having been this day removed from office as Secretary for the Department of War, you are hereby authorized and empowered to act as Secretary of war *ad interim,* and will immediately enter upon the discharge of the duties pertaining to that office.

Mr. Stanton has been instructed to transfer to you all the records, books, papers, and other public property now in his custody and charge.

Respectfully, yours,
ANDREW JOHNSON.

then and there being no vacancy in said office of Secretary of the Department of War; whereby said Andrew Johnson, President of the United States, did then and there commit and was guilty of a high misdemeanor in office.

ART. III. That said Andrew Johnson, President of the United States, on the 21st day of February, A.D. 1868, at Washington, in the District of Columbia, did commit and was guilty of a high misdemeanor in office in this, that without authority of law, while the Senate of the United States was then and there in session, he did appoint one Lorenzo Thomas to be Secretary for the Department of War *ad interim,* without the advice and consent of the Senate, and with intent to violate the Constitution of the United States, . . .

ART. IV. That said Andrew Johnson, President of the United States, . . . did unlawfully conspire with one Lorenzo Thomas, and with other persons to the House of Representatives unknown, with intent, by intimidation and threats, unlawfully to hinder and prevent Edwin M. Stanton, then and there the Secretary for the Department of War, . . . from holding said office of Secretary for the Department of War, contrary to and in violation of the Constitution of the United States and of the provisions of an act entitled "An act to define and punish certain conspiracies," approved July 31, 1861; . . .

ART. V. That said Andrew Johnson, President of the United States, . . . did unlawfully conspire with one Lorenzo Thomas, and with other persons to the House of Representatives unknown, to prevent and hinder the execution of an act entitled "An act regulating the tenure of certain civil offices," passed March 2, 1867.

ART. VI. That said Andrew Johnson, President of the United States, . . . did unlawfully conspire with one Lorenzo Thomas by force to seize, take, and possess the property of the United States in the Department of War, and then and there in the custody and charge of Edwin M. Stanton, Secretary for said Department, contrary to the provisions of an act entitled "An act to define and punish certain conspiracies," approved July 31, 1861, and with intent to violate and disregard an act entitled "An act regulating the tenure of certain civil offices," passed March 2, 1867; . . .

ART. VII. That said Andrew Johnson, President of the United States, . . . did unlawfully conspire with one Lorenzo Thomas with intent unlawfully to seize, take, and possess the property of the United States in the Department of War, in the custody and charge of Edwin M. Stanton, Secretary for said Department, with intent to violate and disregard the act entitled "An act regulating the tenure of certain civil offices, passed March 2, 1867; . . .

ART. VIII. That said Andrew Johnson, President of the United States, . . . with intent unlawfully to control the disbursement of the moneys appropriated for the military service and for the Department of War, . . . did unlawfully, and in violation of the Constitution of the United States, and without the advice and consent of the Senate of the United States, . . . there being no vacancy in the office of Secretary for the Department of War, and with intent to violate and disregard the act aforesaid, then and there issue and deliver to one Lorenzo Thomas a letter of authority, . . .

ART. IX. That said Andrew Johnson, President of the United States, on the 22d day of February, A.D. 1868, . . . in disregard of the Constitution and the laws of the United States duly enacted, as Commander in Chief of the Army of the United States, did bring before himself then and there William H. Emory, a major-general by brevet in the Army of the United States, actually in command of the Department of Washington and the military forces thereof, and did then and there, as such Commander in Chief, declare to and instruct said Emory that part of a law of the United States, passed March 2, 1867, entitled "An Act making appropriations for the support of the Army for the year ending June 30, 1868, and for other purposes," especially the second section thereof, which provides, among other things, that "all orders and instructions relating to military operations issued by the President or Secretary of War shall be issued through the General of the Army, and in case of his inability through the next in rank," was unconstitutional . . . with intent thereby to induce said Emory, in his official capacity as commander of the Department of Washington, to violate the provisions of said act and to take and receive, act upon, and obey such orders as he, the said Andrew Johnson, might make and give, and which should not be issued through the General of the Army of the United States, according to the provisions of said act, . . .

March 3, 1868

The following additional articles of impeachment were agreed to, viz:

ART. X. That said Andrew Johnson, President of the United States, unmindful of the high duties of his office and the dignity and proprieties thereof, and of the harmony and courtesies which ought to exist and be maintained between the executive and legislative branches of the Government of the United States, . . . did attempt to bring into disgrace, ridicule, hatred, contempt, and reproach the Congress of the United States and the several branches thereof, to impair and destroy the regard and respect of all the good people of the United States for the Congress and legislative power thereof (which all officers of the Government ought inviolably to preserve and maintain), and to excite the odium and resentment of all the good people of the United States against Congress and the laws by it duly and constitutionally enacted; and, in pursuance of his said design and intent,

Senator Ross' Account –

The hours seemed to pass with oppressive tedium awaiting the time for the assembling of the Senate and the beginning of the vote. It came at last, and found the galleries thronged to their utmost with a brilliant and eager auditory. Tickets of admission were at an enormous premium. Every chair on the floor was filled with a Senator, a Cabinet officer, a member of the President's counsel, or a representative, for the House had adjourned and its anxious members had at once thronged to the Senate chamber. Every foot of available standing room in the area and about the senatorial seats was occupied.

A profound sensation was apparent on the entrance of Senator James W. Grimes, of Iowa, the war Governor of his State and a great leader of his party, now stricken with a fatal illness and supported to his seat on the arms of employees and officials of the Senate. Inspired by a stern sense of duty, characteristic of the man, he had insisted on being taken from a bed of sickness at the imminent risk of his life to record his vote. . . .

Pages were flitting from place to place with messages to and from Senators and members. Little groups were gathered here and there in subdued conversation, discussing the situation and the probable result and its attendant consequences. The intensity of public interest was increased by the general impression that the entire official incumbency and patronage of the Government in all its departments, financial and political, had been pledged in advance and on condition of the removal of the President. . . .

The venerable Chief Justice, who had so ably and impartially presided through the many tedious weeks of the trial now about to close, was in his place, called the Court to order, and enjoined absolute silence on the part of spectators. The voting then commenced. . . . The call proceeded in alphabetical order. . . .

Then, in the order of the vote, came Senator Grimes. As he rose to his feet, supported by friends on either side, the scene became at once pathetic and heroic, . . . In his then physical condition, and in view of the personal and public enmities which the vote he was about to give would inevitably engender, it was apparent that he was about to perform the last important public act of his life—that a long and conspicuous career of usefulness to his country must now close. But though physically enfeebled by the fatal illness that was upon him, there was no sign of hesitancy or weakness. His vote was "not guilty." . . .

The call then went on down the alphabet with unvarying responses of "guilty," till the name of the uncounted Senator [Ross] was reached . . . on the call of the name of that Senator, the great audience became again hushed into absolute silence. It was as though conscious of an impending crisis. Every fan was folded, not a foot moved, not the rustle of a garment, not a whisper was heard. . . .

It was understood that, on whichever side that vote should be cast, so would be the result of the count. Upon it seemed to depend at once the end or continuance of the existing administration and its policies, and the realization or the crushing of the hopes and plans of those who desired to see the institution of a new, and as they undoubtedly believed, a better order of things. . . .

The vote was being taken on the eleventh and last article of impeachment. It had been ordered by a majority of the Senate, that the vote should not be taken on the first article in its order, as two conspicuous Senators classed with the majority had previously announced in a caucus of the Senate that they could not vote for the conviction of the President on the charges contained in that article, but would so vote on others. So it was ordered that the vote be taken first on the eleventh article or count in the indictment.

The Chief Justice, with apparent emotion, propounded the query, "How say you, Senator Ross, is the respondent, Andrew Johnson, guilty or not guilty under this article?"

At this point the intensity with which the gaze of the audience was centred upon the figure then on the floor was beyond description or comparison. . . . Not only were the occupants of the galleries bending forward in intense and breathless silence and anxiety to catch the verdict, but the Senators in their seats leaned over their desks, many with hand to ear, that not a syllable or intonation in the utterance of the verdict should be lost.

Conscious that I was at that moment the focus of all eyes, and conscious also of the far-reaching effect, especially upon myself, of the vote I was about to give, it is something more than a simile to say that I almost literally looked down into my open grave. Friends, position, fortune, everything that makes life desirable to an ambitious man, were about to be swept away by the breath of my mouth, perhaps forever. Realizing the tremendous responsibility which an untoward combination of conditions seemed to have put upon me, it is not strange that my answer was carried waveringly over the air and failed to reach the limits of the audience, or that a repetition was called for by distant Senators on the opposite side of the chamber. Then the verdict came—"Not guilty"—in a voice that could not be misunderstood.

The die was cast. The best, or the worst, was known. The historic trial of the age was practically ended. American institutions had successfully endured a strain that would have wrecked any other form of government. . . .

The call went on down the alphabet. Two additional votes were cast for acquittal. . . .

As the end was reached the Chief Justice announced that the President was acquitted of the charges contained in the eleventh article.

An adjournment of the Court was then taken for ten days, when votes were had on the second and third articles, still omitting the first for obvious reasons; but, as had been generally anticipated, the result was the same. The remaining eight articles of the impeachment were never put to test of vote.

war

Civil War dead, outside Dunkard Church, Antietam, Maryland, September 1862.

Chapter Three: War

3.1 A Soldier's Solemn Duty

When the Virginia Company of London first set up its colony in North America in 1607 they organized it essentially as a military outpost. The company fed, clothed and housed the colonists, and set the rules that each person was expected to follow. The military officer in charge tried to rule with an iron grip, but was not always successful. Private soldiers and others were expected to obey him to the death. But in 1609 dissension led to the removal of Capt. John Smith. The winter famine 1609–1610 reduced the population from 500 to 60, while discipline remained a recurrent problem. What follows is the "Instructions of the Marshall for the Better Enabling of a Private Soldier to the Executing of His Duty in this Present Colony," dated June 22, 1611.

Questions

What are the duties of a private soldier in this new colony? How is he expected to conduct himself off duty? What is the authority of the officer? What troubles may have led to the issuance of these rules? Who would—and who would not—want to submit to such military duty? What advantages and disadvantages might there be in establishing this sort of discipline? How does this military service contrast with a citizens' militia, such as the Minute Men of Revolutionary War fame?

It is requisite that he who will enter into this function of a soldier, that he dedicate himself wholly for the planting and establishing of true religion, the honor of his Prince, the safety of his country, and to learn the art which he professes, which is in this place to hold war and the service requisite to the subsisting of a colony. There be many men of mean descent, who have this way attained to great dignity, credit, and honor.

SOURCE: "Articles, Laws, and Orders . . . for the Colony in Virginia" (London, 1611), reprinted in *Tracts and Other Papers Relating Principally to the Colonies in North America* (Washington, D.C., 1836–1844), III, 9–13, 56–62.

Having thus dedicated himself with a constant resolution, he ought to be diligent, careful, vigilant, and obedient, and principally to have the fear of God and his honor in greatest esteem.

He must be careful to serve God privately and publicly; for all professions are there unto tied, that carry hope with them to prosper, and none more highly than the soldier, for he is ever in the mouth of death, and certainly he that is thus religiously armed, fights more confidently and with greater courage.

He must not set his mind overgreedily upon his belly and continual feeding, but rest himself contented with such provisions as may be conveniently provided, by his own labor purchase, or his means reach unto; above all things he must eschew that detestable vice of drunkenness.

He must be true-hearted to his captain and obey him and the rest of the officers of the camp, town, or fort with great respect, for by the very oath which he takes he does bind himself and promises to serve his Prince, and obey his officers: for the true order of war is fitly resembled to true religion ordained of God, which binds the soldier to observe justice, loyalty, faith, constance, patience, silence, and, above all, obedience, through the which is easily obtained the perfection in arms.

He shall continue at his work until the drum beats and that his captain, his officer, or overseers of the work, gives order unto a cessation for the time, and for the same purpose attends to lead him in, whom he shall orderly and comely follow into the camp, town, or fort, by his said captain, officer, or overseer him meeting, to be conducted unto the church to hear divine service, after which he may repay to his house or lodging to prepare for his dinner, and to repose him until the drum shall call him forth again in the afternoon, when so (as before) he shall accompany his chief officer unto the field, or where else the work lies, and there to follow his easy task until again the drum beats to return home; at which time according as in the forenoon, he shall follow his chief officer unto the church to hear divine service and after dispose of himself as he shall best please, and as his own business shall require.

3.2 Closing Scenes and Curtain Calls

As the fighting in the Revolutionary War stopped and the final curtain came down, the participants made their last observations and commentaries. The last battle occurred in 1781 at Yorktown, Virginia, where the British Lord Cornwallis surrendered to General Washington. Two years of negotiation was capped by the signing of a treaty in 1783.

There follows now a series of comments by participants in the Revolutionary War. These express the mood of foot soldiers at a moment of fatigue and relief, of generals in their despair and triumph, and of statesmen, politicians and a ruling monarch in elation and disgust.

The statements are by: Anne Rawle, Pennsylvania Quaker and stepdaughter of a prominent Loyalist; Capt. Samuel Graham, a redcoat officer, recalling the surrender at Yorktown; a rebel officer describing the same event; Sir Nathaniel Wraxall, who was in London in 1781, remembering the words of wartime Prime Minister Lord North; Philip Freneau, celebrated poet of the American Revolution; John Hamilton, a Charleston Loyalist, writing to a friend in London March 31, 1782; Thomas Paine in a work called The Crisis *in 1793, offering his*

"Thoughts on the Peace and Probable Advantages Thereof"; Sgt. Joseph P. Martin, an enlisted man from Connecticut, describing the moment of his discharge after eight years' service; Benjamin Franklin, a peace negotiator, writing to a friend from France on July 27, 1783; Samuel Curwen, an American businessman who spent the war years in England, returning to his home town of Boston on September 25, 1783; Lt. Col. Ben Tallmadge describing General Washington's farewell to his officers in Fraunces' Tavern in lower Manhattan, on November 25, 1783.

Questions

What did the Revolutionary War seem to mean to each of these participants? Revolutions have a way of producing unexpected results. Are any expressed in the following excerpts?

How did the soldiers of both sides react at Yorktown?

What conduct should a great nation and its leaders demonstrate when they lose a major war? Did Britain do herself justice in this regard?

Did the Revolution meet the high expectations of the American rebels?

Anna Rawle –

October 24 It is too true that Cornwallis is taken. [Colonel Tench] Tiligman is just arrived with dispatches from Washington which confirm it. B[enjamin] S[hoemaker] came here and shewed us some papers; long conversations we often have together on the melancholy situation of things.

October 25 I suppose, dear Mammy, thee would not have imagined this house to be illuminated last night, but it was. A mob surrounded it; broke the shutters and the glass of the windows, and were coming in; none but forlorn women here. We for a time listened for their attacks in fear and trembling till, finding them grow more loud and violent, not knowing what to do, we ran into the yard. Warm Whigs of one side, and [James] Hartley's of the other (who were treated even worse than we), rendered it impossible for us to escape that way. We had not been there many times before we were drove back by the sight of two men climbing the fence. We thought the mob were coming in thro' there, but it proved to be Coburn and Bob Shewell, who called to us not to be frightened, and fixed lights up at the windows, which pacified the mob, and after three huzzas they moved off. A number of men came in afterwards to see us. French and J. B. nailed boards up at the broken pannels, or it would not have been safe to have gone to bed. Coburn and Shewell were really very kind; had it not been for them I really believe the house would have been pulled down. Even the firm Uncle [William] Fisher was obliged to submit to have his windows illuminated, for they had pickaxes and iron bars with which they had done considerable injury to his house. . . . In short it was

SOURCES: Sir Nathaniel W. Wraxall, *Historical and Posthumous Memoirs, 1772–1789*, Henry B. Wheatley, ed. (New York, 1884), II, 137–142; Philip Freneau, *Poems Written and Published during the American Revolutionary War* (3d edn. 1824), II, 56; Benjamin Talmadge, *Memoir of Col. Benj. Talmadge;* Moncure Conway, ed., *The Writings of Thomas Paine* (New York: G. P. Putnam's Sons, 1894–96), I, 370–75, passim.

the most alarming scene I ever remember. For two hours we had the disagreeable noise of stones banging about, glass crashing, and the tumultuous voices of a large body of men, as they were a long time at the different houses in the neighbourhood. At last they were victorious, and it was one general illumination throughout the town. As we had not the pleasure of seeing any of the gentlemen in the house, nor the furniture cut up, and goods stolen, nor been beat, nor pistols pointed at our breasts, we may count our sufferings slight compared to many others. Mr Gibbs was obliged to make his escape over a fence, and while his wife was endeavouring to shield him from the rage of one of the men, she received a violent bruise in the breast and a blow in the face which made her nose bleed. Ben Shoemaker was here this morning; tho' exceedingly threatened he says he came off with the loss of four panes of glass. Some Whig friends put candles in the windows which made his peace with the mob, and they retired. John Drinker has lost half the goods out of his shop and been beat by them; in short the sufferings of those they pleased to style Tories would fill a volume and shake the credulity of those who were not here on that memorable night, and today Philadelphia makes an uncommon appearance, which ought to cover the Whigs with eternal confusion. . . .

Samuel Graham—

Drums were beat, but the colors remained in their cases—an idle retaliation for a very idle sight which had been put by our people on the American garrison of Charleston, and the regiments having formed in columns at quarter distance the men laid down their arms.

It is a sorry reminiscence, this. Yet the scene made a deep impression at the moment, for the mortification and unfeigned sorrow of the soldiers will never fade from my memory. Some went so far as to shed tears, while one man, a corporal, who stood near me, embraced his firelock and then threw it on the ground exclaiming, 'May you never get so good a master again!'

Nevertheless, to do them justice, the Americans behaved with great delicacy and forbearance, while the French, by what motive actuated I will not pretend to say, were profuse in their protestations of sympathy. . . . When I visited their lines . . . immediately after our parade had been dismissed, I was overwhelmed with the civility of my late enemies.

Rebel Officer—

The British officers in general behaved like boys who had been whipped at school. Some bit their lips, some pouted, others cried. Their round, broad-brimmed hats were well adapted to the occasion, hiding those faces they were ashamed to show. The foreign regiments made a more military appearance, and the conduct of their officers was far more becoming men of fortitude.

Nathaniel Wraxall—

After perusing the account of Lord Cornwallis's surrender at Yorktown, it was impossible not to feel a lively curiosity to know how the King had received the intelligence, as well as how he had expressed himself in his note to Lord George Germain on the first communication of so painful an event. He gratified our wish by reading it to us, observing, at the same time, that it did the highest honour to his Majesty's fortitude, firmness and consistency of character. The words made an impression on my memory which the lapse of more than thirty years has not erased, and I shall here commemorate its tenor as serving to show how that prince felt and wrote under one of the most afflicting as well as humiliating occurrences of his reign. The billet ran nearly to this effect:

"I have received with sentiments of the deepest concern the communication which Lord George Germain has made me of the unfortunate result of the operations in Virginia. I particularly lament it on account of the consequences connected with it and the difficulties which it may produce in carrying on the public business or in repairing such a misfortune. But I trust that neither Lord George Germain nor any member of the Cabinet will suppose that it makes the smallest aleration in those principles of my conduct which have directed me in past time and which will always continue to animate me under every event in the prosecution of the present contest."

Not a sentiment of despondency or of despair was to be found in the letter, the very handwriting of which indicated composure of mind. Whatever opinion we may entertain relative to the practicability of reducing America to obedience by force of arms at the end of 1781, we must admit that no sovereign could manifest more calmness, dignity or self-command than George III displayed in this reply.

Philip Freneau –

When a certain great king, whose initial is G.
Shall force stamps upon paper, and folks to drink tea;
When these folks burn his tea and stampt paper, like stubble,
You may guess that this king is then coming to trouble.
But when a petition he treads under his feet,
And sends over the ocean an army and fleet;
When that army, half starved, and frantic with rage,
Shall be cooped up with a leader whose name rhymes with cage;
When that leader goes home dejected and sad,
You may then be assured the king's prospects are bad.
But when B. and C. with their armies are taken,
This king will do well if he saves his own bacon.
In the year seventeen hundred and eighty and two,
A stroke he shall get that will make him look blue;
In the years eighty-three, eighty-four, eighty-five,
You hardly shall know that the king is alive;
In the year eighty-six the affair will be over,
And he shall eat turnips that grow in Hanover.
The face of the lion shall then become pale,
He shall yield fifteen teeth, and be sheared of his tail.
O king, my dear king, you shall be very sore;
The Stars and the Lily shall run you on shore,
And your Lion shall growl—but never bite more.

John Hamilton –

I was in a State of Despondence for some time until his Majesty's speech arrived when it revived my Spirits, but what was my astonishment when I Read Lord George

G[ermai]n's and Lord North's speech in parliament; surely they can never be so weak as to give up this Country.

Our Country is lost in dissipation, luxury and faction. There is no publick Spirit or virtue left either to reward merrit or punish offences. Remove all Such wretches from power and leav either Execution of affairs to the brave, zealous Loyalists, who have lost their fortunes and Risk'd their lives in defence of their King and Country; such are the men who will save their Country from Ruin and distruction. . . .

Notwithstanding all our Misfortunes, Great Britain can never, must never relinquish America. The last man and shilling must be expended before she gives America her independence; if she looses America, she looses all her West Indies and must Revert again to her insular Situation, which hardly make her visible on the face of the Earth.

Thomas Paine –

"The times that tried men's souls" are over—and the greatest and completest revolution the world ever knew, gloriously and happily accomplished.

But to pass from the extremes of danger to safety, from the tumult of war to the tranquility of peace, though sweet in contemplation, requires a gradual composure of the senses to receive it. Even calmness has the power of stunning, when it opens too instantly upon us. The long and raging hurricane that should cease in a moment, would leave us in a state rather of wonder than enjoyment; and some moments of recollection must pass, before we could be capable of tasting the felicity of repose. There are but few instances in which the mind is fitted for sudden transitions: it takes in its pleasures by reflection and comparison and those must have time to act, before the relish for new scenes is complete. . . .

To see it in our power to make a world happy—to teach mankind the art of being so—to exhibit on the theatre of the universe a character hitherto unknown—and to have, as it were, a new creation intrusted to our hands, are honors that command reflection and can neither be too highly estimated nor too gratefully received.

In this pause then of recollection, while the storm is ceasing, and the long agitated mind vibrating to a rest, let us look back on the scenes we have passed and learn from experience what is yet to be done.

Never, I say, had a country so many openings to happiness as this. Her setting out in life, like the rising of a fair morning, was unclouded and promising. Her cause was good. Her principles just and liberal. Her temper serene and firm. Her conduct regulated by the nicest steps, and everything about her wore the mark of honor. It is not every country (perhaps there is not another in the world) that can boast so fair an origin. Even the first settlement of America corresponds with the character of the Revolution. Rome, once the proud mistress of the universe, was originally a band of ruffians. Plunder and rapine made her rich, and her oppression of millions made her great. But America need never be ashamed to tell her birth, nor relate the stages by which she rose to empire.

Joseph P. Martin –

'The old man,' our captain, came into our room . . . and . . . handed us our discharges, or rather furloughs. . . . I confess, after all, that my anticipation of the happiness I should experience upon such a day as this was not realized. . . . We had lived together as a family of brothers for several years (setting aside some little family squabbles, like most other families); had shared with each other the hardships, dangers, and sufferings incident to a soldier's life, had sympathized with each other in trouble and sickness; had assisted in bearing each other's burdens, or strove to make them lighter by council and advice; had endeavored to conceal each other's faults, or make them appear in as good a light as they would bear. In short, the soldiery, each in his particular circle of acquaintance, were as strict a band of brotherhood as Masons, and I believe as faithful to each other. And now we were to be (the greater part of us) parted forever, as unconditionally separated as though the grave lay between us. This, I say, was the case with the most; I will not say all. There were as many genuine misanthropists among the soldiers . . . as of any other class of people whatever, and some in our corps of miners. But we were young men and had warm hearts. I question if there was a corps in the army that parted with more regret than ours did, the New Englanders in particular. Ah! it was a serious time!

Some of the soldiers went off for home the same day that their fetters were knocked off; others stayed and got their final settlement certificates, which they sold to procure decent clothing and money sufficient to enable them to pass with decency through the country, and to appear something like themselves when they arrived among their friends. I was among those . . . I . . . sold some of them and purchased some decent clothing and then set off. . . .

Benjamin Franklin –

I join with you most cordially in rejoicing at the return of peace. I hope it will be lasting, and that mankind will at length, as they call themselves reasonable creatures, have reason and sense enough to settle their differences without cutting throats; for, in my opinion, *there never was a good war or a bad peace.* What vast additions to the conveniences and comforts of living might mankind have acquired, if the money spent in wars had been employed in works of public utility! What an extension of agriculture, even to the tops of our mountains; what rivers rendered navigable or joined by canals; what bridges, aqueducts, new roads and other public works, edifices and improvements, rendering England a complete paradise, might have been obtained by spending those millions in doing good which in the last war we have been spent in doing mischief; in bringing misery into thousands of families, and destroying the lives of so many thousands of working people, who might have performed the useful labor!

Samuel Curwen –

September 25 Arrived at Boston, and at half past three o'clock landed at the end of Long Wharf, after an absence of nine years and five months, occasioned by an execrable and never enough to be lamented civil war, excited by ambitious, selfish wicked men here and in England, to the disgrace, dishonour, disparagement and distress of these extensive territories. By plunder and rapine some few have accumulated wealth, but many more in numbers are greatly injured in their circumstances; some have to lament over the wrecks of their departed wealth and estates, of which pitiable number I am; my affairs having sunk into irretrievable ruin. . . .

Friday, 10 June 1785 I again departed, presuming never more to repossess my late estate nor effects and twill be well if any part of them shall revert, and am this day June 10 at half past four P.M. going on board the ship *Astra* accompanied only by Mr Ward, intending for London, where and in the country or at least in some foreign parts, I must in the 70th year of my age spend the remainder of my days.

Ben Tallmadge –

At twelve o'clock the officers repaired to Fraunces Tavern in Pearl Street, where General Washington had appointed to meet them and to take his final leave of them. We had been assembled but a few moments when His Excellency entered the room. His emotion, too strong to be concealed, seemed to be reciprocated by every officer present.

After partaking of a slight refreshment, in almost breathless silence, the General filled his glass with wine, and turning to his officers, he said, 'With a heart full of love and gratitude, I now take leave of you. I most devoutly wish that your latter days may be as prosperous and happy as your former ones have been glorious and honorable.'

After the officers had takan a glass of wine, General Washington said, 'I cannot come to each of you, but shall feel obliged if each of you will come and take me by the hand.'

General Knox, being nearest to him, turned to the Commander-in-Chief, who, suffused in tears, was incapable of utterance, but grasped his hand, when they embraced each other in silence. In the same affectionate manner, every officer in the room marched up to, kissed, and parted with his General-in-Chief.

Such a scene of sorrow and weeping I had never before witnessed, and hope I may never be called upon to witness again. . . . Not a word was uttered to break the solemn silence . . . or to interrupt the tenderness of the . . . scene. The simple thought that we were then about to part from the man who had conducted us through a long and bloody war, and under whose conduct the glory and independence of our country had been achieved, and that we should see his face no more in this world, seemed to me utterly insupportable.

But the time of separation had come, and waving his hand to his grieving children around him, he left the room, and passing through a corps of light infantry who were paraded to receive him, he walked silently on to Whitehall, where a barge was in waiting. We all followed in mournful silence to the wharf, where a prodigious crowd had assembled to witness the departure of the man who, under God, had been the great agent in establishing the glory and independence of these United States. As soon as he was seated, the barge put off into the river, and when out in the stream, our great and beloved General waived his hat and bid us a silent adieu.

3.3 Another War with England?

The War of 1812 resulted from an accumulation of grievances between the United States and England that had been festering since the end of the Revolutionary War. Today the most commonly held belief about that conflict is that it had to do chiefly with maritime issues—the impressment of American merchant seamen into the Royal Navy. But clearly it was more complex than that, involving objectives of both nations regarding trade and the future of Canada. For a time the U.S. attempted to apply trade restrictions helping to bring about a resolution of differences, but they failed. War was declared June 18, 1812 and ended two years later, with the Battle of New Orleans.

The issue of whether or not to go to war with the former mother country stirred intense debate in House of Representatives. On December 10 and 11, 1811, John Randolph Jr. (1773–1833) of Roanoke, Virginia, squared off against Richard M. Johnson of Kentucky. Though Randolph spoke in a high soprano voice, he was regarded as a brilliant orator, noted for his sarcasm and for defending lost causes. He opposed Jefferson's Embargo Act of 1807, Madison's presidential candidacy in 1808, and the nation's entry into the war, which cost him re-election in 1813. He eventually returned to the House and was elected to the Senate years later. Johnson, a lesser-known figure, was one of the "War Hawks" who, along with fellow Kentuckian, Henry Clay, dominated Congress from 1810 to 1812. In the selections that follow, the clerk sometimes paraphrases the speakers.

Questions

Summarize Randolph's arguments. Why does he criticize his Republican (Jeffersonian) colleagues? To what purpose does he raise the slavery question? Does he oppose attacking the British? Why?

Summarize Johnson's arguments. How does he justify attacking Canada? What is his reply to the slavery question?

Enumerate all the different causes and objectives for going to war or opposing war again with England. Based on these brief items what can you tell about the causes of war? From the standpoint of either man, what did the war accomplish?

John Randolph, Jr.—

Our people will not submit to be taxed for this war of conquest and dominion. The Government of the United States was not calculated to wage offensive foreign war—it was instituted for the common defense and general welfare; and whosoever should embark it in a war of offense, would put it to a test which it was by no means calculated to endure. Make it out that Great Britain had instigated the Indians on the late occasion, and he was ready for battle; but not for dominion. He was unwilling, however, under present circumstances, to take Canada, at the risk of the Constitution—to embark in a common cause with France and be dragged at the wheels of the car of some Burr or Bonaparte. For a gentleman from Tennessee or Gennessee, or Lake Champlain, there may be some prospect of advantage. Their hemp would bear a great price by the exclusion of foreign supply. In that too the great importers were deeply interested. The upper country on the Hudson and the Lakes would be enriched by the supplies for the troops, which they alone could furnish. They would have the exclusive market; to say nothing of the increased preponderance from the acquisition of Canada. . . .

Mr. Randolph dwelt on the danger arising from the black population. He said he would touch this subject as tenderly as possible—it was with reluctance that he touched it at all—but in cases of great emergency, the State physician must not be deterred by a sickly, hysterical humanity from probing the wound of his patient—he must not be withheld by a fastidious and mistaken humanity from representing his true situation to his friends, or even to the sick man himself, where the occasion called for it. What was the situation of the slaveholding States? During the war of the Revolution, so fixed were their habits of subordination, that when the whole Southern country was overrun by the enemy, who invited them to desert, no fear was ever entertained of an insurrection of the slaves. . . . But should we therefore be unobservant spectators of the progress of society within the last twenty years—of the silent but powerful change wrought by time and chance, upon its composition and temper? When the fountains of the great deep of abomination were broken up, even the poor slaves had not escaped the general deluge. The French Revolution had polluted even them. Nay, there had not been wanting men in [the French Assembly] . . . to preach upon that floor to a crowded audience of blacks in the galleries—teaching them that they are equal to their masters; in other words, advising them to cut their throats. Similar doctrines were disseminated by peddlers from New England and elsewhere, throughout the Southern country—and masters had been found so infatuated, as by their lives and conversation, by a general contempt of order, morality, and religion, unthinkingly to cherish these seeds of self-destruction to them and their families. What was the consequence? Within the last ten years, repeated alarms of insurrection among the slaves—some of them awful indeed. From the spreading of this infernal doctrine, the whole Southern country had been thrown into a state of insecurity. Men dead to the operation of moral causes, had taken away from the poor slave his habits of loyalty and obedience to his master, which lightened his servitude by a double operation; beguiling his own cares and disarming his master's suspicions and severity; and now, like true empirics in politics, you are called upon to trust to the mere physical strength of the

Source: The Debates and Proceedings in the Congress of the United States, Twelfth Congress, First Session (Washington, D.C., 1853), 447–51, 454–60.

fetter which holds him in bondage. You have deprived him of all moral restraint, you have tempted him to eat of the fruit of the tree of knowledge, just enough to perfect him in wickedness; you have opened his eyes to his nakedness; you have armed his nature against the hand that has fed him, that has clothed him, that has cherished him in sickness; that hand, which before he became a pupil of your school, he had been accustomed to press with respectful affection. You have done all this—and then show him the gibbet and the wheel, as incentives to a sullen, repugnant obedience. God forbid, sir, that the Southern States should ever see an enemy on their shores, with these infernal principles of French fraternity in the van! While talking of taking Canada, some of us were shuddering for our own safety at home. He spoke from facts, when he said that the nightbell never tolled for fire in Richmond that the mother did not hug her infant more closely to her bosom. . . .

Before this miserable force of ten thousand men was raised to take Canada, he begged them to look at the state of defense at home—to count the cost of the enterprise before it was set on foot, not when it might be too late—when the best blood of the country should be spilt, and nought but empty coffers left to pay the cost. . . . He would beseech the House, before they ran their heads against this poet, Quebec, to count the cost. His word for it, Virginia planters would not be taxed to support such a war—a war which must aggravate their present distresses, in which they had not the remotest interest. . . . He called upon those professing to be Republicans to make good the promises held out by their Republican predecessors when they came into power—promises, which for years afterwards they had honestly, faithfully fulfilled. We had vaunted of paying off the national debt, of retrenching useless establishments; and yet had now become as infatuated with standing armies, loans, taxes, navies, and war, as ever were the Essex Junto. What Republicanism is this?

Richard M. Johnson—

I feel rejoiced that the hour of resistance is at hand, and that the President, in whom the people have so much confidence, has warned us of the perils that await them, and has exhorted us to put on the armor of defense, to gird on the sword, and assume the manly and bold attitude of war. . . . For the first time since my entrance into this body, there now seems to be but one opinion with a great majority—that with Great Britain war is inevitable; that the hopes of the sanguine as to a returning sense of British justice have expired; that the prophecies of the discerning have failed; and, that her infernal system has driven us to the brink of a second revolution, as important as the first. Upon the Wabash, through the influence of British agents, and within our territorial sea by the British navy, the war has already commenced. Thus, the folly, the power, and the tyranny of Great Britain, have taken from us the last alternative of longer forbearance.

We must now oppose the further encroachments of Great Britain by war, or formally annul the Declaration of our Independence, and acknowledge ourselves her devoted colonies. The people whom I represent will not hesitate which of the two courses to choose; and, if we are involved in war, to maintain our dearest rights, and to preserve our independence, I pledge myself to this House, and my constituents to this nation, that they will not be wanting in valor, nor in their proportion of men and money to prosecute the war with effect. Before we relinquish the conflict, I wish to see Great Britain renounce the piratical system or paper blockade; to liberate our captured seamen on board her ships of war; to relinquish the practice of impressment on board our merchant vessels; to repeal her Orders in Council; and cease, in every other respect, to violate the neutral rights; to treat us to an independent people. The gentleman from Virginia [Mr. Randolph] has objected to the destination of this auxiliary force—the occupation of the Canadas, and the other British possessions upon our borders where our laws are violated, the Indians stimulated to murder our citizens, and where there is a British monopoly of the peltry and fur trade. I should not wish to extend the boundary of the United States by war if Great Britain would leave us to the quiet enjoyment of independence; but, considering her deadly and implacable enmity, and her continued hostility, I shall never die contented until I see her expulsion from North America, and her territories incorporated with the United States. . . .

The gentleman from Virginia says we are identified with the British in religion, in blood, in language, and deeply laments our hatred to that country, who can boast of so many illustrious characters. This deep rooted enmity to Great Britain arises from her insidious policy, the offspring of her perfidious conduct towards the United States. Her disposition is unfriendly; her enmity is implacable; she sickens at our prosperity and happiness. If obligations of friendship do exist, why does Great Britain rend those ties asunder, and open the bleeding wounds of former conflicts? Or does the obligation of friendship exist on the part of the United States alone? I have never thought that the ties of religion, of blood, of language, and of commerce, would justify or sanctify insult and injury—on the contrary, that a premeditated wrong from the hand of a friend created more sensibility, and deserved the greater chastisement and the higher execration. . . . For God's sake let us not again be told of the ties of religion, of laws, of blood, and of customs, which bind the two nations together, with a view to extort our love for the English government, and more especially, where the same gentleman [Randolph], has acknowledged that we have ample cause of war against that nation—let us not be told of the freedom of that corrupt government, whose hands are washed alike in the blood of her own illustrious statesmen, for a manly opposition to tyranny, and the citizens of every other clime.

Twenty-eight years have elapsed, and the only remedy which we have attempted against these crying enormities has been negotiation and remonstrance, and so far from producing any beneficial effect, Great Britain has made new innovations and urged new pretensions, until the neutral rights of the United States are entirely destroyed. . . . May the wrath of this nation kindle into a flame and become a consuming fire! Though slow to anger, may her indignation be like the rushing of mighty waters and the volcanic eruptions of Hecla!

3.4 Reflections on War

The enlightened thinker and statesman Thomas Jefferson often pondered the meaning of war and peace. The major conflicts that he witnessed during his lifetime (1743–1826)—the American Revolutionary War, the French Revolutionary and Napoleonic wars, the War of 1812, the Russo-Turkish War—gave him ample food for thought. In addition, he was a keen student of history and had read broadly on past wars. For one who normally professed great optimism about the human condition, Jefferson's conclusions concerning war were fairly pessimistic. Barbarism and despotism, it seemed, were ever at war with civilization and enlightenment.

Though not a soldier, Jefferson had several personal encounters with war, none of them very successful. As governor of Virginia during the War for Independence he proved ineffectual in mobilizing manpower and resources, and in stymieing the redcoats. When he tried as President (after 1807) to avoid war with Britain by using economic policy and applying diplomatic pressure, his actions did not prevent war so much as postpone it. The following selections reflect his thinking at various intervals over a period of a quarter of a century, from 1797 to 1821.

Questions

What was Jefferson's opinion about Europe and America as potential sources of war?

What did he conclude about warfare from his studies of natural history and history? How much of what he writes is specific to individual conflicts, how much to an overall appraisal of human nature? Does he have a better opinion of revolution than of other forms of armed strife? Did his perceptions change over time, or do they seem static?

How would he have viewed war during the last century? Do natural or social scientists today support his assumptions about human nature?

To James Madison, 1797 –

In the whole animal kingdom I recollect no family but man, steadily and systematically employed in the destruction of itself. . . . If to this we add, that as to other animals, the lions and tigers are mere lambs compared with man as a destroyer, we must conclude that nature has been able to find in man alone a sufficient barrier against the too great multiplication of other animals and of man himself, an equilibrating power against the fecundity of generation.

To John Adams, 1822 –

To turn to the news of the day, it seems that the Cannibals of Europe are going to eating one another again. A war between Russia and Turkey is like the battle of the kite and snake. Whichever destroys the other, leaves a destroyer the less for the world. This pugnacious humor of mankind seems to be the law of his nature, one of the obstacles to too great multiplication provided in the mechanism of the Universe. The cocks of the henyard kill one another up. Bears, bulls, rams, do the same. And the horse, in his wild state, kills all the young males, until worn down with age and war, some vigorous youth kills him, and takes to himself the Harem of females. I hope we shall prove how much happier for man the Quaker policy is, and that the life of the feeder, is better than that of the fighter; and it is some consolation that the desolation by these maniacs of one part of the earth is the means of improving it in other parts. . . .

To Dr. Benjamin Rush, 1803 –

Tremendous times in Europe! How mighty this battle of lions and tigers! With what sensations should the common herd of cattle look on it? With no partialities, certainly. If they can so far worry one another as to destroy their power for tyrannizing, the one over the earth, the other the waters, the world may perhaps enjoy peace, till they recruit again.

To Colonel Duane, 1813 –

It is true that I am tired of practical politics, and happier while reading the history of ancient than of modern times. The total banishment of all moral principle from the code which governs the intercourse of nations . . . , sickens my soul unto death. I turn from the contemplation with loathing, and take refuge in the histories of other times, where, if they also furnished their Tarquins, their Catalines and Caligulas, their stories are handed to us under the brand of a Livy, a Sallust and a Tacitus, and we are comforted with the reflection that the condemnation of all succeeding generations has confirmed the censures of the historian, and consigned their memories to everlasting infamy, a solace we cannot have with the Georges and Napoleons but by anticipation.

To Ketocton Baptist Association, 1808 –

The moral principles and conventional usages which have heretofore been the bond of civilized nations . . . have now given way to force, the law of Barbarians, and the nineteenth century dawns with the Vandalism of the fifth.

To J. Maury, 1812 –

We consider the overwhelming power of England on the ocean, and of France on the land, as destructive of the prosperity and happiness of the world, and wish both to be reduced only to the necessity of observing moral duties. We believe no more in Bonaparte's fighting merely for the liberty of the seas, than in Great Britain's fighting for the liberties of mankind. The object of both is the same, to draw to themselves the power, the wealth and the resources of other nations.

1813 –

Our lot happens to have been cast in an age when two of the most powerful nations of the world, abusing their force and to whom circumstances have given a temporary superiority over others, the one by land, the other by sea, throwing off all the bonds [and] restraints of morality and all regard to pride of national character, forgetting the mutability of fortune and the inevitable doom which the laws of nature pronounce against departures from justice, individual or national—have dared to treat her reclamations with derision and to substitute force instead of reason as the umpire of nations, degrading themselves thus from the character of lawful societies into lawless bands of robbers and pirates, they are ravaging [and] abusing their brief ascendancy by desolating the world with blood and rapine. Against such banditti, war had become preferable [and] less ruinous than peace, for their peace was a war on one side only.

To Adams, 1821 –

I shall not die without a hope that light and liberty are on steady advance. We have seen, indeed, once within the records of history, a complete eclipse of the human mind continuing for centuries. And this, too, by swarms of the same northern barbarians, conquering and taking possession of the countries and governments of the civilized world. Should this be again attempted, should the same northern hordes, allured again by the corn, wine, and oil of the south, be able to settle their swarms in the countries of their growth, the art of printing alone, and the vast dissemination of books, will maintain the mind where it is, and raise the conquering ruffians to the level of the conquered, instead of degrading these to that of their conquerors. And even should the cloud of barbarism and despotism again obscure the science and liberties of Europe, this country remains to preserve and restore light and liberty to them. In short, the flames kindled on the 4th of July, 1776, have spread over too much of the globe to be extinguished by the feeble engines of despotism; on the contrary, they will consume these engines and all who work them.

3.5 Hands Off America!

In 1823 Great Britain asked for U.S. cooperation in issuing a statement to prevent a dangerous situation from developing in Latin America. Spain was threatening, with the help of other European powers, to recover its lost colonies in the New World—it once claimed most of the area from Mexico to the tip of South America. Secretary of State John Quincy Adams advised President James Monroe to reject the British offer and, instead, issue a unilateral statement. Monroe, in his annual message of December 2, 1823 (excerpted below), then proclaimed what came to be known as the Monroe Doctrine.

Monroe's statement went beyond Britain's request. It warned Spain against attempting to interfere with the independence movement in Latin America and it told Russia to back off from enlarging its sphere in the Pacific Northwest. Ironically, it also warned Britain to keep its hands off Cuba.

The Monroe Doctrine had a double message: it demanded that Europe not interfere in America, and it promised that the U.S. would not interfere in Europe. It implied that the U.S. had a natural zone of interest in the Americas. When first issued, this unilateral statement scarcely made a ripple anywhere in the world. Few U.S. citizens understood its meaning then. President Polk invoked it in the 1840s, Lincoln did so during the Civil War in an effort to push France out of Mexico, and Theodore Roosevelt in the 1890s enlarged its scope by giving the U.S. power to resolve the international problems of the Americas. Thereafter Americans have taken the doctrine very much to heart—at least the part of it that warns off Europe—and have regarded it almost as sacred, something akin to a Constitutional principle.

Questions

What exactly did President Monroe say in his message? What pledges and warnings did he imply? Did he intend to use military force to back them up?

What does the U.S. believe is its proper role in Central America today? How is that view related to the Monroe Doctrine?

Fellow-citizens of the Senate and House of Representatives:

. . . At the proposal of the Russian Imperial Government, made through the minister of the Emperor residing here, a full power and instructions have been transmitted to the minister of the United States at St. Petersburg to arrange by amicable negotiation the respective rights and interests of the two nations on the northwest coast of this continent. A similar proposal had been made by His Imperial Majesty to the government of Great Britain, which has likewise been acceded to. The government of the United States has been desirous, by this friendly proceeding, of manifesting the great value which they have invariably attached to the friendship of the Emperor and their solicitude to cultivate the best understanding with his government. In the discussions to which this interest has given rise and in the arrangements by which they may terminate, the occasion has been judged proper for asserting, as a principle in which the rights and interests of the United States are involved, that the American continents, by the free and independent condition which they have assumed and maintain, are henceforth not to be considered as subjects for future colonization by any European powers. . . .

In the wars of the European powers in matters relating to themselves we have never taken any part, nor does it comport with our policy so to do. It is only when our rights are invaded or seriously menaced that we resent injuries or make preparation for our defense. With the

SOURCE: James D. Richardson, ed., *Messages and Papers of the Presidents, 1789–1897* (Washington, D.C.: Government Printing Office, 1897).

movements in this hemisphere we are of necessity more immediately connected, and by causes which must be obvious to all enlightened and impartial observers. The political system of the allied powers is essentially different in this respect from that of America. This difference proceeds from that which exists in their respective governments; and to the defense of our own, which has been achieved by the loss of so much blood and treasure, and matured by the wisdom of their most enlightened citizens, and under which we have enjoyed unexampled felicity, this whole nation is devoted. We owe it, therefore, to candor and to the amicable relations existing between the United States and those powers to declare that we should consider any attempt on their part to extend their system to any portion of this hemisphere as dangerous to our peace and safety. With the existing colonies or dependencies of any European power we have not interfered and shall not interfere. But with the governments who have declared their independence and maintained it, and whose independence we have, on great consideration and on just principles, acknowledged, we could not view any interposition for the purpose of oppressing them, or controlling in any other manner their destiny, by any European power in any other light than as the manifestation of an unfriendly disposition toward the United States. In the war between those new Governments and Spain we declared our neutrality at the time of their recognition, and to this we have adhered, and shall continue to adhere, provided no change shall occur which, in the judgment of the competent authorities of this Government, shall make a corresponding change on the part of the United States indispensable to their security.

The late events in Spain and Portugal shew that Europe is still unsettled. Of this important fact no stronger proof can be adduced than that the allied powers should have thought it proper, on any principle satisfactory to themselves, to have interposed by force in the internal concerns of Spain. To what extent such interposition may be carried, on the same principle, is a question in which all independent powers whose governments differ from theirs are interested, even those most remote, and surely none more so than the United States. Our policy in regard to Europe, which was adopted at an early stage of the wars which have so long agitated that quarter of the globe, nevertheless remains the same, which is, not to interfere in the internal concerns of any of its powers; to consider the government *de facto* as the legitimate government for us; to cultivate friendly relations with it, and to preserve those relations by a frank, firm, and manly policy, meeting in all instances the just claims of every power, submitting to injuries from none. But in regard to those continents circumstances are eminently and conspicuously different. It is impossible that the allied powers should extend their political system to any portion of either continent without endangering our peace and happiness; nor can anyone believe that our southern brethren, if left to themselves, would adopt it of their own accord. It is equally impossible, therefore, that we should behold such interposition in any form with indifference. If we look to the comparative strength and resources of Spain and those new Governments, and their distance from each other, it must be obvious that she can never subdue them. It is still the true policy of the United States to leave the parties to themselves, in the hope that other powers will pursue the same course.

3.6 Democracy and War

After travelling extensively in America in 1831–1832, the French aristocrat Alexis de Tocqueville (1805–1859) published a work entitled Democracy in America *(1835 and 1840) that is now considered the greatest work by a foreign observer of American life. It was a study of the "equality of condition" that he saw in this country, not always approvingly, but always acutely. Tocqueville set out ostensibly to study the prison system of the United States, but travelled widely and observed many things. Almost nothing about government escaped his notice.*

In the course of his writings he expressed opinons about war and the military. The army seemed conspicuous by its absence. And yet the very existence of an army, however small and invisible, presented a potential problem to him. That is, although civilians in a democratic nation were fond of peace, their armies and navies were fond of war. A democratic nation is less fully caught up in the spirit of military glory than an aristocracy, but war poses a problem, nevertheless. The reason is that democracies need armies, like any other nations, but, he argued, standing armies create a particular threat to the stability and well being of civilian government.

Questions

Why, according to Tocqueville, is the military in a democracy such as the United States prone to making war? And why is it easier for the nation to start wars than to stop them?

How much of a prophet did Tocqueville turn out to be? Examine in particular the case of the Mexican War and the Civil War (or, for that matter, other wars that have followed more recently).

The same interests, the same fears, the same passions that deter democratic nations from revolutions deter them also from war; the spirit of military glory and the spirit of revolution are weakened at the same time and by the same causes. The ever increasing numbers of men of property who are lovers of peace, the growth of personal wealth which war so rapidly consumes, the mildness of manners, the gentleness of heart, those tendencies to pity which are produced by the equality of conditions, that coolness of understanding which renders men comparatively insen-

SOURCE: Alexis de Tocqueville, *Democracy in America*, Francis Bowen, ed. (2 vols., 7th edn., Boston: J. Allyn Co., 1882).

sible to the violent and poetical excitement of arms, all these causes concur to quench the military spirit. I think it may be admitted as a general and constant rule that among civilized nations the warlike passions will become more rare and less intense in proportion as social conditions are more equal.

War is nevertheless an occurrence to which all nations are subject, democratic nations as well as others. Whatever taste they may have for peace, they must hold themselves in readiness to repel aggression, or, in other words, they must have an army. Fortune, which has conferred so many peculiar benefits upon the inhabitants of the United States, has placed them in the midst of a wilderness, where they have, so to speak, no neighbors; a few thousand soldiers are sufficient for their wants. But this is peculiar to America, not to democracy.

The equality of conditions and the manners as well as the institutions resulting from it do not exempt a democratic people from the necessity of standing armies, and their armies always exercise a powerful influence over their fate. It is therefore of singular importance to inquire what are the natural propensities of the men of whom these armies are composed.

Among aristocratic nations, especially among those in which birth is the only source of rank, the same inequality exists in the army as in the nation; the officer is noble, the soldier is a serf; the one is naturally called upon to command, the other to obey. . . . Thus one man is born to the command of a regiment, another to that of a company. When once they have reached the utmost object of their hopes, they stop of their own accord and remain contented with their lot.

There is, besides, a strong cause that in aristocracies weakens the officer's desire of promotion. Among aristocratic nations an officer, independently of his rank in the army, also occupies an elevated rank in society; the former is almost always, in his eyes, only an appendage to the latter. A nobleman who embraces the profession of arms follows it less from motives of ambition than from a sense of the duties imposed on him by his birth. . . .

In democratic armies all the soldiers may become officers, which makes the desire of promotion general and immeasurably extends the bounds of military ambition. The officer, on his part, sees nothing that naturally and necessarily stops him at one grade more than at another; and each grade has immense importance in his eyes because his rank in society almost always depends on his rank in the army. Among democratic nations it often happens that an officer has no property but his pay and no distinction but that of military honors; consequently, as often as his duties change, his fortune changes and he becomes, as it were, a new man. What was only an appendage to his position in artistocratic armies has thus become the main point, the basis of his whole condition. . . .

In democratic armies the desire of advancement is almost universal: it is ardent, tenacious, perpetual; it is strengthened by all other desires and extinguished only with life itself. But it is easy to see that, of all armies in the world, those in which advancement must be slowest in time of peace are the armies of democratic countries. As the number of commissions is naturally limited while the number of competitors is almost unlimited, and as the strict law of equality is over all alike, none can make rapid progress; many can make no progress at all. Thus the desire of advancement is greater and the opportunities of advancement fewer there than elsewhere. All the ambitious spirits of a democratic army are consequently ardently desirous of war, because war makes vacancies and warrants the violation of that law of seniority which is the sole privilege natural to democracy.

We thus arrive at this singular consequence, that, of all armies, those most ardently desirous of war are democratic armies, and of all nations, those most fond of peace are democratic nations; and what makes these facts still more extraordinary is that these contrary effects are produced at the same time by the principle of equality.

All the members of the community, being alike, constantly harbor the wish and discover the possibility of changing their condition and improving their welfare; this makes them fond of peace, which is favorable to industry and allows every man to pursue his own little undertakings to their completion. On the other hand, this same equality makes soldiers dream of fields of battle, by increasing the value of military honors in the eyes of those who follow the profession of arms and by rendering those honors accessible to all. In either case the restlessness of the heart is the same, the taste for enjoyment is insatiable, the ambition of success as great; the means of gratifying it alone are different.

These opposite tendencies of the nation and the army expose democratic communities to great dangers. When a military spirit forsakes a people, the profession of arms immediately ceases to be held in honor and military men fall to the lowest rank of the public servants; they are little esteemed and no longer understood. The reverse of what takes place in aristocratic ages then occurs; the men who enter the army are no longer those of the highest, but of the lowest class. Military ambition is indulged only when no other is possible. Hence arises a circle of cause and consequence from which it is difficult to escape: the best part of the nation shuns the military profession because that profession is not honored, and the profession is not honored because the best part of the nation has ceased to follow it.

It is then no matter of surprise that democratic armies are often restless, ill-tempered, and dissatisfied with their lot, although their physical condition is commonly far better and their discipline less strict than in other countries. The soldier feels that he occupies an inferior position, and his wounded pride either stimulates his taste for hostilities that would render his services necessary or gives him a desire for revolution, during which he may hope to win by force of arms the political influence and personal importance now denied him.

The composition of democratic armies makes this last-mentioned danger much to be feared. In democratic communities almost every man has some property to preserve; but democratic armies are generally led by men without property, most of whom have little to lose in civil broils. The bulk of the nation is naturally much more afraid of revolutions than in the ages of aristocracy, but the leaders of the army much less so.

Moreover, as among democratic nations (to repeat what I have just remarked) the wealthiest, best-educated, and ablest men seldom adopt the military profession, the army, taken collectively, eventually forms a small nation by itself, where the mind is less enlarged and habits are more rude than in the nation at large. Now, this small uncivilized nation has arms in its possession and alone knows how to use them; for, indeed, the pacific temper of the community increases the danger to which a democratic people is exposed from the military and turbulent spirit of the army. Nothing is so dangerous as an army in the midst of an unwarlike nation; the excessive love of the whole community for quiet continually puts the constitution at the mercy of the soldiery.

It may therefore be asserted, generally speaking, that if democratic nations are naturally prone to peace from their interests and their propensities, they are constantly drawn to war and revolutions by their armies. Military revolutions, which are scarcely ever to be apprehended in aristocracies, are always to be dreaded among democratic nations. . . .

When a nation perceives that it is inwardly affected by the restless ambition of its army, the first thought which occurs is to give this inconvenient ambition an object by going to war. I do not wish to speak ill of war: war almost always enlarges the mind of a people and raises their character. In some cases it is the only check to the excessive growth of certain propensities that naturally spring out of the equality of conditions, and it must be considered as a necessary corrective to certain inveterate diseases to which democratic communities are liable.

War has great advantages, but we must not flatter ourselves that it can diminish the danger I have just pointed out. That peril is only suspended by it, to return more fiercely when the war is over; for armies are much more impatient of peace after having tasted military exploits. War could be a remedy only for a people who were always athirst for military glory.

I foresee that all the military rulers who may rise up in great democratic nations will find it easier to conquer with their armies than to make their armies live at peace after conquest. There are two things that a democratic people will always find very difficult, to begin a war and to end it.

Again, if war has some peculiar advantages for democratic nations, on the other hand it exposes them to certain dangers which aristocracies have no cause to dread to an equal extent. I shall point out only two of these.

Although war gratifies the army, it embarrasses and often exasperates that countless multitude of men whose minor passions every day require peace in order to be satisfied. Thus there is some risk of its causing, under another form, the very disturbance it is intended to prevent.

No protracted war can fail to endanger the freedom of a democratic country. Not indeed that after every victory it is to be apprehended that the victorious generals will possess themselves by force of the supreme power, after the manner of Sulla and Caesar; the danger is of another kind. War does not always give over democratic communities to military government, but it must invariably and immeasurably increase the powers of civil government; it must almost compulsorily concentrate the direction of all men and the management of all things in the hands of the administration. If it does not lead to despotism by sudden violence, it prepares men for it more gently by their habits. All those who seek to destroy the liberties of a democratic nation ought to know that war is the surest and the shortest means to accomplish it. This is the first axiom of the science.

One remedy, which appears to be obvious when the ambition of soldiers and officers becomes the subject of alarm, is to augment the number of commissions to be distributed by increasing the army. This affords temporary relief, but it plunges the country into deeper difficulties at some future period. To increase the army may produce a lasting effect in an aristocratic there confined to one class of men, and the ambition of each individual stops, as it were, at a certain limit, so that it may be possible to satisfy all who feel its influence. But nothing is gained by increasing the army among a democratic people, because the number of aspirants always rises in exactly the same ratio as the army itself. Those whose claims have been satisfied by the creation of new commissions are instantly succeeded by a fresh multitude beyond all power of satisfaction; and even those who were but now satisfied soon begin to crave more advancement, for the same excitement prevails in the ranks of the army as in the civil classes of democratic society, and what men want is, not to reach a certain grade, but to have constant promotion. Though these wants may not be very vast, they are perpetually recurring. Thus a democratic nation, by augmenting its army, allays only for a time the ambition of the military profession, which soon becomes even more formidable because the number of those who feel it is increased. . . .

The remedy for the vices of the army is not to be found in the army itself, but in the country. Democratic nations are naturally afraid of disturbance and of despotism; the object is to turn these natural instincts into intelligent, deliberate, and community, because military ambition is lasting tastes. When men have at last learned to make a peaceful and profitable use of freedom and have felt its blessings, when they have conceived a manly love of order and have freely submitted themselves to discipline, these same men, if they follow the profession of arms, bring into it, unconsciously and almost against their will, these same habits and manners. The general spirit of the nation, being infused into the spirit peculiar to the army, tempers the opinions and desires engendered by military life, or represses them by the mighty force of public opinion. Teach the citizens to be educated, orderly, firm, and free and the soldiers will be disciplined and obedient.

Any law that, in repressing the turbulent spirit of the army, should tend to diminish the spirit of freedom in the nation and to overshadow the notion of law and right would defeat its object; it would do much more to favor than to defeat the establishment of military tyranny.

After all, and in spite of all precautions, a large army in the midst of a democratic people will always be a source of great danger. The most effectual means of diminishing that danger would be to reduce the army, but this is a remedy that all nations are not able to apply.

3.7 A Decision for War

James K. Polk (1795–1849) was an expansionist and proud of it. He won election in 1844 by openly favoring Manifest Destiny, including the acquisition of Texas, California and New Mexico. He supported the annexation of Texas in 1845 and took a belligerent stance against Mexico in 1846. The Texans asserted that their boundaries extended south to the Rio Grande, a doubtful conclusion that Polk shared.

Few presidents have kept diaries, so the discovery of Polk's diary is considered a rare documentary find. A particularly interesting entry is that of May 9, 1846, concerning a cabinet meeting on the Mexican issue. His decision to go to war against Mexico seems to precede any provocation by Mexico. When diplomacy failed, he sent troops into the disputed border area in 1846, claiming that blood had been shed on U.S. territory. Fighting started in the disputed territory between the Rio Grande and the Nueces River. Congressman Abe Lincoln introduced his famous "spot resolution," asking to be shown the spot on American soil *where blood had been shed. Polk blamed the war on the Mexicans and urged Congress to declare war. It did so on May 13, 1846. The Mexican War lasted until February 2, 1848.*

Questions

Examine the diary entry carefully, assessing the position of the President and his cabinet members.

Did the President seem to think that the Mexicans were engaging in provocations in U.S. territory? State your evidence. If your answer is no, what are the implications of his implying otherwise?

Is this a presidential provocation? If so, have there been other wars where such provocations played a major role?

The Cabinet held a regular meeting today; all the members present. I brought up the Mexican question. . . . The subject was very fully discussed. All agreed that if the Mexican forces at Matamoras committed any act of hostility on General Taylor's forces I should immediately send a message to Congress recommending an immediate declaration of war. I stated to the Cabinet that up to this time, as they knew, we had heard of no open act of aggression by the Mexican army, but that the danger was imminent that such acts would be committed. I said that in my opinion we had ample cause of war, and . . . that I thought it was my duty to send a message to Congress very soon and recommend definitive measures. I told them that I thought I ought to make such a message by Tuesday next, that the country was excited and impatient on the subject, and if I failed to do so I would not be doing my duty. I then propounded the distinct question to the Cabinet and took their opinions individually, whether I should make a message to Congress on Tuesday, and whether in that message I should recommend a declaration of war against Mexico. All except the Secretary of the Navy gave their advice in the affirmative. Mr. Bancroft dissented but said if any act of hostility should be committed by the Mexican forces he was then in favor of immediate war. Mr. Buchanan said he would feel better satisfied in his course if the Mexican forces had or should commit any act of hostility, but that as matters stood

SOURCE: Milo M. Quaife, ed., *The Diary of James K. Polk* (New York, 1910), I, 384–86.

we had ample cause of war against Mexico, and he gave his assent to the measure.

About 6 o'clock P.M. General R. Jones, the Adjutant General of the army, called and handed to me dispatches received from General Taylor by the Southern mail which had just arrived, giving information that a part of the Mexican army had crossed the Del Norte, and attacked and killed and captured two companies of dragoons of General Taylor's army consisting of 63 officers and men. The dispatch also stated that he had on that day (26th April) made a requisition on the Governors of Texas and Louisiana for four Regiments each, to be sent to his relief at the earliest practicable period. . . . I immediately summoned the Cabinet to meet at 7½ O'Clock this evening. . . . The Cabinet was unanimously of opinion, and it was so agreed, that a message should be sent to Congress on Monday laying all the information in my possession before them and recommending vigorous and prompt measures to enable the Executive to prosecute the war.

3.8 The "Slave Power" War

The Mexican War provoked strong opposition, chiefly among those who charged that it represented a conspiracy of the "aggressive slaveocracy" of the South that wanted new territory where slaves could produce cotton. There was little hard evidence for the "slave-power" thesis, but many believed it. Henry David Thoreau went to jail rather than pay taxes to support the slave owners (see Chapter 2, Power). Whigs, such as congressmen Abraham Lincoln of Illinois and Thomas Corwin of Ohio, and Sen. Daniel Webster denounced the war. Charles Sumner, a prominent Boston politician and founder of the Free-Soil party, presented the Massachusetts legislature with a special Report on the War with Mexico. *It helped launch him on a career as a leading political abolitionist, free-soiler and Radical Republican. Excerpts from an impassioned speech by Representative Corwin and from Sumner's report capture the antiwar fervor.*

Questions

Was Corwin right about the patriotic zeal that the war would evoke in Mexico? How much support did the war actually receive from southern politicians and slave owners? By contrast, how much encouragement did it get from westerners who had no interest in slavery? What does this tell you about Sumner's thesis? Are Americans particularly prone to conspiracy theories?

Rep. Thomas Corwin –

I did hope . . . we might get peace, and avoid the slaughter, the shame, the crime, of an aggressive unprovoked war. But now you have overrun half of Mexico—you have exasperated and irritated her people—you claim indemnity for all expenses incurred in doing this mischief, and boldly ask her to give up New Mexico and California; and, as a bribe to her patriotism, seizing on her property, you offer three millions to pay the soldiers she has called out to repel your invasion, on condition that she will give up to you at least one-third of her whole territory. . . .

What is the territory, Mr. President, which you propose to wrest from Mexico? It is consecrated to the heart of the Mexican by many a well-fought battle with his old Castilian master. His Bunker Hills, and Saratogas, and Yorktowns, are there! The Mexican can say, "There I bled for liberty! And shall I surrender that consecrated home of my affections to the Anglo-Saxon invaders? What do they want with it? They have Texas already. They have possessed themselves of the territory between the Nueces and the Rio Grande. What else do they want? To what shall I point my children as memorials of that independence which I bequeath to them when those battlefields shall have passed from my possession?"

Sir, had one come and demanded Bunker Hill of the people of Massachusetts, had England's Lion ever showed himself there, is there a man over thirteen and under ninety who would not have been ready to meet him? Is there a river on this continent that would not have run red with blood? Is there a field but would have been piled high with the unburied bones of slaughtered Americans before these consecrated battlefields of liberty should have been wrested from us? But this same American goes into a sister republic and says to poor, weak Mexico, "Give up your territory, you are unworthy to possess it; I have got one-half already, and all I ask of you is to give up the other!" . . . The Senator from Michigan says he must have this. Why, my worthy Christian brother, on what principle of justice? "I want room!"

Sir, look at this pretence of want of room. With twenty millions of people, you have about one thousand millions of acres of land, inviting settlement by every conceivable argument, bringing them down to a quarter of a dollar an acre, and allowing every man to squat where he pleases. But the Senator from Michigan says we will be two hundred millions in a few years, and we want room. If I were a Mexican I would tell you, "Have you not room in your own country to bury your dead men? If you come into mine, we will greet you with bloody hands, and welcome you to hospitable graves."

Why, says the chairman of this Committee on Foreign Relations, it is the most reasonable thing in the world! We ought to have the Bay of San Francisco. Why? Because it is the best harbor on the Pacific! It has been my fortune, Mr. President, to have practised a good deal in criminal courts in the course of my life, but I never yet heard a thief, arraigned for stealing a horse, plead that it was the best horse that he could find in the country! We want California. What for? Why, says the Senator from Michigan, we will have it; and the Senator from South Carolina, with a very mistaken view, I think, of policy, says you can't keep our people from going there. I don't desire to prevent them. Let them go and seek their happiness in whatever country or clime it pleases them. All I ask of them is, not to require this Government to protect them

SOURCE: Congressional Globe, Twenty-ninth Congress, Second Session, pp. 216–17.

with that banner consecrated to war waged for principles—eternal, enduring truth. Sir, it is not meet that our old flag should throw its protecting folds over expeditions for lucre or for land. But you will say you want room for your people. This has been the plea of every robber chief from Nimrod to the present hour.

Charles Sumner—

Origin and Cause of the War. To answer these inquiries, it will be proper, in the first place, to consider the origin and cause of the war. History and official documents have already placed these in a clear light. They are to be found in two important acts of our government, both of which were in flagrant violation of the Constitution of the United States. The first is the annexation of the foreign State of Texas, and its incorporation into our Union, by joint resolutions of Congress. This may be called the remote cause. The immediate cause was the order from the President, bearing date January 13, 1846, to General Taylor, to break up his camp at Corpus Christi, the extreme western point of the territory actually possessed by Texas, and march upon the Rio Grande. This, which was in itself an act of war, took place during the session of Congress, but without its knowledge or direction. Let us endeavor to comprehend the character and consequences of these acts.

The Annexation of Texas. The history of the annexation of Texas cannot be fully understood without reverting to the early settlement of that province by citizens of the United States. Mexico, on achieving her independence of the Spanish crown, by a general ordinance, worthy of imitation by all Christian nations, had decreed the abolition of human slavery within her dominions, embracing the Province of Texas. . . . At this period, citizens of the United States had already begun to remove into Texas, hardly separated, as it was, by the River Sabine from the slave-holding State of Louisiana. The idea was early promulgated that this extensive province ought to become a part of the United States. Its annexation was distinctly agitated in the Southern and Western States in 1829; and it was urged on the ground of the strength and extension it would give to the "Slave Power," and the fresh market it would open for the sale of slaves.

The suggestion of this idea had an important effect. A current of emigration soon followed from the United States. Slaveholders crossed the Sabine, with their slaves, in defiance of the Mexican ordinance of freedom. . . . A Declaration of Independence, a farcical imitation of that of our fathers, was put forth, not by persons acting in a Congress or in a representative character, but by about *ninety individuals,*—all, except two, from the United States,—acting for themselves, and recommending a similar course to their fellow-citizens. In a just cause the spectacle of this handful of adventurers, boldly challenging the power of Mexico, would excite our sympathy, perhaps our admiration. But successful rapacity, which seized broad and fertile lands, while it opened new markets for slaves, excites no sentiment but that of abhorrence.

The work of rebellion sped. Citizens of the United States joined its fortunes, not singly, but in numbers, even in armed squadrons. Our newspapers excited the *lust* of *territorial* robbery in the public mind. . . . During all this period the United States were at peace with Mexico. A proclamation from our government, forbidding these hostile preparations within our borders, is undeniable evidence of their existance, while truth compels us to record its impotence in upholding the sacred duties of neutrality between Mexico and the insurgents. The Texan flag waved over an army of American citizens. Of the six or eight hundred who won the battle of San Jacinto, scattering the Mexican forces and capturing their general, not more than fifty were citizens of Texas, having grievances of their own to redress on that field.

This victory was followed by the recognition of the independence of Texas by the United States; while the new State took its place among the nations of the earth. . . .

Certainly our sister republic might feel aggrieved by this conduct. It might justly charge our citizens with disgraceful robbery, while, in seeking the extension of slavery, they repudiated the great truths of American freedom. Meanwhile Texas slept on her arms, constantly expecting new efforts from Mexico to regain her former power. The two combatants regarded each other as enemies. Mexico still asserted her right to the territory wrested from her, and refused to acknowledge its independence. Texas turned for favor and succor to England. The government of the United States, fearing it might pass under the influence of this power, made overtures for its annexation to our country. This was finally accomplished by joint resolutions of Congress, in defiance of the Constitution. . . .

Movement of General Taylor form Corpus Christi to the Rio Grande. This was the state of things when, by an order bearing date 13th January, 1846, during the session of Congress, and without any consultation with that body, General Taylor was directed, by the President of the United States, to occupy the east bank of the Rio Grande, being the extreme western part of the territory claimed by Texas, the boundary of which had been designated as an "open question," to be determined by "negotiation." . . .

War Ensues. These were acts of war, accomplished without bloodshed; but they were nevertheless acts of unquestioned hostility 'gainst Mexico. Blockade! . . . On the 26th of April a small body of American troops, under the command of Captain Thornton, encountered Mexican troops at a place twenty miles north of General Taylor's camp. *Here was the first collision of arms.* The report of this was hurried to Washington. Rumor, with a hundred tongues, exaggerated the danger of the American army under General Taylor, and produced an insensibility to the aggressive character of his movement. All concurred in a desire to rescue him from the perilous position which, with the unquestioning obedience of a soldier, he had fearlessly occupied. It was under the influence of this feeling that the untoward act of May 13th was pressed through Congress, by which it was declared that "war exists by the act of Mexico". . . . This disastrous condition still continues. War is still waged; and our armies, after repeated victories achieved on Mexican soil, are still pursuing the path of conquest. . . .

It is a War to Strengthen the "Slave Power." But it is not merely proposed to open new markets for slavery: it is also designed to confirm and fortify the "Slave Power." Here is a distinction which should not fail to be borne in mind. Slavery is odious as an institution, if viewed in the light of morals and Christianity. On this account alone we should refrain from rendering it any voluntary support. But it has been made the basis of a political combination, to which has not inaptly been applied the designation of the "Slave Power." . . .

Disregarding the sentiments of many of the great framers of that instrument, who notoriously considered slavery as *temporary*, they proclaim it a *permanent* institution. . . . And it is urged that, as new free States are admitted into the Union, other slave States should be admitted, in order to preserve, in the Senate, what is called the "balance of power"? . . .

The object of the bold measure of annexation was not only to extend slavery, but to strengthen the "Slave Power." The same object is now proposed by the Mexican war. This is another link in the gigantic chain by which our country and the Constitution are to be bound to the Slave Power." . . .

It is a War Against the Free States. Regarding it as a war to strengthen the "Slave Power," we are conducted to a natural conclusion, that it is virtually, and in its consequences, a war against the free States of the Union. Conquest and robbery are attempted in order to obtain a political control at home; and distant battles are fought, less with a special view of subjugating Mexico than with the design of overcoming the power of the free States, under the Constitution. . . .

Criminality of the War. And it is also a violation of the fundamental law of Heaven, of that great law of Right which is written by God's own finger on the heart of man. His Excellency said nothing beyond the truth when, in his message, he declared that "an offensive and unnecessary war was the highest crime which man can commit against society." It is so; for all the demons of Hate are then let loose in mad and causeless career? . . . The war is a crime, and all who have partaken in the blood of its well-fought fields have aided in its perpetration. It is a principle of military law that the soldier shall not question the orders of his superior. If this shall exonerate the army from blame, it will be only to press with accumulated weight upon the government, which has set in motion this terrible and irresponsible machine. . . .

Resolves. Concerning the Mexican War, and the Institution of Slavery.

Resolved, That the present war with Mexico has its primary origin in the unconstitutional annexation to the United States of the foreign State of Texas, while the same was still at war with Mexico; that it was unconstitutionally commenced by the order of the President, to General Taylor, to take military possession of territory in dispute between the United States and Mexico, *and in the occupation of Mexico;* and that it is now waged ingloriously,—by a powerful nation against a weak neighbor. . . .

Resolved, That such a war of conquest, so hateful in its objects, so wanton, unjust, and unconstitutional in its origin and character, must be regarded as a war against freedom, against humanity, against justice, against the Union, against the Constitution, and *against the Free States;* and that a regard for the true interests and the highest honor of the country, not less than the impulses of Christian duty, should arouse all good citizens to join in efforts to arrest this gigantic crime, by withholding supplies, or other voluntary contributions, for its further prosecution, by calling for the withdrawal of our army within the established limits of the United States, and in every just way aiding the country to retreat from the disgraceful position of aggression which it now occupies towards a weak, distracted neighbor and sister republic.

Resolved, That our attention is directed anew to the wrong and "enormity" of slavery, and to the tyranny and usurpation of the "Slave Power," as displayed in the history of our country, particularly in the annexation of Texas, and the present war with Mexico; and that we are impressed with the unalterable conviction that a regard for the fair fame of our country, for the principles of morals, and for that righteousness which exalteth a nation, sanctions and requires all constitutional efforts for the abolition of slavery within the limits of the United States, while loyalty to the Constitution, and just self-defence, make it specially incumbent on the people of the free States to co-operate in strenuous exertions to restrain and over throw the "Slave Power."

3.9 Secession and Union

For a brief moment in the winter of 1861 the nation had split apart but was not yet fighting a civil war. Seven states had withdrawn from the Union to form the Confederate States of America. On February 18, Jefferson Davis was sworn in as its provisional President and gave his inaugural address in Montgomery, Alabama. (Later he would be elected to a full term and give a second address.) On March 4, Lincoln was sworn in as sixteenth President of the United States and delivered his first inaugural in Washington, D.C.

The speeches are a study in contrast, touching the same issues but coming to opposite conclusions. Lincoln announces that he has no intention of interfering with slavery where it exists, calls for peace and declares that, since the Union is inviolable, he will not accept the right of secession. Davis, claiming that the states preceded the Union, asserts the right of secession. The secession of the South, in his view, is a revolution no different from the colonial break with England. The Confederacy will not attack the Union, he promises, but will respond in kind, if attacked. Both men invoke God as a witness of their honorable and peaceable intentions.

Lincoln's speech is the more memorable. He was one of the great orators of the English language, possessing the rare gift of voicing not only his own sentiments but those of millions of plain and inarticulate people. Davis lacked that talent. Although a radical in earlier years, he had mellowed and there was nothing of the "fire-eater" in his words.

Questions

What qualities make Lincoln's address the more memorable? What did he want of the Confederacy? Was he sincere in saying he would not attack slavery where it existed?

Was Davis honest in saying the Confederacy would not attack the Union? What did he want of the Union at this juncture? Why is his speech less memorable than Lincoln's?

Jefferson Davis –

Called to the difficult and responsible station of Chief Magistrate of the Provisional Government which you have instituted, I approach the discharge of the duties assigned to me with humble distrust of my abilities, but with a sustaining confidence in the wisdom of those who are to guide and aid me in the administration of public affairs, and an abiding faith in the virtue and patriotism of the people. . . .

Our present political position has been achieved in a manner unprecedented in the history of nations. It illustrates the American idea that governments rest on the consent of the governed, and that it is the right of the people to alter or abolish them at will whenever they become destructive of the ends for which they were established. The declared purpose of the compact of the Union from which we have withdrawn was to "establish justice, insure domestic tranquility, provide for the common defense, promote the general welfare, and secure the blessings of liberty to ourselves and our posterity"; and when, in the judgment of the sovereign States composing this Confederacy, it has been perverted from the purposes for which it was ordained, and ceased to answer the ends for which it was established, a peaceful appeal to the ballot-box declared that, so far as they are concerned, the Government created by that compact should cease to exist. In this they merely asserted the right which the Declaration of Independence of July 4, 1776, defined to be "inalienable." . . .

The right solemnly proclaimed at the birth of the United States, and which has been solemnly affirmed and reaffirmed in the Bills of Rights of the States subsequently admitted into the Union of 1789, undeniably recognizes in the people the power to resume the authority delegated for the purposes of government. Thus the sovereign States here represented have proceeded to form this Confederacy; and it is by abuse of language that their act has been denominated a revolution. They formed a new alliance, but within each State its government has remained; so that the rights of person and property have not been disturbed. . . . Doubly justified by the absence of wrong on our part, and by wanton aggression on the part of others, there can be no cause to doubt that the courage and patriotism of the people of the Confederate States will be found equal to any measure of defense which their honor and security may require.

An agricultural people, whose chief interest is the export of commodities required in every manufacturing country, our true policy is peace, and the freest trade which our necessities will permit. It is alike our interest and that of all those to whom we would sell, and from whom we would buy, that there should be the fewest practicable restrictions upon the interchange of these commodities. There can, however,

SOURCE: Jefferson Davis, *The Rise and Fall of the Confederate Government* (New York: D. Appleton and Co., 1881), I, 232–236; and James D. Richardson, ed., *Messages and Papers of the Presidents, 1789–1897* (Washington, D.C. Government Printing Office, 1897), VI, 5–12.

be but little rivalry between ours and any manufacturing or navigating community, such as the Northeastern States of the American Union. . . .

We have entered upon the career or independence, and it must be inflexibly pursued. Through many years of controversy with our late associates of the Northern States, we have vainly endeavored to secure tranquility and obtain respect for the rights to which we were entitled. As a necessity, not a choice, we have resorted to the remedy of separation, and henceforth our energies must be directed to the conduct of our own affairs, and the perpetuity of the Confederacy which we have formed. If a just perception of mutual interest shall permit us peaceably to pursue our separate political career, my most earnest desire will have been fulfilled. But if this be denied to us, and the integrity of our territory and jurisdiction be assailed, it will but remain for us with firm resolve to appeal to arms and invoke the blessing of Providence on a just cause.

As a consequence of our new condition and relations, and with a view to meet anticipated wants, it will be necessary to provide for the speedy and efficient organization of branches of the Executive department having special charge of foreign intercourse, finance, military affairs, and the postal service. For purposes of defense, the Confederate States may, under ordinary circumstances, rely mainly upon the militia; but it is deemed advisable, in the present condition of affairs, that there should be a well-instructed and disciplined army, more numerous than would usually be required on a peace establishment. I also suggest that, for the protection of our harbors and commerce on the high seas, a navy adapted to those objects will be required. . . .

With a Constitution differing only from that of our fathers in so far as it is explanatory of their well-known intent, freed from sectional conflicts, which have interfered with the pursuit of the general welfare, it is not unreasonable to expect that States from which we have recently parted may seek to unite their fortunes to ours under the Government which we have instituted. For this your Constitution makes adequate provision; but beyond this, if I mistake not the judgment and will of the people, a reunion with the States from which we have separated is neither practicable nor desirable. . . .

Actuated solely by the desire to preserve our own rights, and promote our own welfare, the separation by the Confederate States has been marked by no aggression upon others, and followed by no domestic convulsion. Our industrial pursuits have received no check, the cultivation of our fields has progressed as heretofore, and, even should we be involved in war, there would be no considerable diminution in the production of the staples which have constituted our exports, and in which the commercial world has an interest scarcely less than our own. This common interest of the producer and consumer can only be interrupted by exterior force which would obstruct the transmission of our staples to foreign markets—a course of conduct which would be as unjust, as it would be detrimental, to manufacturing and commercial interests abroad.

Should reason guide the action of the Government from which we have separated, a policy so detrimental to the civilized world, the Northern States included, could not be dictated by even the strongest desire to inflict injury upon us; but, if the contrary should prove true, a terrible responsibility will rest upon it, and the suffering of millions will bear testimony to the folly and wickedness of our aggressors. In the mean time there will remain to us, besides the ordinary means before suggested, the well-known resources for retaliation upon the commerce of an enemy.

Experience in public stations, of subordinate grade to this which your kindness has conferred, has taught me that toil and care and disappointment are the price of official elevation. . . . Your generosity has bestowed upon me an undeserved distinction, one which I neither sought nor desired. Upon the continuance of that sentiment, and upon your wisdom and patriotism, I rely to direct and support me in the performance of the duties required at my hands.

We have changed the constituent parts, but not the system of government. The Constitution framed by our fathers is that of these Confederate States. . . .

Thus instructed as to the true meaning and just interpretation of that instrument, and ever remembering that all offices are but trusts held for the people, and that powers delegated are to be strictly construed, I will hope by due diligence in the performance of my duties, though I may disappoint your expectations, yet to retain, when retiring, something of the good-will and confidence which welcome my entrance into office.

It is joyous in the midst of perilous times to look around upon a people united in heart. . . . Reverently let us invoke the God of our Fathers to guide and protect us in our efforts to perpetuate the principles which by his blessing they were able to vindicate, establish, and transmit to their posterity. With the continuance of his favor ever gratefully acknowledged, we may hopefully look forward to success, to peace, and to prosperity.

Abraham Lincoln—

Fellow-Citizens of the United States: In compliance with a custom as old as the Government itself, I appear before you to address you briefly and to take in your presence the oath prescribed by the Constitution of the United States to be taken by the President "before he enters on the execution of his office." . . . .

Apprehension seems to exist among the people of the Southern States that by the accession of a Republican Administration their property and their peace and personal security are to be endangered. There has never been any reasonable cause for such apprehension. Indeed, the most ample evidence to the contrary has all the while existed and been open to their inspection. It is found in nearly all the published speeches of him who now addresses you. I do but quote from one of those speeches when I declare that—

I have no purpose, directly or indirectly, to interfere with the institution of slavery in the States where it exists. I believe I have no lawful right to do so, and I have no inclination to do so.

Those who nominated and elected me did so with full knowledge that I had made this and many similar declarations and had never recanted them; and more than this, they placed in the platform for my acceptance, and as a law to themselves and to me, the clear and emphatic resolution which I now read:

Resolved, That the maintenance inviolate of the rights of the States, and especially the right of each State to order and control its own domestic institutions according to its own judgment exclusively, is essential to that balance of power on which the perfection and endurance of our political fabric depend; and we denounce the lawless invasion by armed force of the soil of any State or Territory, no matter under what pretext, as among the gravest of crimes.

I now reiterate these sentiments, and in doing so I only press upon the public attention the most conclusive evidence of which the case is susceptible that the property, peace, and security of no section are to be in any wise endangered by the now incoming Administration. . . .

There is much controversy about the delivering up of fugitives from service or labor. The clause I now read is as plainly written in the Constitution as any other of its provisions:

No person held to service or labor in one State, under the laws thereof, escaping into another, shall in consequence of any law or regulation therein be discharged from such service or labor, but shall be delivered up on claim of the party to whom such service or labor may be due.

It is scarcely questioned that this provision was intended by those who made it for the reclaiming of what we call fugitive slaves; and the intention of the lawgiver is the law. All members of Congress swear their support to the whole Constitution—to this provision as much as to any other. . . .

There is some difference of opinion whether this clause should be enforced by national or by State authority, but surely that difference is not a very material one. If the slave is to be surrendered, it can be of but little consequence to him or to others by which authority it is done? . . .

I take the official oath to-day with no mental reservations and with no purpose to construe the Constitution or laws by any hypercritical rules. . . .

It is seventy-two years since the first inauguration of a President under our National Constitution. During that period fifteen different and greatly distinguished citizens have in succession administered the executive branch of the Government. . . . A disruption of the Federal Union, heretofore only menaced, is now formidably attempted.

I hold that in contemplation of universal law and of the Constitution the Union of these States is perpetual. Perpetuity is implied, if not expressed, in the fundamental law of all national governments. It is safe to assert that no government proper ever had a provision in its organic law for its own termination. . . .

Again: If the United States be not a government proper, but an association of States in the nature of contract merely, can it, as a contract, be peaceably unmade by less than all the parties who made it? One party to a contract may violate it—break it, so to speak—but does it not require all to lawfully rescind it?

Descending from these general principles, we find the proposition that in legal contemplation the Union is perpetual confirmed by the history of the Union itself. The Union is much older than the Constitution. It was formed, in fact, by the Articles of Association in 1774. It was matured and continued by the Declaration of Independence in 1776. It was further matured, and the faith of all the then thirteen States expressly plighted and engaged that it should be perpetual, by the Articles of Confederation in 1778. And finally, in 1787, one of the declared objects for ordaining and establishing the Constitution was *"to form a more perfect Union."*. . .

It follows from these views that no State upon its own mere motion can lawfully get out of the Union; that *resolves* and *ordinances* to that effect are legally void, and that acts of violence within any State or States against the authority of the United

States are insurrectionary or revolutionary, according to circumstances.

I therefore consider that in view of the Constitution and the laws the Union is unbroken, and to the extent of my ability I shall take care, as the Constitution itself expressly enjoins upon me, that the laws of the Union be faithfully executed in all the States. . . .

In doing this there needs to be no bloodshed or violence, and there shall be none unless it be forced upon the national authority. The power confided to me will be used to hold, occupy, and possess the property and places belonging to the Government and to collect the duties and imposts; but beyond what may be necessary for these objects, there will be no invasion, no using of force against or among the people anywhere. Where hostility to the United States in any interior locality shall be so great and universal as to prevent competent resident citizens from holding the Federal offices, there will be no attempt to force obnoxious strangers among the people for that object. . . .

The mails, unless repelled, will continue to be furnished in all parts of the Union. So far as possible the people everywhere shall have that sense of perfect security which is most favorable to calm thought and reflection. The course here indicated will be followed unless current events and experience shall show a modification or change to be proper, and in every case and exigency my best discretion will be exercised, according to circumstances actually existing and with a view and a hope of a peaceful solution of the national troubles and the restoration of fraternal sympathies and affections. . . .

All profess to be content in the Union if all constitutional rights can be maintained. Is it true, then, that any right plainly written in the Constitution has been denied? I think not. Happily, the human mind is so constituted that no party can reach to the audacity of doing this. Think, if you can, of a single instance in which a plainly written provision of the Constitution has ever been denied. If by the mere force of numbers a majority should deprive a minority of any clearly written constitutional right, it might in a moral point of view justify revolution; certainly would if such right were a vital one. But such is not our case. All the vital rights of minorities and of individuals are so plainly assured to them by affirmations and negations, guaranties and prohibitions, in the Constitution that controversies never arise concerning them. But no organic law can ever be framed with a provision specifically applicable to every question which may occur in practical administration. No foresight can anticipate nor any document of reasonable length contain express provisions for all possible questions. Shall fugitives from labor be surrendered by national or by State authority? The Constitution does not expressly say. *May* Congress prohibit slavery in the Territories? The Constitution does not expressly say. *Must* Congress protect slavery in the Territories? The Constitution does not expressly say.

From questions of this class spring all our constitutional controversies, and we divide upon them into majorities and minorities. If the minority will not acquiesce, the majority must, or the Government must cease. There is no other alternative, for continuing the Government is acquiescence on one side or the other. If a minority in such case will secede rather than acquiesce, they make a precedent which in turn will divide and ruin them, for a minority of their own will secede from them whenever a majority refuses to be controlled by such minority. For instance, why may not any portion of a new confederacy a year or two hence arbitrarily secede again, precisely as portions of the present Union now claim to secede from it? All who cherish disunion sentiments are now being educated to the exact temper of doing this. . . .

Plainly the central idea of secession is the essence of anarchy. A majority held in restraint by constitutional checks and limitations, and always changing easily with deliberate changes of popular opinions and sentiments, is the only true sovereign of a free people. . . .

I do not forget the position assumed by some that constitutional questions are to be decided by the Supreme Court, nor do I deny that such decisions must be binding in any case upon the parties to a suit as to the object of that suit. . . . At the same time, the candid citizen must confess that if the policy of the Government upon vital questions affecting the whole people is to be irrevocably fixed by decisions of the Supreme Court, the instant they are made in ordinary litigation between parties in personal actions the people will have ceased to be their own rulers, having to that extent practically resigned their Government into the hands of that eminent tribunal. Nor is there in this view any assault upon the court or the judges. . . .

One section of our country believes slavery is *right* and ought to be extended, while the other believes it is *wrong* and ought not to be extended. This is the only substantial dispute. The fugitive-slave clause of the Constitution and the law for the suppression of the foreign slave trade are each as well enforced, perhaps, as any law can ever be in a community where the moral sense of the people imperfectly supports the law itself. The great body of the people abide by the dry legal obligation in both cases, and a few break over in each. This, I think, can not be perfectly cured, and it would be worse in both cases *after* the separation of the sections than before. . . .

Physically speaking, we can not separate. We can not remove our respective sections from each other nor build an impassable wall between them. A husband and wife may be divorced and go out of the presence and beyond the reach of each other, but the different parts of our country can not do this. They can not but remain face to face, and intercourse, either amicable or hostile, must continue between them. . . .

This country, with its institutions, belongs to the people who inhabit it. Whenever they shall grow weary of the existing Government, they can exercise their *constitutional* right of amending it or their *revolutionary* right to dismember or overthrow it. I can not be ignorant of the fact that many worthy and patriotic citizens are desirous of having the National Constitution amended. While I make no recommendation of amendments, I fully recognize the rightful authority of the people over the whole subject, to be exercised in either of the modes prescribed in the instrument itself; and I should, under existing circumstances, favor rather than oppose a fair opportunity being afforded the people to act upon it. I will venture to add that to me the convention mode seems preferable, in that it allows amendments to originate with the people themselves, instead of only permitting them to take or reject propositions originated by others, not especially chosen for the purpose, and which might not be precisely such as they would wish to either accept or refuse. . . .

The Chief Magistrate derives all his authority from the people, and they have conferred none upon him to fix terms for the separation of the States. The people themselves can do this also if they choose, but the Executive as such has nothing to do with it. His duty is to administer the present Government as it came to his hands and to transmit it unimpaired by him to his successor.

Why should there not be a patient confidence in the ultimate justice of the people? Is there any better or equal hope in the world? In our present differences, is either party without faith of being in the right? If the Almighty Ruler of Nations, with His eternal truth and justice, be on your side of the North, or on yours of the South, that truth and that justice will surely prevail by the judgment of this great tribunal of the American people. . . .

My countrymen, one and all, think calmly and *well* upon this whole subject. Nothing valuable can be lost by taking time. If there be an object to *hurry* any of you in hot haste to a step which you would never take *deliberately,* that object will be frustrated by taking time; but no good object can be frustrated by it. Such of you as are now dissatisfied still have the old Constitution unimpaired, and, on the sensitive point, the laws of your own framing under it; while the new Administration will have no immediate power, if it would, to change either. . . .

3.10 "While God is Marching On"

Wars, especially terrible wars, often evoke Biblical imagery. The Biblical term "Armageddon" was applied in World War I, and "Holocaust" evoked horror in World War II. So it was in the Civil War, when Julia Ward Howe wrote the lyrics of the "Battle-Hymn of the Republic," in 1862.

Howe was an ardent abolitionist. After talking to soldiers in an army camp near Washington, she was impressed by their dedication to the Union cause. At dawn the following morning she awakened with the lyrics to a song in her head. She took up "an old stump of a pen . . . [and] scrawled the verses almost without looking at the paper." Howe set the words to the tune of "John Brown's Body," a moving song of the anti-slavery crusade written by Union soldiers in 1861 (and based on an old southern revival hymn). The "Battle-Hymn" made Howe famous.

The central image of the "Battle-Hymn" appears to come from Isaiah 63.1–6. The verses resemble those of songs sung during the English Civil war in the seventeenth century. Howe sees the Union armies working in the cause of God's truth.

Other Civil War songs had Biblical overtones. A refrain in a popular Union recruiting song is, "We are coming Father Abraham, three hundred thousand more," which gives Pres-

ident Lincoln a Biblical stature. Confederate soldiers also sang patriotic and hymn-like songs, but none is as memorable as the "Battle Hymn."

Questions

What symbols does Howe use for the Union and for the Confederacy? How does she use the grapes of wrath, the serpent, and Christ as symbols? What kind of God is behind this war? Whom does He favor? How will He show His favor? Are there Calvinist or other religious implications in the verses?

Compare this "sacred" vision of the war, with the "profane" vision in the next item, from General Sherman.

Battle-hymn of the Republic

Mine eyes have seen the glory of the coming of the Lord:
He is trampling out the vintage where the grapes of wrath are stored;
He hath loosed the fateful lightning of his terrible swift sword;
His truth is marching on.
I have seen Him in the watch-fires of a hundred circling camps;
They have builded Him an altar in the evening dews and damps;
I can read His righteous sentence by the dim and flaring lamps;
His day is marching on.
I have read a fiery gospel, writ in burnished rows of steel:
"As ye deal with my contemners, so with you my grace shall deal;
Let the Hero, born of woman, crush the serpent with his heel,
Since God is marching on."
He has sounded forth the trumpet that shall never call retreat;
He is sifting out the hearts of men before his judgment-seat:
Oh! be swift my soul, to answer Him! be jubilant, my feet!
Our God is marching on.
In the beauty of the lilies Christ was born across the sea,
With a glory in his bosom that transfigures you and me:
As he died to make men holy, let us die to make men free,
While God is marching on.

SOURCE: Julia Ward Howe, "The Battle-Hymn of the Republic," *Atlantic Monthly*, February 1862.

3.11 "War is All Hell"

General William Tecumseh Sherman of Ohio, a West Point graduate, is considered "the first modern soldier" in American history. Ulysses Grant made him General of the Army in 1864, giving him command of the western armies and encouraging him to force the Confederate armies back to the Atlantic coast. During his famous "March to the Sea," Sherman burned Atlanta and cut a wide swath of destruction in his path through Georgia. This effort by the Union forces is still remembered with bitterness in the South. Sherman's men lived off the land and pillaged and looted as they went. His tactics in mechanized warfare are likened by some to the blitzkrieg tactics of Hilter in World War II. His scorched earth policy against civilian populations certainly shortened the war, but it gave the Civil War the distinction of being "the first modern war."

Sherman was personally likeable; his soldiers called him "Uncle Billy." But he was a contradictory figure. He was noted for his candor, but also for his arrogance and anti-democratic sentiments. (He once declared, "Vox populi, vox humbug.") War to him was "all hell," but it was also, on another occasion, "a grand and beautiful game." Before the March to the Sea, he enjoyed warm personal and professional relations with southerners. He was never a real foe of slavery. Below is his letter to the Mayor and a City Councilman of Atlanta, September 12, 1864.

Questions

What does Sherman mean by "I will ever conduct war with a view to perfect and early success"? How does his view of the Civil War compare with that expressed in the "Battle Hymn of the Republic"?

GENTLEMEN: I have your letter of the 11th, in the nature of a petition to revoke my orders removing all the inhabitants from Atlanta. I have read it carefully, and give full credit to your statements of the distress that will be occasioned, and yet shall not revoke my orders, because they were not designed to meet the humanities of the case, but to prepare for the future struggles in which millions of good people outside of Atlanta have a deep interest. We must have peace, not only at Atlanta, but in all America. To secure this, we must stop the war that now desolates our once happy and favored country. To stop war, we must defeat the rebel armies which are arrayed

SOURCE: Sherman to Mayor James M. Calhoun and City Councilman S. C. Wells, September 12, 1864, in William T. Sherman, *Memoirs* (New York: D. Appleton and Company, 1875), II, 111–12, 125–27.

against the laws and Constitution that all must respect and obey. To defeat those armies, we must prepare the way to reach them in their recesses, provided with the arms and instruments which enable us to accomplish our purpose. . . .

In *your* hands, my dissatisfied fellow-countrymen, and not in *mine,* is the momentous issue of civil war. The Government will not assail *you.* You can have no conflict without being yourselves the aggressors. *You* have no oath registered in heaven to destroy the Government, while *I* shall have the most solemn one to "preserve, protect, and defend it."

I am loath to close. We are not enemies, but friends. We must not be enemies. Though passion may have strained it must not break our bonds of affection. The mystic chords of memory, stretching from every battlefield and patriot grave to every living heart and hearthstone all over this broad land, will yet swell the chorus of the Union, when again touched, as surely they will be, by the better angels of our nature.

You cannot qualify war in harsher terms than I will. War is cruelty, and you cannot refine it; and those who brought war into our country deserve all the curses and maledictions a people can pour out. I know I had no hand in making this war, and I know I will make more sacrifices to-day than any of you to secure peace. But you cannot have peace and a division of our country. If the United States submits to a division now, it will not stop, but will go on until we reap the fate of Mexico, which is eternal war. The United States does and must assert its authority, wherever it once had power; for, if it relaxes one bit to pressure, it is gone, and I believe that such is the national feeling. This feeling assumes various shapes, but always comes back to that of Union. Once admit the Union, once more acknowledge the authority of the national Government, and, instead of devoting your houses and streets and roads to the dread uses of war, I and this army become at once your protectors and supporters, shielding you from danger, let it come from what quarter it may. . . .

We don't want your negroes, or your horses, or your houses, or your lands, or any thing you have, but we do want and will have a just obedience to the laws of the United States. That we will have, and, if it involves the destruction of your improvements, we cannot help it.

You have heretofore read public sentiment in your newspapers, that live by falsehood and excitement; and the quicker you seek for truth in other quarters, the better. I repeat then that, by the original compact of Government, the United States had certain rights in Georgia, which have never been relinquished and never will be; that the South began war by seizing forts, arsenals, mints, custom-houses, etc., etc., long before Mr. Lincoln was installed, and before the South had one jot or tittle of provocation. I myself have seen in Missouri, Kentucky, Tennessee, and Mississippi, hundreds and thousands of women and children fleeing from your armies and desperadoes, hungry and with bleeding feet. . . . Now that war comes home to you, you feel very different. You deprecate its horrors, but did not feel them when you sent car-loads of soldiers and ammunition, and moulded shells and shot, to carry war into Kentucky and Tennessee, to desolate the homes of hundreds and thousands of good people who only asked to live in peace at their old homes, and under the Government of their inheritance. But these comparisons are idle. I want peace, and believe it can only be reached through union and war, and I will ever conduct war with a view to perfect and early success.

3.12 A Civil War Legacy

Below are reprinted three brief statements on the legacy of the Civil War. The first is by Lincoln, expressing his hopes for the future in his Second Inaugural Address, March 4, 1865, a month before his murder. The selection includes some of his immortal phrases.

A contrasting view, as bitter as Lincoln's is moderate, is expressed by Edmund Ruffin (1794–1865). It is excerpted from his diary in April. Ruffin was a prominent Virginia planter and pioneer agricultural scientist who migrated to South Carolina on the eve of the war. As a vocal southern extremist and leading member of the state's militia, he had been given the honor of firing the first shot against Fort Sumter in April 1861. Four years later, when General Lee surrendered, Ruffin penned this last entry into his diary and committed suicide.

Still a third perspective on the heritage of the Civil War is by the young Virginian, Woodrow Wilson, in 1880, while a law student at the University of Virginia. It is an example of what later came to be called the celebration of the Lost Cause.

Questions

Did Lincoln set forth specific plans to encourage his moderate plans for the future? How does his tone here compare with that of his First Inaugural?

Assuming that Ruffin had not succumbed to madness, what could have caused him such extreme despair?

In your opinion, does Wilson successfully reconcile his contradictory view of the War? Explain.

Abraham Lincoln—

Neither party expected for the war the magnitude or the duration which it has already attained. Neither anticipated that the cause of the conflict might cease with, or even before, the conflict itself should cease. Each looked for an easier triumph, and a result less fundamental and astounding. Both read the same Bible, and pray to the same God; and each invokes his aid against the other. It may seem strange that any men should dare to ask a just God's assistance in wringing their bread from the sweat of other men's faces; but let us judge not, that we be not judged. The prayers of both could not be answered—that of neither has been answered fully. . . .

With malice toward none; with charity for all; with firmness in the right, as God

SOURCE: *The Speeches of Abraham Lincoln* (New York, 1908), 410–11; and "The Diary of Edmund Ruffin, 1856–1865" (n.p., n.d.) Library of Congress microfilm LC84.

gives us to see the right, let us strive on to finish the work we are in; to bind up the nation's wounds; to care for him who shall have borne the battle, and for his widow, and his orphan—to do all which may achieve and cherish a just and lasting peace among ourselves, and with all nations.

Edmund Ruffin—

I here declare my unmitigated hatred to Yankee rule—to all political, social and business connections with the Yankees and to the Yankee race. Would that I could impress these sentiments, in their full force, on every living Southerner and bequeath them to every one yet to be born! May such sentiments be held universally in the outraged and down-trodden South, though in silence and stillness, until the now far-distant day shall arrive for just retribution for Yankee usurpation, oppression and atrocious outrages, and for deliverance and vengeance for the now ruined, subjugated and enslaved Southern States! And now with my latest writing and utterance, and with what will be near my latest breath, I here repeat and willingly proclaim my unmitigated hatred to Yankee rule—to all political, social and business connections with Yankees, and the perfidious, malignant and vile Yankee race.

Woodrow Wilson—

Because I love the South, I rejoice in the failure of the Confederacy. . . . Conceive of this Union divided into two separate and independent sovereignties! . . . Slavery was enervating our Southern society. . . . [Nevertheless] I recognize and pay loving tribute to the virtues of the leaders of secession . . . the righteousness of the cause which they thought they were promoting—and to the immortal courage of the soldiers of the Confederacy.

TO BE SOLD on board the Ship *Bance-Island*, on tuesday the 6th of *May* next, at *Ashley-Ferry*; a choice cargo of about 250 fine healthy

NEGROES,

just arrived from the Windward & Rice Coast. —The utmost care has already been taken, and shall be continued, to keep them free from the least danger of being infected with the SMALL-POX, no boat having been on board, and all other communication with people from *Charles-Town* prevented.

Austin, Laurens, & Appleby.

N. B. Full one Half of the above Negroes have had the SMALL-POX in their own Country.

Chapter Four: Race

4.1 Conflict with Native Americans

In the seventeenth century, New Englanders fought wars with Native Americans that had lasting and bitter results. Colonial villages were destroyed, Indians suffered defeat and decline, hatred between the races increased, and whites came to rely upon military force to settle differences. Two conflicts illustrate this evolving history—the Pequot War from 1636 to 1637, and King Philip's War, in 1675–1676.

The Pequot War was essentially a struggle of European colonial farmers against Native American farmers for control of land. The Pequots of the Connecticut Valley were hemmed in between the Mohegans to the west and Narragansetts to the east. Englishmen from Massachusetts Bay bargained with the Mohegans for land, ignoring the authority of the Pequots over than land. Each side was confused as to the other's motives. In addition, the people of Massachusetts were angry about the death of a member of their colony who was probably killed by Narragansetts on Block Island. In 1636, the Massachusetts governor sent John Endicott and ninety men to kill all Indian men on Block Island and to turn upon the Pequots on the mainland. The men refrained from killing but they did burn wigwams and steal food, which enraged the Pequots. An Indian who felt cheated in a land deal induced the Pequots to attack the town of Wethersfield, resulting in the deaths of several settlers. Pequots killed thirty or more pioneers in the coming months, sometimes burning or torturing them.

Colonial authorities authorized a retaliatory raid consisting of 110 men under John Mason and John Underhill, as well as 280 Mohegans and Narragansetts. After a night of prayer, one of the raiders, a Rev. Stone, counselled making a surprise attack on the Indian fort. On May 20 the attackers burned the fort and village, and burned and shot from 400 to 700 Pequots, capturing others. The Pequot nation was destroyed. Farms owned by other Indians groups, even those who fought as allies of the English, also fell into English hands.

King Philip's War erupted in June 1875, when Metacomet ("King Philip"), leader of the Wampanoag tribe, attacked an outpost of Plymouth Colony. It had been preceded by tension over land ownership, and strong Native American resentment against Puritan missionary activities. Indians had suffered loss of land and access to fisheries. Also, Chief Metacomet feared that the English had poisoned his brother. He was repeatedly hauled into court to face criminal charges. The settlers considered the assault on the Plymouth outpost as unprovoked aggression and ferociously attacked the Wampanoags and their allies, the Narragansetts, near Kingston, R.I. Three hundred Indians were killed, mostly women and children. Metacomet did not relish the war but counter-attacked strongly. He was killed in August by an Indian fighting for the English. His severed hands were sent to Boston and his head to Plymouth, amid much rejoicing by the colonists.

The damage from this conflict was far-reaching. An entire generation of Wampanoag men was killed, and many others surrendered. Metacomet's coalition was weakened beyond repair. Twelve New England towns were demolished and fifty or sixty more damaged. Five percent of the adult English males had been killed. The frontier remained closed to further expansion for 75 years. Missionary work declined, owing as much to deep prejudices among whites as to resentment by Indians. Metacomet's wife and son were sold into slavery in the West Indies.

In the first selection that follows, John Underhill discusses Endicott's raid in 1636 and the massacre in the Mystic River fort in May 1637. The second selection is an account of King Philip's War from a work by Increase and Cotton Mather, published in 1676.

Questions

Underhill believes the Pequots were courageous and deserving of mercy. Why then was there such brutality against the Native Americans, including women and children? He is also concerned about the affect of the fighting on the young, impressionable colonial soldiers. Can you imagine what their reactions might have been?

Summarize the Mathers' rationale for the conflict, including their perception of God's intervention. Why was Philip destroyed? Why were these Puritans so stern and contemptuous of Native Americans?

Estimate what have been the long-term consequences of military solutions to Indian-white conflicts.

John Underhill—

The last messenger brought us this intelligence from the sachem, that if we would but lay down our arms, and approach about thirty paces from them, and meet the heathen prince, he would cause his men to do the like, and then we shall come to a parley.

But we seeing their drift was to get our arms, we rather chose to beat up the drum and bid them battle. Marching into a champaign field we displayed our colors; but none would come near us, but standing remotely off did laugh at us for our patience. We suddenly set upon our march, and gave fire to as many as we could come near, firing their wigwams, spoiling their corn, and many other necessaries that they had buried in the ground we raked up, which the soldiers had for booty. Thus we spent the day burning and spoiling the country. Towards night embarked ourselves. The next morning, landing on the Nahanticot shore, where we were served in like nature, no Indians would come near us, but run from us, as the deer from the dogs. . . .

Most courageously these Pequeats behaved themselves. But seeing the fort was too hot for us, we devised a way how we

SOURCES: John Underhill, "News from America" (London, 1638), in *Massachusetts Historical Society Collections*, 3d Series, Vol. VI (Boston, 1837), 10–11, 24–25; Increase Mather, *The History of King Philip's War*, and Cotton Mather, *A History of the Same War* (Boston, 1862), 47–54, 193–195.

might save ourselves and prejudice them. Captain Mason entering into a wigwam, brought out a firebrand, after he had wounded many in the house. Then he set fire on the west side, where he entered; myself set fire on the south end with a train of powder. The fires of both meeting in the centre of the fort, blazed most terribly, and burnt all in the space of half an hour. Many courageous fellows were unwilling to come out, and fought most desperately through the palisadoes, so as they were scorched and burnt with the very flame, and were deprived of their arms—in regard the fire burnt their very bowstrings—and so perished valiantly. Mercy they did deserve for their valor, could we have had opportunity to have bestowed it. Many were burnt in the fort, both men, women, and children. Others forced out, and came in troops to the Indians, twenty and thirty at a time, which our soldiers received and entertained with the point of the sword. Down fell men, women, and children; those that scaped us, fell into the hands of the Indians that were in the rear of us. It is reported by themselves, that there were about four hundred souls in this fort, and not above five of them escaped out of our hands. Great and doleful was the bloody sight to the view of young soldiers that never had been in war, to see so many souls lie gasping on the ground, so thick, in some places, that you could hardly pass along.

Increase and Cotton Mather–

In the latter end of the Year 1674. An *Indian* called *John Sausaman,* who had submitted himself unto, and was taken under the protection of the *English,* perceiving that the *profane Indians* were hatching mischief against the *English,* he faithfully acquainted the Governour of *Plymouth,* with what he knew, and also what his fears were, together with the grounds thereof, withal declaring; that he doubted such and such *Indians,* belonging to *Philip* the Sachem of *Pokanoket* or *Mount-hope,* would murder him; which quickly happened accordingly: for soon after this, *John Sausaman* was barbarously murdered by an *Indian,* called *Tobias* (one of *Philip's* chief Captains and Counsellors) and by his son and another *Indian,* who knocked him on the head and then left him on the Ice on a great Pond. . . . An *Indian* unseen by those three that killed Sausaman, beheld all. . . . The three *Indians* who had committed the murder were apprehended. . . . They had a fair Tryal for their Lives, and . . . *Indians* as well as *English* sate upon the *Jury,* and all agreed to the condemnation of those Murtherers. . . .

No doubt but one reason why the *Indians* murdered *John Sausaman,* was out of hatred against him for his Religion, for he was Christianized and baptiz'd, and was a Preacher amongst the *Indians* . . . but the main ground why they murthered him seems to be, because he discovered their subtle and malicious designs, which they were complotting against the *English, Philip* perceiving that the Court of *Plymouth* had Condemned and Executed one of his Counsellors, being (as is upon strong grounds supposed) conscious of the murder committed upon *John Sausaman,* must needs think that ere long, they would do to him (who had no less deserved it) as they had done to his Counsellor: Wherefore he, contrary to his Covenant and Faith engaged to *Plymouth* Colony, yea, and contrary to his promise unto some in this Colony (for about five years ago, *Philip* made a disturbance in *Plymouth* Colony, but was quieted . . . when he engaged, that if at any time hereafter he should think the *English* among whom he lived did him wrong, he would not cause any disquiet-ment before such time as he had acquainted the *English* of *Massachusets,* but contrary to these solemn engagements he) doth call his Men together and *Arm* them, and refused to come when sent for, by the Authority of *Plymouth,* unto whose Government he had subjected himself. Here upon the *English* in *Plymouth* Jurisdiction, sent a small Army to those Towns next *Mount hope,* in order to reducing *Philip* to his obedience, and for the security of those places which were in great danger, and in no less fear, by reason of the insolency of the Heathen. . . .

August 12 [1676]. This is the memorable day wherein *Philip,* the perfidious and bloudy Author of the war and wofull miseryes that have thence ensued, was taken and slain. And God brought it to pass, chiefly by *Indians* themselves. For one of *Philips* men (being disgusted at him, for killing an *Indian* who had propounded an expedient for peace with the *English*) ran away from him, and coming to Road-Island, informed that *Philip* was now returned again to *Mount-Hope,* and undertook to bring them to the Swamp where he hid himself. . . . Our Souldiers came upon him and surrounded the *Swamp* (where he with seven of his men absconded) Thereupon he betook himself to flight; but as he was coming out of the Swamp, an *English-man* and an *Indian* endeavoured to fire at him, the *English-man* missed of his aime, but the *Indian* shot him through the heart, so as that he fell down dead. The *Indian* who thus killed *Philip,* did formerly belong to Squaw-Sachim of *Pocasset,* being known by the name of *Alderman.* In the beginning of the war, he came to the Governour of *Plymouth,* manifesting his desire to be at peace with the *English,* and immediately withdrew to an Island not having engaged against the *English* nor for them, before this time. Thus when *Philip* had made an end to deal treacherously, his own Subjects dealt treacherously with him. This Wo was brought upon him that spoyled when he was not spoyled. And in that very place where he first contrived and began his mischief, was he taken and destroyed, and there was he (like as Agag was hewed in pieces before the Lord) cut into four quarters, and is now hanged up as a monument of revenging Justice, his head being cut off and carried to *Plymouth,* his Hands were brought to *Boston. So let all thine Enemies perish, O Lord!* When *Philip* was thus slain, five of his men were killed with him, one of which was his chief Captains son, being (as the *Indians* testifie) that very *Indian* who shot the first gun at the *English,* when the War began. So that we may hope that the War in those parts will dye with *Philip.*

4.2 Good Will toward Native Americans

White colonials who sought a mutually satisfactory relationship with Native Americans now seem like a rarity in American history, but they were not entirely unknown, especially in the seventeenth century. Despite the many brutal battles already fought between the races (see Document 4.1), eastern North America was not yet totally a white man's country. Nor were the Native Americans as yet completely caught up in the fierce international rivalries between England and France that would later embitter their relations with Europeans.

William Penn, the proprietor of Pennsylvania, was one prominent white who sought good relations with the Native Americans. While still living in London and organizing his "Holy Experiment" in 1681, he wrote the following friendly letter to the original natives of Pennsylvania, the Delaware Indians. It was delivered by his commissioners. Brimming with Quaker friendliness, the message of the absentee proprietor sets the tone for a treaty Penn would sign with the natives a year later. Pennsylvanians did maintain a fair degree of good will with them until the French and Indian War.

Questions

What idealistic or practical considerations moved Penn to seek the good will of Native Americans? Which Christian beliefs and specifically Quaker beliefs, are demonstrated here? If a few Europeans such as Penn could establish good relations with Native Americans, why not others? What caused this good will to break down in Pennsylvania during the French and Indian War in the 1750s?

My friends—There is one great God and power that hath made the world and all things therein; . . . this great God hath written his law in our hearts, by which we are taught and commanded to live and help, and do good to one another, and not to do harm and mischief one to another. Now this great God hath been pleased to make me concerned in your parts of the world, and the king of the country where I live hath given unto me a great province, but I desire to enjoy it with your love and consent, that we may always live together as neighbors and friends, else what would the great God say to us, who hath made us not to devour and destroy one another, but live soberly and kindly together in the world? Now I would have you well observe, that I am very sensible of the unkindness and injustice that hath been too much exercised towards you by the people of these parts of the world, who sought themselves, and to make great advantages by you, rather than be examples of justice and goodness unto you, which I hear hath been matter of trouble to you, and caused great grudgings and animosities, sometimes to the shedding of blood, which hath made the great God angry; but I am not such a man, as is well known in my own country; I have great love and regard towards you, and I desire to win and gain your love and friendship, by a kind, just, and peaceful life, and the people I send are of the same mind, and shall in all things behave themselves accordingly; and if in anything any shall offend you or your people, you shall have a full and speedy

SOURCE: Samuel Hazard, ed., *Annals of Pennsylvania, from the Discovery of the Delaware* (Philadelphia, 1850), 532–33.

satisfaction for the same, by an equal number of just men on both sides, that by no means you may have just occasion of being offended against them. . . . I have sent my commissioners to treat with you about land, and a firm league of peace. Let me desire you to be kind to them and the people, and receive these presents and tokens which I have sent to you, as a testimony of my good will to you, and my resolution to live justly, peaceably, and friendly with you.

4.3 Savagery, Science and Civilization

Eighteenth-century whites commonly viewed Native Americans as "savages." This early racial stereotype had specific connotations. It mainly implied that Native Americans were backward in intelligence, government, family stability, religion, and an understanding of property values. The opposite of savagery was "civilization."

Many of the notions embodied in the term savage were summarized by George Louis Leclerc, Count de Buffon (1707–1788), a brilliant French naturalist. A major figure in the eighteenth-century European Enlightenment and a pioneer of evolutionary science, de Buffon produced a 44-volume work on natural history filled with information, theories and speculations. The monumental work included the brief characterization of Native Americans that is included below.

Most readers probably accepted the Frenchman's characterization as Gospel. But Thomas Jefferson, who compared it to "the fables of Aesop," disagreed. It moved him to prepare the strong response in defense of Native Americans that is also included below. While differing with the French writer, Jefferson also argues within the framework of the savagery concept.

Questions

Where do you think Buffon and Jefferson acquired their information? Which man seems to have the most accurate data? If Buffon's profile typifies the idea of savagery, what are the basic elements of its opposite, "civilization"? How enlightened or scientific was Jefferson's attitude toward Native Americans; to what degree was he patronizing?

How did the stereotypes of whites toward Native Americans compare with those toward blacks?

Count DeBuffon –

Although the savage of the new world is about the same height as man in our world, this does not suffice for him to constitute an exception to the general fact that all living nature has become smaller on that continent. The savage is feeble, and has small organs of generation; he has neither hair nor beard, and no ardor whatever for his female; although swifter than the European because he is better accustomed to running, he is, on the other hand, less strong in body; he is also less sensitive, and yet more timid and cowardly; he has no vivacity, no activity of mind; the activity of his body is less an exercise, a voluntary motion, than a necessary action caused by want; relieve him of hunger and thirst, and you deprive him of the active principle of all his movements; he will rest stupidly upon his legs or lying down entire days. There is no need for seeking further the cause of the isolated mode of life of these savages and their repugnance for society: the most precious spark of the fire of nature has been refused to them; they lack ardor for their females, and consequently have no love for their fellow men: not knowing this strongest and most tender of all affections, their other feelings are also cold and languid; they love their parents and children but little; the most intimate of all ties, the family connection, binds them therefore but loosely together; between family and family there is no tie at all; hence they have no communion, no commonwealth, no state of society. Physical love constitutes their only morality; their heart is icy, their society cold, and their rule harsh. They look upon their wives only as servants for all work, or as beasts of burden, which they load without consideration with the burden of their hunting, and which they compel without mercy, without gratitude, to perform tasks which are often beyond their strength. They have only few children, and they take little care of them. Everywhere the original defect appears: they are indifferent because they have little sexual capacity, and this indifference to the other sex is the fundamental defect which weakens their nature, prevents its development, and—destroying the very germs of life—uproots society at the same time. Man is here no exception to the general rule. Nature, by refusing him the power of love, has treated him worse and lowered him deeper than any animal.

SOURCE: Jefferson, *Notes on Virginia* (Philadelphia, 1801).

Thomas Jefferson –

The Indian of North America being . . . within our reach, I can speak of him somewhat from my own knowledge, but more from the information of others better acquainted with him, and on whose truth and judgment I can rely. From these sources I am able to say, in contradiction to this representation, that he is neither more defective in ardor, nor more impotent with his female, than the white reduced to the same diet and exercise: that he is brave, when an enterprize depends on bravery; education with him making the point of honor consist in the destruction of an enemy by stratagem, and in the preservation of his own person free from injury; or perhaps this is nature; while it is education which teaches us to honor force more than finesse; that he will defend himself against an host of enemies, always chusing to be killed, rather than to surrender, though it be to the whites, who he knows will treat him well: that in other situations also he meets death with more deliberation, and endures tortures with a firmness unknown almost to religious enthusiasm with us: that he is affectionate to his children, careful of them, and indulgent in the extreme: that his affections comprehend his other connections, weakening, as with us, from circle to circle, as they recede from the center: that his friendships are strong and faithful to the uttermost extremity: that his sensibility is keen, even the warriors weeping most bitterly on the loss of their children, though in general they endeavour to appear superior to human events: that his vivacity and activity of mind is equal to ours in the same situation; hence his eagerness for hunting, and for games of chance. The women are submitted to unjust drudgery. This I believe is the case with every barbarous people. With such, force is law. The stronger sex therefore imposes on the weaker. It is civilization alone which replaces women in the enjoyment of their natural equality. That first teaches us to subdue the selfish passions, and to respect those rights in others which we value in ourselves. Were we in equal barbarism, our females would be equal drudges. The man with them is less strong than with us, but their woman stronger than ours; and both for the same obvious reason: because our man and their woman is habituated to labour, and formed by it. With both races the sex which is indulged with ease is least athletic. An Indian man is small in the hand and wrist for the same reason for which a sailor is large and strong in the arms and shoulders, and a porter in the legs and thighs. —They raise fewer children than we do. The causes of this are to be found, not in a difference of nature, but of circumstance. The women very frequently attending the men in their parties of war and of hunting, child-bearing becomes extremely inconvenient to them. It is said, therefore, that they have learnt the practice of procuring abortion by the use of some vegetable; and that it even extends to prevent conception for a considerable time after. . . . They experience a famine once in every year. With all animals, if the female be badly fed, or not fed at all, her young perish: and if both male and female be reduced to like want, generation becomes less active, less productive. To the obstacles then of want and hazard, which nature has opposed to the multiplication of wild animals, for the purpose of restraining their numbers within certain bounds, those of labour and of voluntary abortion are added with the Indian. No wonder then if they multiply less than we do. . . . The same Indian women, when married to white traders, who feed them and their children plentifully and regularly, who exempt them from excessive drudgery, who keep them stationary and unexposed to accident, produce and raise as many children as the white women. . . . An inhuman practice once prevailed in this country of making slaves of the Indians. (This practice commenced with the Spaniards with the first discovery of America). It is a fact well known with us, that the Indian women so enslaved produced and raised as numerous families as either the whites or blacks among whom they lived. —It has been said, that Indians have less hair than the whites, except on the head. But this is a fact of which fair proof can scarcely be had. With them it is disgraceful to be hairy on the body. They say it likens them to hogs. They therefore pluck the hair as fast as it appears. . . . Nor, if the fact be true, is the consequence necessary which has been drawn from it. Negroes have notoriously less hair than the whites; yet they are more ardent. But if cold and moisture be the agents of nature for diminishing the races of animals, how comes she all at once to suspend their operation as to the physical man of the new world, whom the Count acknowledges to be "about the same size as the man of our hemisphere," and to let loose their influence on his moral faculties? How has this "combination of the elements and other physical causes, so contrary to the enlargement of animal nature in this new world, these obstacles to the development and formation of great germs," been arrested and suspended, so as to permit the human body to acquire its just dimensions, and by what inconceivable process has their action been directed on his mind alone? To judge of the truth of this, to form a just estimate of their genius and mental powers, more facts are wanting, and great allowance to be made for those circumstances of their situation which call for a display of particular talents only. This done, we shall probably find that they are formed in mind as well as in body, on the same module with the "Homo sapiens Europaeus." The principles of their society forbidding all compulsion, they are to be led to duty and to enterprize by personal influence and persuasion. Hence eloquence in council, bravery and address in war, become the foundations of all consequence with them. To these acquirements all their faculties are directed. Of their bravery and address in war we have multiplied proofs, because we have been the subjects on which they were exercised. Of their eminence in oratory we have fewer examples, because it is displayed chiefly in their own councils. Some, however, we have of very superior lustre. I may challange the whole orations of Demosthenes and Cicero, and of any more eminent orator, if Europe has furnished more eminent, to produce a single passage, superior to the speech of Logan, a Mingo chief, to Lord Dunmore, when governor of this state. And, as a testimony of their talents in this line, I beg leave to introduce. . . . Logan, a chief celebrated in peace and war, and long distinguished as the friend of the whites sent by a messenger the following speech. . . . [Logan] to be delivered to Lord Dunmore.

"I appeal to any white man to say, if ever he entered Logan's cabin hungry, and he gave him not meat; if ever he came cold and naked, and he clothed him not. During the course of the last long and bloody war, Logan remained idle in his cabin, an advocate for peace. Such was my love for the whites, that my countrymen pointed as they passed, and said, 'Logan is the friend of white men.' I had even thought to have lived with you, but for the injuries of one man. Col. Cresap, the last spring, in cold blood, and unprovoked, murdered all the relations of Logan, not sparing even my women and children. There runs not a drop of my blood in the veins of any living creature. This called on me to revenge. I have sought it: I have killed many: I have fully glutted my vengeance. For my country. I rejoice at the beams of peace. But do not harbour a thought that mine is the joy of fear. Logan never felt fear. He will not turn on his heel to save his life. Who is there to mourn for Logan?—Not one."

Before we condemn the Indians of this continent as wanting genius, we must consider that letters have not yet been introduced among them. Were we to compare them in their present state with the Europeans North of the Alps, when the Roman arms and arts first crossed those mountains, the comparison would be unequal, because, at that time, those parts of Europe were swarming with numbers; because numbers produce emulation, and multiply the chances of improvement, and one improvement begets another. Yet I may safely ask, How many good poets, how many able mathematicians, how many great inventors in arts or sciences, had Europe North of the Alps then produced? And it was sixteen centuries after this before a Newton could be formed. I do not mean to deny, that there are varieties in the race of man, distinguished by their powers both of body and mind. I believe there are, as I see to be the case in the races of other animals. I only mean to suggest a doubt, whether the bulk and faculties of animals depend on the side of the Atlantic on which their food happens to grow, or which furnishes the elements of which they are compounded? . . .

4.4 Missionary, Go Home!

From the earliest exchanges, some whites tried to convert the Native Americans to Christianity and some Native Americans found the religion interesting and appealing. But few Indians embraced the European's religion on an exclusive basis. Instead, they preferred to incorporate it into their old beliefs.

Indian leaders often regarded Christian missionaries as a threat to cultural survival. When a young evangelist named Cramm appeared at the Seneca nation near Buffalo, New York in 1805 and asked permission to set up a mission on the reservation, Chief Red Jacket firmly rebuffed him. In the following speech, recorded from memory years later by the white artist and explorer George Catlin, the old and highly revered Iroquois leader explains in full detail why he sent the missionary away. Red Jacket died shortly afterward. Ironically, he was given a Christian burial, against his expressed personal wishes.

Questions

Which beliefs does Red Jacket share with whites? With which does he differ? What is his concept of Christianity? Is his argument theological or political; does it involve religious doctrine or something else? What does he fear from white contact, and is he justified?

Friend and brother, it was the will of the Great Spirit that we should meet together this day. He orders all things, and He has given us a fine day for our council. He has taken His garment from before the sun, and caused it to shine with brightness upon us; our eyes are opened, that we see clearly; our ears are unstopped, that we have been able to hear distinctly the words that you have spoken; for all these favours we thank the Great Spirit, and Him only.

Source: Red Jacket, "Reply to Missionary Cram at Buffalo, N.Y., 1805," from Samuel Griswold Goodrich, ed., *Lives of Celebrated American Indians,* (New York: J. M. Allen, 1843).

Brother, this council fire was kindled by you; it was at your request that we came together at this time; we have listened with attention to what you have said. . . . You say you want an answer to your talk, before you leave this place. It is right you should have one, as you are a great distance from home, and we do not wish to detain you; but we will first look back a little, and tell you what our fathers have told us, and what we have heard from the White people.

Brother, listen to what we say. There was a time when our forefathers owned this great land. Their seats extended from the rising to the setting sun. The Great Spirit had made it for the use of Indians. He had created the buffalo, the deer, and other animals for food. He made the bear and the beaver, and their skins served us for clothing. He had scattered them over the country, and taught us how to take them. He had caused the earth to produce corn for bread.

All this He had done for His Red children because he loved them. If we had any disputes about hunting grounds, they were generally settled without the shedding of much blood.

But an evil day came upon us; your forefathers crossed the great waters, and landed on this island. Their numbers were small; they found friends, and not enemies; they told us they had fled from their own country for fear of wicked men, and come here to enjoy their religion. They asked for a small seat; we took pity on them, granted their request, and sat down amongst us; we gave them corn and meat; they gave us poison in return. The White people had now found our country, tidings were carried back, and more came amongst us; yet we did not fear them, we took them to be friends; they called us brothers; we believed them, and gave them a larger seat. At length their numbers had greatly increased; they wanted more land; they wanted our country. Our eyes were opened; and our minds became uneasy. Wars took place; Indians were hired to fight against Indians, and many of our people were destroyed. They also brought strong liquors among us; it was strong and powerful, and has slain thousands.

Brother, our seats were once large, and yours were very small; you have now become a great people, and we have scarcely a place left to spread our blankets; you have got our country, but are not satisfied; you want to force your religion upon us.

Brother, continue to listen. You say that you are sent to instruct us how to worship the Great Spirit agreeably to His mind, and if we do not take hold of the religion which you White people teach, we shall be unhappy hereafter; you say that you are right, and we are lost; how do we know this to be true? We understand that your religion is written in a book; if it was intended for us as well as you, why has not the Great Spirit given it to us, and not only to us, but why did He not give to our forefathers the knowledge of that book, with the means of understanding it rightly? We only know what you tell us about it; how shall we know when to believe, being so often deceived by the White people?

Brother, you say there is but one way to worship and serve the Great Spirit; if there is but one religion, why do you White people differ so much about it? Why not all agree, as you can all read the book?

Brother, we do not understand these things; we are told that your religion was given to your forefathers, and has been handed down from father to son. We also have a religion which was given to our forefathers, and has been handed down to us, their children. We worship that way. It teaches us to be thankful for all the favours we receive; to love each other, and to be united; we never quarrel about religion.

Brother, the Great Spirit has made us all; but He has made a great difference between His White and Red children; He has given us a different complexion and different customs; to you He has given the arts; to these He has not opened our eyes; we know these things to be true. Since He has made so great a difference between us in other things, why may we not conclude that He has given us a different religion according to our understanding? The Great Spirit does right: He knows what is best for his children; we are satisfied.

Brother, we do not wish to destroy your religion, or take it from you. We want only to enjoy our own.

Brother, you say you have not come to get our land or our money, but to enlighten our minds. I will now tell you that I have been at your meetings, and saw you collecting money from the meeting. I cannot tell what this money was intended for, but suppose it was for your minister, and if should conform to your way of thinking, perhaps you may want some from us. . . .

Brother you have now heard our answer to your talk, and this is all we have to say at present. As we are going to part, we will come and take you by the hand, and hope the Great Spirit will protect you on your journey, and return you safe to your friends.

4.5 Resisting the "Long Knives"

One of the great "patriot chiefs" was the Shawnee leader Tecumseh. He rose to prominence when General William H. Harrison came before the Native Americans of the Old Northwest with sweeping land-grabbing proposals. To stop Harrison and his "Long Knives," Tecumseh proposed an equally sweeping plan of political and military resistance. He would create a unified, independent Indian confederation with its center in what is now Indiana, and with its influence ranging from the Great Lakes to the Gulf of Mexico. It would employ military force to uphold Indian authority and halt the piecemeal disposal of land. To make the plan work, Tecumseh would have to unify many Native American groups unaccustomed to working together. He had as a trusted co-worker his brother, the Prophet, a religious leader who urged a return to older Native American traditions and religious practices. Travelling thousands of miles to sell his message, Tecumseh appeared in the South before a joint Choctaw and Chickasaw council in 1812, where he presented his case. But it was defeated by the Choctaw orator Pushmataha, whose argument favoring accommodation to the whites carried the day.

In the War of 1812 Tecumseh joined the redcoat soldiers to fight the Americans. He died in a skirmish with Harrison in 1813. With him died the idea of an independent Native Amer-

ican nation. But the proposal is remembered as perhaps the boldest ever put forward in support of Native American resistance in the United States. The speeches of Tecumseh and Pushmataha are reprinted below.

Questions

What evils did Tecumseh wish to resist? How did he propose going about it? What did he hope to accomplish? What arguments did Pushmataha offer in opposition? Did the two speakers disagree about the means or the ends of resistance? Why do you think the Choctaw prevailed? Had Tecumseh prevailed, how might history have been different?

Tecumseh –

In view of questions of vast importance, have we met together in solemn council tonight. Nor should we here debate whether we have been wronged and injured, but by what measures we should avenge ourselves. . . . The whites are already nearly a match for us all united, and too strong for any one tribe alone to resist; so that unless we support one another with our collective and united forces; unless every tribe unanimously combines to give a check to the ambition and avarice of the whites, they will soon conquer us apart and disunited, and we will be driven away from our native country and scattered as autumnal leaves before the wind. . . .

Sleep no longer, o Choctaws and Chickasaws, in false security and delusive hopes. Our broad domains are fast escaping from our grasp. Every year our white intruders become more greedy, exacting, oppressive, and overbearing. Every year contentions spring up between them and our people and when blood is shed we have to make atonement whether right or wrong, at the cost of the lives of our greatest chiefs, and the yielding up of large tracts of our lands. Before the pale-faces came among us, we enjoyed the happiness of unbounded freedom, and were acquainted with neither riches, wants, nor oppression. How is it now? Wants and oppressions are our lot; for are we not controlled in everything, and dare we move without asking, by your leave? Are we not being stripped day by day of the little that remains of our ancient liberty? Do they not even now kick and strike us as they do their black-faces? How long will it be before they will tie us to a post and whip us, and make us work for them in cornfields as they do them? Shall we wait for that moment or shall we die fighting before submitting to such ignominy? . . . The annihilation of our race is at hand unless we unite in one common cause against the common foe. Think not, brave Choctaws and Chickasaws, that you can remain passive and indifferent to the common danger, and thus escape the common fate. Your people too, will soon be as falling leaves and scattering clouds before their blighting breath. You too will

SOURCE: H. B. Cushman, *History of the Chocktaw, Chicasaw, and Natchez Indians* (Greenville, Texas, 1899), 303 ff.

be driven away from your native land and ancient domains as leaves are driven before the wintry storms.

Have we not for years had before our eyes a sample of their designs, and are they not sufficient harbingers of their future determinations? Will we not soon be driven from our respective countries and the graves of our ancestors? Will not the bones of our dead be plowed up, and their graves be turned into fields? Shall we calmly wait until they become so numerous that we will no longer be able to resist oppression? Will we wait to be destroyed in our turn, without making an effort worthy our race? Shall we give up our homes, our country, bequeathed to us by the Great Spirit, the graves of our dead, and everything that is dear and sacred to us without a struggle? I know you will cry with me. Never! Never! Then let us by unity of action destroy them all, which we now can do, or drive them back whence they came. War or extermination is now our only choice. Which do you choose, brave Choctaws and Chickasaws, to assist in the just cause of liberating our race from the grasp of our faithless invaders and heartless oppressors. The white usurpation in our common country must be stopped or we, its rightful owners, be forever destroyed and wiped out as a race of people. I am now at the head of many warriors backed by the strong arm of English soldiers. Choctaws and Chickasaws, you [have] too long borne with grievous usurpation inflicted by the arrogant Americans.

Be no longer their dupes. If there be one here tonight who believes that his rights will not sooner or later, be taken from him by the avaricious American pale-faces, his ignorance ought to excite pity, for he knows little of the character of our common foe. And if there be one among you mad enough to undervalue the growing power of the white race among us, let him tremble in considering the fearful woes he will bring down upon our entire race, if by his criminal indifference he assists the designs of our common enemy against our common country. Then listen to the voice of duty, of honor, of nature, and of your endangered country. Let us form one body, one heart, and defend to the last warrior our country, our homes, our liberty, and the graves of our fathers.

Choctaws and Chickasaws, you are among the few of our race who sit indolently at ease. You have indeed enjoyed the reputation of being brave, but will you be indebted for it more from report than fact? Will you let the whites encroach upon your domains even to your very door before you will assert your rights in resistance? Let no one in this council imagine that I speak more from malice against the pale-face Americans than just grounds of complaint. Complaint is just toward friends who have failed in their duty; accusation is against enemies guilty of injustice; especially when such great acts of injustice have been committed by them upon our race, of which they seem to have no manner of regard, or even to reflect. They are a people fond of innovations, quick to contrive and quick to put their schemes into effectual execution, no matter how great the wrong and injury to us; while we are content to preserve what we already have. Their designs are to enlarge their possessions by taking yours in turn; and will you, can you longer dally, o Choctaws and Chickasaws? Do you imagine that people will not continue longest in the enjoyment of peace who timely prepare to vindicate themselves, and manifest a determined resolution to do themselves right whenever they are wronged? Far otherwise. Then haste to the relief of our common cause, as by consanguinity of blood you are bound; lest the day be not far distant when you will be left singlehanded and alone to the cruel mercy of our most inveterate foe.

Pushmataha –

It was not my design in coming here to enter into a disputation with anyone. But I appear before you, my warriors and my people, not to throw in my plea against the accusations of Tecumseh; but to prevent your forming rash and dangerous resolutions upon things of highest importance, through the instigations of others. I have myself learned by experience, and I also see many of you, o Choctaws and Chickasaws, who have the same experience of years that I have, the injudicious steps of engaging in an enterprise because it is new. Nor do I stand up before you tonight to contradict the many facts alleged against the American people, or to raise my voice against them in useless accusations. The question before us now is not what wrongs they have inflicted upon our race, but what measures are best for us to adopt in regard to them; and though our race may have been unjustly treated and shamefully wronged by them, yet I shall not for that reason alone advise you to destroy them unless it was just and expedient for you so to do; nor would I advise you to forgive them, though worthy of your commiseration, unless I believe it would be to the interest of our common goal. We should consult more in regard to our future welfare than our present. What people, my friends and countrymen, were so unwise and inconsiderate as to engage in a war of their own accord, when their own strength, and even the aid of others, was judged unequal to the task? . . . My friends and fellow countrymen! you now have no just cause to declare war against the American people, or wreak your vengeance upon them as enemies, since they have ever manifested feelings of friendship toward you. It is besides inconsistent with your national glory and with your honor, as a people, to violate your solemn treaty; and a disgrace to the memory of your forefathers, to wage war against the American people merely to gratify the malice of the English.

The war, which you are now contemplating against the Americans, is a flagrant breach of justice; yea, a fearful blemish on your honor and also that of your fathers, and which you will find if you will examine it carefully and judiciously, forbodes nothing but destruction to our entire race. It is a war against a people whose territories are now far greater than our own, and who are far better provided with all necessary implements of war, with men, guns, horses, wealth, far beyond that of all our race combined, and where is the necessity or wisdom to make war upon such a people? Where is our hope of success, if thus weak and unprepared we should declare it against them? . . . And though we will not permit ourselves to be made slaves, or, like inexperienced warriors, shudder at the thought of war, yet I am not so insensible and inconsistent as to advise you to cowardly yield to the outrages of the whites, or willfully to connive at their unjust encroachments; but only not yet to have recourse to war, but to send ambassadors to our Great Father at Washington, and lay before him our grievances, without betraying too great eagerness for war, or manifesting any tokens of pusillanimity. . . .

. . . Hear me, o my countrymen, if you begin this war it will end in calamities to us from which we are now free and at a distance; and upon whom of us they will fall, will only be determined by the uncertain and hazardous event. Be not, I pray you, guilty of rashness, which I never as yet have known you to be; therefore, I implore you, while healing measures are in the election of us all, not to break the treaty, nor violate your pledge or honor, but to submit our grievances, whatever they may be, to the Congress of the United States, according to the articles of the treaty existing between us and the American people. If not, I here invoke the Great Spirit, who takes cognizance of oaths, to bear me witness, that I shall endeavor to avenge myself upon the authors of this war, by whatever methods you shall set me an example. . . .

Let us, my countrymen, not forget it now, nor in short space of time precipitately determine a question in which so much is involved. It is indeed the duty of the prudent, so long as they are not injured, to delight in peace. But it is the duty of the brave, when injured, to lay peace aside, and to have recourse to arms; and when successful in these, to then lay them down again in peaceful quiet; thus never to be elevated above measure by success in war, nor delighted with the sweets of peace to suffer insults. For he who, apprehensive of losing the delight, sits indolently at ease, will soon be deprived of the enjoyment of that delight which interesteth his fears; and he whose passions are inflamed by military success, elevated too high by a treacherous confidence, hears no longer the dictates of judgement.

Many of the schemes, though unadvisedly planned, through the more unreasonable conduct of an enemy, which turn out successfully; but more numerous are those which, though seemingly founded on mature counsel, draw after them a disgraceful and opposite result. This proceeds from the great inequality of spirit with which an exploit is projected, and with which it is put into actual execution. For in council we resolve, surrounded with security; into execution we faint, through the prevalence of fear. Listen to [the] voice of prudence, o, my countrymen, ere you rashly act. But do as you may, know this truth, enough for you to know, I shall join our friends, the Americans, in this war.

4.6 The Cortina War

For years after the Mexican War, Mexicans in the borderland area faced rampant racial prejudice, injustice and violent confrontations with Anglos. From Brownsville, Texas, to Los Angeles, California, the scene was one of repeated instances of land grabbing, legal discrimination, banditry, vigilante justice, murder, cattle rustling, and ranger action.

The Mexican Americans responded in various ways, including taking up banditry. Historians now believe that banditry, in the context that then existed in the borderland, represents a form of "primitive political rebellion." One such rebel was Juan N. Cortina, the "Red Robber of the Rio Grande." Cortina was born in 1822 to a wealthy landed family near Brownsville. He had fought for Mexico in the Mexican War and became a U.S. citizen under the Treaty of Guadalupe Hidalgo. A man of hot temper and physical courage, he resented the injustices suffered by Mexicans. When he witnessed a marshall pistol-whipping a Mexican he liberated him. Cortina was indicted for cattle stealing. Along with 50 or 60 followers, he set out for Mexico. While in Brownsville he raised the Mexican flag and liberated some prisoners whom he thought were unjustly imprisoned, killing the jailer in the process. Vengeful Anglo-Texans seized a friend of Cortina's, an innocent elderly man, and lynched him.

Cortina's band swelled to 1,200 followers. For a year or more, the entire border from Laredo to the mouth of the Rio Grande was engulfed in the "Cortina War." The conflict in southern Texas and northern Mexico continued until 1860, when American military units, led by Robert E. Lee, crossed into Mexico and stopped the raids. Cortina, however, eluded him. Later, Cortina was appointed military governor of Tamaulpias and an army general, and played a major role in the politics of northern Mexico for decades. As such he may have headed an international cattle rustling operation.

Cortina did not reform the system or change the conduct of the Yankees, but Mexican Americans enshrined him as a popular Mexican hero. He was the subject of corridos, *ballads glorifying the deeds of folk heroes, that are still sung today in that region.*

In 1859, while holding out in Cameron County, Texas, the bandit chieftain issued a flaming proclamation. In it, he appealed to Mexicans to rise up and cast off their oppressors, and to Anglo-American authorities to bring the wrong-doers to justice. He called for the formation of a secret society of Mexicans. Most of this manifesto, reprinted from a U.S. Congressional report, appears below. The flowery language may have originated with the unknown translator, since Cortina was known to be illiterate.

Questions

List Cortina's grievances. What did he want both of the Mexicans and of the Yankees? What remedies did he propose and how viable do they seem, given the circumstances? How did he view the Yankees of South Texas? What do you make of his appeal to Sam Houston at the end of his proclamation?

There are, doubtless, persons so overcome by strange prejudices, men without confidence or courage to face danger in an undertaking in sisterhood with the love of liberty, who, examining the merit of acts by a false light, and preferring that of the same opinion contrary to their own, prepare no other reward than that pronounced for the "bandit," for him who,

SOURCE: From 36 Congress, 1 Session, House Executive Document No. 52, "Difficulties on Southwestern Frontier," 79–82.

with complete abnegation of self, dedicates himself to constant labor for the happiness of those who, suffering under the weight of misfortunes, eat their bread, mingled with tears, on the earth which they rated. . . .

Mexicans! When the State of Texas began to receive the new organization which its sovereignty required as an integrant part of the Union, flocks of vampires, in the guise of men, came and scattered themselves in the settlements, without any capital except the corrupt heart and the most perverse intentions. Some, brimful of laws, pledged to us their protection against the attacks of the rest; others assembled in shadowy councils, attempted and excited the robbery and burning of the houses of our relatives on the other side of the river Bravo; while others, to the abusing of our unlimited confidence, when we intrusted them with our titles, which secured the future of our families, refused to return them under false and frivolous pretexts; all, in short, with a smile on their faces, giving the lie to that which their black entrails were meditating. Many of you have been robbed of your property, incarcerated, chased, murdered, and hunted like wild beasts, because your labor was fruitful, and because your industry excited the vile avarice which led them. A voice infernal said, from the bottom of their soul, "kill them; the greater will be our gain!" Ah! this does not finish the sketch of your situation. It would appear that justice had fled from this world, leaving you to the caprice of your oppressors, who become each day more furious toward you; that, through witnesses and false charges, although the grounds may be insufficient, you may be interred in the penitentiaries, if you are not previously deprived of life by some keeper who covers himself from responsibility by the pretence of your flight. There are to be found criminals covered with frightful crimes, but they appear to have impunity until opportunity furnish them a victim; to these monsters indulgence is shown, because they are not of our race, which is unworthy, as they say, to belong to the human species. . . .

Mexicans! Is there no remedy for you? Inviolable laws, yet useless, serve, it is true, certain judges and hypocritical authorities, cemented in evil and injustice, to do whatever suits them, and to satisfy their vile avarice at the cost of your patience and suffering; rising in their frenzy, even to the taking of life, through the treacherous hands of their bailiffs. The wicked way in which many of you have been oftentimes involved in persecution, accompanied by circumstances making it the more bitter, is now well known; these crimes being hid from society under the shadow of a horrid night, those implacable people, with the haughty spirit which suggests impunity for a life of criminality, have pronounced, doubt ye not, your sentence, which is, with accustomed insensibility, as you have seen, on the point of execution.

Mexicans! My part is taken; the voice of revelation whispers to me that to me is entrusted the work of breaking the chains of your slavery, and that the Lord will enable me, with powerful arm, to fight against our enemies, in compliance with the requirements of that Sovereign Majesty, who, from this day forward, will hold us under His protection. On my part, I am ready to offer myself as a sacrifice for your happiness; and counting upon the means necessary for the discharge of my ministry, you may count upon my cooperation, should no cowardly attempt put an end to my days. This undertaking will be sustained on the following bases:

First: A society is organized in the State of Texas, which devotes itself sleeplessly until the work is crowned with success, to the improvement of the unhappy condition of those Mexicans resident therein; exterminating their tyrants, to which end those which compose it are ready to shed their blood and suffer the death of martyrs.

Second: As this society contains within itself the elements necessary to accomplish the great end of its labors, the veil of impenetrable secrecy covers "The Great Book" in which the articles of its constitution are written; while so delicate are the difficulties which must be overcome that no honorable man can have cause for alarm, if imperious exigencies require them to act without reserve.

Third: The Mexicans of Texas repose their lot under the good sentiments of the governor elect of the state, General Houston, and trust that upon his elevation to power he will begin with care to give us legal protection within the limits of his powers.

Mexicans! Peace be with you! Good inhabitants of the State of Texas, look on them as brothers, and keep in mind that which the Holy Spirit saith: "Thou shalt not be the friend of the passionate man; nor join thyself to the madman, lest thou learn his mode of work and scandalize thy soul."

4.7 Slavery Emerges

It is in a way curious that the institution of slavery should have come into existence in the English colonies. As it no longer existed in England in the seventeenth century, it lacked a legal basis. The first blacks in the colonies, those in Virginia, were indentured servants rather than slaves. For the first few generations they remained servants. By the 1660s, though, their rights and social status began slipping, and gradually they became slaves. At the same time, the status of white servants improved. The spread of tobacco as the major cash crop in Virginia, the rise of the slave trade in Europe, and the growers' need for labor had much to do with the rise of slavery.

Emerging slowly over a period of time, the legal basis of slavery had crystallized by the 1660s. The laws passed by the Virginia House of Burgesses from 1630 to 1705 provide insights into this process. They cover matters such as the punishment of sexual relations between blacks and whites, the status of the children of such relationships, and the treatment of non-Christian blacks and of those who forcibly rebelled against their bondage.

Questions

Which racial attitudes of whites toward blacks are revealed in these documents? How did white Virginians reconcile black slavery with their religious faith?

What do these items suggest as to whether blacks accepted or rebelled against their status? What do they tell us about the justice system? How would blacks be treated who were not Christians? How was physical resistance to be handled?

[1630] September 17th, 1630. Hugh David to be soundly whipped, before an assembly of Negroes and others for abusing himself to the dishonor of God and shame of Christians, by defiling his body in lying with a negro; which fault he is to acknowledge next Sabbath day.

[1640] Robert Sweet to do penance in church according to laws of England, for getting a negro woman with child and the woman whipt.

[1661] *Be it enacted* That in case any English servant shall run away in company with any negroes who are incapable of making satisfaction by addition of time, *Be it enacted* that the English so running away in company with them shall serve for the time of the said negroes absence as they are to do for their own by a former act.

[1662] Whereas some doubts have arrisen whether children got by any Englishman upon a negro woman should be slave or ffree, *Be it therefore enacted and declared by this present grand assembly*, that all children borne in this country shalbe held bond or free only according to the condition of the mother, *And* that if any christian shall committ ffornication with a negro man or woman, hee or shee soe offending shall pay double the ffines imposed by the former act. . . .

[1668] Whereas some doubts, have arisen whether negro women set free were still to be accompted tithable according to a former act, *It is declared by this grand assembly* that negro women though permitted to enjoy their Freedom yet ought not in all respects to be admitted to a full fruition of the exemptions and impunities of the England, and are still liable to payment of taxes.

[1669] Whereas the only law in force for the punishment of refractory servants resisting their master, mistress or overseer cannot be inflicted upon negroes, nor the obstinancy of many of them by other than violent means supprest. *Be it enacted and declared by this grand assembly*, if any slave resist his master (or other by his master's order correcting him) and by the extremity of the correction should chance to die, that his death shall not be accompted Felony, but the master (or that other person appointed by the master to punish him) be acquit from molestation, since it cannot be presumed that prepensed malice (which alone makes murder Felony) should induce any man to destroy his own estate.

[1680] *It is hereby enacted by the authority aforesaid*, that from and after the publication of this law, it shall not be lawful for any negro or other slave to carry or arm himself with any club, staff, gun, sword, or any other weapon of defence or offence, nor to go to depart from his master's ground without a certificate from his master, mistress or overseer, and such permission not to be granted but upon particular and necessary occasions; and every negro or slave so offending not having a

SOURCE: W. W. Hening, comp., *Laws of Virginia, 1619–1792* (1823), I–III.

certificate as aforesaid shall be sent to the next constable, who is hereby enjoined and required to give the said negro twenty lashes on his bare back well laid on, and so sent home to his said master, mistress or overseer. *And it is further enacted by the authority aforesaid* that if any negro or other slave shall presume to lift up his hand in opposition against any christian, shall for every such offense, upon due proof made thereof by the oath of the party before a magistrate, have and receive thirty lashes on his bare back well laid on.

[1691] *It is hereby enacted,* that in all such cases upon intelligence of any such negroes, mulattoes, or other slaves lying out, two of their majesties' justices of the peace of that county, whereof one to be of the quorum, where such negroes, mulattoes or other slave shall be, shall be empowered and commanded, and are hereby impowered and commanded, to issue out their warrants directed to the sheriff of the same county to apprehend such negroes, mulattoes, and other slaves, which said sheriff is hereby likewise required upon all such occasions to raise such and so many forces from time to time as he shall think convenient and necessary for the effectual apprehending such negroes, mulattoes and other slaves, and in case any negroes, mulattoes or other slave or slaves lying out as aforesaid shall resist, run away, or refuse to deliver and surrender him or themselves to any person or persons that shall be by lawful authority employed to apprehend and take such negroes, mulattoes or other slaves that in such cases it shall and may be lawful for such person and persons to kill and destroy such negroes, mulattoes, and other slave or slaves by gun or any other ways whatsoever.

[1705] *And it also be enacted, by the authority aforesaid, and it is hereby enacted,* That all servants imported and brought into this country, by sea or land, who were not christians in their native country, (except Turks and Moors in amity with her majesty, and others that can make due proof of their being free in England, or any other christian country, before they were shipped, in order to transportation hither) shall be accounted and be slaves, and as such be here bought and sold notwithstanding a conversion to christianity afterwards. . . .

And for a further prevention of that abominable mixture and spurious issue, which hereafter may increase in this her majesty's colony and dominion, as well by English, and other white men and women intermarrying with negroes or mulattos, as by their unlawful coition with them, *Be it enacted, by the authority aforesaid, and it is hereby enacted,* That whatsoever English, or other white man or woman, being free, shall intermarry with a negro or mulatto man or woman, bond or free, shall, by judgement of the county court, be committed to prison, and there remain, during the space of six months, without bail or mainprize; and shall forfeit and pay ten pounds current money of Virginia, to the use of the parish, as aforesaid. . . .

And if any slave resist his master, or owner, or other person, by his or her order, correcting such slave, and shall happen to be killed in such correction, it shall not be accounted felony; but the master, owner, and every such other person so giving correction, shall be free and acquit of all punishment and accusation for the same, as if such accident had never happened: And also, if any negro, mulatto, or Indian, bond or free, shall at any time, lift his or her hand, in opposition against any christian, not being negro, mulatto, or Indian, he or she so offending, shall, for every such offence, proved by the oath of the party, receive on his or her bare back, thirty lashes, well laid on; cognizable by a justice of the peace for that county wherein such offence shall be committed.

And also be it enacted, by the authority aforesaid, and it is hereby enacted, That no slave go armed with gun, sword, club, staff, or other weapon, nor go from off the plantation and seat of land where such slave shall be appointed to live, without a certificate of leave in writing, for so doing, from his or her master, mistress, or overseer: And if any slave shall be found offending herein, it shall be lawful for any person or persons to apprehend and deliver such slave to the next constable or head-borough, who is hereby enjoined and required, without further order or warrant, to give such slave twenty lashes on his or her bare back, well laid on, and so send him or her home: And all horses, cattle, and hogs, now belonging, or that hereafter shall belong to any slave, or of any slaves mark in this her majesty's colony and dominion, shall be seised and sold by the church-wardens of the parish, wherein such horses, cattle, or hogs shall be, and the profit thereof applied to the use of the poor of the said parish. . . .

And also it is hereby enacted and declared, That baptism of slaves doth not exempt them from bondage; and that all children shall be bond or free, according to the condition of their mothers, and the particular directions of this act. . . .

4.8 Walker's Appeal

Until about 1830 abolitionists offered only moderate, humanitarian arguments against slavery. They proposed colonization and manumission as solutions. Blacks seemed restless but relatively voiceless. Then came a change of mood, marking the end of gradualism and the start of the "immediatist" phase of abolitionism. One sign of change was the publication of William Lloyd Garrison's militant newspaper, the Liberator, *in January, 1831. A second was Nat Turner's slave revolt in Virginia in that same year, when fifty-five whites were killed. A third event signifying a rising opposition to "the peculiar institution" was the publication in 1829 of David Walker's* Appeal.

This incendiary pamphlet, whose full title was Walker's Appeal in Four Articles Together with a Preamble to the Colored Citizens of the World But in Particular and very Expressly to those of the United States of America, *tried to raise black consciousness and stir them to violence against whites.*

Walker (1785–1830), a free black from North Carolina, had recently arrived in Boston and was the owner of a used clothing store. He was literate and used his verbal skills addressing small groups and writing newspaper articles about the condition of blacks. Though never a slave himself, he had travelled widely in the South and understood the conditions of slavery. Walker composed the pamphlet in white heat and published it with his own money. He did not mince words, calling whites cruel and insensitive. Nor was he hesitant to say that blacks were the "most wretched, degraded and abject sort of beings that ever lived since the world began." He cited the Bible and he closed his incendiary appeal by quoting the Declaration of Independence as a justification for violent rebellion. He encouraged slaves to kill their masters.

Walker's pamphlet shocked and angered even sympathetic whites. Moderate abolitionists feared it would alienate whites. Even the militant Garrison hesitated before reprinting it. The author was found dead near his shop in 1830, a probable victim of poisoning.

Questions

What is Walker's message to blacks. How does it differ from his message to whites? What are the religious underpinnings of his beliefs? Would this message be considered radical today?

I know that the blacks, take them half enlightened and ignorant, are more humane and merciful than the most enlightened and refined European that can be found in all the earth. Let no one say that I assert this because I am prejudiced on the side of my colour, and against the whites or Europeans. For what I write, I do it candidly, for my God and the good of both parties: Natural observations have taught me these things; there is a solemn awe in the hearts of the blacks, as it respects *murdering* men; whereas the whites (though they are great cowards) where they have the advantage, or think that there are any prospects of getting it, they murder all before them, in order to subject men to wretchedness and degradation under them. This is the natural result of pride and avarice . . . Should the lives of such creatures be spared? Are God and Mammon in league? What has the Lord to do with a gang of desperate wretches, who go *sneaking about the country like robbers*—light upon his people wherever they can get a chance, binding them with chains and handcuffs, beat and murder them as they would *rattle-snakes?* Are they not the Lord's enemies? Ought they not to be destroyed? Any person who will save such wretches from destruction, is fighting against the Lord, and will receive his just recompense. . . .

Now, I ask you, had you not rather be killed than to be a slave to a tyrant, who takes the life of your mother, wife, and dear little children? Look upon your mother, wife and children, and answer God Almighty; and believe this, that it is no more harm for you to kill a man, who is trying to kill you, than it is for you to take a drink of water when thirsty; in fact, the man who will stand still and let another murder him, is worse than an infidel, and, if he has common sense, ought not to be pitied. . . . Oh! coloured people of these

SOURCE: From David Walker, *Walker's Appeal, in Four Articles: Together with a Preamble to Coloured Citizens of the World* (Boston: D. Walker, 1830).

United States, I ask you, in the name of that God who made us, have we, in consequence of oppression, nearly lost the spirit of man, and, in no very trifling degree, adopted that of brutes? Do you answer no? I ask you, then, what set of men can you point me to, in all the world, who are so abjectedly employed by their oppressors, as we are by our *natural enemies?* How can, Oh! how can those enemies but say that we and our children are not of the *human family,* but were made by our Creator to be an inheritance to them and theirs for ever? How can the slaveholders but say that they can bribe the best coloured person in the country, to sell his brethren for a trifling sum of money, and take that atrocity to confirm them in their avaricious opinion, that we were made to be slaves to them and their children? . . .

Men of colour, who are also of sense, for you particularly is my APPEAL designed. Our more ignorant brethren are not able to penetrate its value. I call upon you therefore to cast your eyes upon the wretchedness of your brethren, and to do your utmost to enlighten them—*go to work and enlighten your brethren!*—Let the Lord see you doing what you can to rescue them and yourselves from degradation. Do any of you say that you and your family are free and happy, and what have you to do with the wretched slaves and other people? So can I say, for I enjoy as much freedom as any of you, if I am not quite as well off as the best of you. Look into our freedom and happiness, and see of what kind they are composed!! They are of the very lowest kind—they are the very *dregs!*—they are the most servile and abject kind, that ever a people was in possession of! If any of you wish to know how FREE you are, let one of you start and go through the southern and western States of this country, and unless you travel as a slave to a white man (a servant is a *slave* to the man whom he serves) or have your free papers (which if you are not careful they will get from you) if they do not take you up and put you in jail, and if you cannot give good evidence of your freedom, sell you into eternal slavery, I am not a living man: or any man of colour, immaterial who he is, or where he came from, if he is *the fourth from the negro race!!* (as we are called) the white Christian of America will serve him the same they will sink him into wretchedness and degradation for ever while he lives. And yet some of you have the hardihood to say that you are free and happy! May God have mercy on your freedom and happiness!! I met a coloured man in the street a short time since, with a string of boots on his shoulders; we fell into conversation, and in the course of which, I said to him, what a miserable set of people we are! He asked, why?—Said I, we are so subjected under the whites, that we cannot obtain the comforts of life, but by cleaning their boots and shoes, old clothes, waiting on them, shaving them &c. Said he, (with the boots on his shoulders) "I am completely happy!!! I never want to live any better or happier than when I get a plenty of boots and shoes to clean!!!" Oh! how can those who are actuated by avarice only, but think, that our Creator made us to be an inheritance to them for ever, when they see that our greatest glory is centered in such mean and low objects? Understand me, brethren, I do not mean to speak against the occupants by which we acquire enough and sometimes scarcely that, to render ourselves and families comfortable through life. I am subjected to the same inconvenience, as you all.—My objections are, to our *gloring* and being *happy* in such low employments; for if we are men, we ought to be thankful to the Lord for the past, and for the future. Be looking forward with thankful hearts to higher attainments than *wielding the razor* and *cleaning boots and shoes.* The man whose aspirations are not *above,* and even *below* these, is indeed, ignorant and wretched enough. I advanced it therefore to you, not as a *problematical,* but as an unshaken and for ever immovable *fact,* that your full glory and happiness, as well as all other coloured people under Heaven, shall never be fully consummated, but with the *entire emancipation of your enslaved brethren all over the world.* You may therefore, go to work and do what you can to rescue, or join in with tyrants to oppress them and yourselves, until the Lord shall come upon you all like a thief in the night. For I believe it is the will of the Lord that our greatest happiness shall consist in working for the salvation of our whole body. When this is accomplished a burst of glory will shine upon you, which will indeed astonish you and the world. Do any of you say this never will be done? I assure you that God will accomplish it—if nothing else will answer, he will hurl tyrants and devils into *atoms* and make way for his people. But O my brethren! I say unto you again, you must go to work and prepare the way of the Lord.

4.9 Of Bondage and Freedom

Frederick Douglass (1817–1895) was the first slave to become a distinguished national figure. Born on a Maryland plantation, he taught himself to read and write, fled to the North as a young man, and became an eloquent abolitionist lecturer and editor. He agitated in Europe against slavery and, when the Civil War broke out, recruited soldiers into the Union army. He backed John Brown and actively supported abolition during the Civil War. In fact, he met Lincoln and urged him to emancipate the slaves. After the war he emerged as a prominent Republican, and served as U.S. consul general in Haiti.

A runaway and still in his twenties in 1845, Douglass published an autobiographical account that was so literate that some whites dismissed it as a fraud—as the work of a white person. He had the remarkable gift of describing and analyzing not only what slavery did to blacks, but how it affected whites, as well. In the following account, Douglass describes a childhood experience.

Questions

How and why did the reading incident shape Douglass' view of slavery and freedom? Why do you suppose Mr. Auld ordered his wife to stop the lessons, and how do you suppose she felt about it? What problems does it suggest white masters and mistresses had to live with?

How does Douglass' perception of slavery differ from that of Fitzhugh, in Document 4.10, below?

I was seldom whipped by my old master, and suffered little from any thing else than hunger and cold. I suffered much from hunger, but much more from cold. In hottest summer and coldest winter, I was kept almost naked—no shoes, no stockings, no jacket, no trousers, nothing on but a coarse tow linen shirt, reaching only to my knees. I had no bed, I must have perished with cold, but that, the coldest nights, I used to steal a bag which was used for carrying corn to the mill. I would crawl into this bag, and there sleep on the cold, damp, clay floor, with my head in and feet out. My feet have been so cracked with the frost, that the pen with which I am writing might be laid in the gashes. . . .

We were not regularly allowanced. Our food was coarse corn meal boiled. This was called *mush*. It was put into a large wooden try or trough, and set down upon the ground. The children were then called, like so many pigs, and like so many pigs they would come and devour the mush; some with oyster-shells, others with pieces of shingle, some with naked hands, and none with spoons. He that ate fastest got most; he that was strongest secured the best place; and few left the trough satisfied.

I was probably between seven and eight years old when I left Colonel Lloyd's plantation. I left it with joy. . . .

SOURCE: Frederick Douglass, *Narrative of the Life of Frederick Douglass, An American Slave, Written by Himself* (New York, 1845).

The ties that ordinarily bind children to their homes were all suspended in my case. I found no severe trial in my departure. My home was charmless; it was not home to me; on parting from it, I could not feel that. . . . I was leaving anything which I could have enjoyed by staying. My mother was dead, my grandmother lived far off, so that I seldom saw her. I had two sisters and one brother, that lived in the same house with me; but the early separation of us from our mother had well nigh blotted the fact of our relationship from our memories. I looked for home elsewhere, and was confident of finding none which I should relish less than the one which I was leaving. If, however, I found in my new home hardship, hunger, whipping, and nakedness, I had the consolation that I should not have escaped any one of them by staying. Having already had more than a taste of them in the house of my old master. . . .

We sailed out of Miles River for Baltimore on a Saturday morning. I remember only the day of the week, for at that time I had no knowledge of the days of the month, nor the months of the year. . . .

We arrived at Baltimore early on Sunday morning, landing at Smith's Wharf, not far from Bowley's Wharf. . . .

Mr. and Mrs. Auld were both at home, and met me at the door with their little son Thomas, to take care of whom I had been given. And here I saw what I had never seen before; it was a white face beaming with the most kindly emotions; it was the face of my new mistress, Sophia Auld. I wish I could describe the rapture that flashed through my soul as I beheld it. It was a new and strange sight to me, brightening up my pathway with the light of happiness. Little Thomas was told, there was his Freddy,—and I was told to take care of little Thomas; and thus I entered upon the duties of my new home with the most cheering prospect ahead. . . . Going to live at Baltimore laid the foundation and opened the gateway, to all my subsequent prosperity. I have ever regarded it as the first plain manifestation of that kind providence which has ever since attended me, and marked my life with so many favors. . . .

. . . From my earliest recollection, I date the entertainment of a deep conviction that slavery would not always be able to hold me within its foul embrace; and in the darkest hours of my career in slavery, this living word of faith and spirit of hope departed not from me, but remained like ministering angels to cheer me through the gloom. This good spirit was from God, and to him I offer thanksgiving and praise. . . .

My new mistress proved to be all she appeared when I first met her at the door,—a woman of the kindest heart and finest feelings. She had never had a slave under her control previously to myself, and prior to her marriage she had been dependent upon her own industry for a living. She was by trade a weaver; and by constant application to her business, she had been in a good degree preserved from the blighting and dehumanizing effects of slavery. I was utterly astonished at her goodness. I scarcely knew how to behave towards her. She was entirely unlike any other white woman I had even seen. I could not approach her as I was accustomed to approach other white ladies. My early instruction was all out of place. The crouching servility, usually so acceptable a quality in a slave, did not answer when manifested toward her. Her favor was not gained by it; she seemed to be disturbed by it. She did not deem it impudent or unmannerly for a slave to look her in the face. The meanest slave was put fully at ease in her presence, and none left without feeling better for having seen her. Her face was made of heavenly smiles, and her voice of tranquil music.

But, alas! this kind heart had but a short time to remain such. The fatal poison of irresponsible power was already in her hands, and soon commenced its infernal work. That cheerful eye, under the influence of slavery, soon became red with rage; that voice, made all of sweet accord, changed to one of harsh and horrid disorder; and that angelic face gave place to that of a demon.

Very soon after I went to live with Mr. and Mrs. Auld, she very kindly commenced to teach me the A, B, C. After I had learned this, she assisted me in learning to spell words of three or four letters. Just at this point of my progress, Mr. Auld found out what was going on and at once forbade Mrs. Auld to instruct me further, telling her, among other things, that it was unlawful, as well as unsafe, to teach a slave to read. To use his own words, further, he said, "If you give a nigger an inch, he will take an ell. A nigger should know nothing but to obey his master—to do as he is told to do. Learning would *spoil* the best nigger in the world. Now," said he, "if you teach that nigger (speaking of myself) how to read, there would be no keeping him. It would forever unfit him to be a slave. He would at once become unmanageable, and of no value to his master. As to himself, it could do him no good, but a great deal of harm. It would make him discontented and unhappy." These words sank deep into my heart, stirred up sentiments within that lay slumbering, and called into existence an entirely new train of thought. It was a new and special revelation, explaining dark and mysterious things, with which my youthful understanding had struggled, but struggled in vain. I now understood what had been to me a most perplexing difficulty—to wit, the white man's power to enslave the black man. It was a grand achievement, and I prized it highly. From that moment, I understood the pathway from slavery to freedom. It was just what I wanted, and I got it at a time when I the least expected it. Whilst I was saddened by the thought of losing the aid of my kind mistress, I was gladdened by the invaluable instruction which, by the merest accident, I had gained from my master. Though conscious of the difficulty of learning without a teacher, I set out with high hope, and a fixed purpose, at whatever cost of trouble, to learn how to read. The very decided manner with which he spoke, and strove to impress his wife with the evil consequences of giving me instruction, served to convince me that he was deeply sensible of the truths he was uttering. It gave me the best assurance that I might rely with the utmost confidence on the results which, he said, would flow from teaching me to read. What he most dreaded, that I most desired. What he most loved, that I most hated. That which to him was a great evil, to be carefully shunned, was to me a great good, to be diligently sought; and the argument which he so warmly urged, against my learning to read, only served to inspire me with a desire and determination to learn. In learning to read, I owe almost as much to the bitter opposition of my master, as to the kindly aid of my mistress. I acknowledge the benefit of both. . . .

I lived in Master Hugh's family about seven years. During this time, I succeeded in learning to read and write. In accomplishing this, I was compelled to resort to various stratagems. I had no regular teacher. My mistress, who had kindly commenced to instruct me, had, in compliance with the advice and direction of her husband, not only ceased to instruct, but had set her face against my being instructed by any one else. It is due, however, to my mistress to say of her, that she did not adopt this course of treatment immediately. She at first lacked the depravity indispensable to shutting me up in mental darkness. It was at least necessary for her to have some training in the exercise of irresponsible power, to make her equal to the task of treating me as though I were a brute.

My mistress was, as I have said, a kind and tender-hearted woman; and in the simplicity of her soul she commenced, when I first went to live with her, to treat me as she supposed one human being ought to treat another. In entering upon the duties of a slaveholder, she did not seem to perceive that I sustained to her the relation of a mere chattel, and that for her to treat me as a human being was not only wrong, but dangerously so. Slavery proved as injurious to her as it did to me. When I went there, she was a pious, warm, and tender-hearted woman. There was no sorrow or suffering for which she had not a tear. She had bread for the hungry, clothes for the naked, and comfort for every mourner that came within her reach. Slavery soon proved its ability to divest her of these heavenly qualities. Under its influence, the tender heart became stone, and the lamblike disposition gave way to one of tiger-like fierceness. The first step in her downward course was in her ceasing to instruct me. She now commenced to practise her husband's precepts. She finally became even more violent in her opposition than her husband himself. She was not satisfied with simply doing as well as he had commanded; she seemed anxious to do better. Nothing seemed to make her more angry than to see me with a newspaper. She seemed to think that here lay the danger. I have had her rush at me with a face made all up of fury, and snatch from me a newspaper, in a manner that fully revealed her apprehension. She was an apt woman; and a little experience soon demonstrated, to her satisfaction, that eduction and slavery were incompatible with each other.

From this time I was most narrowly watched. If I was in a separate room any considerable length of time, I was sure to be suspected of having a book, and was at once called to give an account of myself. All this, however, was too late. The first step had been taken. Mistress, in teaching me the alphabet, had given me the *inch*, and no precaution could prevent me from taking the *ell*. . . .

4.10 The Dred Scott Decision

Once the Supreme Court handed down its decision in Dred Scott *v.* Sanford *in 1857, a civil war between the North and South was probably unavoidable. Dred and Harriet Scott were slaves who had filed a suit for their freedom in Missouri back in 1846. They argued that their master had taken them to Minnesota and other places where slavery had been prohibited by the Missouri Compromise, and that they were, therefore, free. The Court ruled otherwise.*

The Dred Scott *decision was one of the most sweeping and momentous in our history. The High Court ruled that Congress could not stop slaves from entering any unorganized territory. Slavery, in effect, now had no legal boundaries, no geographic limits. Efforts to pass laws restricting bondage in the new states would be futile. Slaves could be introduced into the North, even where for a generation they had been prohibited. Blacks were not American citizens and could not become free individuals, not even by leaving the deep South and settling in the North. To regard them as free might undermine the slave-owners rights of property. The Court went out of its way to demean blacks by saying they had been held "so far inferior that they had no rights which the white man was bound to respect."*

The decision dashed the hopes of free-soilers and abolitionists that the government would stop slavery. It held out to planters the message that slavery would be vigorously defended and extended. The ruling produced a storm of opposition.

The fateful decision, excerpted below, was written by Roger B. Taney (1777–1864) of Maryland. A prominent Jacksonian, he had been appointed to succeed James Marshall as Chief Justice in 1835.

Questions

Exactly what had the Constitution of 1787 said, or not said, about slavery? Were the terms "slave" or "slavery" used? Did the document directly or indirectly uphold any aspects of bondage such as the slave trade and the fugitive slave law? Was it fundamentally a "slave-owners constitution"?

How had Congress dealt with slavery in the Missouri Compromise of 1820, the Compromise of 1850 and the Kansas-Nebrasks Act of 1854?

Exactly what was Taney's decision, and on what grounds did he base it? What was the political fallout from Dred Scott?

The question is simply this: Can a negro, whose ancestors were imported into this country, and sold as slaves, become a member of the political community formed and brought into existence by the Constitution of the United States, and as such become entitled to all the rights, and privileges, and immunities, guaranteed by that instrument to the citizen? One of which rights is the privilege of suing in a court of the United States in the cases specified in the Constitution.

It will be observed, that the plea applies to that class of persons only whose ancestors were negros of the African race, and imported into this country, and sold and held as slaves. The only matter in issue before the court, therefore, is, whether the descendants of such slaves, when they shall be emancipated, or who are born of parents who had become free before their birth, are citizens of a State, in the sense in which the word citizen is used in the Constitution of the United States. And this being the only matter in dispute on the pleadings, the court must be understood as speaking in this opinion of that class only, that is of persons who are the descendants of Africans who were imported into this country and sold as slaves. . . .

We proceed to examine the case as presented by the pleadings.

The words "people of the United States" and "citizens" are synonymous terms, and mean the same thing. . . . The question before us is, whether the class of persons described in the plea in abatement compose a portion of this people, and are constituent members of this sovereignty? We think they are not, and that they are not included, and were not included to be included, under the word "citizens" in the Constitution, and can, therefore, claim none of the rights and privileges which that instrument provides for and secures to citizens of the United States. On the contrary, they were at that time considered as a subordinate and inferior class of beings, who had been subjugated by the dominant race, and whether emancipated, or not, yet remained subject to their authority, and had no rights or privileges but such as those who held the power and the government might choose to grant them. . . .

SOURCE: 19 Howard 393 (1857).

In discussing this question, we must not confound the rights of citizenship which a state may confer within its own limits, and the rights of citizenship as a member of the Union. It does not by any means follow, because he has all rights and privileges of a citizen of a State, that he must be a citizen of the United States. He may have all of the rights and privileges of a State, and yet not be entitled to the rights and privileges of a citizen in any other State. For, previous to the adoption of the Constitution of the United States, every State had the undoubted right to confer on whomsoever it pleased the character of a citizen, and to endow him with all its rights. But this character, of course, was confined to the boundaries of the State, and gave him no rights or privileges in other States beyond those secured to him by the laws of nations and the comity [mutual jurisdiction] of States. Nor have the several States surrendered the power of conferring these rights and privileges by adopting the Constitution of the United States. Each State may still confer them upon an alien, or any one it thinks proper, or upon any class or description of persons; yet he would not be a citizen in the sense in which that word is used in the Constitution of the United States, nor entitled to sue as such in one of its courts, nor to the privileges and immunities of a citizen in the other States. The rights which he would acquire would be restricted to the State which gave them. . . .

The question then arises, whether the provisions of the Constitution, in relation to the personal rights and privileges to which the citizen of a State should be entitled, embraced the negro African race, at that time in this country, or who might afterwards be imported, who had then or should afterwards be made free in any State; and to put it in the power of a single State to make him a citizen of the United States, and endue him with the full rights of citizenship in every other State without their consent. Does the Constitution of the United States act upon him whenever he shall be made free under the laws of a State, and raised there to the rank of a citizen, and immediately clothe him with all the privileges of a citizen in every other State, and in its own courts?

The court think the affirmative of these propositions cannot be maintained. And if it cannot, the plaintiff in error could not be a citizen of the State of Missouri, within the meaning of the Constitution of the United States, and, consequently, was not entitled to sue in its courts. . . .

It is difficult at this day to realize the state of public opinion in relation to that unfortunate race, which prevailed in the civilized and enlightened portions of the world at the time of the Declaration of Independence, and when the Constitution of the United States was framed and adopted. . . .

They had for more than a century before been regarded as beings of an inferior order; and altogether unfit to associate with the white race, either in social or political relations; and so far inferior that they had no rights which the white man was bound to respect; and that the negro might justly and lawfully be reduced to slavery for his benefit. . . . This opinion was at that time fixed and universal in the civilized portion of the white race. It was regarded as an axiom in morals as well as in politics, which no one thought of disputing, or supposed to be open to dispute; and men in every grade and position in society daily and habitually acted upon it in their private pursuits, as well as in matters of public concern, without doubting for a moment the correctness of this opinion . . .

But there are two clauses in the Constitution which point directly and specifically to the negro race as a separate class of persons, and show clearly that they were not regarded as a portion of the people or citizens of the Government then formed.

One of these clauses reserves to each of the thirteen States the right to import slaves until the year 1808, if he thinks it proper. And the importation which it thus sanctions was unquestionably of persons of the race of which we are speaking, as the traffic in slaves in the United States had always been confined to them. And by the other provision the States pledge themselves to each other to maintain the right of property of the master, by delivering up to him any slave who may have escaped from his service, and be found within their respective territories. . . . And these two provisions show, conclusively, that neither the description of persons therein referred to, not their descendants, were embraced in any of the other provisions of the Constitution; for certainly these two clauses were not intended to confer on them or their posterity the blessings of liberty, or any of the personal rights so carefully provided for the citizen. . . .

The Act of Congress, upon which the plaintiff relies, declares that slavery and involuntary servitude, except as a punishment for crime, shall be forever prohibited in all that part of the territory ceded by France, under the name of Louisiana, which lies north of thirty-six degrees thirty minutes north latitude, and not included within the limits of Missouri. And the difficulty which meets us at the threshold of this part of the inquiry is, whether Congress was authorized to pass this law under any of the powers granted to it by the Constitution; for if the authority is not given by that instrument, it is the duty of this court to declare it void and inoperative, and incapable of conferring freedom upon any one who is held as a slave under the laws of any one of the States.

The counsel for the plaintiff has laid much stress upon that article in the Constitution which confers on Congress the power "to dispose of and make all needful rules and regulations respecting the territory or other property belonging to the United States," but, in the judgment of the court, that provision has no bearing on the present controversy, and the power there given, whatever it may be, is confined, and was intended to be confined, to the territory which at that time belonged to, or was claimed by, the United States. . . .

If this clause is construed to extend to territory acquired by the present Government from a foreign nation, outside of the limits of any charter from the British Government to a colony, it would be difficult to say, why it was deemed necessary to give the Government the power to sell any vacant lands belonging to the sovereignty which might be found within it; and if this was necessary, why the grant of this power should precede the power to legislate over it and establish a Government there; and still more difficult to say, why it was deemed necessary so specially and particularly to grant the power to make needful rules and regulations in relation to any personal or movable property it might acquire there. For the words, *other property* necessarily, by every known rule of interpretation, must mean property of a different description from territory or land. And the difficulty would perhaps be insurmountable in endeavoring to account for the last member of the sentence, which provides that "nothing in this Constitution shall be so construed as to prejudice any claims of the United States or any particular State," or to say how any particular State could have claims in or to a territory ceded by a foreign Government, or to account for associating this provision with the preceding provisions of the clause, with which it would appear to have no connection. . . .

But the power of Congress over the person or property of a citizen can never be a mere discretionary power under our Constitution and form of Government. The powers of the Government and the rights and privileges of the Citizen are regulated and plainly defined by the Constitution itself. And when the Territory becomes a part of the United States, the Federal Government enters into possession in the character impressed upon it by those who created it. It enters upon it with its powers over the citizen strictly defined, and limited by the Constitution, from which it derives its own existence, and by virtue of which alone it continues to exist and act as a Government and sovereignty. It has no power of any kind beyond it; and it cannot, when it enters a Territory of the United States, put off its character, and assume discretionary or despotic powers which the Constitution has denied to it. It cannot create for itself a new character separated from the citizens of the United States, and the duties it owes them under the provisions of the Constitution. The Territory being a part of the United States, the Government and the citizen both enter it under the authority of the Constitution, with their respective rights defined and marked out; and the Federal Government can exercise no power over his person or property, beyond what that instrument confers, nor lawfully deny any right which it has reserved. . . .

The rights of private property have been guarded with equal care. Thus the rights of property are united with the rights of person, and placed on the same ground by the fifth amendment to the Constitution. . . . An Act of Congress which deprives a person of the United States of his liberty or property merely because he came himself or brought his property into a particular Territory of the United States, and who had committed no offense against the laws, could hardly be dignified with the name of due process of law. . . .

And this prohibition is not confined to the States, but the words are general, and extend to the whole territory over which the Constitution gives it power to legislate, including those portions of it remaining under territorial government, as well as that covered by States. . . .

It seems, however, to be supposed, that there is a difference between property in a slave and other property, and that different rules may be applied to it in expounding the Constitution of the United States. And the laws and usages of nations, and the writings of eminent jurists upon the relation of master and slave and their mutual rights and duties, and the powers which governments may exercise over it, have been dwelt upon in the argument.

But . . . if the Constitution recognizes the right of property of the master in a slave, and makes no distinction between that description of property and other property owned by a citizen, no tribunal, acting under the authority of the United States, whether it be legislative, executive, or judicial, has a right to draw such a distinction, or deny to it the benefit of the provisions and guarantees which have been provided for the protection of private property against the enroachments of the Government.

Now . . . the right of property in a slave is distinctly and expressly affirmed in the Constitution. The right to traffic in it, like an ordinary article of merchandise and property, was guaranteed to the citizens of the United States, in every State that might desire it, for twenty years. And the Government in express terms is pledged to protect it in all future time, if the slave escapes from his owner. . . . And no word can be found in the Constitution which gives Congress a greater power over slave property, or which entitles property of that kind to less protection than property of any other description. The only power conferred is the power coupled with the duty of guarding and protecting the owner in his rights.

Upon these considerations, it is the opinion of the court that the Act of Congress which prohibited a citizen from holding and owning property of this kind in the territory of the United States north of the line therein mentioned, is not warranted by the Constitution, and is therefore void; and that neither Dred Scott himself, nor any of his family, were made free by being carried into this territory; even if they had been carried there by the owner, with the intention of becoming a permanent resident.

4.11 Justifying Slavery

It is difficult to accept today that thousands of white Americans before the Civil War vigorously defended slavery, even to the death. That defense went through various stages. Early on, the planter class argued that black bondage was a necessary evil; later they justified it as a positive good. Biblical and historical justifications were offered. The main problem was squaring slavery with democracy and personal liberty. Some apologists searched for comparisons between the United States and ancient Greece, where slavery existed alongside democracy. Others provided constitutional arguments. Or they sought "scientific" proofs that blacks were destined, by reason of inferior mental and physical traits, to serve whites. In the background, was a practical consideration, namely that slave labor produced profits for white planters. In general apologists tried to say that bondage benefitted both *whites and blacks.*

In the tense days preceding the Civil War (in the year of the Dred Scott decision) George Fitzhugh of Virginia wrote a "sociological" defense of slavery entitled Cannibals All! *In it he remarks on the good things that masters do for slaves. He attacks the northern wage system while defending black slavery—a favorite motif of apologists.*

Questions

According to Fitzhugh, who are the "cannibals?" Why does he think slavery is better than the wage system? How does Fitzhugh reconcile democracy and slavery?

What is his concept of "sociology," and how does it compare to the one commonly used today?

What racial beliefs and stereotypes does Fitzhugh employ here? How do they compare with stereotypes regarding Native Americans (Document 4.3, above) and other minorities?

The Universal Trade. We are, all, North and South, engaged in the White Slave Trade, and he who succeeds best, is esteemed most respectable. It is far more cruel than the Black Slave Trade, because it exacts more of its slaves, and neither protects nor governs them. We boast, that it exacts more, when we say, "that the *profits* made from employing free labor are greater than those from slave labor." The profits made from free labor, are the amount of the products of such labor, which the employer, by means of the command which capital or skill gives him, takes away, exacts or "exploitates" from the free laborer. The profits of slave labor are that portion of the products of such labor which the power of the matter enables him to appropriate. These profits are less, because the master allows the slave to retain a larger share of the results of his own labor, than do the employers of free labor. But we not only boast that the White Slave Trade is more exacting and fraudulent (in fact, though not intention,) than Black Slavery; but we also boast, that it is more cruel, in leaving the laborer to take care of himself and family out of the pittance which skill or capital have allowed him to retain. When the day's labor is ended, he is free, but is overburdened with the cares of family and household, which makes his freedom an empty and delusive mockery. But his employer is really free, and may enjoy the profits made by others' labor, without a care, or a trouble, as to their well-being. The negro slave is free, too, when the labors of the day are over, and free in mind as well as body; for the master provides food, raiment, house, fuel, and everything else necessary to the physical well-being of himself and family. . . .

Now, reader, if you wish to know yourself—to "descent on your own deformity"—read on. But if you would cherish self-conceit, self-esteem, or self-appreciation, throw down our book; for we will dispel illusions which have promoted your happiness, and shew you that what you have considered and practiced as virtue, is little better than moral Cannibalism. . . . Throwing the negro slaves out of the account, and society is divided in Christendom into four classes: The rich, or independent respectable people, who live well and labor not at all; the professional and skillful respectable people, who do a little light work, for enormous wages; the poor hard-working people, who support every body, and starve themselves; and the poor thieves, swindlers and sturdy beggars, who live like gentlemen, without labor, on the labor of other people. The gentlemen exploitate, which being done on a large scale, and requiring a great many victims, is highly respectable—whilst the rogues and beggars take so little from others, that they fare little better than those who labor. . . .

SOURCE: George Fitzhugh, *Cannibals All! or Slaves Without Masters* (Richmond, 1857), 25–32.

Probably, you are a lawyer, or a merchant, or a doctor, who have made by your business fifty thousand dollars, and retired to live on your capital. But, mark! not to spend your capital. That would be vulgar, disreputable, criminal. That would be, to live by your own labor; for your capital is your amassed labor. That would be, to do as common working men do; for they take the pittance which their employers leave them, to live on. They live by labor; for they exchange the results of their own labor for the products of other people's labor. It is, no doubt, an honest, vulgar way of living; but not at all a respectable way. The respectable way of living is, to make other people work for you, and to pay them nothing for so doing—and to have no concern about them after their work is done. Hence, white slave-holding is much more respectable than negro slavery—for the master works nearly as hard for the negro, as he for the master. But you, my virtuous, respectable reader, exact three thousand dollars per annum from white labor, (for your income is the product of white labor,) and make not one cent of return in any form. You retain your capital, and never labor, and yet live in luxury on the labor of others. Capital commands labor, as the master does the slave. Neither pays for labor; but the master permits the slave to retain a larger allowance from the proceeds of his own labor, and hence "free labor is cheaper than slave labor." You, with the command over labor which your capital gives you, are a slave owner—a master, without the obligations of a master. They who work for you, who create your income, are slaves, without the rights of slaves. Slaves without a master! whilst you were engaged in amassing your capital, in seeking to become independent, you were in the White Slave Trade. . . . The men without property, in free society, are theoretically in a worse condition than slaves. Practically, their condition corresponds with this theory, as history and statistics every where demonstrate. The capitalists, in free society, live in ten times the luxury and show that Southern masters do, because the slaves to capital work harder and cost less, than negro slaves.

The negro slaves of the South are the happiest, and, in some sense, the freest people in the world. The children and the aged and infirm work not at all, and yet have all the comforts and necessaries of life provided for them. They enjoy liberty, because they are oppressed neither by care nor labor. The women do little hard work, and are protected from the despotism of their husbands by their masters. The negro men and stout boys work, on the average, in good weather, not more than nine hours a day. The balance of their time is spent in perfect abandon. Besides, they have their Sabbaths and holidays. White men, with so much of license and liberty, would die of ennui; but negros luxuriate in corporeal and mental repose. With their faces upturned to the sun, they can sleep at any hour; and quiet sleep is the greatest of human enjoyments. "Blessed be the man who invented sleep." 'Tis happiness in itself—and results from contentment with the present, and confident assurance of the future. We do not know whether free laborers ever sleep. They are fools to do so; for, whilst they sleep, the wily and watchful capitalist is devising means to ensnare and exploitate them. The free laborer must work or starve. He is more of a slave than the negro, because he works longer and harder for less allowance than the slave, and has no holiday, because the cares of life with him begin when its labors end. He has no liberty, and not a single right. . . .

Free laborers have not a thousandth part of the rights and liberties of negro slaves. Indeed, they have not a single right or a single liberty, unless it be the right or liberty to die. But the reader may think that he and other capitalists and employers are freer than negro slaves. Your capital would soon vanish, if you dared indulge in the liberty and abandon of negroes. You hold your wealth and position by tenure of constant watchfulness, care and circumspection. You never labor; but you are never free.

Where a few own the soil, they have unlimited power over the balance of society, until domestic slavery comes in, to compel them to permit this balance of society to draw a sufficient and comfortable living from "terra mater." Free society, asserts the right of a few to the earth—slavery, maintains that it belongs, in different degrees, to all.

But, reader, well may you follow the slave trade. It is the only trade worth following, and slaves are the only property worth owning. All other is worthless, a mere *caput mortuum,* except in so far as it vests the owner with the power to command the labors of others—to enslave them. Give you a palace, ten thousand acres of land, sumptuous clothes, equipage and every other luxury; and with your artificial wants, you are poorer than Robinson Crusoe, or the lowest working man, if you have no slaves to capital, or domestic slaves. Your capital will not bring you an income of a cent, nor supply one of your wants, without labor. Labor is indispensable to give value to property, and if you owned every thing else, and did not own labor, you would be poor. . . .

"Property in man" is what all are struggling to obtain. Why should they not be obliged to take care of man, their property, as they do of their horses and their hounds, their cattle and their sheep. Now, under the delusive name of liberty, you work him "from morn to dewy eve"—from infancy to old age—then turn him out to starve. You treat your horses and hounds better. Capital is a cruel master. The free slave trade, the commonest, yet the cruellest of trades.

4.12 Lincoln as Emancipator

If Abraham Lincoln's signature on the Emancipation Proclamation appears wobbly, it is not because he was unsure of himself, as has been charged, but because he had been shaking hands with well-wishers all day. And yet, as one examines his stance on blacks and on slavery it is at worst ambiguous, and at best gradually evolving. This is certainly true from 1858 to 1862.

In 1858, while running for the U.S. Senate in Illinois, Lincoln engaged the incumbent Sen. Stephen Douglas in a series of debates. Brief excerpts from the debates of June through October appear below. Lincoln was born into a pioneer farm family in Kentucky in 1809, but was raised in Indiana and Illinois. He was self educated, achieved success as an attorney, and served in the Illinois legislature and the U.S. Congress. He lost the senatorial election bid, but the campaign gained him national attention for his run for the presidency two years later.

As wartime President, Lincoln issued the Emancipation Proclamation in 1862—to take effect the following January (excerpted below). He had hoped to do so earlier but was leery of alienating those border states that remained in the Union. He saw in it the possibility of encouraging blacks to bolt their masters. The Proclamation was also popular abroad, and prevented Britain and France from supporting the Confederacy. Lincoln timed its release to occur after a Union victory at Antietam, so as to strengthen its impact. He hoped it would undermine more radical abolitionist measures being considered in Congress. He deliberately meant for it to have only limited impact.

Slavery was finally and officially ended not by presidential decree, but by passage of the Thirteenth Amendment. This revolutionary proposal was introduced into Congress in 1863 with Lincoln's active support, and became law in 1865.

Lincoln's detractors see in him a tendency toward weak and vacillating views on slavery: an overt belief in white supremacy, an unwillingness to flatly defend black rights, a cautiousness about confronting the institution of slavery in the South, a flirtation with such impractical ideas as deporting slaves to some unnamed country. They remark that he backed into the Emancipation Proclamation, timing it carefully so that it would sound better than it really was. And yet, he clearly opposed slavery, and there was something significant about his wartime leadership, his pragmatic handling of the issues, and his vigorous support, finally, of the Thirteenth Amendment.

Questions

What conditions prevailed in the country in 1858 as Lincoln debated Doublas? Describe his views on the extension of slavery into the territories; on ending slavery where it already existed; on the future of the Union; on the social equality or inequality of whites and blacks under slavery; on the political rights of blacks during and after slavery; and on the preservation of the Union.

What had changed by 1862? What were his views on the border states and the states of the Confederacy?

In the end, how justified is Lincoln's reputation as the Great Emancipator? Did he intend to liberate the blacks, or was he thrust in the role of emancipator unwillingly or accidentally? Did he hold any consistent views on these issues over time, or did his views shift or evolve from one position to another, depending on practical considerations? Can he be forgiven for wavering? Explain.

At Springfield, Illinois, June 16, 1858—

We are now far into the fifth year since a policy was initiated with the avowed object and confident promise of putting an end to slavery agitation. Under the operation of that policy, that agitation has not only not ceased, but has constantly augmented. In my opinion, it will not cease until a crisis shall have been reached and passed. "A house divided against itself cannot stand." I believe this government cannot endure permanently half slave and half free. I do not expect the Union to be dissolved—I do not expect the house to fall—but I do expect it will cease to be divided. It will become all one thing, or all the other. Either the opponents of slavery will arrest the further spread of it, and place it where the public mind shall rest in the belief that it is in the course of ultimate extinction; or its advocates will push it forward till it shall become alike lawful in all the States, old as well as new, North as well as South.

At Chicago, Illinois, July 10, 1858—

I protest, now and forever, against that counterfeit logic which presumes that because I do not want a negro woman for a slave, I do necessarily want her for a wife. My understanding is that I need not have her for either; but, as God made us separate, we can leave one another alone, and do one another much good thereby. There are white men enough to marry all the white women, and enough black men to marry all the black women, and in God's name let them be so married.

At Springfield, Illinois, July 17, 1858—

My declaration upon this subject of negro slavery may be misrepresented, but cannot be misunderstood. I have said that I do not understand the Declaration [of Independence] to mean that all men were created equal in all respects. They are not our equal in color; but I suppose that it does mean to declare that all men are equal in some respects; they are equal in their right to "life, liberty, and the pursuit of happiness." Certainly the negro is not our equal in color—perhaps not in many other respects; still, in the right to put into his mouth the bread that his own hands have earned, he is the equal of every other man, white or black. In pointing out that more has been given you, you cannot be justified in taking away the little which has been given him. All I ask for the negro is that if you do not like him, let him alone. If God gave him but little, that little let him enjoy.

At Ottawa, Illinois, August 21, 1858—

I have no purpose to introduce political and social equality between the white and the black races. There is a physical difference between the two, which, in my judgment will probably forever forbid their living together upon the footing of perfect equality; and inasmuch as it becomes a necessity that there must be a difference, I, as well as Judge Douglas, am in favor of the race to which I belong having the superior position. I have never said anything to the contrary, but I hold that, notwithstanding all this, there is no reason in the world why

SOURCES: John Nicolay and John Hay, eds., *Complete Works of Abraham Lincoln* (12 vols., Lincoln Memorial University, n.p., 1894), VII, 161-164; *The Speeches of Abraham Lincoln* (New York, 1908), pp. 52-53, 72, 91-92, 94-95, 151-52, 163, 185-86, 200, 204.

the negro is not entitled to all the natural rights enumerated in the Declaration of Independence—the right to life, liberty, and the pursuit of happiness. I hold that he is as much entitled to these as the white man. I agree with Judge Douglas he is not my equal in many respects—certainly not in color, perhaps not in moral or intellectual endowment. But in the right to eat the bread, without the leave of anybody else, which his own hand earns, he is my equal and the equal of Judge Douglas, and the equal of every living man.

At Charleston, Illinois, September 18, 1858—

Judge Douglas has said to you that he has not been able to get from me an answer to the question whether I am in favor of negro citizenship. So far as I know, the judge never asked me the question before. He shall have no occasion to ever ask it again, for I tell him very frankly that I am not in favor of negro citizenship. . . . My opinion is that the different States have the power to make a negro citizen under the Constitution of the United States, if they choose. The Dred Scott decision decides that they have not that power. If the State of Illinois had that power, I should be opposed to the exercise of it. That is all I have to say about it.

At Galesburg, Illinois, October 7, 1858—

The judge has alluded to the Declaration of Independence, and insisted that negroes are not included in that Declaration; and that it is a slander upon the framers of that instrument to suppose that negroes are meant therein; and he asks you: Is it possible to believe that Mr. Jefferson, who penned the immortal paper, could have supposed himself applying the language of that instrument to the negro race, and yet held a portion of that race in slavery? Would he not at once have freed them? I only have to remark upon this part of the judge's speech, . . . that I believe the entire records of the world, from the date of the Declaration of Independence up to within three years ago, may be searched in vain for one single affirmation, from one single man, that the negro was not included in the Declaration of Independence; . . . I will remind Judge Douglas and his audience that while Mr. Jefferson was the owner of slaves, as undoubtedly he was, in speaking upon this very subject, be used the strong language that "he trembled for his country when he remembered that God was just."

At Quincy, Illinois, October 13, 1858—

I suggest that the difference of opinion, reduced to its lowest terms, is no other than the difference between the men who think slavery is a wrong and those who do not think it wrong. The Republican party think it wrong—we think it is a moral, a social, and a political wrong. We think it is a wrong not confining itself merely to the persons or the States where it exists, but that it is a wrong which in its tendency, to say the least, affects the existence of the whole nation.

Emancipation Proclamation—

Whereas on the 22d day of September, A.D. 1862, a proclamation was issued by the President of the United States, containing among other things, the following, to wit:

"That on the 1st day of January, A.D. 1863, all persons held as slaves within any State or designated part of a State the people whereof shall then be in rebellion against the United States shall be then, thenceforward, and forever free; and the executive government of the United States, including the military and naval authority thereof, will recognize and maintain the freedom of such persons and will do no act or acts to repress such persons, or any of them, in any efforts they may make for their actual freedom.

"That the executive will on the 1st day of January aforesaid, by proclamation, designate the States and parts of States, if any, in which the people thereof, respectively, shall then be in rebellion against the United States; and the fact that any State or the people thereof shall on that day be in good faith represented in Congress of the United States by members chosen thereto at elections wherein a majority of the qualified voters of such States shall have participated shall, in the absence of strong countervailing testimony, be deemed conclusive evidence that such State and the people thereof are not then in rebellion against the United States."

Now, therefore, I, Abraham Lincoln, President of the United States, by virtue of the power in me vested as Commander-in-Chief of the Army and Navy of the United States in time of actual armed rebellion against the authority and government of the United States, and as a fit and necessary war measure for suppressing said rebellion, do, on this 1st day of January, A.D. 1863, and in accordance with my purpose so to do, publicly proclaimed for the full period of one hundred days from the first day above mentioned, order and designate as the States and parts of States wherein the people therof, respectively, are this day in rebellion against the United States the following, to wit:

Arkansas, Texas, Louisiana (except the parishes of St. Bernard, Plaquemines, Jefferson, St. John, St. Charles, St. James, Ascension, Assumption, Terrebonne, Lafourche, St. Mary, St. Martin, and Orleans, including the city of New Orleans), Mississippi, Alabama, Florida, Georgia, South Carolina, North Carolina, and Virginia (except the forty-eight counties designated as West Virginia, and also the counties of Berkeley, Accomac, Northhampton, Elizabeth City, York, Princess Anne, and Norfolk, including the cities of Norfolk and Portsmouth), and which excepted parts are for the present left precisely as if this proclamation were not issued.

And by virtue of the power and for the purpose aforesaid, I do order and declare that all persons held as slaves within said designed States and parts of States are, and henceforward shall be, free; and that the Executive Government of the United States, including the military and naval authorities thereof, will recognize and maintain the freedom of said persons.

And I hereby enjoin upon the people so declared to be free to abstain from all violence, unless in necessary self-defense; and I recommend to them that, in all cases when allowed, they labor faithfully for reasonable wages.

And I further declare and make known that such persons of suitable condition will be received into the armed service of the United States to garrison forts, positions, stations, and other places, and to man vessels of all sorts in said service.

And upon this act, sincerely believed to be an act of justice, warranted by the Constitution upon military necessity, I invoke the considerate judgment of mankind and the gracious favor of Almighty God.

4.13 White Supremacy

The Civil War and Reconstruction did little to alter white perceptions of blacks in the North or South. If anything, white racial views were even more negative than before. In the mid-1870s Reconstruction was winding down. Yankee troops still occupied the South, blacks still had an active, though declining, role in governmental affairs, and the Republican party still had a dominant position in politics. White supremacists, having used terror and intimidation to alter conditions, were now beginning to mobilize politically, as well. In 1874 and 1875 they were particularly outraged at a Radical Reconstruction civil rights bill pending in Congress. The resolution and the newspaper items shown below originated in Mississippi, Georgia, and Alabama in those years. They reveal the sense of rage—as well as the racial perceptions.

Questions

What racial attitudes are reflected in these newspaper items? What do the whites seem to want of the blacks? Who are their current villains and heroes? How do the whites justify violence?

Alabama Democrat Resolution, 1874—

Resolved, That we, the people . . . for the protection of our dearest and most sacred interests, our homes, our honor, the purity and integrity of our race, and to conserve the peace and tranquility of the country, accept the issue of race thus defiantly tendered and forced upon us, notwithstanding our determination and repeated efforts to avoid it; and further

Resolved, That nothing is left to the white man's party but social ostracism of all those who act, sympathize or side with the negro party, or who support or advocate the odious, unjust, and unreasonable measure known as the civil rights bill; and that from henceforth we will hold all such persons as enemies of our race, and we will not in the future have intercourse with them in any of the social relations of life.

SOURCE: W. L. Fleming, ed., *Documentary History of Reconstruction* (Cleveland: Arthur H. Clark Co., 1906), II, 387–88, 394–95.

Georgia Editorial, 1874—

Let there be White Leagues formed in every town, village and hamlet of the South, and let us organize for the great struggle which seems inevitable. The radicalism of the republican party must be met by the radicalism of white men. We have no war to make against the United States Government, but against the republican party our hate must be unquenchable, our war interminable and merciless. Fast fleeting away is the day of wordy protests and idle appeals to the magnanimity of the republican party. By brute force they are endeavoring to force us into acquiescence to their hideous programme. We have submitted long enough to indignities, and it is time to meet brute-force with brute-force . . . . It will not do to wait till radicialism has fettered us to the car of social equality before we make an effort to resist it. The signing of the [Civil Rights] bill will be a declaration of war against the southern whites. It is our duty to ourselves, it is our duty to our children, it is our duty to the white race whose prowess subdued the wilderness of this continent, whose civilization filled it with cities and towns and villages, whose mind gave it power and grandeur, and whose labor imparted to it prosperity, and whose love made peace and happiness dwell within its home, to take the gage of battle the moment it is thrown down. If the white democrats of the North are men, they will not stand idly by and see us borne down by northern radicals and half-barbarous negroes. But no matter what they may do, it is time for us to organize. We have been temporizing long enough. Let northern radicals understand that military supervision of southern elections and the civil-rights bill mean war, that war means bloodshed, and that we are terribly in earnest, and even they, fanatical as they are, may retrace their steps before it is too late.

Mississippi Editorial, 1875—

. . . [T]he present campaign . . . is, so far as the white people and land-owners are concerned, a battle for the control of their own domestic affairs; a struggle to regain a mastery that has been ruthlessly torn from them by selfish white schemers and adventurers, through the instrumentality of an ignorant horde of another race which has been as putty in their hands, molded to our detriment and ruin.

The present contest is rather a revolution than a political campaign—it is the rebellion, if you see fit to apply that term, of a down-trodden people against an absolutism imposed by their own hirelings, and by the grace of God we will cast it off next November, or cast off the willfully and maliciously ignorant tools who eat our bread, live in our houses, attend the schools that we support, come to us for aid and succor in their hour of need, and yet are deaf to our appeals when we entreat them to assist us in throwing off a galling yoke that has been borne until further endurance is but the basest of cowardice. . . .

We favor a continuance of the canvass upon the broad and liberal basis that has heretofore characterized it, that is, we favor appealing to the negro by everything good and holy to forsake his idols and unite with us in ridding the State of a way that we despise; but at the same time that we extend the olive-branch and plead for alliance and amity, we should not hesitate to use the great and all-powerful weapon that is in our control; we should not falter in the pledge to ourselves and our neighbors to discharge from our employ and our friendship forever, every laborer who persists in the diabolical war that has been waged against the white man and his interests ever since the negro has been a voter.

Chapter Five: Nationality and Religion

5.1 No Toleration of Evil

A stubborn streak of intolerance ran through the Puritan mind. It was directed against other religious sects, people who adopted "heretical" beliefs and those who succumbed to sins of the flesh. This tendency to come down hard against "wickedness" is exemplified and justified in a sermon by Nathaniel Ward in 1647 in his book, The Simple Cobbler of Aggawam. *Ward was a Cambridge educated lawyer and preacher, an Anglican by upbringing. He was excluded from that church because of his Puritanism and went to New England to serve as minister of Ipswich, Massachusetts (whose Indian name was Aggawam) from 1634 to 1648. Afterward he returned to England.*

Questions

If the Puritans did not seek religious liberty, what did they want? What are Ward's justifications for intolerance? Are they Biblical, theological or political? What sort of population and community life would he need to enforce such views?

Do similar sentiments still motivate religious leaders in this country?

I dare aver that God does nowhere in His word tolerate Christian states to give toleration to such adversaries of His truth, if they have power in their hands to suppress them. . . .

If the devil might have his free option, I believe he would ask nothing else but liberty to enfranchise all false religions and to embondage the truth; nor should he need. It is much to be feared that lax tolerations upon state pretenses and planting necessities will be the next subtle stratagem he will spread to dista[s]te the truth of God and supplant the peace of the churches. Tolerations in things tolerable, exquisitely drawn out by the lines of the scripture and pencil of the spirit, are the sacred favors of truth, the due latitudes of love, the fair compartiments of Christian fraternity; but irregular dispensations, dealt forth by the facilities of men, are the frontiers of error, the redoubts of schism, the perilous irritaments of carnal and spiritual enmity.

My heart has naturally detested four things: the standing of the Apocrypha in the Bible; foreigners dwelling in my country to crowd out native subjects into the corners of the earth; alchemized coins; tolerations of divers religions, or of one religion in segregant shapes. He that willingly assents to the last, if he examines his heart by daylight, his conscience will tell

SOURCE: Nathaniel Ward, *The Simple Cobbler of Aggawam in America* (Boston: James Munroe & Co., 1843), 1–11, 13, 21–23, 52–55, 78–79.

him he is either an atheist or a heretic or a hypocrite, or at best a captive to some lust. Poly-piety is the greatest impiety in the world. True religion is *ignis probationis* ["fire of proof"], which doth *congregare homogenea & segregare heterogenea* ["unite the homogeneous and separate the heterogeneous"]. . . . but God? The power of all religion and ordinances lies in their purity, their purity in their simplicity; then are mixtures pernicious. I lived in a city where a Papist preached in one church, a Lutheran in another, a Calvinist in a third; a Lutheran one part of the day, a Calvinist the other, in the same pulpit. The religion of that place was but motley and meager, their affections leopard-like. . . .

That state is wise that will improve all pains and patience rather to compose than tolerate differences in religion. There is no divine truth but hath much celestial fire in it from the spirit of truth, nor no irreligious untruth without its proportion of antifire from the spirit of error to contradict it: the zeal of the one, the virulency of the other, must necessarily kindle combustions. Fiery diseases seated in the spirit embroil the whole frame of the body; others more external and cool are less dangerous. They which divide in religion, divide in God; they who divide in Him, divide beyond *genus generalissimum* ["the most general genus"], where there is no reconciliation without atonement: that is, without uniting in Him who is one, and in His truth which is also one. . . .

Concerning tolerations I may further assert:

That persecution of true religion and toleration of false are the *Jannes* and *Jambres* to the kingdom of Christ, whereof the last is far the worst. Augustine's tongue had not owed his mouth one pennyrent though it had never spake word more in it but this; *Nullum malum pejus libertate errandi* ["No evil is worse than liberty for the erring"].

He that is willing to tolerate any religion or discrepant way of religion besides his own, unless it be in matters merely indifferent, either doubts of his own or is not sincere in it.

He that is willing to tolerate any unsound opinion, that his own may also be tolerated, though never so sound, will for a need hang God's Bible at the devil's girdle.

Every toleration of false religions or opinions hath as many errors and sins in it as all the false religions and opinions it tolerates; and one sound, one more.

That state that will give liberty of conscience in matters of religion must give liberty of conscience and conversation in their moral laws, or else the fiddle will be out of tune and some of the strings crack.

He that will rather make an irreligious quarrel with other religions than try the truth of his own valuable arguments and peaceable sufferings, either his religion or himself is irreligious.

Experience will teach churches and Christians that it is far better to live in a state united, though somewhat corrupt, than in a state whereof some part is incorrupt and all the rest divided.

I am not altogether ignorant of the eight rules given by orthodox divines about giving tolerations, yet with their favor I dare affirm:

That there is no rule given by God for any state to give an affirmative toleration to any false religion or opinion whatsoever; they must connive in some cases, but may not concede in any.

That the state of England (so far as my intelligence serves) might in time have prevented with ease, and may yet without any great difficulty deny both toleration, and connivances *salva Republica* ["without violation of the state"].

That if the state of England shall either willingly tolerate or weakly connive at such courses, the church of that kingdom will sooner become the devil's dancing-school than God's temple, the civil state a bear-garden than an exchange, the whole realm a *pays bas* than an England. And what pity it is that the country which hath been the staple of truth to all Christendom should now become the aviary of errors to the whole world, let every fearing heart judge. . . .

I take liberty of conscience to be nothing but a freedom from sin and error. . . . And liberty of error nothing but a prison for conscience. Then small will be the kindness of a state to build such prisons for their subjects.

The scripture says there is nothing makes free but Truth. And Truth says there is no Truth but one: If the states of the world would make it their sumoperous care to preserve this one Truth in its purity and authority it would ease them of all other political cares. I am sure Satan makes it his grand, if not only task, to adulterate Truth; falsehood is his sole scepter whereby he first ruffled, and ever since ruined the world. . . .

Let all considerate men beware of ungrounded opinions in religion. Since I knew what to fear, my timorous heart has dreaded three things: a blazing star appearing in the air; a state comet, I mean a favorite rising in a kingdom; a new opinion spreading in religion. These are exorbitancies, which is a formidable word. A vacuum and an exorbitancy are mundicidious evils. Concerning novelties of opinions, I shall express my thoughts in these brief passages: First that truth is the best boon God ever gave the world; there is nothing in the world any further than truth makes it so; it is better than any created *Ens* or *Bonum*, which are but truth's twins. Secondly, the least truth of God's kingdom doth in its place uphold the whole kingdom of His Truths; take away the least *vericulum* ["javelin"] out of the world, and it unworlds all potentially, and may unravel the whole texture actually, if it be not conserved by an arm of extraordinary power. Thirdly, the least evangelical truth is more worth than all the civil truths in the world, that are merely so. Fourthly, that truth is the parent of all liberty, whether political or personal: so much untruth, so much thralldom (John 8. 32).

Hence it is that God is so jealous of His truths, that He hath taken order in His due justice: First, that no practical sin is so sinful as some error in judgment; no men so accursed with indelible infamy and dedolent impenitency as authors of heresy. Secondly, that the least error, if grown sturdy and pressed, shall set open the spittle-door of all the squint-eyed, wry-necked, and brazen-faced errors that are or ever were of that litter; if they be not enough to serve its turn, it will beget more, though it hath not one crust of reason to maintain them. Thirdly, that that state which will permit errors in religion shall admit errors in policy unavoidably. Fourthly, that that policy which will suffer irreligious errors shall suffer the loss of so much liberty in one kind or other: I will not exempt Venice, Rhaguse, the Netherlands, or any. . . .

A Word of Ireland (Not of the nation universally, nor of any man in it that has so much as one hair of Christianity or humanity growing on his head or beard, but only of the truculent cut-throats, and such as shall take up arms in their defense.)

These *Irish* anciently called *Antropophagi* (man-eaters) have a tradition among them:

That when the devil showed our Savior all the kingdoms of the earth and their glory, he would not show him Ireland, but reserved it for himself. It is probably true, for he has kept it ever since for his own peculiar. The old fox foresaw it would eclipse the glory of all the rest. He thought it wisdom to keep the land for a Boggards for his unclean spirits employed in this hemisphere, and the people, to do his son and heir, I mean the Pope, that service for which Louis XI kept his barber Oliver, which makes them so blood-thirsty. They are the very offal of men, dregs of mankind, reproach of Christendom, the bots that crawl on the beast's tail. I wonder Rome itself is not ashamed of them.

I beg upon my hands and knees that the expedition against them may be undertaken while the hearts and hands of our soldiery are hot, to whom I will be bold to say briefly: Happy is he that shall reward them as they have served us, and cursed be he that shall do that work of the Lord negligently. Cursed be he that holds back his sword from blood. Yea, cursed be he that makes not his sword stark drunk with Irish blood, that does not recompense them double for their hellish treachery to the English, that makes them not heaps upon heaps, and their country a dwelling place for dragons, an astonishment to nations. Let not that eye look for pity, nor that hand to be spared, that pities or spares them; and let him be accursed that curses them not bitterly.

5.2 Full Liberty of Conscience

If Puritanism produced a hard-nosed Nathaniel Ward, it also brought forth a Roger Williams. He too was Cambridge educated and had studied law and the ministry. He believed not only in toleration but complete liberty of conscience and separation of church and state.

Williams had serious differences with the establishment in England and New England. He openly repudiated Anglicanism, defended the Indians' title to their lands, and urged separation of church and state. He was formally banished from Massachusetts, and left to form Providence (later Rhode Island). Cotton Mather likened him to a windmill he had heard about that caught fire in a dangerous storm. "The stone at length by its rapid motion became so intensely hot as to fire the mill, from whence the flames . . . did set a whole town on fire. . . . [He was] a preacher that had less light than fire in him. . . ."

Returning to England in 1643, Williams published a full-blown attack on the principles of the Massachusetts Bay Colony as expounded by John Cotton. It was called Bloudy Tenent of Persecution *and was published in 1644. The preface follows.*

Later Williams returned to the colonies and served several terms as president of the colony of Rhode Island. It became a haven for people of various beliefs, many of them very contentious. The preface is followed by a letter he wrote to the town of Providence in 1655 in response to people who thought that the government should have no authority over its citizens.

Questions

What are Williams's arguments against religious conformity? In addition to toleration, what did he believe in? What were the limits of his beliefs?

Today it is said that toleration rests on indifference in matters of faith. Was this Williams's attitude?

What is his vision of population and community life? Compare his belief system with Ward's. How could Puritanism hope to survive if so many persons of different religions could freely enter New England and pray as they liked?

Preface, 1644–

First, That the blood of so many hundred thousand soules of Protestants and Papists, split in the Wars of present and former Ages, for their respective Consciences, is not required nor accepted by Jesus Christ the Prince of Peace.

Secondly, Pregnant Scripturs and Arguments are throughout the Worke proposed against the Doctrine of persecution for the cause of Conscience.

Thirdly, Satisfactorie Answers are given to Scriptures, and objections produced by Mr. Calvin, Beza, Mr. Cotton, and the Ministers of the New English Churches and others former and later, tending to prove the Doctrine of persecution for cause of Conscience.

Fourthly, The Doctrine of persecution for cause of Conscience, is proved guilty of all the blood of the Soules crying for vengeance under the Altar.

Fifthly, All Civill States with their Officers of justice in their respective constitutions and administrations are proved essentially Civill, and therefore not Judges, Governours or Defendours of the Spirituall or Christian state and Worship.

Sixtly, It is the will and command of God, that (since the comming of his Sonne the Lord Jesus) a permission of the most Paganish, Jewish, Turkish, or Antichristian consciences and worships, bee granted to all men in all Nations and Countries: and they are onely to bee fought against with that Sword which is only (in Soule matters) able to conquer, to wit, the Sword of Gods Spirit, the Word of God.

Seventhly, The state of the Land of Israel, the Kings and people thereof in Peace & War, is proved figurative and ceremoniall, and no patterne nor president for any Kingdome or civill state in the world to follow.

Eightly, God requireth not an uniformity of Religion to be inacted and in-

SOURCES: Samuel L. Caldwell and J. R. Bartlett, eds., *Publications of the Narragansett Club* (Providence, Rhode Island, 1867–1874), III, 3–4, and VI, 278–279; Roger Williams, *The Bloudy Tenent of Persecution* (1644).

forced in any civill state; which inforced uniformity (sooner or later) is the greatest occasion of civill Warre, ravishing of conscience, persecution of Christ Jesus in his servants, and of the hypocrisie and destruction of millions of souls.

Ninthly, in holding an inforced uniformity of Religion in a civill state, wee must necessarily disclaime our desires and hopes of the Jewes conversion to Christ.

Tenthly, An inforced uniformity of Religion throughout a Nation or civill state, confounds the Civill and Religious, denies the principles of Christianity and civility, and that Jesus Christ is come in the Flesh.

Eleventhly, The permission of other consciences and worships then a state professeth, only can (according to God) procure a firme and lasting peace, (good assurance being taken according to the wisedome of the civill state for uniformity of civill obedience from all sorts.)

Twelfthly, lastly, true civility and Christianity may both flourish in a state or Kingdome, notwithstanding the permission of divers and contrary consciences, either of Jew or Gentile.

Letter, 1655—

That ever I should speak or write a title, that tends to such an infinite liberty of conscience, is a mistake, and which I have ever disclaimed and abhorred. To prevent such mistakes, I shall at present only propose this case: There goes many a ship to sea, with many hundred souls in one ship, whose weal and woe is common, and is a true picture of a common-wealth, or a human combination or society. It hath fallen out sometimes, that both papists and protestants, Jews and Turks, may be embarked in one ship; upon which supposal I affirm, that all the liberty of conscience, that ever I pleaded for, turns upon these two hinges—that none of the papists, protestants, Jews, or Turks, be forced to come to the ship's prayers or worship, nor compelled from their own particular prayers or worship, if they practice any, I further add, that I never denied, that notwithstanding this liberty, the commander of this ship ought to command the ship's course, yea, and also command that justice, peace and sobriety, be kept and practiced, both among the seamen and all the passengers. If any of the seamen refuse to perform their services, or passengers to pay their freight; if any refuse to help, in person or purse, towards the common charges or defence; if any refuse to obey the common laws and orders of the ship, concerning their common peace or preservation; if any shall mutiny and rise up against their commanders and officers; if any should preach or write that there ought to be no commanders or officers, because all are equal in Christ, therefore no masters nor officers, no laws nor orders, nor corrections nor punishments;—I say, I never denied, but in such cases, whatever is pretended, the commander or commanders may judge, resist, compel and punish such transgressors, according to their deserts and merits. This if seriously and honestly minded, may, if it so please the Father of lights, let in some light to such as willingly shut not their eyes.

I remain studious of your common peace and liberty.

5.3 Hardships of the Scots-Irish

America prides itself on the role that immigrants have played in its history, but the welcome mat is not always out to them. In the second quarter of the eighteenth century German immigrants from the Palatine area and people of Scottish and Scots-Irish background from northern Ireland landed in the colonies. The Scots-Irish were driven from their homeland by economic stagnation after the end of Queen Anne's War in 1713. Some went inland to settle, while others stayed in the coastal cities of New York, Boston, and Philadelphia where their labor was in demand.

The bunching up of non-English migrants in Boston (pop. 13,000 in 1720) disturbed the English colonists, who were always suspicious of outsiders. The newcomers were Protestants, but poor. Bostonians feared that they might become a drain on the public. The town government drafted restrictive ordinances against them. While these regulations were usually mild enough (as the following selections show), sometimes, as in 1729, the crowd resorted to mob violence. These laws hint at the type of nativist pressures that would become typical in the next century.

Questions

What did the English Bostonians want of the immigrants and how did they propose to control their entry? What skills did the immigrants bring? What clues do you get as to how the poor were treated in those days?

[October 28, 1717] At a meeting of ye Select men. . . . Voted. That the Select men will defray ye charge of Sending [out of the city] Severall persons Strangers who have Obtruded into this Town. [Among these] James Goodwin from Ireland who arrived here wth Capt Douglis ab^{t} a moneth before, was on ye 28th of Septr Last warned to depart.

SOURCE: *Records of Boston Selectmen, 1716 to 1736*, in *A Report of the Record Commissioners of the City of Boston* (Boston: Rockwell and Churchill, 1885), 29, 200, 312–13, 318.

[May 4, 1723] The Inhabitants According to Adjornment being Assembled. . . . Whereas great numbers of Persons have very lately bin Transported from Ireland into this Province, many of which. . . . Are now Resident in this Town whose Circomstances and Condition are not known, Some of which if due care be not taken may become a Town Charge or be otherwise prejuditial to the well fair & Prosperity of the Place. for Remedy whereof Ordered That Every Person now Resident here, that hath within the Space of three years last past bin brought from Ireland, or for the future Shal come from thence hither, Shal come and Enter his name and Occupation with the Town Clerk, and if marryed the number and Age of his Children and Servants. . . .

[September 9, 1730] William fryland & francis Clinton Joyners from Ireland are admitted to Reside and Inhabit within this Town and have Liberty to Exercise their Callings haveing [given] Security to Indemnifie the Town to the Satisfaction of the Select men according to Law.

[August 16, 1736] At a meeting of the Select men . . . Mr. James Wimble Informs, That Capt. Benedict Arnold . . . is just arrived from Cork with Passengers. . . . Accordingly the Master Capt. Arnold was sent for Who appear'd and gave Information, That he came from Ireland about Twelve Weeks ago, and that he is Bound to Philadelphia with his Passengers, Who in all, are one Hundred and Twenty, Hopes to Sail in a few days, as soon as he can Recruit with Water and Provissions, and Promises That the Passengers which came ashore Yesterday shall repair aboard again to day. . . .

[September 1, 1736] John White Cordwainer Informs that he has taken One John Wallace into his Family as a Journey man, Who was lately imported by Capt. Beard from Ireland.

5.4 Sinners in the Hands of an Angry God

Perhaps the most famous American sermon is "Sinners in the Hands of an Angry God." It was delivered on a hot July Sunday in 1741 in the Congregational church in the village of Enfield, Massachusetts. The pastor, Jonathan Edwards, read it in a flat tone of voice, scarcely glancing at his audience, with none of the bold hand gestures or body movements normally associated with hell-fire and brimstone preaching. And yet his words frightened and deeply moved the congregation. Preachers have been studying the sermon ever since.

This sermon was an expression of the "Great Awakening," a religious revival movement that swept through the colonies from about 1730 to 1750. People had been drifting toward secularism and rationalism, preferring to think less about sin and hell and more about worldly things. They came to believe in free will, labelled by the orthodox Calvinist clergy as the sin of Arminianism. Then came the awakening. This burst of evangelical fervor gave rise to wild and wooly revival meetings in churches and camp meetings. It led to many conversions, but also to heated discussions and schisms in most churches. Some parishioners favored the new passionate mood, while others shied away in disgust, hoping for a return to the more dignified style.

Edwards (1703–1758) was a philosopher and an important theologian. He was raised a Presbyterian and was an undergraduate and ministerial student at Yale. After assisting his grandfather, pastor of Northampton church, he himself became pastor there in 1729, serving for 25 years. His self-appointed mission was to resist liberal thought and conduct, especially among the young. He stressed the importance of knowledge of the Bible. Yet he also had a scholarly and scientific turn of mind (he wrote a learned treatise on spiders at age twelve). By turns a rationalist and a mystic, he regarded an intuitive conversion experience as the most important of all human experiences. It was based on a concept of an arbitrary and supreme God.

Late in life he had a falling out with his parishioners and became a missionary to the Indians. He was chosen to become head of Princeton but died shortly after being installed. What follows is most of the second part and the conclusion of the famous sermon.

Questions

How does Edwards get his point across? Examine his use of imagery—pressure from above, an insect, a bow and arrow, the pit of hell, etc. God is angry, but is there also any love in Him? What do you think was in the hearts and minds of the listeners that made them so receptive to this message? How were sinners supposed to avoid going to hell?

What was the significance of the Great Awakening and Edwards's place in it?

How do you think a modern audience would react to such a sermon, and why? How do you think this sermon compares with that of tv evangelists you may have seen? Explain.

The use may be of awakening to unconverted persons in this congregation. This that you have heard is the case of every one of you that are out of Christ. That world of misery, that lake of burning brimstone, is extended abroad under you. There is the dreadful pit of the glowing flames of the wrath of God; there is hell's wide gaping mouth open; and you have nothing to stand upon, nor any thing to take hold of. There is nothing between you and hell but the air; it is only the power and mere pleasure of God that holds you up.

You probably are not sensible of this; you find you are kept out of hell, but do not see the hand of God in it; but look at other things, as the good state of your bodily constitution, your care of your own life, and the means you use for your own preservation. But indeed these things are nothing; if God should withdraw his hand, they would avail no more to keep you from falling, than the thin air to hold up a person that is suspended in it.

Your wickedness makes you as it were heavy as lead, and to tend downwards with

SOURCE: Samuel Austin, ed., *The Works of President Edwards* (6 v.; Worcester, Mass.: Isaiah Thomas, 1808), II, 72–79.

great weight and pressure towards hell; and if God should let you go, you would immediately sink and swiftly descend and plunge into the bottomless gulf, and your healthy constitution, and your own care and prudence, and best contrivance, and all your righteousness, would have no more influence to uphold you and keep you out of hell, that a spider's web would have to stop a falling rock. Were it not that so is the sovereign pleasure of God, the earth would not bear you one moment; for you are a burden to it; the creation groans with you; the creature is made subject to the bondage of your corruption, not willingly; the sun does not willingly shine upon you to give you light to serve sin and Satan; the earth does not willingly yield her increase to satisfy your lusts; nor is it willingly a stage for your wickedness to be acted upon; the air does not willingly serve you for breath to maintain the flame of life in your vitals, while you spend your life in the service of God's enemies. God's creatures are good, and were made for men to serve God with, and do not willingly subserve to any other purpose, and groan when they are abused to purposes so directly contrary to their nature and end. And the world would spew you out, were it not for the sovereign hand of him who hath subjected it in hope. . . .

The wrath of God is like great waters that are dammed for the present; they increase more and more, and rise higher and higher, till an outlet is given; and the longer the stream is stopped, the more rapid and mighty is its course, when once it is let loose. It is true, that judgment against your evil work has not been executed hitherto; the floods of God's vengeance have been withheld; but your guilt in the mean time is constantly increasing, and you are every day treasuring up more wrath; the waters are continually rising, and waxing more and more mighty; and there is nothing but the mere pleasure of God, that holds the waters back, that are unwilling to be stopped, and press hard to go forward. If God should only withdraw his hand from the floodgate, it would immediately fly open, and the fiery floods of the fierceness and wrath of God, would rush forth with inconceivable fury, and would come upon you with omnipotent power; and if your strength were ten thousand times greater than it is, yea, ten thousand times greater than the strength of the stoutest, sturdiest devil in hell, it would be nothing to withstand or endure it.

The bow of God's wrath is bent, and the arrow made ready on the string, and justice bends the arrow at your heart, and strains the bow, and it is nothing but the mere pleasure of God, and that of an angry God, without any promise or obligation at all, that keeps the arrow one moment from being made drunk with your blood.

Thus are all you that never passed under a great change of heart, by the mighty power of the Spirit of God upon your souls; all that were never born again, and made new creatures, and raised from being dead in sin, to a state of new, and before altogether unexperienced light and life, (however you may have reformed your life in many things, and may have had religious affections, and may keep up a form of religion in your families and closets, and in the houses of God, and may be strict in it,) you are thus in the hands of an angry God; it is nothing but his mere pleasure that keeps you from being this moment swallowed up in everlasting destruction. . . .

The God that holds you over the pit of hell, much as one holds a spider, or some loathsome insect, over the fire, abhors you, and is dreadfully provoked; his wrath towards you burns like fire; he looks upon you as worthy of nothing else, but to be cast into the fire; he is of purer eyes than to bear to have you in his sight; you are ten thousand time so abominable in his eyes, as the most hateful and venomous serpent is in ours. You have offended him infinitely more than ever a stubborn rebel did his prince: and yet it is nothing but his hand that holds you from falling into the fire every moment: it is ascribed to nothing else, that you did not go to hell the last night; that you was suffered to awake again in this world, after you closed your eyes to sleep; and there is no other reason to be given, why you have not dropped into hell since you arose in the morning, but that God's hand has held you up. . . .

O sinner! consider the fearful danger you are in: it is a great furnace of wrath, a wide and bottomless pit, full of the fire of wrath, that you are held over in the hand of that God, whose wrath is provoked and incensed as much against you, as against many of the damned in hell: you hang by a slender thread, with the flames of divine wrath flashing about it, and ready every moment to singe it, and burn it asunder. . . .

And consider here more particularly several things concerning that wrath that you are in such danger of.

1. Whose wrath it is. It is the wrath of the infinite God. If it were only the wrath of man, though it were of the most potent prince, it would be comparatively little to be regarded. The wrath of kings is very much dreaded, especially of absolute monarchs, that have the possessions and lives of their subjects wholly in their power, to be disposed of at their mere will. Prov. xx.2, "The fear of a king is as the roaring of a lion: whoso provoketh him to anger, sinneth against his own soul." The subject that very much enrages an arbitrary prince, is liable to suffer the most extreme torments that human art can invent, or human power can inflict. But the greatest earthly potentates, in their greatest majesty and strength, and when clothed in their greatest terrors, are but feeble, despicable worms of the dust, in comparison of the great and almighty Creator and King of heaven and earth: it is but little that they can do, when most enraged, and when they have exerted the utmost of their fury. All the kings of the earth before God, are as grasshoppers; they are nothing, and less than nothing: both their love and their hatred is to be despised. The wrath of the great King of kings, is as much more terrible than theirs, as his majesty is greater. Luke xii. 4, 5, "And I say unto you, my friends, Be not afraid of them that kill the body, and after that have no more that they can do. But I will forewarn you whom you shall fear: fear him, which after he hath killed, hath power to cast into hell; yea, I say unto you, Fear him."

2. It is the fierceness of his wrath that you are exposed to. We often read of the fury of God; as in Isaiah lix. 18: "According to their deeds, accordingly he will repay fury to his adversaries." So Isaiah lxvi. 15, "For behold, the Lord will come with fire, and with his chariots like a whirlwind, to render his anger with fury, and his rebuke with flames of fire." And so in many other places. So we read of God's fierceness, Rev. xix. 15. There we read of "the wine-press of the fierceness and wrath of Almighty God." The words are exceedingly terrible: if it had only been said, "the wrath of God," the words would have implied that which is infinitely dreadful: but it is not only said so, but "the fierceness and wrath of God:" the fury of God! the fierceness of Jehovah! Oh how dreadful must that be! Who can utter or conceive what such expressions

carry in them! But it is not only said so, but "the fierceness and wrath of Almighty God." . . .

Consider this, you that are here present, that yet remain in an unregenerate state. That God will execute the fierceness of his anger, implies, that he will inflict wrath without any pity: when God beholds the ineffable extremity of your case, and sees your torment so vastly disproportioned to your strength, and sees how your poor soul is crushed, and sinks down, as it were, into an infinite gloom; he will have no compassion upon you, he will not forbear the executions of his wrath, or in the least lighten his hand; there shall be no moderation or mercy, nor will God then at all stay his rough wind; he will have no regard to your welfare, nor be at all careful lest you should suffer too much in any other sense, than only that you should not suffer beyond what strict justice requires: nothing shall be withheld, because it is so hard for you to bear. Ezek. viii. 18, "Therefore will I also deal in fury; mine eye shall not spare, neither will I have pity; and though they cry in mine ears with a loud voice, yet will I not hear them." Now God stands ready to pity you; this is a day of mercy; you may cry now with some encouragement of obtaining mercy: but when once the day of mercy is past, your most lamentable and dolorous cries and shrieks will be in vain; you will be wholly lost and thrown away of God, as to any regard to your welfare. . . .

How awful are those words, Isaiah lxiii. 3, which are the words of the great God: "I will tread them in mine anger, and trample them in my fury, and their blood shall be sprinkled upon my garments, and I will stain all my raiment." It is perhaps impossible to conceive of words that carry in them greater manifestations of these three things, viz., contempt and hatred, and fierceness of indignation. If you cry to God to pity you, he will be so far from pitying you in your doleful case, or showing you the least regard or favor, that instead of that he will only tread you under foot: and though he will know that you cannot bear the weight of omnipotence treading upon you, yet he will not regard that, but he will crush you under his feet without mercy. . . .

3. The misery you are exposed to is that which God will inflict to that end, that he might show what that wrath of Jehovah is. God hath had it on his heart to show to angels and men, both how excellent his love is, and also how terrible his wrath is. . . . When the great and angry God hath risen up and executed his awful vengeance on the poor sinner, and the wretch is actually suffering the infinite weight and power of his indignation, then will God call upon the whole universe to behold that awful majesty and mighty power that is to be seen in it. Isa. xxxiii. 12, 13, 14, "And the people shall be as the burnings of lime, as thorns cut up shall they be burnt in the fire. Hear, ye that are afar off, what I have done; and ye that are near, acknowledge my might. The sinners in Zion are afraid; fearfulness hath surprised the hypocrites," &c.

Thus it will be with you that are in an unconverted state, if you continue in it; the infinite might, and majesty, and terribleness, of the Omnipotent God shall be magnified upon you in the ineffable strength of your torments: you shall be tormented in the presence of the holy angels, and in the presence of the Lamb; and when you shall be in this state of suffering, the glorious inhabitants of heaven shall go forth and look on the awful spectacle, that they may see what the wrath and fierceness of the Almighty is; and when they have seen it, they will fall down and adore that great power and majesty. . . .

4. It is everlasting wrath. It would be dreadful to suffer this fierceness and wrath of Almighty God one moment; but you must suffer it to all eternity: there will be no end to this exquisite, horrible misery: when you look forward, you shall see a long forever, a boundless duration before you, which will swallow up your thoughts, and amaze your soul; and you will absolutely despair of ever having any deliverance, any end, any mitigation, any rest at all; you will know certainly that you must wear out long ages, millions of millions of ages, in wrestling and conflicting with this Almighty merciless vengeance; and then when you have so done, when so many ages have actually been spent by you in this manner, you will know that all is but a point to what remains. So that your punishment will indeed be infinite. . . .

How dreadful is the state of those that are daily and hourly in danger of this great wrath and infinite misery! But this is the dismal case of every soul in this congregation that has not been born again, however moral and strict, sober and religious, they may otherwise be. Oh that you would consider it, whether you be young or old! There is reason to think, that there are many in this congregation now hearing this discourse, that will actually be the subjects of this very misery to all eternity. We know not who they are, or in what seats they sit, or what thoughts they now have. It may be they are now at ease, and hear all these things without much disturbance, and are now flattering themselves that they are not the persons; promising themselves that they shall escape. If we knew that there was one person, and but one, in the whole congregation, that was to be the subject of this misery, what an awful thing it would be to think of! If we knew who it was, what an awful sight would it be to see such a person! How might all the rest of the congregation lift up a lamentable and bitter cry over him! But alas! Instead of one, how many is it likely will remember this discourse in hell! And it would be a wonder, if some that are now present should not be in hell in a very short time, before this year is out. And it would be no wonder if some persons, that now sit here in some seats of this meeting-house in health, and quiet and secure, should be there before to-morrow morning.

5.5 A Deist Views Organized Religion

Tom Paine enjoyed enormous popularity after writing Common Sense *and* The Crisis *during the Revolutionary War era (see chapter 2, above). Later, he worked for a Congressional committee, served as clerk to the Pennsylvania assembly, and sailed to his native England, where he wrote* The Rights of Man *in defense of the French Revolution. He then visited*

France to experience the revolutionary turmoil first hand. Ironically, the French Revolution regime threw him in jail. Partly to offset the spread of atheism in France, he penned The Age of Reason *(1794), a statement of religious belief. Ironically, while some readers regarded it as an affirmation of religion, others denounced it as the work of an atheist. Paine's popularity melted away. A century later, Theodore Roosevelt dismissed him as "a filthy little atheist."*

The Age of Reason *was an attack on* organized *religion, although many regarded it as an attack on religion itself. In essence, it is a statement favoring deism, a religious belief system common to many Enlightenment thinkers, based on science and rooted in a faith in human reason and progress. A selection from this work follows.*

Questions

How does deism differ from atheism and agnosticism? Since deism was a popular belief, why did this work infuriate so many people?

Why are Paine's views still so unpopular among some groups? Does the controversy over deism have any parallels today? What role does agnosticism—and, for that matter, atheism—play in American culture?

It has been my intention for several years past to publish my thoughts upon Religion. I am well aware of the difficulties that attend the subject; and from that consideration had reserved it to a more advanced period of life. I intended it to be the last offering I should make to my fellow-citizens of all nations, and that at a time when the purity of the motive that induced me to it could not admit of a question, even by those who might disapprove the work. . . .

I believe in one God, and no more; and I hope for happiness beyond this life.

I believe in the equality of man, and I believe that religious duties consist in doing justice, loving mercy, and endeavoring to make our fellow-creatures happy.

SOURCE: Thomas Paine, *The Age of Reason: Being an Investigation of a True and of a Fabulous Theology* (1794).

But lest it should be supposed that I believe many other things in addition to these, I shall, in the progress of this work, declare the things I do not believe and my reasons for not believing them.

I do not believe in the creed professed by the Jewish church, by the Roman church, by the Greek church, by the Turkish church, by the Protestant church, nor by any church that I know of. My own mind is my own church.

All national institutions of churches—whether Jewish, Christian, or Turkish—appear to me no other than human inventions set up to terrify and enslave mankind and monopolize power and profit.

I do not mean by this declaration to condemn those who believe otherwise. They have the same right to their belief as I have to mine. But it is necessary to the happiness of man that he be mentally faithful to himself. Infidelity does not consist in believing or in disbelieving; it consists in professing to believe what he does not believe.

It is impossible to calculate the moral mischief, if I may so express it, that mental lying has produced in society. When a man has so far corrupted and prostituted the chastity of his mind as to subscribe his professional belief to things he does not believe, he has prepared himself for the commission of every other crime. He takes up the trade of priest for the sake of gain, and in order to *qualify* himself for that trade, he begins with a perjury. Can we conceive anything more destructive to morality than this?

Soon after I had published the pamphlet, COMMON SENSE, in America, I saw the exceeding probability that a revolution in the system of government would be followed by a revolution in the system of religion. The adulterous connection of church and state, wherever it had taken place, whether Jewish, Christian, or Turkish, had so effectually prohibited, by pains and penalties, every discussion upon established creeds and upon first principles of religion, that until the system of government should be changed those subjects could not be brought fairly and openly before the world; but that whenever this should be done, a revolution in the system of religion would follow. . . .

As to the Christian system of faith, it appears to me as a species of atheism; a sort of religious denial of God. It professes to believe in a man rather than in God. It is a compound made up chiefly of manism, with but little deism, and is as near to atheism as twilight is to darkness. It introduces between man and his Maker an opaque body, which it calls a Redeemer, as the moon introduces her opaque self between the earth and the sun; and it produces by this means a religious or an irreligious eclipse of light. It has put the whole orb of reason into shade. . . .

That which is now called natural philosophy, embracing the whole circle of science of which astronomy occupies the chief place, is the study of the works of God, and of the power and wisdom of God and is works, and is the true theology.

As to the theology that is now studied in its place, it is the study of human opinions and of human fancies *concerning* God. It is not the study of God himself in the works that he has made, but in the works or writings that man has made; and it is not among the least of the mischiefs that the Christian system has done to the world that it has abandoned the original and beautiful system of theology, like a beautiful innocent, to distress and reproach, to make room for the hag of superstition.

The book of Job and the 19th Psalm, which even the church admits to be more ancient than the chronological order in which they stand in the book called the Bible, are theological orations conformable to the original system of theology. The internal evidence of those orations proves to a demonstration that the study and contemplation of the works of creation, and of the power and wisdom of God revealed and manifested in those works, make a great part of the religious devotion of the times in which they were written; and it was this devotional study and contemplation that led to the discovery of the principles upon which what are now called sciences are established; and it is to the discovery of these principles that almost all the arts that contribute to the convenience of human life owe their existence. . . .

It is a fraud of the Christian system to call the sciences *human inventions;* it is only the application of them that is human.

Every science has for its basis a system of principles as fixed and unalterable as those by which the universe is regulated and governed. Man cannot make principles; he can only discover them.

For example. Every person who looks at an almanac sees an account when an eclipse will take place, and he sees also that it never fails to take place according to the account there given. This shows that man is acquainted with the laws by which the heavenly bodies move. But it would be something worse than ignorance were any church on earth to say that those laws are a human invention.

It would also be ignorance or something worse to say that the scientific principles, by the aid of which man is enabled to calculate and foreknow when an eclipse will take place, are a human invention. Man cannot invent anything that is eternal and immutable, and the scientific principles he employs for this purpose must be, and are, of necessity, as eternal and immutable as the laws by which the heavenly bodies move, or they could not be used as they are to ascertain the time when, and the manner how, an eclipse will take place. . . .

It is from the study of the true theology that all our knowledge of science is derived, and it is from that knowledge that all the arts have originated.

The Almighty lecturer, by displaying the principles of science in the structure of the universe, has invited man to study and to imitation. It is as if he had said to the inhabitants of this globe that we call ours: "I rendered the starry heavens visible, to teach him science and the arts. He can now provide for his own comfort, AND LEARN FROM MY MUNIFICENCE TO BE KIND TO EACH OTHER." . . .

Having now extended the subject to a greater length than I first intended, I shall bring it to a close by abstracting a summary from the whole.

First—That the idea or belief of a word of God existing in print, or in writing, or in speech, is inconsistent in itself for the reasons already assigned. These reasons, among others, are the want of a universal language; the mutability of language; the errors to which translations are subject; the possibility of totally suppressing such a word; the probability of altering it, or of fabricating the whole, and imposing it upon the world.

Secondly—That the creation we behold is the real and ever-existing word of God in which we cannot be deceived. It proclaimeth his power, it demonstrates his wisdom, it manifests his goodness and beneficence.

Thirdly—That the moral duty of man consists in imitating the moral goodness and beneficence of God manifested in the creation towards all his creatures. That seeing, as we daily do, the goodness of God to all men, it is an example calling upon all men to practice the same towards each other; and consequently that everything of persecution and revenge between man and man, and everything of cruelty to animals is a violation of moral duty.

I trouble not myself about the manner of future existence. I content myself with believing, even to positive conviction, that the power that gave me existence is able to continue it in any form and manner he pleases, either with or without this body; and it appears more probable to me that I shall continue to exist hereafter than that I should have had existence, as I now have, before that existence began.

It is certain that in one point all nations of the earth and all religions agree. All believe in a God. The things in which they disagree are the redundancies annexed to that belief; and, therefore, if ever a universal religion should prevail, it will not be believing anything new, but in getting rid of redundancies and believing as man believed at first. Adam, if ever there was such a man, was created a Deist; but in the meantime let every man follow, as he has a right to do, the religion and the worship he prefers. . . .

5.6 Separating Church and State

Separation of church and state is now taken for granted by Americans as a cherished and fundamental principle of government. And yet, as we have seen (Documents 5.1 and 5.2) it had a difficult birth, and was still in its infancy immediately prior to the writing of the federal Constitution.

In the revolutionary generation of the 1770s and 1780s, the battle over religious liberty concerned two basic issues. One was whether public officials should be forced to swear a religious test oath before taking office (see Document 5.7). A second was whether any one church should be the established church, whether all churches should be supported equally, or whether all churches should be disestablished.

The struggle for the complete separation of church and state was particularly intense in Virginia. A milestones in this contest was the "Declaration of Rights" passed by the Virginia Convention of 1776 which supported the general idea of religious liberty. Nevertheless, on the eve of the Revolution, the Anglican church remained the established church in Virginia and elsewhere. The law still mandated church attendance and encouraged universal support of the established church. A year later the Virginia liberals managed to repeal these statutes. In 1779 they also managed, against conservative opposition, to have the church disestablished (i.e., deprived of its official sanction). That meant that churches were finally disestablished in all states from Pennsylvania south—although northward, in some New England states, Congregational churches remained established for a decade after the adoption of the new constitution. (The Bill of Rights applied only to the federal government, not the states.)

In Virginia in the 1780s, religious conservatives like Patrick Henry and George Washington tried to place all Christian churches on an equal footing and give them all tax support. In 1786, Thomas Jefferson, along with James Madison, George Mason and others, blocked this move. They prepared a bill, "The Virginia Statute of Religious Liberty," providing for full religious freedom and equality without exceptions. Although bitterly opposed by the Episcopalian and Presbyterian clergy and their allies, it was enacted in 1786. The entire law is reprinted below.

Jefferson considered it one of his most important accomplishments, along with founding the University of Virginia and co-authoring the Declaration of Independence. It set a precedent for the First Amendment: "Congress shall make no law respecting an establishment of religion, or prohibiting the free exercise thereof. . . ." The struggle in Virginia in the 1770s was prelude also to the writing of Article VI of the federal Constitution: "no religious test shall ever be required as a qualification to any office or public trust under the United States."

Questions

How does the Virginia Statute compare with the First Amendment? It includes a lengthy justification. What philosophical arguments does Jefferson offer for this religious principle?

What are some issues today involving the separation of church and state?

I. WHEREAS Almighty God hath created the mind free; that all attempts to influence it by temporal punishments or burthens, or by civil incapacitations, tend only to beget habits of hypocrisy and meanness, and are a departure from the plan of the Holy author of our religion, who being Lord both of body and mind, yet chose not to propagate it by coercions on either, as was in his Almighty power to do; that the impious presumption of legislators and rulers, civil as well as ecclesiastical, who being themselves but fallible and uninspired men, have assumed dominion over the faith of others, setting up their own opinions and modes of thinking as the only true and infallible, and as such endeavouring to impose them on others, hath established and maintained false religions over the greatest part of the world, and through all time; that to compel a man to furnish contributions of money for the propagation of opinions which he disbelieves, is sinful and tyrannical; that even the forcing him to support this or that teacher of his own religious persuasion, is depriving him of the comfortable liberty of giving his contributions to the particular pastor whose morals he would make his pattern, and whose powers he feels most persuasive to righteousness, and is withdrawing from the ministry those temporary rewards, which proceeding from an approbation of their personal conduct, are an additional incitement to earnest and unremitting labours for the instruction of mankind; that our civil rights have no dependence on our religious opinions, any more than our opinions in physics or geometry; that therefore the proscribing any citizen as unworthy the public confidence by laying upon him an incapacity of being called to offices of trust and emolument, unless he profess or renounce this or that religious opinion, is depriving him injuriously of those privileges and advantages to which in common with his fellow-citizens he has a natural right, that it tends only to corrupt the principles of that religion it is meant to encourage, by bribing

SOURCE: W. W. Henning, ed., *Statues at Large of Virginia*, XII, 84 ff.

with a monopoly of worldly honours and emoluments, those who will externally profess and conform to it; that though indeed these are criminal who do not withstand such temptation, yet neither are those innocent who lay the bait in their way; that to suffer the civil magistrate to intrude his powers into the field of opinion, and to restrain the profession or propagation of principles on supposition of their ill tendency, is a dangerous fallacy, which at once destroys all religious liberty, because he being of course judge of that tendency will make his opinions the rule of judgment, and approve or condemn the sentiments of others only as they shall square with or differ from his own; that it is time enough for the rightful purposes of civil government, for its officers to interfere when principles break out into overt acts against peace and good order; and finally, that truth is great and will prevail if left to herself, that she is the proper and sufficient antagonist to error, and has nothing to fear from the conflict, unless by human interposition disarmed of her natural weapons, free argument and debate, errors ceasing to be dangerous when it is permitted freely to contradict them.

II. *Be it enacted by the General Assembly,* that no man shall be compelled to frequent or support any religious worship, place or ministry whatsoever, nor shall be enforced, restrained, molested, or burthened in his body or goods, nor shall otherwise suffer on account of his religious opinions or belief; but that all men shall be free to profess, and by argument to maintain, their opinion in matters of religion, and that the same shall in no wise diminish, enlarge or affect their civil capacities.

III. And though we well know that this assembly, elected by the people for the ordinary purposes of legislation only, have no power to restrain the acts of succeeding assemblies, constituted with powers equal to our own, and that therefore to declare this act to be irrevocable would be of no effect in law; yet as we are free to declare, and do declare, that the rights hereby asserted are of the natural rights of mankind, and that if any act shall hereafter be passed to repeal the present, or to narrow its operation, such act will be an infringement of natural right.

5.7 A Jew Petitions for Religious Equality

While the Philadelphia convention was in session hammering out the new federal constitution, it received a letter from Jonas Phillips, dated September 7, 1787. Phillips was a Jew who had applied for public office, only to be turned down on religious grounds. He urged the meeting to eliminate this injustice. Many Catholics voiced similar complaints. Since the con-

vention was meeting behind closed doors, the public did not yet know that the problem raised by Phillips had already been laid to rest in Article VI of the Constitution. It did not apply to the states, however, where similar restrictions continued to prevail for many years. The letter is useful in understanding not only the constitutional issue, but also the state of Jewish life in America.

Questions

Precisely what did Article VI say about religious tests for serving in office? Which states retained restrictive religious requirements after 1789, and for how long?

What do you suppose were Phillips's politics, ideology and social status? What clues can you find here as to the place of Jews in American society at that time?

Sires: With leave and submission I address myself to those in whom there is wisdom, understanding and knowledge. They are the honorable personages appointed and made overseers of a part of the terrestrial globe of the earth, namely the 13 United States of America, in convention assembled, the Lord preserve them amen.

I, the subscriber, being one of the people called Jews, of the city of Philadelphia, a people scattered and dispersed among all nations, do behold with concern that among the laws in the Constitution of Pennsylvania, there is a clause, Section 10, to wit—'I do believe in one God, the Creator and governor of the Universe and Rewarder of the good and punisher of the wicked; and I do acknowledge the Scriptures of the Old and New Testament to be given by divine inspiration.' To swear and believe that the New Testament was given by divine inspiration is absolutely against the religious principles of a Jew, and is against his conscience to take any such oath. By the above law a Jew is deprived of holding any public office, or place of government, which is contradictory to the bill of rights [of Pennsylvania], Section—'That all men have a natural and unalienable right to worship almighty God according to the dictates of their own conscience and understanding; that no man ought or of right can be compelled to attend any religious worship or creed, or support any place of worship or maintain any minister contrary to or against his own free will and consent; nor can any man who acknowledges the being of a God be justly deprived or abridged of any civil right as a citizen on account of his religious sentiments or peculiar mode of religious worship; and that no authority can or ought to be vested in or assumed by any power whatever that shall in any case interfere or in any manner control the right of conscience in the free exercise of religious worship.'

It is well known among all the citizens of the 13 United States that the Jews have been true and faithful whigs, and during the late contest with England they have

SOURCE: Jonas Phillips, September 7, 1787, from Herbert Friedenwald, ed., "A Letter of Jonas Phillips to the Federal Convention," American Jewish Historical Society *Publications* (New York, 1894), II, 108–110.

been foremost in aiding and assisting the states with their lives and fortunes. They have supported the cause, have bravely fought and bled for liberty which they cannot enjoy.

Therefore, if the honorable convention shall in their wisdom think fit, and alter the said oath and leave out the words, to wit—'and I do acknowledge the scripture of the New Testament to be given by divine inspiration'—then the Israelites will think themselves happy to live under a government where all religious societies are on an equal footing. I solicit this favor for myself, my children and posterity, and for the benefit of all the Israelites throughout the 13 United States of America.

My prayers are unto the Lord. May the people of these states rise up as a great and young lion. May they prevail against their enemies. May the degrees of honor of his Excellency, the president of the Convention, George Washington, be exalted and raised up. May everyone speak of his glorious exploits. May God prolong his days among us in this land of liberty. . . . May God extend peace to them and their seed after them, so long as the sun and moon endureth. May the almighty God of our father, Abraham, Isaac and Jacob, indue this noble Assembly with wisdom, judgment and unanimity in their counsels. And may they have the satisfaction to see that their present toil and labor for the welfare of the United States may be approved of through all the world and particularly by the United States of America—is the ardent preyer of

Your most devoted obedient servant,
Jonas Phillips

5.8 Defining Nationality

In most parts of the world, national identity was shaped before the state was formed. That is, songs, legends, heroes and heroines, stories, poetry, literature and art usually preceded the existence of the nation. Here in America, it was otherwise. First the government was formed, and then the culture was produced that defined the nation. This curious process has fascinated both Americans and Europeans. Many have wondered whether we came to define our nationality by gaining our independence from Britain, pioneering on the frontier, passing through the immigrant experience, or from other influences. The earliest significant effort to explore this cultural issue occurs in a work entitled Letters of An American Farmer, *published by J. Hector St. John de Crévecoeur in 1782. Crévecoeur (1735–1813) was born in France, served under General Montcalm in the French and Indian War, travelled through the Great Lakes and Ohio Valley, and in 1769 settled on a farm in Orange County, New York. Although a Tory during the Revolutionary era, he wrote what was essentially a glowing tribute to the emerging nation.*

What follows is a selection from his chapter entitled, "What is an American?" It is noteworthy because, among other things, it anticipates the twentieth-century metaphor of the "melting pot."

Questions

What importance does Crévecoeur ascribe to the frontier in shaping American nationhood? What importance does he give to immigration and the immigrant experience?

He writes of a process of ethnic "melting." But in truth how much of American culture, despite the input of other cultures, was anything but Anglo-Saxon? Would "tossed salad" be a more appropriate image than "melting pot"?

What, in your opinion, are the defining characteristics of American nationality today?

What then is the American, this new man? He is either an European, or the descendant of an European, hence that strange mixture of blood, which you will find in no other country. I could point out to you a family whose grandfather was an Englishman, whose wife was Dutch, whose son married a French woman, and whose present four sons have now four wives of different nations. *He* is an American, who leaving behind him all his ancient prejudices and manners, receives new ones from the new mode of life he has embraced, the new government be obeys, and the new rank he holds. He becomes an American by being received in the broad lap of our great *Alma Mater*. Here individuals of all nations are melted into a new race of men, whose labours and posterity will one day cause great changes in the world. Americans are the western pilgrims, who are carrying along with them that great mass of arts, sciences, vigour, and industry which began long since in the east; they will finish the great circle. The Americans were once scattered all over Europe; here they are incorporated into one of the finest systems of population which has ever appeared, and which will hereafter become distinct by the power of the different climates they inhabit. The American ought therefore to love this country much better than that wherein either he or his forefathers were born. Here the rewards of his industry follow with equal steps the progress of his labour; his labour is founded on the basis of nature, *self-interest;* can it want a stronger allurement? Wives and children, who before in vain demanded of him a morsel of bread, now, fat and frolicsome, gladly help their father to clear those fields whence exuberant crops are to arise to feed and to clothe them all; without any part being claimed, either by a despotic prince, a rich abbot, or a mighty lord. Here religion demands but little of him; a small voluntary salary to the minister, and gratitude to God; can be refuse these? The American is a new man, who acts upon new principles; he must therefore entertain new ideas, and form new opinions. From involuntary idleness, servile dependence, penury, and useless labour, he has passed to toils of a very different nature, rewarded by ample subsistence.—This is an American. . . .

Now we arrive near the great woods, near the last inhabited districts; there men seem to be placed still farther beyond the

SOURCE: Hector St. John de Crévecoeur, *Letters of an American Farmer* (1782).

reach of government, which in some measure leaves them to themselves. How can it pervade every corner; as they were driven there by misfortunes, necessity of beginnings, desire of acquiring large tracks of land, idleness, frequent want of economy, ancient debts; the re-union of such people does not afford a very pleasing spectacle. When discord, want of unity and friendship; when either drunkenness or idleness prevail in such remote districts; contention, inactivity, and wretchedness must ensue. There are not the same remedies to these evils as in a long established community. The few magistrates they have, are in general little better than the rest; they are often in a perfect state of war; that of man against man, sometimes decided by blows, sometimes by means of the law; that of man against every wild inhabitant of these venerable woods, of which they are come to dispossess them. There men appear to be no better than carnivorous animals of a superior rank, living on the flesh of wild animals when they can catch them, and when they are not able, they subsist on grain. He who would wish to see America in its proper light, and have a true idea of its feeble beginnings and barbarous rudiments, must visit our extended line of frontiers where the last settlers dwell. . . . They are a kind of forlorn hope, preceding by ten or twelve years the most respectable army of veterans which come after them. In that space, prosperity will polish some, vice and the law will drive off the rest, who uniting again with others like themselves will recede still farther; making room for more industrious people, who will finish their improvements, convert the loghouse into a convenient habitation, and rejoicing that the first heavy labours are finished, will change in a few years that hitherto barbarous country into a fine fertile, well regulated district. Such is our progress, such is the march of the Europeans toward the interior parts of this continent. In all societies there are off-casts; this impure part serves as our precursors or pioneers; my father himself was one of that class, but he came upon honest principles, and was therefore one of the few who held fast; by good conduct and temperance, he transmitted to me his fair inheritance, when not above one in fourteen of his contemporaries had the same good fortune. . . .

But to return to our back-settlers. I must tell you, that there is something in the proximity of the woods, which is very singular. It is with men as it is with the plants and animals that grow and live in the forests; they are entirely different from those that live in the plains. I will candidly tell you all my thoughts but you are not to expect that I shall advance any reasons. By living in or near the woods, their actions are regulated by the wildness of the neighbourhood . . . they soon become professed hunters; this is the progress; once hunters, farewell to the plough. The chase renders them ferocious, gloomy, and unsociable; a hunter wants no neighbour. . . . they go oftener to the woods. That new mode of life brings along with it a new set of manners, which I cannot easily describe. These new manners being grafted on the old stock, produce a strange sort of lawless profligacy, the impressions of which are indelible. The manners of the Indian natives are respectable, compared with this European medley. Their wives and children live in sloth and inactivity; and having no proper pursuits, you may judge what education the latter receive. . . . To all these reasons you must add, their lonely situation, and you cannot imagine what an effect on manners the great distances they live from each other has! Consider one of the last settlements in its first view: of what is it composed? Europeans who have not that sufficient share of knowledge they ought to have, in order to prosper; people who have suddenly passed from oppression, dread of government, and fear of laws, into the unlimited freedom of the woods. This sudden change must have a very great effect on most men, and on that class particularly. Eating of wild meat, whatever you may think, tends to alter their temper: though all the proof I can adduce, is, that I have seen it: and having no place of worship to resort to, what little society this might afford, is denied them. The Sunday meetings, exclusive of religious benefits, were the only social bonds that might have inspired them with some degree of emulation in neatness. Is it then surprising to see men thus situated, immersed in great and heavy labours, degenerate a little? It is rather a wonder the effect is not more diffusive.

Europe contains hardly any other distinctions but lords and tenants; this fair country alone is settled by freeholders, the possessors of the soil they cultivate, members of the government they obey, and the framers of their own laws, by means of their representatives. This is a thought which you have taught me to cherish; our difference from Europe, far from diminishing, rather adds to our usefulness and consequence as men and subjects. Had our forefathers remained there, they would only have crouded it, and perhaps prolonged those convulsions which had shook it so long. Every industrious European who transports himself here, may be compared to a sprout growing at the foot of a great tree; it enjoys and draws but a little portion of sap; wrench it from the parent roots, transplant it, and it will become a tree bearing fruit also. . . .

There is room for every body in America; has he any particular talent, or industry? he exerts it in order to procure a livelihood, and it succeeds. Is he a merchant? the avenues of trade are infinite; is he eminent in any respect? he will be employed and respected. Does he love a country life? pleasant farms present themselves; he may purchase what he wants, and thereby become an American farmer. Is he a labourer, sober and industrious? he need not go many miles, nor receive many informations before he will be hired, well fed at the table of his employer, and paid four or five times more than he can get in Europe. Does he want uncultivated lands? thousands of acres present themselves, which he may purchase cheap. Whatever be his talents or inclinations, if they are moderate, he may satisfy them. I do not mean that every one who comes will grow rich in a little time; no, but he may procure an easy, decent maintenance, by his industry. Instead of starving he will be fed, instead of being idle he will have employment; and these are riches enough for such men as come over here. The rich stay in Europe, it is only the middling and the poor that emigrate. Would you wish to travel in independent idleness, from north to south, you will find easy access, and the most cheerful reception at every house; society without ostentation, good cheer without pride, and every decent diversion which the country affords, with little expence. It is no wonder that the European who has lived here a few years, is desirous to remain; Europe with all its pomp, is not to be compared to this continent, for men of middle stations, or labourers.

An European, when he first arrives, seems limited in his intentions, as well as in his views; but he very suddenly alters his scale; two hundred miles formerly appeared a very great distance, it is now but a trifle; he no sooner breathes our air than he forms schemes, and embarks in designs he never would have thought of in his own country. There the plenitude of society confines many useful ideas, and often extinguishes the most laudable schemes which here ripen into maturity. Thus Europeans become Americans.

But how is this accomplished in that croud of low, indigent people, who flock here every year from all parts of Europe? I will tell you; they no sooner arrive than they immediately feel the good effects of that plenty of provisions we possess: they fare on our best food, and are kindly entertained; their talents, character, and peculiar industry are immediately inquired into; they find countrymen every where disseminated, let them come from whatever part of Europe. Let me select one as an epitome of the rest; he is hired, he goes to work, and works moderately; instead of being employed by a haughty person, he finds himself with his equal, placed at the substantial table of the farmer, or else at an inferior one as good; his wages are high, his bed is not like that bed of sorrow on which he used to lie: if he behaves with propriety, and is faithful, he is caressed, and becomes as it were a member of the family. He begins to feel the effects of a sort of resurrection; hitherto he had not lived, but simply vegetated; he now feels himself a man, because he is treated as such; the laws of his own country had overlooked him in his insignificancy; the laws of this cover him with their mantle.

5.9 Catholicism in America

The following documents relate to the status of Catholics in pre-Civil War America, from the 1830s to the 1850s. They consist of an observation by the Frenchman Alexis de Tocqueville, a letter by Archbishop John Hughes, and song lyrics and poetry by anonymous nativists.

Tocqueville writes as a European aristocrat witnessing life in democratic America in the 1830s. The fact that he was a Catholic observing Catholics give his words extra weight.

For centuries Roman Catholics were political and social outcasts in America—witness the waves of nativism that washed over the country with each new influx of Catholic immigrants. Anti-Catholic nativism was especially strong in the 1840s and 1850s and again in the 1880s. It continued to have considerable impact on American politics in the twentieth century. Not until the election of John F. Kennedy in 1960 did the political climate improve decisively for Catholics.

Nativists developed paranoid fears that Catholic immigrants would "capture" the American West. "The Pilgrim's Legacy," a popular hymn sung to the opening of anti-Catholic meetings, was sold widely for use in churches and at home.

Partly to help their people escape nativist outbursts such as these, some eastern Catholic leaders tried to stimulate western colonization, especially in the late 1840s and 1850s. Catholic clergy from the U.S. and Canada met at Buffalo, New York in 1856 to encourage this move. But the most powerful figure in American Catholicism at that time, Archbishop John Hughes of New York, firmly opposed the plan, and it had minimal success. Here, in a statement prepared by Hughes in 1857 but never issued, the clergyman explains his strong objections to western colonization. In passing, he comments on the impoverished condition of American Catholics in the wake of the Irish famine of 1847 and 1848. It is a notable document because it flies in the face of the popular concept of encouraging poor people to go West to make their fortune.

Questions

In what condition did Tocqueville find his Catholic co-religionists? If they were adapting successfully, what was the secret of their success? Did he seem to have a good grasp on American religion generally?

How did Protestant nativists justify their intense hatred toward Catholics in the 1840s? Which symbols and traditions were they drawing on? What did they hope to achieve and by what means?

Why did Hughes object to western colonization? What did he think of the Irish immigrants, and what did he hope they would achieve in America?

What picture do you get from these documents about the overall status of Catholicism? Are there still lingering signs of anti-Catholic sentiment in this country? How is it expressed?

Alexis de Tocqueville –

I showed in my former volume how the American clergy stand aloof from secular affairs. This is the most obvious, but not the only, example of their self-restraint. In America, religion is a distinct sphere, in which the priest is sovereign, but out of which he takes care never to go. Within its limits, he is master of the mind; beyond them, he leaves men to themselves, and surrenders them to the independence and instability which belong to their nature and their age. I have seen no country in which Christianity is clothed with fewer forms, figures, and observances than in the United States; or where it presents more distinct, simple, and general notions to the mind. Although the Christians of America are divided into a multitude of sects, they all look upon their religion in the same light. This applies to Roman Catholicism as well as to the other forms of belief. There are no Romish priests who show less taste for the minute individual observances, for extraordinary or peculiar means of salvation, or who cling more to the spirit, and less to the letter, of the law, than the Roman Catholic priests of the United States. . . . Yet the Roman Catholics of America are very submissive and very sincere.

Another remark is applicable to the clergy of every communion. The American ministers of the Gospel do not attempt to draw or to fix all the thoughts of man upon the life to come; they are willing to surrender a portion of his heart to the cares of the present; seeming to consider the goods of this world as important, though secondary, objects. If they take no part themselves in productive labor, they are at least interested in its progress, and they applaud its results; and whilst they never cease to point to the other world as the great object of the hopes and fears of the believer, they do not forbid him honestly to court prosperity in this. . . .

All the American clergy know and respect the intellectual supremacy exercised by the majority: they never sustain any but necessary conflicts with it. They take no share in the altercations of parties, but they readily adopt the general opinions of their country and their age: and they allow themselves to be borne away without opposition in the current of feeling and opinion by which everything around them is carried along. They endeavor to amend their contemporaries, but they do not quit fellowship with them. . . .

Thus it is, that, by respecting all democratic tendencies not absolutely contrary to herself, and by making use of several of them for her own purposes, Religion sustains a successful struggle with that spirit of individual independence which is her most dangerous opponent.

America is the most democratic country in the world, and it is at the same time (according to reports worthy of belief) the country in which the Roman Catholic religion makes most progress. At first sight, this is surprising.

Two things must here be accurately distinguished: equality inclines men to wish to form their own opinions; but, on the other hand, it imbues them with the taste and the idea of unity, simplicity, and impartiality in the power which governs society. Men living in democratic times are therefore very prone to shake off all religious authority; but if they consent to subject themselves to any authority of this kind, they choose at least that it should be single and uniform. Religious powers not radiating from a common centre are naturally repugnant to their minds; and they almost as readily conceive that there should be no religion, as that there should be several.

At the present time, more than in any preceeding age, Roman Catholics are seen to lapse into infidelity, and Protestants to be converted to Roman Catholicism. If the Roman Catholic faith be considered within the pale of the Church, it would seem to be losing ground; without that pale, to be gaining it. Nor is this difficult of explanation. The men of our days are naturally little disposed to believe; but, as soon as they have any religion, they immediately find in themselves a latent instinct which urges them unconsciously towards Catholicism. Many of the doctrines and practices of the Romish Church astonish them; but they feel a secret admiration for its discipline, and its great unity attracts them. If Catholicism could at length withdraw itself from the political animosities to which it has given rise, I have hardly any doubt but that the same spirit of the age which appears to be so opposed to it would become so favorable as to admit of its great and sudden advancement. . . .

. . . I am inclined to believe . . . our posterity will tend more and more to a division into only two parts,—some relinquishing Christianity entirely, and others returning to the Church of Rome.

Archbishop Hughes–

There is no people in the world, whether at home or abroad, so overdosed with counsel and advice as the Irish. Their friends advise them, their enemies advise them, those who are indifferent about their welfare advise them in like manner.

The last gentle advice that has been rendered to them in this country emanates from what is called the Buffalo Convention. The good intentions of those who composed that spontaneous and self-constituted assembly, it is unnecessary to question. . . .

Without questioning the purity of motives of any one connected with this meeting, one may be allowed to say that it was a most superfluous, unnecessary and unprofitable assemblage. It has added no single new idea to the common stock of information by which individual emigrants might be guided in the selection of their future homes. It has repeated what was known before, that there is a great deal of waste land, fertile withal, in the Eastern and Western provinces of Canada and on the Western boundaries of the present United States. It has also proclaimed what was sufficiently known before, that in the Eastern large cities, whether of the seaboard or of the immediate neighborhood of the interior, there are great numbers of Irish emigrants who have to struggle against all the miseries incident to their condition. . . . Having said thus much we have abridged the whole amount of new light which the discussion of the question in the Buffalo Convention has shed on this very important topic.

Next however the convention volunteers its benevolent advice and thereby assumes the responsibility which should induce conscientious persons familiar with the whole subject to pause and hesitate before they offered it to the very few who may be imposed upon and deceived by their silly theories. . . .

Still advice, like politeness, costs but little to those who administer it, though it should prove very dear to such as may be misled and deceived by its erroneousness. The writer of this is acquainted with the circumstances of Catholics both in the East and in the West, and nothing on earth could induce him to give such advice as has emanated from the Buffalo Convention in regard to Catholic emigrants in this country. It may happen that persons misled by that advice will commemorate it in the bitterness of disappointment by tears on their cheeks and maledictions on their lips.

Again if those members of the Buffalo Convention who are not anchored to their present domicile by bonds which cannot be sundered were in earnest, one might expect that they would offer themselves as leaders and pioneers to exhibit the practical reality of happiness which they have so gorgeously painted in the idea of owning land, more or less, in the Western country. This however is a test to which it does not appear that a single member of the convention was equal. Their language is in substance as addressed to their Catholic fellow countrymen, "Go you, we stay." It is difficult to perceive that if this advice is good for their neighbors it should not be good for themselves also.

It must not be inferred that the writer is opposed to the diffusion of emigrants into those portions of the country in which land may be obtained and in which living is cheap and labor has its fair recompense. But there is a natural process by which this result is perpetually going on. Poor emigrants not finding employment in one place seek it in another. And then when they go westward especially, acquire a certain practical knowledge of the production of the soil or the mines in the neighborhoods in which they find themselves. With this necessary knowledge, as a far more important capital than the limited amount which they may have economized from their labors, they sometimes acquire a title to lands, or in other interests by which their temporal prosperity is increased. But the idea of disturbing the minds of those who may be already established, whether in the East or in the West by a gilded and exaggerated report of theoretical blessings, which are in reserve for them, provided they can acquire the nominal ownership of 60 or 100 acres of uncultivated land, not unfrequently teeming with fever and ague—remote from the church—remote from the school—remote [from] the Post Office—remote from the physician—remote from the neighbors—this idea is dangerous, just so far as any Catholic emigrant is liable to be misled and deceived thereby. Then besides, our convention have [*sic*] understood that capital, more or less will be necessary, for those who shall be found simple enough to follow their advice. This being the case, that advice is tendered to those who, wherever they are located whether in the East or in the West, have been already, to some extent, successful in their industrial efforts. One might suppose that if they are doing well, it would be unwise for them to give up the certainty which they have for the uncertainty which is proposed to them.

But passing from this class our attention is directed to another, the condition of which has exercised the deep reflection and roused the benevolence of the Buf. Convention. We mean the hundreds and thousands who in New York, Boston, Philadelphia, and New Orleans are living in the proverbial wretchedness usually associated with the idea of a residence in cellars and in garrets. Now this class could not but improve their condition by a change to the open fields of the rural districts. But then the convention has not been able to devise any practical system of ways and means by which this [*sic*] could be transported to better homes, even if they themselves were willing to go. A great majority of them are entirely unfit by any sudden transition to enter on the multifarious industry which a settlement on wild land pre-supposes. They know not how to use the axe, if the land is to be cleared of timber. They know not how to hew and shape the logs necessary for the construction of their first rude cabin. They know not how to guide the plough in the prairies. They are inexpert in almost every element necessary to carry out the impractical ideal of their Buffalo advisers. But even if this were not the case the Buffalo Convention has not suggested any adequate means, either for their transportation to the west, or for the means of living there until the combined fruitfulness of the earth and their own labor should furnish them with the sustenance of life. Suppose they were skilful in clearing the wild land of timber, the Buffalo Convention has not told us who shall provide them with an axe—who shall construct their first cabin—who shall provide them with a plough, and other necessary farming utensils. . . .

The Pilgrim's Legacy

The Mayflower, on New England's coast,
has furled her tattered sail,

And through her chafed and moaning
  shrouds December breezes wail,
Yet on that icy deck, Behold! A meek but
  dauntless band,
Who, for the right to worship God, have
  left their native land;
And to a dreary wilderness, this glorious
  boon they bring,
A Church without a bishop, and a state
  without a king.
Then prince and prelate, hope no more to
  bend them to your sway,
Devotion's fire enflames their breasts, and
  freedom points the way,
And in their brave heart's estimate, 'twere
  better not to be,
Then quail beneath a despot where a soul
  cannot be free;
And therefore o'er the wintry wave, those
  exiles come to bring
A church without a bishop and a state
  without a king.
And still their spirit, in their sons, with
  freedom walks abroad,
The BIBLE is our only creed, our only *monarch,* God!
The hand is raised—the word is spoke—
  the solemn pledge is given
And boldly on our banner floats, in the free
  air of heaven,
The motto of our sainted sires, and loud
  we'll make it ring,
A church without a bishop and a state
  without a king.

We've Conquered America

Lo! O'er America's beautiful soil
Is scattered the legion who gathers the
  spoil;
The scorned and degraded of Europe's high
  powers
Their land have deserted to desecrate ours.
They come o'er the foam of the wild
  sweeping sea,
To darken the land, the bright land of the
  free,
And with soul-galling shackles of bigotry
  bind
The noble, the God-like, the Glorious mind.
O Sons of America, list to the cry!
The loud fearful warning that rings in the
  sky;
Will ye bend to the yoke of bondage so
  vile?
Shall idols your altars most sacred defile?
Arouse ye, arouse ye, O men of the North!
Let the south send her champions fear-
  lessly forth,
And the east and the west, let them gird on
  the sword,
And away to the strife in the night of the
  Lord.

5.10 The Mormon Struggle

Mormonism is now regarded as a respectable branch of Protestantism, but it started out very differently. Mormons were once widely scorned for practicing polygamy, organizing a religious despotism and maintaining an excessive political solidarity against non-Mormons.

They committed acts and lived a life-style that appeared, to most Americans, as unpatriotic, immoral, paranoid and un-American.

Mormonism—officially known as the Church of Jesus Christ of Latter-Day Saints—was founded in 1830 in New York by Joseph Smith and his disciples. Persecuted by mobs, public officials and religious enemies, the Mormons were forced to leave New York and make their way west, first to Illinois and finally to Utah. Founder Smith was lynched in 1844. His followers arrived in Utah in 1848 under the leadership of Brigham Young. In 1850, no sooner were the Mormons granted territorial status with Young as governor, than the conflict resumed in earnest.

At a church meeting in September 1851, Young charged the federal government with encouraging the murder of Smith seven years earlier. A non-Mormon tried to set the record straight. He was Judge Perry E. Brocchus, an easterner, who had come to the Mormons representing a nationwide organization trying to obtain marble blocks for the Washington monument that was then under construction. Young sparred with Brocchus, defended his original remarks and insulted the memory of the late President Zachary Taylor. It was a war of words and symbols rather than a substantive fight, but it fully illustrated the intensity of feeling on both sides. Although the breach was patched over, a few years later Young would refuse to accept orders from the government in Washington. Polygamy had surfaced publicly and was officially denounced. Federal troops would be sent to quell the "Mormon War" in 1857. Not until 1896, after the Mormons had renounced polygamy, did Utah achieve statehood.

Questions

What clue do we have that polygamy, though not openly mentioned, was on the minds of both Brocchus and Young? Why did Young express extreme hatred of the late Zachary Taylor? What part did patriotism seem to have played in this argument? Basically, what did these two men want of each other?

Has Mormonism fully lived down its status as an outsider, or are there still lingering traces of it? Explain.

Governor Young's Summary—

He expressed his everlasting gratitude for the kindness and hospitality of our people to him when sick and a stranger. He bore testimony to the peacefulness of the inhabitants of the territory, and their submission to the tribunals of their own choice, and prayed to God that all the United States might soon have such tribunals as were in this territory, and then it would always bring peace to the hearts of those who had to be judged. He hoped there would be no litigation. . . . He ap-

SOURCES: *Congressional Globe*, Appendix, 32d Cong., 1st Sess., p. 88; and Mss. entitled "Journal of Discourses," "Journal History of the Church of Jesus Christ of Latter-day Saints," September 8, 19, 1851; "Comprehensive History of the Church of Jesus Christ of Latter-day Saints," and the "Millennial Star," in the Archives of the Church of Jesus Christ of Latter-day Saints.

peared before his audience, under a commission by the board of managers of the National Washington Monument, to ask the territory to contribute a block of marble toward the erection of that building. He cursorily reviewed the career and character of George Washington. He then referred to the oration of Hon. D. W. Wells on the 24th of July, and objected to some portions of it. The government made no imperative demand for 500 of our best men for service in the Mexican War, and had no evil intentions in asking for them, nor was it responsible for the persecutions in Missouri and Illinois. President Polk expressed decided disapprobation of those deeds, he (Brocchus) felt indignant about them, and he believed the mass of the people, at the time, boiled with rage towards the perpetrators. The federal government had not injured us. The president could not lay a private wrong before congress. To those states [i.e. Missouri and Illinois], we should look for redress. The speaker regretted to hear in our midst such expressions as that the United States were a stink in our nostrils. He was pained to hear it said that the government of the United States was going to hell as fast as possible. He said that if the people of Utah could not offer a block [i.e. of marble] for the Washington Monument in full fellowship with the United States, it were better to leave it unquarried in the bosom of its native mountain. He directed a portion of his discourse towards the ladies, and libertine as he boasted himself, strongly recommended them to become virtuous.

Young's Reply to Brocchus—

Judge Brocchus is either profoundly ignorant, or willfully wicked, one of the two. . . . It is well known to every man in this community, and has become a matter of history throughout the enlightened world, that the government of the United States looked on the scenes of robbing, driving, and murdering of this people and said nothing about the matter, but by silence gave sanction to the lawless proceedings. Hundreds of women and children have been laid in the tomb prematurely in consequence thereof, and their blood cries to the Father for vengeance against those who have caused or consented to their death. George Washington was not dandled in the cradle of ease, but schooled to a life of hardship in exploring and surveying the mountains and defending the frontier settlers, even in his early youth, from the tomahawk and the scalping knife. It was God that dictated him and enabled him to assert and maintain the independence of the country. It is the same God that leads this people. I love the government and the Constitution of the United States, but I do not love the damned rascals who administer the government.

I know Zachary Taylor, he is dead and damned, and I cannot help it. I am indignant at such corrupt fellows as Judge Brocchus coming here to lecture us on morality and virtue. I could buy a thousand of such men and put them into a bandbox. Ladies and gentlemen, here we learn principle and good manners. It is an insult to this congregation to throw out such insinuations. I say it is an insult and I will say no more.

Judge Brocchus Report to President—

As the life, character, and services of Washington were intimately blended with everything relating to the Government and institutions of the United States, the occasion was supposed to be an appropriate one to disabuse the minds of the Mormon people of the false prejudicial opinions they entertained towards the people and Government of the United States, and thus to arrest that flow of seditious sentiment which was so freely pouring forth from their bosoms towards the country to which they owed their highest patriotism and their best affections. We have remained there up to this period, and submitted in silence to almost every species of indignity and mortification rather than take any step that would produce discord and involve the territorial government in difficulties. It was in this spirit that we preserved silence, until the favorable opportunity, above alluded to, was presented, when we unanimously concurred in the opinion that it was not only a matter of right, but also of duty, to have the attention of the people directed to the errors of their opinions in holding the Government of the United States and her citizens as enemies to them, and the seekers of their ruin and extermination. Such opinions were daily inculcated by the leaders of the Church upon the fanatical credulity of the masses of the people. They were taught to believe that the General Government sympathized with those whom they regarded as their persecutors in the State of Illinois and Missouri, and desired their overthrow and utter destruction. The natural result of such convictions was a feeling of deep-seated hostility towards the Government and people of the United States, which was every day becoming more deep and inveterate under the teachings of their spiritual leaders. We believed that to confront and remove those false impressions, thus shamefully instilled into the popular mind, would be to dry up the fountain of seditious sentiment in the Territory. . . . It was in pursuance of this design that the address above alluded to was made. In the course of that address the speaker endeavored, in good faith, only to correct erroneous opinions in regard to the Government from which he held his commission, without indulging in terms of invective and rebuke. His remonstrances against these opinions, and the hostile feelings resulting from them, were calm and dispassionate, and in good faith intended to effect the salutary purpose of producing peace and concord between the various branches of the Government and good will towards the United States.

The address was entirely free from any allusions, even the most remote, to the peculiar religion of the community, or to any of their domestic or social customs. It contained not a single expression of bravado or unkindness or harsh rebuke, or any sentiment that could have been tortured into a design on the part of the speaker to inflict wantonly a wound upon the hearts of his hearers.

At the close of the address, the Governor arose and denounced the speaker with great violence, as "profoundly ignorant, or willfully wicked"—strode the stage madly—assumed various theatrical attitudes—declared he "was a greater man than ever George Washington was"—"that he knew more than ever George Washington did"—that "he was the man that could handle the sword"—and "that if there was any more discussion, there would be pulling of hair and cutting of throats." Referring to a remark of the speaker, that the United States Government was humane and kindly disposed [towards] them, he said, "I know the United States did not murder our wives and children, burn our houses, and rob us of our property, but they stood by and saw it done, and never opened their mouths, the d----d soundrels." By this time the passions of the people was lashed into a fury like his own. . . .

Those of us present felt the personal danger that surrounded us. If the Governor had but pointed his finger towards us, as an indication of wish, we have no doubt we would have been massacred before leaving the house. The Governor declared afterwards "that if he had crooked his finger, we would have been torn to pieces."

Gov. Young To P. Brocchus—

Great Salt Lake City, Sept. 19, 1851. Dear Sir,—Ever wishing to promote the peace, love, and harmony of the people, and to cultivate the spirit of charity and benevolence to all, and especially towards strangers, I propose, and respectfully invite your honour to meet our public assembly at the Bowery, on Sunday evening next, at 10 A.M., and address the same people from the stand that you addressed on the 8th inst., at our General Conference; and if your honour shall then and there explain, satisfy, or apologize to the satisfaction of the ladies who heard your address on the 8th, so that those feelings of kindness which you so dearly prized in your address can be reciprocated by them. I shall esteem it a duty and a pleasure to make every apology and satisfaction for my observation which you as a gentleman can claim or desire at my hands.

Should your honour please to accept of this kind and benevolent invitation, please answer by the bearer, that public notice may be given, and widely extended, that the house may be full. And believe me, sir, most sincerely and respectfully, your friend and servant, Brigham Young.

Hon. P. E. Brocchus, Asste. Justice.

P.S.—Be assured that no gentleman will be permitted to make any repay to your address on that occasion. B.Y.

Judge Brocchus' Reply—

My sole design in the branch of my remarks which seems to be the source of offense, was to vindicate the government of the United States from those feelings of prejudice and that spirit of defection which seemed to pervade the public sentiment. That duty I attempted to perform, in a manner faithful to the government of which I am a citizen, and to which I owe a patriotic allegiance, without unjustly causing a chord to vibrate painfully in the bosom of my hearers. Such a duty, I trust, I shall ever be ready to discharge with the fidelity that belongs to a true American citizen—with firmness, with boldness, with dignity—always observing a due respect towards other parties, whether assailants or neutrals.

It was not my intention to insult, or offer disrespect to my audience and farthest possible was it from my design, to excite a painful or unpleasant emotion in the hearts of the ladies who honoured me with their presence and their respectful attention on the occasion.

In conclusion, I will remark, that at the time of the delivery of my speech, I did not conceive that it contained anything deserving the censure of a just-minded person. My subsequent reflections have fully confirmed me in that impression.

5.11 "America Letters"

Many thousands of Europeans were persuaded to migrate to America because of letters they received from relatives and friends already settled in the new land. These were called "America letters." Generally they were written for one of three reasons: to help arrange for others to make the move; to ask for financial help for starting a business in America or making some other costly change; and to overcome loneliness and alienation by staying in touch with friends and loved ones left behind.

These letters are valuable historical documents because they created the image of America in the minds of the common people of Europe. They reveal how the immigrants were assimilating and accommodating to their new lives. Native-born Americans often feared the impact of immigration on America—what they frequently ignored was the impact of America on the immigrant. It is difficult to know how typical any one letter was. Those reprinted in the European press usually had a bias of encouraging or discouraging overseas migration. Some writers were literate and expressive, while others were not. The occupation of the writers and their geographic locations had considerable bearing on the tone of the letters.

The two sample letters reprinted below are by Norwegian immigrants. They express opposite points of view. The first, dated April 22, 1835, is from Gjert Gregoriussen Hovland who had settled near Rochester, New York and later moved to Illinois. His communication is said to have touched off a wave of emigration from Norway. The second, by Hans Olsen Thorud, January 27, 1851, from Buffalo, New York, carries a more sour message. Its effect is unknown.

Questions

As a farmer, what was Hovland looking for? What did he want for his children in the way of government structure, religion, etc.? How was he coping with the language problem? Had he been an artisan or merchant, or an illiterate individual, how different might his goals and perceptions be?

What experiences or biases might have shaped Thorud's negative view?

If you wanted to know how typical these America letters are, how might you go about it?

Compare the immigrant experience of those days with what you know of the immigrant experience today. Is your family in possession of any immigrant letters? How do they compare with these letters and what do they tell you about your own family?

Gjert Hovland—

I must take this opportunity to let you know that we are in the best of health, and that we—both my wife and I—find ourselves exceedingly well satisfied. Our son attends the English school, and talks English as well as the native-born. Nothing has made me more happy and contented than the fact that we left Norway and journeyed to this country. . . .

Such excellent plans have been developed here that, even though one be infirm, no one need suffer want. Competent men are elected whose duty it is to see that no needy persons, either in the cities or in the country, shall have to beg for their living. If a man dies and is survived by a widow and children who are unable to support themselves—as is often the case—they have the privilege of petitioning these officials. To each one will then be given every year as much as is needed of clothes and food, and no discrimination will be shown between the native-born and those from foreign countries. These things I have learned through daily observation, and I do not believe there can be better laws and arrangements for the benefit and happiness of the common man in the whole world. I have talked with a sensible person who has traveled in many countries, who has lived here twenty-six years, and has full knowledge of the matter; both of him and of other reliable persons I have made inquiries, for I wish to let everyone learn the truth.

When assemblies are held to elect officials who are to serve the country, the vote of the common man carries just as much authority and influence as does that of the rich and powerful man. Neither in the matter of clothes nor in seats are distinctions to be observed, whether one be a farmer or a clerk. The freedom which the one enjoys is just as good as that of the other. So long as he comports himself honestly he will be subjected to no interference. Everybody has the liberty to travel about in the country, wherever he wishes, without any passports or papers. Everyone is permitted to engage in whatever business he finds most desirable, in trade or commerce, by land or by water. But if anyone is found guilty of crime, he will be prosecuted and severely punished for it.

No duties are levied upon goods which are produced in the country and brought to the city by water or by land. In case of death, no registration is required; the survivor, after paying the debts, is free to dispose of the property for himself and his family just as he desires. There is no one here who snatches it away, like a beast of prey, wanting only to live by the sweat of others and to make himself the heir to the money of others. No, everyone must work for his living here, and it makes no difference whether he is of low or of high estate. It would heartily please me if I could learn that everyone of you who are in need and have little chance of gaining support for yourselves and your families would make up your mind to leave Norway and to come to America, for, even if many more were to come, there would still be room here for all. For all those who are willing to work there is no lack of employment and business here. It is possible for all to live in comfort and without suffering want. I do not believe that any of those who suffer under the oppression of others and who must rear their children under straightened circumstances could do better than to help the latter to come to America. . . . I should like to talk to many persons in Norway for a little while, but we do not wish to live in Norway. We lived there altogether too long. Nor have I talked with

SOURCE: *Mississippi Valley Historical Review*, 9:71–74 (June 1922), reprinted by permission of the Organization of American Historians.

any immigrant in this country who wished to return.

We left our home in Norway on June 24, 1831. Sailing from Gottenborg on July 30, we landed in America September 18, and by October 4 we had reached this place in the interior where we now live. The day after my arrival I began to work for an American. In December I went and bought myself fifty acres of land. I put up a house which we moved into in the month of March, 1832. I then set to work with the greatest will and pleasure, for the land was covered with trees. In the fall I planted about one barrel of wheat and in the spring of 1833 we planted about half a bushel of Indian corn and three bushels of potatoes (the latter in May). The next fall we harvested fifteen barrels of wheat, six barrels of Indian corn, and fourteen barrels of potatoes. Wheat, which is grown almost everywhere, is used for one's daily food. It costs from three to four dollars a barrel, corn costs from one and one-half to two dollars a barrel, and potatoes fifty cents a barrel. Oats are a dollar a barrel, being used not for human food, but for the cattle and horses. We purchased a cow in April of the first year that we were here for eighteen dollars, from which we milked six *kander* (Norwegian measure) a day and sometimes more. A pound of butter costs, in the towns, from eight to twelve *skillings,* salt pork from four to eight *skillings* a pound, and meat four *skillings* a pound.

A hired man engaged for a whole year receives from eight to twelve dollars per month in addition to board, washing, and lodging. A servant girl receives one dollar a week, or fifty dollars a year, besides board, washing, and lodging, and is not required to do heavy or outside work, but only work within the house. A laborer engaged to work the soil receives from one-half to one dollar a day and free board.

I can also inform you that the land is measured off with a pole eight ells and six inches long, this being called a *rod*. An acre measure sixteen rods in length by ten in breadth. One hundred acres, here called a *lot,* makes a piece of land of considerable size. I am certain that from fifty acres here, we harvest many times more than from a *gaard* in Norway. I believe that an acre is something more than a *tönde sœd* in Norway; an acre is sown with two bushels of wheat.

Six families of the Norwegians who had settled in this place sold their farms last summer and moved farther west in the country to a place which is called *Ellenaais* [Illinois]. We and another Norwegian family have also sold our farms and intend to journey, this May, to that state, where land can be bought at a better price, and where it is easier for one to get started. The supply of trees there is only sufficient to meet one's actual needs. Cattle can be fed there at little cost, for one can cut as much hay there as one needs. There is an untold amount of land which the United States own and which is reserved by an established law at a set price for the one who first buys it from the government. It is called public land, and is sold for $1.25 per acre. Land thus bought and paid for is held in allodial possession for the purchaser and his heirs. Whether native-born or foreign, one is free to do with it whatever one pleases. . . .

Excellent order and good laws exist here, and the country is governed by wise authorities. . . .

In America one associates with good and kindly people. Everyone has the freedom to practice that teaching and religion which he himself favors. Nor are there any taxes to be paid here, except for the land one owns, and not even that tax is large. Nor are there other useless expenditures for the support of persons—as in many places in Europe—who are of no benefit, but much rather to the harm of the country. For the fifty acres which I have sold I paid annually one dollar in taxes.

There is much more of which I could write to you, but I will close for this time, with hearty greetings from my wife and son and myself to you, my relatives and acquaintances.

Hans Thorud—

Dear friends and countrymen, consider carefully what you are doing before you decide to come here. Please do not expect to find roasted pigs, with knives and forks in their backs, ready for anyone to eat. Moreover, the high daily wages supposed to be paid here are nothing but a fable. . . . The work is very hard, as you have to accomplish in one day here what you get three days to do in Norway. . . . Roads are bad, at times quite impassable, and most of the Norwegians and other nationals have lost their money before they reach their destination. Then they can only become beggars. Besides there are just as many taxes here as in Norway: poor tax, city tax, business tax, school tax, and so on. What you are quite sure to get here is a sickly body; Norwegians suffer particularly from the ague.

G g GIRL.

G is a Girl,
With a quiet look;
She sits in a chair,
And reads in a book.

Chapter Six: Women And The Family

6.1 Women for Virginia

When the Virginia Company of London decided to convert its military and trading outpost into a permanent settlement in 1618, they naturally thought of introducing families. The Company began recruiting women for Virginia and favoring the institution of marriage. A Company official writing from England to the resident governor on August 12, 1622 explains the new policy and how it will be implemented.

Questions

In what way did the Virginia Company intend to encourage marriage and the family? Would the new policies improve on the existing situation? How was the recruitment of women to be paid for, and how was their welfare to be looked after?

There come now over in this ship, and are immediately to follow in some others many hundreds of people, to whom as we here think ourselves bound to give the best encouragement for their going, there is no way left to increase the plantation, but by abundance of private undertakers; so we think you obliged to give all possible furtherance and assistance, for the good entertaining and well settling of them, that they may both thrive and prosper and others by their welfare be drawn after them. This is the way that we conceive most effectual for the engaging of this state, and securing of Virginia, for in the multitude of people is the strength of a kingdom. The allotting out of the settling of private persons, we leave unto your wisdom and judgment; not doubting but you will find out some course as shall give content to reasonable minds; not suffering any to plant or set down anywhere but with so sufficient a number of able men and well provided, as may, not in their own, but in your judgments (who shall be therefore accountable), defend themselves from any assaults of the Indians. In which regard, as also for their better civil government, we think it fit that the houses and buildings be so contrived together as may make if not handsome towns yet compact and orderly villages; that this is the most proper and successful manner of proceeding in new plantations.

We send you in this ship one widow and eleven maids for wives for the people in Virginia: there hath been especial care had

SOURCE: "Letter to the Governor and Council in Virginia," August 12, 1622, by the Treasurer and Council for the Virginia Company," in Susan M. Kingsbury, ed., in *The Records of the Virginia Company of London* (Washington, D.C.: Government Printing Office, 1933), III, 492–94.

in the choice of them; for there hath not any one of them been received but upon good commendations. We pray you all therefore in general to take them into your care; and more especially we recommend that at their first landing they may be housed, lodged, and provided for of diet till they be married; for such was the haste of sending them away, as that straightened with time we had no means to put provisions aboard. And in case they cannot be presently married we desire they may be put to several households that have wives till they can be provided of husbands. There are nearly fifty more which are shortly to come, are sent by certain worthy gentlemen, who taking into their consideration that the plantation can never flourish till families be planted, and the respect of wives and children fix the people on the soil. Therefore have given this fair beginning: for the reimbursing of whose charges it is ordered that every man that marries them give 120 weight of the best leaf tobacco for each of them, and in case any of them die, that proportion must be advanced to it upon those that survive. That marriage be free according to the law of nature, yet would we not have these maids deceived and married to servants, but only to such free men or tenants as have means to maintain them. We pray you therefore to be fathers to them in this business, not enforcing them to marry against their wills; neither send we them to be servants, save in case of extremity, for we would have their condition so much bettered as multitudes may be allured thereby to come unto you. And you may assure such men as marry those women that the first servants sent over by the company shall be consigned to them; it being our intent to preserve families, and to prefer married men before single persons.

6.2 A Puritan Childhood

Before pediatricians and psychiatrists started advising parents on how to raise their children, preachers often assumed this role. The Puritan clergyman Cotton Mather (1663–1728) wrote a piece entitled, "Some Special Points Relating to the Education of My Children," in which he set forth his views on child rearing. Interestingly, he speaks not only as a pastor preaching to his flock, but as a father faced with the perennial problems of educating and disciplining his own offspring.

Questions

What is Mather's view of childhood, and how good a psychologist is he? Does he understand children? How good a father do you imagine him to have been?

Compare Mather's views on rearing children with Benjamin Wadsworth's, in the following selection.

How does Mather's view of childhood compare with current thinking? Are you surprised at anything you read here?

Cotton Mather—

I. I pour out continual prayers and cries to the God of all grace for them, that He will be a Father to my children, and bestow His Christ and His Grace upon them, and guide them with His councils, and bring them to His glory. And in this action I mention them distinctly, every one by name, unto the Lord.

II. I begin betimes to entertain them with delightful stories, especially scriptural ones, and still conclude with some lesson of piety, bidding them to learn that lesson from the story. . . .

III. When the children at any time accidentally come in my way, it is my custom to let fall some sentence or other that may be monitory and profitable to them. This matter proves to me a matter of some study and labor and contrivance. But who can tell what may be the effect of a continual dropping?

IV. I essay betimes to engage the children in exercises of piety, and especially secret prayer, for which I give them very plain and brief directions, and suggest unto them the petitions which I would have them to make before the Lord and which I therefore explain to their appprehension and capacity. And I often call upon them, "Child, don't you forget every day to go alone and pray as I have directed you!"

SOURCE: Worthington C. Ford, ed., *The Diary of Cotton Mather*, in *Massachusetts Historical Society Collections* (7th series; 1911), VII, 534–37.

V. Betimes I try to form in the children a temper of benignity. I put them upon doing of services and kindnesses for one another and for other children. I applaud them when I see them delight in it. I upbraid all aversion to it. I caution them exquisitely against all revenges of injuries. I instruct them to return good offices for evil ones. I show them how they will by this goodness become like to the good God and His glorious Christ. . . .

VI. As soon as 'tis possible, I make the children learn to write. And when they can write, I employ them in writing out the most agreeable and profitable things that I can invent for them. In this way I propose to freight their minds with excellent things, and have a deep impression made upon their minds by such things.

VII. I mightily endeavor it that the children may betimes be acted by principles of reason and honor. I first beget in them an high opinion of their father's love to them, and of his being best able to judge what shall be good for them. Then I make them sensible, 'tis a folly for them to pretend unto any wit and will of their own; they must resign all to me, who will be sure to do what is best; my word must be their law. I cause them to understand that it is an hurtful and a shameful thing to do amiss. . . .

The first chastisement which I inflict for an ordinary fault is to let the child see and hear me in an astonishment, and hardly able to believe that the child could do so base a thing, but believing that they will never do it again. I would never come to give a child a blow, except in case of obstinacy or some gross enormity. To be chased for a while out of my presence I would make to be looked upon as the sorest punishment in the family.

I would by all possible insinuations gain this point upon them, that for them to learn all the brave things in the world is the bravest thing in the world. I am not fond of proposing play to them, as a reward of any diligent application to learn what is good, lest they should think diversion to be a better and a nobler thing than diligence. I would have them come to propound and expect at this rate: "I have done well, and now I will go to my father; he will teach me some curious thing for it." I must have them count it a privilege to be taught; and I sometimes manage the matter so that my refusing to teach them something is their punishment. . . .

VIII. Though I find it a marvellous advantage to have the children strongly biassed by principles of reason and honor (which, I find, children will feel sooner than is commonly thought for), yet I would neglect no endeavors to have higher principles infused into them. I therefore betimes awe them with the eye of God upon them. I show them how they must love Jesus Christ, and show it by doing what their parents require of them. . . . Heaven and Hell I set before them as the consequences of their behavior here.

IX. When the children are capable of it, I take them alone, one by one; and after my charges unto them to fear God and serve Christ and shun sin, I pray with them in my study and make them the witnesses of the agonies, with which I address the throne of grace on their behalf.

X. I find much benefit, by a particular method, as of catechising the children, so of carrying the repetition of the public sermons unto them. The answers of the catechism I still explain with abundance of brief questions, which make them to take in the meaning of it; and I see that they do so. And when the sermons are to be repeated, I choose to put every truth into a question, to be answered still with "yes" or "no". In this way I awaken their attention as well as enlighten their understanding. And in this way I have an opportunity to ask, "Do you desire such or such a grace of God?" and the like. Yea, I have an opportunity to demand, and perhaps to obtain, their consent unto the glorious articles of the new covenant. . . .

6.3 The Well-Ordered Family

Often, when the clergy write about family life they reveal more about their biases, hopes and fears than they do about the realities of daily life. Benjamin Wadsworth, a Congregational minister, in 1712 delivered a sermon on his vision of a well-ordered family. In it he describes the proper relationships of husbands and wives, children and parents, servants and masters. Portions of the sermon follow.

Questions

Wadsworth's ideal marriage partners are not equal; what are they expected to offer each other? Is there anything wrong in your opinion, with the relationship of children to parents? Does anything in the idealized puritanical household surprise you?

About Family Prayer

Family prayer is a duty. A family should pray to God for family mercies which are needed, and praise Him for family benefits which are enjoyed. *The neglect of family prayer* expose one to God's displeasure. . . .

If you cannot find time to serve God, do not think that He will find time to save you.

Your honest, lawful business will not suffer for your taking time for family prayer. You should *pray* as well as work for your daily bread. In all your ways acknowledge Him (that is; God) and He shall direct your paths.

About the Duties of Husbands and Wives

Concerning the duties of this relation we may assert a few things. *It is their duty to dwell together with one another.* Surely they should dwell together; if one house cannot hold them, surely they are not affected to each other as they should be. They should have a very great and tender love and affection to one another. This is plainly commanded by God. This duty of love is mutual; it should be performed by each, to each of them. When, therefore, they quarrel or disagree, then they do the Devil's work; he is pleased at it, glad of it. But such contention provokes God; it dishonors Him; it is a vile example before inferiors in the family; it tends to prevent family prayer.

As to outward things. If the one is sick, troubled or distressed, the other should manifest care, tenderness, pity, and compassion, and afford all possible relief and succor. They should likewise unite their prudent counsels and endeavors, comfortably to maintain themselves and the family under their joint care.

Husband and wife should be patient one toward another. If both are truly pious, yet neither of them is perfectly holy, in such cases a patient, forgiving, forbearing spirit is very needful. You, therefore, that are husbands and wives, do not aggravate every error or mistake, every wrong or hasty word, every wry step as though it were a willfuly designed intolerable crime; for this would soon break all to pieces: but rather put the best construction on things, and bear with and forgive one another's failings.

The husband's government ought to be gentle and easy, and the wife's obedience ready and cheerful. The husband is called the head of the woman. It belongs to the head to rule and govern. Wives are part of the house and family, and ought to be under the husband's government. Yet his government should not be with rigor,

SOURCE: Benjamin Wadsworth, *A Well-Ordered Family* (2d edn.; Boston, 1719), 4–5, 22–59, 99–121.

haughtiness, harshness, severity, but with the greatest love, gentleness, kindness, tenderness that may be. Though he governs her, he must not treat her as a servant, but as his own flesh; he must love her as himself.

Those husbands are much to blame who do not carry it lovingly and kindly to their wives. O man, if your wife is not so young, beautiful, healthy, well-tempered, and qualified as you would wish; if she did not bring a large estate to you, or cannot do so much for you, as some other women have done for their husbands; yet she is your wife, and the great God commands you to love her, not be bitter, but kind to her. What can be more plain and expressive than that?

Those wives are much to blame who do not carry it lovingly and obediently to their own husbands. O woman, if your husband is not as young, beautiful, healthy, so well-tempered, and qualified as you could wish; if he has not such abilities, riches, honors, as some others have; yet he is your husband, and the great God commands you to love, honor, and obey him. Yea, though possibly you have greater abilities of mind than he has, was of some high birth, and he of a more common birth, or did bring more estate, yet since he is your husband, God has made him your head, and set him above you, and made it your duty to love and revere him.

Parents should act wisely and prudently in the matching of their children. They should endeavor that they may marry someone who is most proper for them, most likely to bring blessings to them.

About the Duties of Parents and Children –

They should love their children, and carefully provide for their outward supply and comfort while unable to provide for themselves. As soon as the mother perceives herself with child, she should be careful not to do anything injurious to herself or to the child God has formed in her. Mothers also, if they are able, should suckle their children; and yet through sloth or niceness neglect to suckle them, it seems very criminal and blameworthy.

Yet by way of caution I might say, let wisdom and prudence sway, more than fond or indulgent fancy, in feeding and clothing your children. Too much niceness and delicateness in these things is not good; it tends not to make them healthy in their bodies, nor serviceable and useful in their generation, but rather the contrary.

Parents should bring up their children to be diligent in some lawful business. It is true, time for lawful recreation now and then is not altogether to be denied them. Yet for them to do little or nothing else but play in the streets, especially when almost able to earn their living, is a great sin and shame. They should by no means be brought up in idleness, or merely to learn fashions, ceremonious compliments, and to dress after the newest mode. Such folly as this ruins many children. Boys and girls should be brought up diligently in such business as they are capable of, and as is proper for them. Christians are bid to be not slothful in business. And if Christians should be thus diligent in business, surely they should be brought up to it while young. Train up a child in the way wherein he should go.

Parents should teach their children good manners. A civil, respectful, courteous behavior is comely and commendable; those who will not put suitable marks of respect and honor on others, especially on superiors, or those in authority, do not imitate the commendable examples of the godly recorded in Scripture.

Parents should instruct their children in the only true religion taught in the Scriptures. You should bring them up in the nurture and admonition of the Lord. You should also teach them to be sober, chaste, and temperate, to be just to all and bountiful to the poor as they have opportunity and ability.

Parents should govern their children well; restrain, reprove, correct them as there is occasion. A Christian householder should rule well his own house. Children should not be left to themselves, to a loose end to do as they please, but should be under tutors and governors, not being fit to govern themselves. Children being bid to obey their parents in all things plainly implies that parents should give suitable precepts to and maintain a wise government over their children, so carry it, as their children may both fear and love them. You should reprove them for their faults. He that spares the rod, hates his son. Yet on the other hand, a father should pity his children. You should by no means carry it ill to them, you should not frown, be harsh, morose, faulting, and blaming them when they do not deserve it, but do behave themselves well. Again, you should never be cruel or barbarous in your corrections; and if milder ones will reform them, more severe ones should never be used. You should not suffer your children needlessly to frequent taverns nor to be abroad unseasonable on nights, lest they are drawn into numberless hazards and mischiefs thereby.

About the Duties of Children to Their Parents—

Children should love their parents. If children duly consider, they will find they have abundant cause to love their parents, they are very vile if they neglect it.

Children should fear their parents. Children should fear both, fear to offend, grieve, disobey, or displease either of them. The great God of Heaven bids children fear their parents; if therefore they fear them not, they rebel against God.

Children should patiently bear and grow better by the needful corrections their parents give them. O child, if you are not bettered by the correction of parents, you are in danger of being terribly destroyed. Children should be faithful and obedient to their parents. . . . When children are disobedient to parents, God is often provoked to leave them to those sins which bring them to great shame and misery in this world. Alas, children, if you once become disobedient to parents, you do not know what vile abominations God may leave you to fall into. When persons have been brought to die at the gallows for their crimes, how often have they confessed that disobedience to parents led them to those crimes?

Children should be very willing and ready to support and maintain their indigent parents. If our parents are poor, aged, weak, sickly, and not able to maintain themselves, we are bound in duty and conscience to do what we can to provide for them, nourish, support, and comfort them.

About the Duties of Masters to Their Servants—

Masters should suitably provide for the bodily support and comfort of their servants. Servants are part of their household. Masters should keep their servants diligently employed. Indeed, they should allow them sufficient time to eat, drink, sleep; on proper occassions some short space for relaxation and diversion may be very advisable. To be sure, servants should be allowed time for prayer and Bible reading. But though time should be allowed for these things, yet we may say, in general, servants should be kept diligently employed. Do not let your servants be idle; oversee them carefully.

About the Duty of Servants to Their Masters—

Servants should fear their masters. Servants should honor their masters. Servants should obey their masters, be diligent and faithful in their service and to their interest. The word of God is very plain and expressive for this. You that are servants, take your Bibles, frequently read these plain commands of the great God, that out of obedience to His supreme indisputable authority you may be moved and quickened, conscientiously to obey your masters, and to be faithful to their interest. . . .

6.4 A Woman's War Memoir

While in her twenties, Sarah Osborn (b. 1756) worked as a cook and washerwoman for the Continental Army, travelling voluntarily with her husband, a commissary sergeant in the Third New York Regiment. In 1837, as a spry 81-year-old widow she applied for her husband's army pension. She swore out a deposition, part of which follows. Her account includes mention of a scalping, a court-martial, the treason of Benedict Arnold, maltreatment of black soldiers, an exchange of quips with Washington, and the British surrender at Yorktown. Many of her comments have been verified by other evidence. Her husband, a blacksmith in civilian life, was a loutish fellow and a bigamist. She was awarded a double pension, one for this husband, and another for a second one not mentioned in this application. Considering her troubles, she deserved the money. Sarah Benjamin lived to be well over 100 years of age.

Questions

What role did this colonial wife—a household servant—play, and how does it compare with the role pictured by Wadsworth in the previous document? What insights does Osborn provide about the experiences of servants during wartime?

This is an early example of what historians now call "oral history." What benefits and what disadvantages does this type of evidence have? How would you test the memory of the subject?

[A]fter deponent had married said Osborn, he informed her that he was returned during the war, and that he desired deponent to go with him. Deponent declined until she was informed by Captain Gregg that her husband should be put on the commissary guard, and that she should have the means of conveyance either in a wagon or on horseback. That deponent then in the same winter season in sleighs accompanied her husband and the forces under command of Captain Gregg on the east side of the Hudson river to Fishkill, then crossed the river and went down to West Point. There remained till the river opened in the spring, when they returned to Albany. . . .

Deponent, accompanied by her said husband and the same forces, returned during the same season to West Point. Deponent recollects no other females in company but the wife of Lieutenant Forman and of Sergeant Lamberson. Deponent was well acquainted with Captain Gregg and repeatedly saw the bare spot on his head where he had been scalped by the Indians. Captain Gregg had turns of being shattered in his mind and at such times would frequently say to deponent, "Sarah, did you ever see where I was scalped?" showing his head at the same time. Captain Gregg informed the deponent also of the circumstances of his being scalped: that he and two more went out pigeon hunting and were surprised by the Indians, and that the two men that were with him were killed dead, but that he escaped by reason of the tomahawk glancing on the button of his hat; that when he came to his senses, he crept along and laid his [head near] one of the dead men, and while there, his dog came to his relief, and by means of his dog, [caught the attention of] the two fishermen who were fishing near the fort.

Deponent further says that she and her husband remained at West Point till the departure of the army for the South, a term of perhaps one year and a half, but she cannot be positive as to the length of time. While at West Point, deponent lived at Lieutenant Foot's, who kept a boarding-house. Deponent was employed in washing and sewing for the soldiers. Her said husband was employed about the camp. She well recollects the uproar occasioned when word came that a British officer had been taken as a spy. She understood at the time that Major André was brought up on the opposite side of the river and kept there till he was executed. On the return of the bargemen who assisted Arnold to escape, deponent recollects seeing two of them, one by the name of Montecu, and other by the name of Clark. That they said Arnold told them to hang up their dinners, for he had to be at Stony Point in so many minutes, and when he got there he hoisted his pocket handkerchief and his sword and said, "Row on boys," and that they soon arrived in Haverstraw Bay and found the British ship. That Arnold jumped on board, and they were all invited, and they went aboard and had their choice to go or stay. And some chose to stay and some to go and did accordingly.

When the army were about to leave West Point and go south, they . . . traveled all night in a direct course for Philadelphia. Deponent was part of the time on horseback and part of the time in a wagon. Deponent's said husband was still serving as one of the commissary's guard. A man by the name of Burke was hung about this time for alleged treason, but more especially for insulting Adjutant Wendell, the prosecutor against Burke, as deponent understood and believed at the time. . . .

SOURCE: Sarah Osborn deposition, U.S. National Archives, Record Group 15, Records of the Veterans Administration, microfilm, M804, M805, M898.

In their march for Philadelphia, they were under command of Generals Washington and Clinton, Colonel Van Schaick, Captain Gregg, Captain Parsons, Lieutenant Forman, Sergeant Lamberson, Ensign Clinton, one of the general's sons. They continued their march to Philadelphia, deponent on horseback through the streets, and arrived at a place towards the Schuylkill where the British had burnt some houses, where they encamped for the afternoon and night. Being out of bread, deponent was employed in baking the afternoon and evening . . . next day they continued their march from day to day till they arrived at Baltimore, where deponent and her said husband and the forces under command of General Clinton, Captain Gregg, and several other officers, all of whom she does not recollect, embarked on board a vessel and sailed down the Chesapeake. There were several vessels along, and deponent was in the foremost. . . . They continued sail until they had got up the St. James River as far as the tide would carry them, about twelve miles from the mouth, and then landed, and the tide being spent, they had a fine time catching sea lobsters, which they ate.

They, however, marched immediately for a place called Williamsburg, as she thinks, deponent alternately on horseback and on foot. There arrived, they remained two days till the army all came in by land and then marched for Yorktown, or Little York as it was then called. The York troops were posted at the right, the Connecticut troops next, and the French to the left. In about one day or less than a day, they reached the place of encampment about one mile from Yorktown. Deponent was on foot and the other females above named and her said husband still on the commissary's guard. Deponent's attention was arrested by the appearance of a large plain between them and Yorktown and an entrenchment thrown up. She also saw a number of dead Negroes lying round their encampment, whom she understood the British had driven out of the town and left to starve, or were first starved and then thrown out. Deponent took her stand just back of the American tents, say about a mile from the town, and busied herself washing, mending, and cooking for the soldiers, in which she was assisted by the other females; some men washed their own clothing. She heard the roar of the artillery for a number of days, and the last night the Americans threw up entrenchments . . . deponent cooked and carried in beef, and bread, and coffee (in a gallon pot) to the soldiers in the entrenchment.

On one occasion when deponent was thus employed carrying in provisions, she met General Washington, who asked her if she "was not afraid of the cannonballs?". . . .

They dug entrenchments nearer and nearer to Yorktown every night or two till the last. While digging that, the enemy fired very heavy till about nine o'clock next morning, then stopped, and the drums from the enemy beat excessively. . . .

The drums continued beating, and all at once the officers hurrahed and swung their hats, and deponent asked them, "What is the matter now?"

One of them replied, "Are not you soldier enough to know what it means?"

Deponent replied, "No."

They then replied, "The British have surrendered."

Deponent, having provisions ready, carried the same down to the entrenchments that morning, and four of the soldiers whom she was in the habit of cooking for ate their breakfasts.

Deponent stood on one side of the road and the American officers upon the other side when the British officers came out of the town and rode up to the American officers and delivered up [their swords, which the deponent] thinks were returned again, and the British officers rode right on before the army, who marched out beating and playing a melancholy tune, their drums covered with black handkerchiefs and their fifes with black ribbands tied around them, into an old field and there grounded their arms and then returned into town again to await their destiny. Deponent recollects seeing a great many American officers, some on horseback and some on foot, but cannot call them all by name. Washington, Lafayette, and Clinton were among the number. The British general at the head of the army was a large, portly man, full face, and the tears rolled down his cheeks as he passed along. She does not recollect his name, but it was not Cornwallis. She saw the latter afterwards and noticed his being a man of diminutive appearance and having cross eyes. . . .

After two or three days, deponent and her husband, Captain Gregg, and others who were sick or complaining embarked on board a vessel from Yorktown, not the same they came down in, and set sail up the Chesapeake Bay and continued to the Head of Elk, where they landed . . . they arrived at Pompton Plains in New Jersey. Deponent does not recollect the county. They were joined by the main body of the army under General Clinton's command, and they set down for winter quarters. Deponent and her husband lived a part of the time in a tent made of logs but covered with cloth, and a part of the time at a Mr. Manuel's near Pompton Meetinghouse. She busied herself during the winter in cooking and sewing as usual. Her said husband was on duty among the rest of the army and held the station of corporal from the time he left West Point.

In the opening of spring, they marched to West Point and remained there during the summer, her husband still with her. In the fall they came up a little back of Newburgh to a place called New Windsor and put up huts on Ellis's lands and again sat down for winter quarters, her said husband still along and on duty. The York troops and Connecticut troops were there. In the following spring or autumn they were all discharged. Deponent and her husband remained in New Windsor in a log house built by the army until the spring following. Some of the soldiers boarded at their house and worked round among the farmers, as did her said husband also.

Deponent and her husband spent certainly more than three years in the service, for she recollects a part of one winter at West Point and the whole of another winter there, another winter at Pompton Plains, and another at New Windsor. And her husband was the whole time under the command of Captain Gregg as an enlisted soldier holding the station of corporal to the best of her knowledge.

In the winter before the army were disbanded at New Windsor, on the twentieth of February, deponent had a child by the name of Phebe Osborn, of whom the said Aaron Osborn was the father. A year and five months afterwards, on the ninth day of August at the same place, she had another child by the name of Aaron Osborn, Jr., of whom the said husband was the father. The said Phebe Osborn afterwards married a man by the name of William Rockwell and moved into the town of Dryden, Tompkins County, New York, where he died, say ten or twelve years ago, but her said daughter yet lives near the same place on the west side of Ithaca, in the town of Enfield. Her son Aaron Osborn, Jr., lived in Blooming Grove, Orange County, New York, had fits and was crazy, and became a town charge, and finally died there at the age of about thirty years.

About three months after the birth of her last child, Aaron Osborn, Jr., she last saw her said husband, who then left her at New Windsor and never returned. He had been absent at intervals before this from deponent, and at one time deponent understood he was married again to a girl by the name of Polly Sloat above Newburgh about fifteen or sixteen miles. Deponent got a horse and rode up to inquire into the truth of the story. She arrived at the girl's father's and there found her said husband, and Polly Sloat, and her parents. Deponent was kindly treated by the inmates of the house but ascertained for a truth that her husband was married to said girl. After remaining overnight, deponent determined to return home and abandon her said husband forever, as she found he had conducted in such a way as to leave no hope of reclaiming him. . . . Deponent heard of him afterwards up the Mohawk River and that he had married again. Deponent, after hearing of this second unlawful marriage of her said husband, married herself to John Benjamin of Blooming Grove, Orange County, New York, whose name she now bears.

About twenty years ago, deponent heard that her said husband Osborn died up the Mohawk, and she has no reason to believe to the contrary to this day. Deponent often saw the discharge of her said husband Osborn and understood that he drew a bounty in lands in the lake country beyond Ithaca, but her husband informed her that he sold his discharge and land together in Newburgh to a merchant residing there whose name she cannot recollect. Her son-in-law, said Rockwell, on hearing of the death of Osborn, went out to see the land and returned saying that it was a very handsome lot. But said Rockwell being now dead, she can give no further information concerning it. Deponent was informed more than forty years ago and believes that said Polly Sloat, Osborn's second wife above mentioned, died dead drunk, the liquor running out of her mouth after she was dead. Osborn's third wife she knows nothing about.

After deponent was thus left by Osborn, she removed from New Windsor to Blooming Grove, Orange County, New York, about fifty years ago, where she had been born and brought up, and, having married Mr. Benjamin as above stated, she continued to reside there perhaps thirty-five years, when she and her husband Benjamin removed to Pleasant Mount, Wayne County, Pennsylvania, and there she has resided to this day. Her said husband, John Benjamin, died there ten years ago last April, from which time she has continued to be and is now a widow.

6.5 Women in a Democracy

The Frenchman Alexis de Tocqueville studied the family and the status of women in America during his travels here in 1831. He tried to compare the behavior and lifestyles of young women, before and during marriage, here and in Europe. He found, among other things, that when the young American woman marries she undergoes a dramatic loss of independence. He reports and analyzes these facets in his classic work, Democracy in America. *An excerpt from his chapter, "Young Women in a Democracy," appears below. (See also Documents 3.5 and 5.10.)*

Questions

What are Tocqueville's biases and prejudices about gender? What differences does he see in young American women compared to European women. Which traits please him most and which cause him concern? How is the virtue of women defended in America? What did he say happened to the independence of American women when they married, and why?

Does anything he describes in the 1830s still hold true in America today? Are morals still "the work of women"?

No free communities ever existed without morals; and, as I observed in the former part of this work, morals are the work of women. Consequently, whatever affects the condition of women, their habits and their opinions, has great political importance in my eyes.

Amongst almost all Protestant nations, young women are far more the mistresses of their own actions than they are in Catholic countries. This independence is still greater in Protestant countries like England, which have retained or acquired the right of self-government; freedom is then infused into the domestic circle by political habits and by religious opinions. In the United States, the doctrines of Protestantism are combined with great political liberty and a most democratic state of society; and nowhere are young women surrendered so early or so completely to their own guidance.

Long before an American girl arrives at the marriageable age, her emancipation from maternal control begins: she has scarcely ceased to be a child, when she already thinks for herself, speaks with freedom, and acts on her own impulse. The great scene of the world is constantly open to her view: far from seeking to conceal it from her, it is every day disclosed

SOURCE: Alexis de Tocqueville, *Democracy in America,* Part II, Book Three, Chapter 39.

more completely, and she is taught to survey it with a firm and calm gaze. Thus the vices and dangers of society are early revealed to her; as she sees them clearly, she views them without illusion, and braves them without fear; for she is full of reliance on her own strength, and her confidence seems to be shared by all around her. . . .

I have been frequently surprised, and almost frightened, at the singular address and happy boldness with which young women in America contrive to manage their thoughts and their language, amidst all the difficulties of free conversation; a philosopher would have stumbled at every step along the narrow path which they trod without accident and without effort. It is easy, indeed, to perceive that, even amidst the independence of early youth, an American woman is always mistress of herself: she indulges in all permitted pleasures, without yielding herself up to any of them; and her reason never allows the reins of self-guidance to drop, though it often seems to hold them loosely.

In France, where traditions of every age are still so strangely mingled in the opinions and tastes of the people, women commonly receive a reserved, retired, and almost conventual education, as they did in aristocratic times; and then they are suddenly abandoned, without a guide and without assistance, in the midst of all the irregularities inseparable from democratic society.

The Americans are more consistent. They have found out that, in a democracy, the independence of individuals cannot fail to be very great, youth premature, tastes ill-restrained, customs fleeting, public opinion often unsettled and powerless, paternal authority weak, and marital authority contested. Under these circumstances, believing that they had little chance of repressing in woman the most vehement passions of the human heart, they held that the surer way was to teach her the art of combating those passions for herself. As they could not prevent her virtue from being exposed to frequent danger, they determined that she should know how best to defend it; and more reliance was placed on the free vigor of her will than on safeguards which have been shaken or overthrown. Instead then of inculcating mistrust of herself, they constantly seek to enhance her confidence in her own strength of character. . . .

Although the Americans are a very religious people, they do not rely on religion alone to defend the virtue of woman; they seek to arm her reason also. . . .

I am aware that an education of this kind is not without danger; I am sensible that it tends to invigorate the judgment at the expense of the imagination, and to make cold and virtuous women instead of affectionate wives and agreeable companions to man. Society may be more tranquil and better regulated, but domestic life has often fewer charms. These, however, are secondary evils, which may be braved for the sake of higher interests. At the stage at which we are now arrived, the choice is no longer left to us; a democratic education is indispensable to protect women from the dangers with which democratic institutions and manners surround them.

In America, the independence of woman is irrecoverably lost in the bonds of matrimony. If an unmarried woman is less constrained there than elsewhere, a wife is subjected to stricter obligations. The former makes her father's house an abode of freedom and of pleasure; the latter lives in the home of her husband as if it were a cloister. Yet these two different conditions of life are perhaps not so contrary as may be supposed, and it is natural that the American women should pass through the one to arrive at the other.

Religious communities and trading nations entertain peculiarly serious notions of marriage: the former consider the regularity of woman's life as the best pledge and most certain sign of the purity of her morals; the latter regard it as the highest security for the order and prosperity of the household. The Americans are, at the same time, a puritanical people and a commercial nation; their religious opinions, as well as their trading habits, consequently lead them to require much abnegation on the part of women, and a constant sacrifice of her pleasures to her duties, which is seldom demanded of her in Europe. . . .

Upon her entrance into the world, a young American woman finds these notions firmly established; she sees the rules which are derived from them; she is not slow to perceive that she cannot depart for an instant from the established usages of her contemporaries, without putting in jeopardy her peace of mind, her honor, nay, even her social existence; and she finds the energy required for such an act of submission in the firmness of her understanding, and in the virile habits which her education has given her. It may be said that she has learned, by the use of her independence, to surrender it without a struggle and without a murmur when the time comes for making the sacrifice.

But no American woman falls into the toils of matrimony as into a snare held out to her simplicity and ignorance. She had been taught beforehand what is expected of her, and voluntarily and freely enters upon this engagement. She supports her new condition with courage, because she chose it. As, in America, paternal discipline is very relaxed and the conjugal tie very strict, a young woman does not contract the latter without considerable circumspection and apprehension. Precocious marriages are rare. American women do not marry until their understandings are exercised and ripened; whereas, in other countries, most women generally only begin to exercise and ripen their understandings after marriage.

I by no means suppose, however, that the great change which takes place in all the habits of women in the United States, as soon as they are married, ought solely to be attributed to the constraint of public opinion; it is frequently imposed upon themselves by the sole effort of their own will. When the time for choosing a husband is arrived, that cold and stern reasoning power which has been educated and invigorated by the free observation of the world teaches an American woman that a spirit of levity and independence in the bonds of marriage is a constant subject of annoyance, not of pleasure; it tells her that the amusements of the girl cannot become the recreations of the wife, and that the sources of a married woman's happiness are in the home of her husband. . . .

The same strength of purpose which the young wives of America display, in bending themselves at once and without repining to the austere duties of their new condition, is no less manifest in all the great trials of their lives. In no country in the world are private fortunes more precarious than in the United States. It is not uncommon for the same man, in the course of his life, to rise and sink again through all the grades which lead from opulence to poverty. American women support these vicissitudes with calm and unquenchable energy: it would seem that their desires contract as easily as they expand with their fortunes.

The greater part of the adventurers who migrate every year to people the Western wilds belong, as I observed in the former part of this work, to the old Anglo-American race of the Northern States. Many of these men, who rush so boldly onwards in pursuit of wealth, were already in the enjoyment of a competency in their own part of the country. They take their wives along with them, and make them share the countless perils and privations which always attend the commencement of these expeditions. I have often met, even on the verge of the wilderness, with young women who, after having been brought up amidst all the comforts of the large towns of New England, had passed, almost without any intermediate stage, from the wealthy abode of their parents to a comfortless hovel in a forest. Fever, solitude, and a tedious life had not broken the springs of their courage. Their features were impaired and faded, but their looks were firm; they appeared to be at once sad and resolute. I do not doubt that these young American women had amassed, in the education of their early years, that inward strength which they displayed under these circumstances. . . .

6.6 Her Proper Place

Angelina and Sarah Grimké (1805–1879; 1792–1873) were the daughters of a prominent slave-owning family in South Carolina. Although their parents were Anglicans, they had become Quakers when they moved to Philadelphia. The evil of slavery aroused them and they decided to speak out publicly against it. In Massachusetts in 1837 they addressed mixed audiences of men and women and described, among things, the sexual abuse of white men against black women. This infuriated the Congregational clergy, who demanded the women be silent. Sarah defended herself and her sister in a Letter on the Equality of the Sexes and the Condition of Women, *published in 1838, while Angelina wrote in a similar vein to Catherine Beecher, a pioneer in woman's education. These documents showed the difficulty of pious Christian women struggling to break the mold of religious teachings. Although the main issue was slavery, the subsidiary issue had became woman's rights. Both the clergymen's pastoral letter and Angelina's letters to Beecher are excerpted below.*

Questions

Summarize Angelina Grimké's arguments, the ministers' reactions, and what you think might be Beecher's position. How does each view the proper role for women in society? Where do they clash, where do they agree? How do they think a religious woman should legitimately deal with human rights and related moral issues?

Conservatives and liberals still disagree on the part that woman should play in achieving social or political reforms. What arguments does each side offer?

Pastoral Letter—

. . . We invite your attention to the dangers which at present seem to threaten the female character with wide-spread and permanent injury.

The appropriate duties and influence of woman are clearly stated in the New Testament. Those duties and that influence are unobtrusive and private, but the source of mighty power. When the mild, dependent, softening influence of woman upon the sternness of man's opinions is fully exercised, society feels the effects of it in a thousand forms. The power of woman is in her dependence, flowing from the consciousness of that weakness which God has given her for her protection, and which keeps her in those departments of life that form the character of individuals and of the nation. There are social influences which females use in promoting piety and the great objects of Christian benevolence which we cannot too highly commend. We appreciate the unostentatious prayers and efforts of woman in advancing the cause of religion at home and abroad; in Sabbath-schools; in leading religious inquirers to the pastors for instruction; and in all such associated effort as becomes the modesty of her sex. . . .

But when she assumes the place and tone of man as a public reformer, our care and protection of her seem unnecessary; we put ourselves in self-defence against her; she yields the power which God has given her for protection, and her character becomes unnatural. . . . We cannot, therefore, but regret the mistaken conduct of those who encourage females to bear an obtrusive and ostentatious part in measures of reform, and countenance any of that sex who so far forget themselves as to itinerate in the character of public lecturers and teachers.—We especially deplore the intimate acquaintance and promiscuous conversation of females with regard to things "which ought not to be named"; by which that modesty and delicacy which is the charm of domestic life, and which constitutes the true influence of woman in society, is consumed, and the way opened, as we apprehend, for degeneracy and ruin. We say these things, not to discourage proper influences against sin, but to secure such reformation as we believe is Scriptural, and will be permanent.

SOURCES: "Pastoral Letter of the General Association of Massachusetts Congregationalist Clergy (Orthodox) to the Churches under Their Care," in the *Liberator* (Boston), August 11, 1837; *Letters to Catherine E. Beecher, in Reply to an Essay on Slavery and Abolitionism, Addressed to A. E. Grimké* (Boston, 1838), excerpts from Letters XI and XII, pp. 103–9, 114–21.

Angelina Grimké—

BROOKLINE, Mass. 8th month, 28th, 1837.

Dear Friend: I come now to that part of thy book, which is, of all others, the most important to the women of this country; thy "general views in relation to the place woman is appointed to fill by the dispensations of heaven." I shall quote paragraphs from thy book, offer my objections to them, and then throw before thee my own views.

Thou sayest, "Heaven has appointed to one sex the *superior*, and to the other the *subordinate* station, and this without any reference to the character or conduct of either." This is an assertion without proof. Thou further sayest, that "it was designed that the mode of gaining influence and exercising power should be *altogether different and peculiar.*" Does the Bible teach this? "Peace on earth, and good will to men, is the character of all the rights and privileges, the influence and the power of *woman.*" Indeed! Did our Holy Redeemer preach the doctrines of *peace to our sex* only? "A *man* may act on Society by the collision of intellect, in public debate; *he* may urge his measures by a sense of shame, by fear and by personal interest; *he* may coerce by the combination of public sentiment; *he* may drive by physical force, and *he* does *not* overstep the boundaries of his sphere." Did Jesus, then, give a different rule of action to men and women? Did he tell his disciples, when he sent them out to preach the gospel, that man might appeal to the fear, and shame, and interest of those he addressed, and coerce by public sentiment, and drive by physical force? "But (that) all the power and all the conquests that are lawful to *woman* are those only which appeal to the kindly, generous, peaceful and benevolent principles?" If so, I should come to a very different conclusion from the one at which thou hast arrived: I should suppose that *woman was the superior,* and *man the subordinate being,* inasmuch as moral power is immeasurably superior to "physical force."

"Woman is to win every thing by peace and love; by making *herself* so much respected, &c. that to yield to *her* opinions, and to gratify *her* wishes, will be the free-will offering of the heart." This principle may do as the rule of action to the fashionable belle,whose idol is *herself;* whose every attitude and smile are designed to win the admiration of others to *herself;* and who enjoys, with exquisite delight, the double-refined incense of flattery which is offered to *her* vanity, by yielding to *her* opinions, and gratifying *her* wishes, because they are *hers.* But to the humble Christian, who feels that it is *truth* which she seeks to recommend to others, *truth* which she wants them to esteem and love, and not herself, this subtle principle must be rejected with holy indignation. Suppose she could win thousands to her opinions, and govern them by her wishes, how much nearer would they be to Jesus Christ, if she presents no higher motive, and points to no higher leader?

"But this is all to be accomplished in the domestic circle." Indeed! "Who made thee a ruler and a judge over all?" I read in the Bible, that Miriam, and Deborah, and Huldah, were called to fill *public stations* in Church and State. I find Anna, the prophetess, speaking in the temple "unto all them that looked for redemption in Jerusalem." During his ministry on earth, I see women following him from town to town, in the most public manner; I hear the woman of Samaria, on her return to the city, telling the *men* to come and see a man who had told her all the things that ever she did. I see them even standing on Mount Calvary, around his cross, in the most exposed situation; but He never *rebuked* them; He never told them it was unbecoming *their sphere in life* to mingle in the crowds which followed his footsteps. . . . And it shall come to pass in the last days, said *God,* I will pour out my spirit upon *all* flesh: and your sons and your *daughters shall prophesy*. . . . And on my servants and on my *handmaidens,* I will pour out in those days of my spirit; and *they shall prophesy*." . . .

I find, too, that Philip had four daughters which did *prophesy;* . . . On examination, too, it appears that the very same word, *Diakonos,* which, when applied to Phoebe, Romans xvi. 1, is translated *servant,* when applied to Tychicus, Ephesians vi. 21, is rendered *minister.* Ecclesiastical History informs us, that this same Phoebe was pre-eminently useful, as a minister in the Church, and that female ministers suffered martyrdom in the first ages of Christianity. And what, I ask, does the Apostle mean when he says in Phillipians [*sic*] iv. 3.— "Help those women who labored with me in the gospel"? Did these holy women of old perform all their gospel labors in "the domestic and social circle"? I trow not.

Thou sayest, "the moment woman begins to feel the promptings of ambition, or the thirst for power, her aegis of defence is gone." Can man, then, retain his aegis when he indulges these guilty passions? Is it woman only who suffers this loss?

"All the generous promptings of chivalry, all the poetry of romantic gallantry, depend upon woman's retaining her place as *dependent* and *defenceless,* and making no claims, and maintaining no rights, but what are the gifts of honor, rectitude and love."

I cannot refrain from pronouncing this sentiment as beneath the dignity of any woman who names the name of Christ. No woman, who understands her dignity as a moral, intellectual and accountable being, cares aught for any attention or any protection, vouchsafed by "the promptings of chivalry, and the poetry of romantic gallantry." Such a one loathes such littleness, and turns with disgust from all such silly insipidities. Her noble nature is insulted by such paltry, sickening adulation, and she will not stoop to drink the foul waters of so turbid a stream. If all this sinful foolery is to be withdrawn from our sex, with all my heart I say, *the sooner the better.* . . .

"A woman may seek the aid of cooperation and combination among her own sex, to assist her in her appropriate offices of piety, charity," &c. *Appropriate* offices! Ah! here is the great difficulty. What are they? Who can point them out? Who has ever attempted to draw a line of separation between the duties of men and women, as *moral* beings, without committing the grossest inconsistencies on the one hand, or running into the most arrant absurdities on the other?

"Whatever, in any measure, throws a woman into the attitude of a combatant, either for herself or others—whatever binds her in a party conflict—whatever obliges her in any way to exert coercive influences, throws her out of her appropriate sphere." If, by a *combatant,* thou meanest one who "drives by *physical force,*" then I say, *man* has no more right to appear as *such* a combatant than woman; for all the pacific precepts of the gospel were given to *him,* as well as to her. If, by a *party conflict,* thou meanest a struggle for power, either civil or ecclesiastical, a thirst for the praise and the honor of man, why, then I would ask, is this the proper sphere of *any* moral, accountable being, man or woman? If, by *coercive influences,* thou meanest the use of force or of fear, such as slaveholders and warriors employ, then, I repeat, that *man* has no more right to exert these than *woman.* All such influences are repudiated by the precepts and examples of Christ, and his apostles; so that, after all, this appropriate sphere of woman is *just as appropriate* to man. . . .

6.7 Separate Spheres for Men and Women

Thomas R. Dew, a teacher at William and Mary College in Virginia, was best known as a pro-slavery pamphleteer. As a conservative, in 1835 he also wrote a "Dissertation on the Characteristic Differences between the Sexes, and on the Position and Influence of Women in Society." In it he argued that society would be better off by maintaining separate spheres for men and women. A portion follows.

Questions

What benefits did Dew find in the two separate spheres for men and women? Did the sexes benefit equally from the separation?

Today, family life seems more difficult than ever. Were conservatives like Dew right after all that the spheres should remain separate? Have we lost something by merging sexual roles, and is it possible to get back what we lost? How so?

The relative position of the sexes in the social and political world, may certainly be looked upon as the result of organization. The greater physical strength of man, enables him to occupy the foreground in the picture. He leaves the domestic scenes; he plunges into the turmoil and bustle of an active, selfish world; in his journey through life, he has to encounter innumerable difficulties, hardships and labors which constantly beset him. His mind must be nerved against them. Hence courage and boldness are his attributes. . . . He is the shield of woman, destined by nature to guard and protect her. Her inferior strength and sedentary habits confine her within the domestic circle; she is kept aloof from the bustle and storm of active life; she is not familiarized to the out of door dangers and hardships of a cold and scuffling world: timidity and modesty are her attributes. . . . She must rely upon the strength of others; man must be engaged in her cause. How is he to be drawn over to her side? Not by menace—not by force; for weakness cannot, by such means, be expected to triumph over might. No! It must be by conformity to that character which circumstances demand for the sphere in which she moves; by the exhibition of those qualities which delight and fascinate—which are calculated to win over to her side the proud lord of creation,

SOURCE: *Southern Literary Messenger* (Richmond, Va.), I (May 1835), 493–512.

and to make him an humble suppliant at her shrine. Grace, modesty and loveliness are the charms which constitute her power. . . . Her attributes are rather of a passive than active character. Her power is more emblematical of that of divinity: it subdues without an effort, and almost creates by mere volition; whilst man must wind his way through the difficult and intricate mazes of philosophy; with pain and toil, tracing effects to their causes, and unraveling the deep mysteries of nature—storing his mind with useful knowledge, and exercising, training and perfecting his intellectual powers, whilst he cultivates his strength and hardens and matures his courage; all with a view of enabling him to assert his rights, and exercise a greater sway over those around him. Woman we behold dependant [sic] and weak; but out of that very weakness and dependance [sic] springs an irresistible power. She may pursue her studies too—not however with a view of triumphing in the senate chamber—not with a view to forensic display—not with a view of leading armies to combat, or of enabling her to bring into more formidable action the physical power which nature has conferred on her. No! It is but the better to perfect all those feminine graces, all those fascinating attributes, which render her the centre of attraction, and which delight and charm all who breathe the atmosphere in which she moves. . . .

6.8 The Birth of the Woman's Movement

The basic yardstick for measuring feminist complaints and achievements in American history is the "Declaration of Sentiments" issued by the first woman's convention in July, 1848. Gathering in the Wesleyan chapel in the small northern New York town of Seneca Falls, some 260 women and 40 men gathered to hear complaints and make demands for the improvement of the status of women. The meeting's organizers were Lucretia Mott, a teacher, Quaker minister and mother of six, and Elizabeth Cady Stanton, a prominent antislavery and temperance advocate, who would become the leading advocate for nineteenth-century feminism.

The Seneca Falls declaration fired the opening salvo of the woman's rights movement in the U.S. All resolutions were drafted by Stanton except the last, which Mott added at the final session. Clearly the statement is modeled after the Declaration of Independence of 1776. Many complaints are addressed, but the centerpiece is the demand for suffrage. Allowing women to vote was considered controversial even at that meeting.

Questions

Compare the Seneca Falls Declaration with the Declaration of Independence of July 4, 1776. What grievances did the feminists point to, and how did they propose to bring about improvements? The authors refer to a different code of morals for men and women. What, if anything, is wrong with a double standard?

This declaration charges men with trying to destroy women's confidence in themselves and weakening their self-respect. How did men do this? And if women were brainwashed, as the statement indicates, how could they get out of the situation in which they were accomplices to their own subjugation? Is this condition still a problem? Explain.

Since male voters held the key to women's liberation, what arguments could women invent to convince them *to share power and give women the vote?*

What has changed since 1848 and what remains the same?

When, in the course of human events, it becomes necessary for one portion of the family of man to assume among the people of the earth a position different from that which they have hitherto occupied, but one to which the laws of nature and of nature's God entitle them, a decent respect to the opinions of mankind requires that they should declare the causes that impel them to such a course.

We hold these truths to be self-evident: that all men and women are created equal; that they are endowed by their Creator with certain inalienable rights; that among these are life, liberty, and the pursuit of happiness; that to secure these rights governments are instituted, deriving their just powers from the consent of the governed. Whenever any form of government becomes destructive of these ends, it is the right of those who suffer from it to refuse allegiance to it, and to insist upon the institution of a new government, laying its foundation on such principles, and organizing its powers in such form, as to them shall seem most likely to effect their safety and happiness. Prudence, indeed, will dictate that governments long established should not be changed for light and transient causes; and accordingly all experience hath shown that mankind are more disposed to suffer, while evils are sufferable, than to right themselves by abolishing the forms to which they were accustomed. But when a long train of abuses and usurpations, pursuing invariably, the same object, evinces a design to reduce them under absolute despotism, it is their duty to throw off such government, and to provide new guards for their future security. Such has been the patient sufferance of the women under this government, and such is now the necessity which constrains them to demand the equal station to which they are entitled.

The history of mankind is a history of repeated injuries and usurpations on the part of man toward woman, having in direct object the establishment of an ab-

SOURCE: Elizabeth Cady Stanton, Susan B. Anthony, and Matilda Joslyn Gage, eds., *History of Woman Suffrage* (New York, 1881), I, 70–73.

solute tyranny over her. To prove this, let facts be submitted to a candid world.

He has never permitted her to exercise her inalienable right to the elective franchise.

He has compelled her to submit to laws, in the formation of which she had no voice.

He has withheld from her rights which are given to the most ignorant and degraded men—both natives and foreigners.

Having deprived her of this first right of a citizen, the elective franchise, thereby leaving her without representation in the halls of legislation, he has oppressed her on all sides.

He has made her, if married, in the eye of the law, civilly dead.

He has taken from her all right in property, even to the wages she earns.

He has made her, morally, an irresponsible being, as she can commit many crimes with impunity, provided they be done in the presence of her husband. In the covenant of marriage, she is compelled to promise obedience to her husband, he becoming, to all intents and purposes, her master—the law giving him power to deprive her of her liberty, and to administer chastisement.

He has so framed the laws of divorce, as to what shall be the proper causes, and in case of separation, to whom the guardianship of the children shall be given, as to be wholly regardless of the happiness of women—the law, in all cases, going upon the false supposition of the supremacy of man, and giving all power into his hands.

After depriving her of all rights as a married woman, if single, and the owner of property, he has taxed her to support a government which recognizes her only when her property can be made profitable to it.

He has monopolized nearly all the profitable employments, and from those she is permitted to follow, she receives but a scanty remuneration. He closes against her all the avenues to wealth and distinction which he considers most honorable to himself. As a teacher of theology, medicine, or law, she is not known.

He has denied her the facilities for obtaining a thorough education, all colleges being closed against her.

He allows her in Church, as well as State, but a subordinate position, claiming Apostolic authority for her exclusion from the ministry, and, with some exceptions, from any public participation in the affairs of the Church.

He has created a false public sentiment by giving to the world a different code of morals for men and women, by which moral delinquencies which exclude women from society, are not only tolerated, but deemed of little account in man.

He has ursurped the prerogative of Jehovah himself, claiming it as his right to assign for her a sphere of action, when that belongs to her conscience and to her God.

He has endeavored, in every way that he could, to destroy her confidence in her own powers, to lessen her self-respect, and to make her willing to lead a dependent and abject life.

Now, in view of this entire disfranchisement of one-half the people of this country, their social and religious degradation—in view of the unjust laws above mentioned, and because women do feel themselves aggrieved, oppressed, and fraudulently deprived of their most sacred rights, we insist that they have immediate admission to all the rights and privileges which belong to them as citizens of the United States.

In entering upon the great work before us, we anticipate no small amount of misconception, misrepresentation, and ridicule; but we shall use every instrumentality within our power to effect our object. We shall employ agents, circulate tracts, petition the State and National legislatures, and endeavor to enlist the pulpit and the press in our behalf. We hope this Convention will be followed by a series of Conventions embracing every part of the country.

Resolutions

Whereas, The great precept of nature is conceded to be, that "man shall pursue his own true and substantial happiness." Blackstone in his Commentaries remarks, that this law of Nature being coeval with mankind, and dictated by God himself, is of course superior in obligation to any other. It is binding over all the globe, in all countries and at all times; no human laws are of any validity if contrary to this, and such of them as are valid, derive all their force, and all their validity, and all their authority, mediately and immediately, from this original; therefore,

Resolved, That such laws as conflict, in any way, with the true and substantial happiness of woman, are contrary to the great precept of nature and of no validity, for this is "superior in obligation to any other."

Resolved, That all laws which prevent woman from occupying such a station in society as her conscience shall dictate, or which place her in a position inferior to that of man, are contrary to the great precept of nature, and therefore of no force or authority.

Resolved, That woman is man's equal—was intended to be so by the Creator, and the highest good of the race demands that she should be recognized as such.

Resolved, That the women of this country ought to be enlightened in regard to the laws under which they live, that they may no longer publish their degradation by declaring themselves satisfied with their present position, nor their ignorance, by asserting that they have all the rights they want.

Resolved, That inasmuch as man, while claiming for himself intellectual superiority, does accord to woman moral superiority, it is pre-eminently his duty to encourage her to speak and teach, as she has an opportunity, in all religious assemblies.

Resolved, That the same amount of virtue, delicacy, and refinement of behavior that is required of woman in the social state, should also be required of man, and the same transgressions should be visited with equal severity on both man and woman.

Resolved, That the objection of indelicacy and impropriety, which is so often brought against woman when she addresses a public audience, comes with a very ill-grace from those who encourage, by their attendance, her appearance on the stage, in the concert, or in feats of the circus.

Resolved, That woman has too long rested satisfied in the circumscribed limits which corrupt customs and a perverted application of the Scriptures have marked out for her, and that it is time she should move in the enlarged sphere which her great Creator has assigned her.

Resolved, That it is the duty of the women of this country to secure to themselves their sacred right to the elective franchise.

Resolved, That the equality of human rights results necessarily from the fact of the identity of the race in capabilities and responsibilities.

Resolved, therefore, That, being invested by the Creator with the same capabilities, and the same consciousness of responsibility for their exercise, it is demonstrably the right and duty of woman, equally with man, to promote every righteous cause by every righteous means; and especially in regard to the great subjects of morals and religion, it is self-evidently her right to participate with her brother in teaching them, both in private and in public, by writing and by speaking, by any instrumentalities proper to be used, and in any assemblies proper to be held; and this being a self-evident truth growing out of the divinely implanted principles of human nature, any custom or authority adverse to it, whether modern or wearing the hoary sanction of antiquity, is to be regarded as a self-evident falsehood, and at war with mankind.

Resolved, That the speedy success of our cause depends upon the zealous and untiring efforts of both men and women, for the overthrow of the monopoly of the pulpit, and for the securing to woman an equal participation with men in the various trades, professions, and commerce.

6.9 The Dress Controversy

Some feminists believed that women's fashions were impractical, uncomfortable and symbolic of an inferior social status. To them, clothing clearly indicated that women were less free than men. To dramatize the problem, one of them, Amelia Bloomer, tried popularizing a new outfit for girls and women, a short skirt and loose pants gathered at the ankles. A few feminists wore these "bloomers" even in the face of public ridicule. (The outfit was later redesigned for female athletes and was still worn in the twentieth century.) On the surface, the issue seemed trivial, but would not die easily. Elizabeth Cady Stanton and her cousin, Gerrit Smith, exchanged friendly correspondence on the subject in 1855. Smith was a wealthy land owner and social reformer who was sympathetic to the feminist movement.

Questions

How important was the dress issue? Since it aroused ridicule, was it worth the trouble, or did it merely detract from more serious complaints by feminists? Was Stanton serious about women dressing like men; was she right?

What would the early feminists make of dress styles today? Interestingly, the controversy over women's clothing remains current. In your opinion, do women's fashions today symbolize the social inferiority of women? Why?

G. Smith to E. C. Stanton—

PETERBORO, *December* 1, 1855.

My Dear Friend:— . . . The object of the "Woman's Rights Movement" is nothing less than to recover the rights of woman—nothing less than to achieve her independence. . . .

What if a nation in the heart of Europe were to adopt, and uniformly adhere to, the practice of cutting off one of the hands of all their new-born children? It would from this cause be reduced to poverty, to helpless dependence upon the charity of surrounding nations, and to just such a measure of privileges as they might see fit to allow it, in exchange for its forfeited rights. Very great, indeed, would be the folly of this strange nation. But a still greater folly would it be guilty of, should it, notwithstanding this voluntary mutilation, claim all the wealth, and all the rights, and all the respect, and all the independence which it enjoyed before it entered upon this systematic mutilation.

Now, this twofold folly of this one-hand nation illustrates the similar twofold folly of some women. Voluntarily wearing, in common with their sex, a dress which imprisons and cripples them, they nevertheless, follow up this absurdity with the greater one of coveting and demanding a social position no less full of admitted rights, and a relation to the other sex no less full of independence, than such position and relation would naturally and necessarily have been, had they scorned a dress which leaves them less than half their personal power of self-subsistence and usefulness. . . . But the handful of women of whom I am here complaining—the woman's rights women—persevere just as blindly and stubbornly as do other women, in wearing a dress that both marks and makes their impotence, and yet, O amazing inconsistency! they are ashamed of their dependence, and remonstrate against its injustice. They claim that the fullest measure of rights and independence and dignity shall be accorded to them, and yet they refuse to place themselves in circumstances corresponding with their claim. . . .

I admit that the dress of woman is not the primal cause of her helplessness and degradation. That cause is to be found in the false doctrines and sentiments of which the dress is the outgrowth and symbol. On the other hand, however, these doctrines and sentiments would never have become the huge bundle they now are, and they would probably have all languished, and perhaps all expired, but for the dress. . . .

Were woman to throw off the dress, which, in the eye of chivalry and gallantry, is so well adapted to womanly gracefulness and womanly helplessness, and to put on a dress that would leave her free to work her own way through the world, I see not but that chivalry and gallantry would nearly or quite die out. No longer would she present herself to man, now in the bewitching character of a play-

SOURCES: Gerrit Smith to Elizabeth Cady Stanton and others, December 1, 1855; and Stanton to Smith, December 11, 1855, from Elizabeth Cady Stanton, Susan B. Anthony, and Matilda Joslyn Gage, eds., *History of Woman Suffrage* (New York, 1881), I, 836–42.

thing, a doll, an idol, and now in the degraded character of his servant. But he would confess her transmutation into his equal; and, therefore, all occasion for the display of chivalry and gallantry toward her on the one hand, and tyranny on the other, would have passed away. Only let woman attire her person fitly for the whole battle of life—that great and often rough battle, which she is as much bound to fight as man is, and the common sense expressed in the change will put to flight all the nonsensical fancies about her superiority to man, and all the nonsensical fancies about her inferiority to him. No more will then be heard of her being made of a finer material than man is made of; and, on the contrary, no more will then be heard of her being but the complement of man. . . . No more will it then be said that there is sex in mind—an original sexual difference in intellect. What a pity that so many of our noblest women make this foolish admission! It is made by the great majority of the women who plead the cause of woman.

I am amazed that the intelligent women engaged in the "Woman's Rights Movement," see not the relation between their dress and the oppressive evils which they are striving to throw off. I am amazed that they do not see that their dress is indispensable to keep in countenance the policy and purposes out of which those evils grow. I hazard nothing in saying, that the relation between the dress and degradation of an American woman, is as vital as between the cramped foot and degradation of a Chinese woman; as vital as between the uses of the inmate of the harem and the apparel and training provided for her. Moreover, I hazard nothing in saying, that an American woman will never have made her most effectual, nor, indeed, any serviceable protest against the treatment of her sex . . . so long as she consents to have her own person clothed in ways so repugnant to reason and religion. . . .

Women are holding their meetings; and with great ability do they urge their claim to the rights of property and suffrage. But, as in the case of the colored man, the great needed change is in himself, so, also, in the case of woman, the great needed change is in herself. Of what comparative avail would be her exercise of the right of suffrage, if she is still to remain the victim of her present false notions of herself and of her relations to the other sex?—false notions so emphatically represented and perpetuated by her dress? Moreover, to concede to her the rights of property would be to benefit her comparatively little, unless she shall resolve to break out from her clothes-prison, and to undertake right earnestly, as right earnestly as a man, to get property. . . .

I am not unaware that such views as I have expressed in this letter will be regarded as serving to break down the characteristic delicacy of woman. I frankly admit that I would have it broken down; and that I would have the artificial and conventional, the nonsensical and pernicious thing give place to the natural delicacy which would be common to both sexes. As the delicacy, which is made peculiar to one of the sexes, is unnatural, and, therefore, false, this, which would be common to both, would be natural, and, therefore, true. I would have no characteristic delicacy of woman, and no characteristic coarseness of man. On the contrary, believing man and woman to have the same nature, and to be therefore under obligation to have the same character, I would subject them to a common standard of morals and manners. The delicacy of man should be no less shrinking than that of woman, and the bravery of woman should be one with the bravery of man. . . .

But if woman is of the same nature and same dignity with man, and if as much and as varied labor is needed to supply her wants as to supply the wants of man, and if for her to be, as she so emphatically is, poor and destitute and dependent, is as fatal to her happiness and usefulness and to the fulfillment of the high purposes of her existence, as the like circumstances would be to the honor and welfare of man, why then put her in a dress which compels her to be a pauper—a pauper, whether in ribbons or rags? Why, I ask, put her in a dress suited only to those occassional and brief moods, in which man regards her as his darling, his idol, and his angel; or to that general state of his mind in which he looks upon her as his servant, and with feelings certainly much nearer contempt than adoration. Strive as you will to elevate woman, nevertheless the disabilities and degradation of this dress, together with that large group of false views of the uses of her being and of her relations to man, symbolized and perpetuated, as I have already said, by this dress, will make your striving vain. . . .

Affectionately yours,
GERRIT SMITH.

E. C. Stanton to G. Smith—

SENECA FALLS, *Dec.* 21, 1855.

MY DEAR COUSIN:— . . . I thank you, in the name of woman, for having said what you have on so many vital points. You have spoken well for a man whose convictions on this subject are the result of reason and observation; but they alone whose souls are fired through personal experience and suffering can set forth the height and depth, the source and center of the degradation of women; they alone can feel a steadfast faith in their own native energy and power to accomplish a final triumph over all adverse surroundings, a speedy and complete success. You say you have but little faith in this reform, because the changes we propose are so great, so radical, so comprehensive; whilst they who have commenced the work are so puny, feeble, and undeveloped. . . .

We who have spoken out, have declared our rights, political and civil; but the entire revolution about to dawn upon us by the acknowledgment of woman's social equality, have been seen and felt but by the few. The rights, to vote, to hold property, to speak in public, are all-important; but there are great social rights, before which all others sink into utter insignificance. The cause of woman is, as you admit, a broader and a deeper one than any with which you compare it; and this, to me, is the very reason why it must succeed. It is not a question of meats and drinks, of money and lands, but of human rights—the sacred right of a woman to her own person, to all her God-given powers of body and soul. . . . [W]hen woman shall stand on an even pedestal with man—when they shall be bound together, not by withes of law and gospel, but in holy unity and love, then, and not till then, shall our efforts at minor reforms be crowned with complete success. Here, in my opinion, is the starting-point; here is the battleground where our independence must be fought and won. A true marriage relation has far more to do with the elevation of woman than the style and cut of her dress. Dress is a matter of taste, of fashion; it is changeable, transient, and may be doffed or donned at the will of the individual; but institutions, supported by laws, can be overturned but by revolution. We have no reason to hope that pantaloons would do more for us than they have done for man himself. The negro slave enjoys the most unlimited freedom in his attire, not surpassed even by the fashions of Eden in its palmiest days; yet in spite of his dress, and his manhood, too, he is a slave still. Was the old Roman in his toga less of a man than he now is in swallow-tail and tights? Did the flowing robes of Christ Himself render His life less grand and beautiful? In regard to dress, where you claim to be so radical, you are far from consistent. . . .

I fully agree with you that woman is terribly cramped and crippled in her present style of dress. I have not one word to utter in its defense; but to me, it seems that if she would enjoy entire freedom, she should dress just like man. . . . Disguised as a man, the distinguished French woman, "George Sand," has been able to see life in Paris, and has spoken in political meetings with great applause, as no woman could have done. In male attire, we could travel by land or sea; go through all the streets and lanes of our cities and towns by night and day, without a protector; get seven hundred dollars a year for teaching, instead of three, and ten dollars for making a coat, instead of two or three, as we now do. . . .

. . . Talk not to us of chivalry, that died long ago. . . . In social life, true, a man in love will jump to pick up a glove or bouquet for a silly girl of sixteen, whilst at home he will permit his aged mother to carry pails of water and armfuls of wood, or his wife to lug a twenty-pound baby, hour after hour, without ever offering to relieve her. . . . If a short dress is to make the men less gallant than they now are, I beg the women at our next convention to add at least two yards more to every skirt they wear. . . .

Affectionately yours,
ELIZABETH CADY STANTON.

Chapter Seven: Community

7.1 A Model of Christian Community

As the Arabella *rode the waves of the Atlantic Ocean in 1630, Governor John Winthrop delivered a lecture to his fellow Puritans establishing the solemn objectives he thought they should pursue in Massachusetts. In this lecture, called "A Model of Christian Charity," he drew attention to the covenant they had with one another and with God. They must pursue their affairs "always having before our eyes our commission and community in the work, our community as members of the same body." The Puritans were operating under a "special overruling providence." They would jointly establish a "city upon a hill" for the entire world to emulate. Many speech makers have since used this compelling metaphor to signify the special "mission of America."*

The Arabella *represents the start of the Great Migration that would bring thousands from England to New England. Winthrop was a rich gentleman farmer and college-educated lawyer. From 1630 until his death in 1647 he dominated the Massachusetts Bay Company. He defended his community against the influence of dissidents like Roger Williams (see Chapter 5).*

Questions

What did Winthrop mean by "community"? How did he make use of the Bible in his plans? What was the connection between church and state? What would happen to the colonists if they failed to work together? How were the rich and the poor supposed to relate to one another in that community?

What is a good general definition of the term "community," and how do most people define it today? Why is it difficult to agree on such a concept?

Is it less or more difficult to establish a new community today? Why?

God Almighty in His most holy and wise providence hath so disposed of the condition of mankind as in all times some must be rich, some poor; some high and eminent in power and dignity, others mean and subjection.

SOURCE: John Winthrop, *The Winthrop Papers* (5 v.; Boston: Massachusetts Historical Society, 1931), II, 282–295.

The reason hereof:

First to hold conformity with the rest of His works, being delighted to show forth the glory of His wisdom in the variety and differences of the creatures and the glory of His power, in ordering all these differences for the preservation and good of the whole, and the glory of His greatness: that as it is the glory of princes to have many officers, so this great King will have many stewards, counting Himself more honored in dispensing His gifts to man by man than if He did it by His own immediate hand.

Secondly, that He might have the more occasion to manifest the work of His Spirit: first, upon the wicked in moderating and restraining them, so that the rich and mightly should not eat up the poor, nor the poor and despised rise up against their superiors and shake off their yoke; secondly, in the regenerate, in exercising His graces in them—as in the great ones, their love, mercy, gentleness, temperance, etc., in the poor and inferior sort, their faith, patience, obedience, etc.

Thirdly, that every man might have need of other, and from hence they might be all knit more nearly together in the bond of brotherly affection. From hence it appears plainly that no man is made more honorable than another or more wealthy, etc., out of any particular and singular respect to himself, but for the glory of his creator and the common good of the creature man. . . . All men being thus (by divine providence) ranked into two sorts, rich and poor, under the first are comprehended all such as are able to live comfortably by their own means duly improved, and all others are poor, according to the former distribution.

There are two rules whereby we are to walk, one towards another: justice and mercy. . . .

. . . We may frame these conclusions.

All true Christians are of one body in Christ (1 Cor. 12. 12, 13, 17).

The ligaments of this body which knit together are love.

No body can be perfect which wants its proper ligaments.

All the parts of this body being thus united are made so contiguous in a special relation as they must needs partake of each other's strength and infirmity, joy, and sorrow, weal and woe (1 Cor. 12. 26). If one member suffers all suffer with it, if one be in honor, all rejoice with it. . . .

From the former considerations arise these conclusions:

This love among Christians is a real thing, not imaginary. . . .

It rests in the love and welfare of its beloved, for the full and certain knowledge of these truths concerning the nature, use, and excellency of this grace. That which the holy ghost has left recorded (1 Cor. 13) may give full satisfaction which is needful for every true member of this lovely body of the Lord Jesus, to work upon their hearts, by prayer, meditation, and continual exercise at least of the special power of this grace until Christ be formed in them and they in him all in each other knit together by this bond of love.

It rests now to make some application of this discourse by the present design which gave the occasion of writing it. Herein are four things to be propounded: the persons, the work, the end, and the means.

1. For the persons, we are a company professing ourselves fellow members of Christ, in which respect only, though we were absent from each other many miles, and had our employments as far distant, yet we ought to account ourselves knit together by this bond of love, and live in the exercise of it, if we would have comfort of our being in Christ. . . .

2. For the work we have in hand, it is by mutual consent, through a special overruling providence and a more than an ordinary approbation of the churches of Christ, to seek out a place of cohabitation and consortship, under a due form of government both civil and ecclesiastical. In such cases as this, the care of the public

must oversway all private respects by which not only conscience but mere civil policy doth bind us; for it is a true rule that particular estates cannot subsist in the ruin of the public.

3. The end is to improve our lives to do more service to the Lord, the comfort and increase of the body of Christ whereof we are members, that ourselves and posterity may be the better preserved from the common corruptions of this evil world, to serve the Lord and work out our salvation under the power and purity of His holy ordinances.

4. For the means whereby this must be effected, they are twofold: a conformity with the work and the end we aim at; these we see are extraordinary, therefore we must not content ourselves with usual ordinary means. Whatsoever we did or ought to have done when we lived in England, the same must we do, and more also where we go. That which the most in their churches maintain as a truth in profession only, we must bring into familiar and constant practice: as in this duty of love we must love brotherly without dissimulation, we must love one another with a pure heart fervently, we must bear one another's burdens, we must not look only on our own things but also on the things of our brethren. . . .

Thus stands the cause between God and us: we are entered into covenant with Him for this work; we have taken out a commission, the Lord hath given us leave to draw our own articles. We have professed to enterprise these actions upon these and these ends; we have hereupon besought Him of favor and blessing. Now if the Lord shall please to hear us and bring us in peace to the place we desire, then hath He ratified this covenant and sealed our Commission, [and] will expect a strict performance of the articles contained in it. But if we shall neglect the observation of these articles which are the ends we have propounded, and dissembling with our God, shall fall to embrace this present world and prosecute our carnal intentions, seeking great things for ourselves and our posterity, the Lord will surely break out in wrath against us, be revenged of such a perjured people, and make us know the price of the breach of such a covenant.

Now the only way to avoid this shipwreck and to provide for our posterity is to follow the counsel of Micah: to do justly, to love mercy, to walk humbly with our God. For this end, we must be knit together in this work as one man. We must entertain each other in brotherly affection; we must be willing to abridge ourselves of our superfluities, for the supply of others' necessities; we must uphold a familiar commerce together in all meekness, gentleness, patience and liberality. We must delight in each other, make others' conditions our own, rejoice together, mourn together, labor and suffer together: always having before our eyes our commission and community in the work, our community as members of the same body. So shall we keep the unity of the spirit in the bond of peace, the Lord will be our God and delight to dwell among us, as His own people, and will command a blessing upon us in all our ways, so that we shall see much more of His wisdom, power, goodness, and truth than formerly we have been acquainted with. We shall find that the God of Israel is among us, when ten of us shall be able to resist a thousand of our enemies, when He shall make us a praise and glory, that men shall say of succeeding plantations: "The Lord make it like that of New England." For we must consider that we shall be as a city upon a hill, the eyes of all people are upon us. So that if we shall deal falsely with our God in this work we have undertaken, and so cause Him to withdraw His present help from us, we shall be made a story and a by-word through the world: we shall open the mouths of enemies to speak evil of the ways of God and all professors for God's sake; we shall shame the faces of many of God's worthy servants, and cause their prayers to be turned into curses upon us, till we be consumed out of the good land whither we are going.

And to shut up this discourse with that exhortation of Moses, that faithful servant of the Lord in his last farewell to Israel (Deut. 30). Beloved, there is now set before us life, and good, death and evil in that we are commanded this day to love the Lord our God, and to love one another, to walk in his ways and to keep his commandments and his ordinance, and his laws, and the articles of our covenant with him that we may live and be multiplied, and that the Lord our God may bless us in the land whither we go to possess it. But if our hearts shall turn away so that we will not obey, but shall be seduced and worship other Gods, our pleasures, and profits, and serve them; it is propounded unto us this day, we shall surely perish out of the good land whither we pass over this vast sea to possess it.

Therefore let us choose life, that we and our seed may live; by obeying His voice, and cleaving unto Him, for He is our life, and our prosperity.

7.2 The Dedham Covenant

In 1636 the founding fathers of Dedham, Massachusetts, bound themselves together in Christian love—forever. The Dedham Covenant embraced all signers, plus some added later, for a total of 124 people. It excluded outsiders. The document set down conditions for land ownership and for dealing with disputes.

Questions

Do the New England villages represent the "golden age" of community life in American history? What other places have such a good reputation and why? What status do small towns occupy in America today? What is your personal favorite type of community and why?

Historian Kenneth A. Lockridge calls Dedham a "Christian Closed Utopian Corporate Community." What do you think he means?

One: We whose names are hereunto subscribed do, in the fear and reverence of our Almighty God, mutually and severally promise amongst ourselves and to each other to profess and practice one truth according to that most perfect rule, the foundation whereof is everlasting love.

Two: That we shall by all means labor to keep off from us all such as are contrary minded, and receive only such unto us as may be probably of one heart with us, as that we either know or may well and truly be informed to walk in a peaceable conversation with all meekness of spirit, for the edification of each other in the knowledge and faith of the Lord Jesus, and the mutual encouragement unto all temporal comforts in all things, seeking the good of each other, out of which may be derived true peace.

Three: That if at any time differences shall rise between parties of our said town, that then such party or parties shall presently refer all such differences unto some one, two, or three others of our said society, to be fully accorded and determined without any further delay, if it possibly may be.

Four: That every man that now, or at any time hereafter, shall have lots in our said town shall pay his share in all such rates of money and charges as shall be imposed on him rateably in proportion with other men, as also become freely subject unto all such orders and constitutions as shall be necessarily had or made, now or at any time hereafter from this day forward, as well for loving and comfortable society in our said town as also for the prosperous and thriving condition of our said fellowship, especially respecting the fear of God, in which we desire to begin and continue whatsoever we shall by His loving favor take into hand.

Five: And for the better manifestation of our true resolution herein, every man so received to subscribe hereunto his name, thereby obliging both himself and his successors after him forever, as we have done.

SOURCE: Don Gleason Hill, ed., *Early Records of the Town of Dedham* (Dedham, Mass., 1896), III, 2–3. *A New England Town, The First Hundred Years: Dedham, Massachusetts, 1636–1736* (New York: W. W. Norton & Company, Inc., 1970), 17.

7.3 The Growth of Plymouth Plantation

William Bradford (1590–1675) was governor of Plymouth Colony for three decades. He wrote a classic work, History of Plymouth Plantation, *between 1630 and 1651, in which he touches on many community problems. One problem concerns community growth—the problem of how to maintain unity and stability when the newer settlers seek more land and tend to disperse.*

Questions

The tendency of town settlers to move away to new land and start new communities weakened community bonds. How did the early New Englanders deal with this challenge? In general, how did private or family objectives conflict with community objectives? Do they still cause conflict today?

. . . Also the people of the Plantation began to grow in their outward estates, by reason of the flowing of many people into the country, especially into the Bay of the Massachusetts. By which means corn and cattle rose to a great price, by which many were much enriched and commodities grew plentiful. And yet in other regards this benefit turned to their hurt, and this accession of strength to their weakness. For now as their stocks increased and the increase vendible, there was no longer any holding them together, but now they must of necessity go to their great lots. They could not otherwise keep their cattle, and having oxen grown they must have land for plowing and tillage. And no man now thought he could live except he had cattle and a great deal of ground to keep them, all striving to increase their stocks. By which means they were scattered all over the Bay quickly and the town in which they lived compactly till now was left very thin and in a short time almost desolate.

And if this had been all, it had been less, though too much; but the church must also be divided, and those that had lived so long together in Christian and comfortable fellowship must now part and suffer many divisions. First, those that lived on their lots on the other side of the Bay, called Duxbury, they could not long bring their wives and children to the public worship and church meetings here, but with such burden as, growing to some competent number, they sued to be dismissed and become a body of themselves. And so they were dismissed about this time, though very unwillingly. But to touch this sad matter, and handle things together that fell out afterward: to prevent any further scattering from this place and weakening of the same, it was thought best to give out some good farms to special persons that would promise to live at Plymouth, and likely to be helpful to the church or commonwealth, and so tie the lands to Plymouth as farms for the same; and there they might keep their cattle and tillage by some servants and retain their dwellings here. And so some special lands granted at a place generally called Green's Harbor, where no allotments had been in the former division, a place very well meadowed and fit to keep and rear cattle good store. But alas, this remedy proved worse than the disease; for within a few years those that had thus got footing there rent themselves away, partly by force and partly wearing the rest with importunity and pleas of necessity, so as they must either suffer them to go or live in continual opposition and contention. And others still, as they conceived themselves straitened or to want accommodation, broke away under one pretence or other, thinking their own

SOURCE: William Bradford, *History of Plymouth Plantation* (Boston, 1856), 302–4.

conceived necessity and the example of others a warrant sufficient for them. And this I fear will be the ruin of New England, at least of the churches of God there, and will provoke the Lord's displeasure against them.

7.4 Witchcraft in Salem

Clearly, Salem, Massachusetts did not represent the utopian vision of a "city upon a hill" in 1692. In that year, community life turned sour as witchcraft trials swept through the town like a virus epidemic. Nineteen men and women were convicted and hanged, and another man was pressed to death by heavy rocks. The root cause of this tragedy—and whether it represents an indictment of all of Puritanism, or was a localized and temporary deviation—has never been fully settled.

The Salem witch hunt has been explained in various ways: as a reflection of totalitarianism and thought control; as mob rule; as the abnormal behavior of adolescent girls; as a mass hysteria caused by the eating of bread contaminated by an hallucinogenic fungus, ergot, (similar to LSD); as an early case of "spiritualism" (attempting to contact the netherworld); or as an instance of age and sex discrimination (one harmless old woman was executed on flimsy evidence).

To some interpreters, these legal proceedings have been dismissed as unrepresentative of Puritan life, a tragic mistake of a backwater town. To others, they are the essence of the warped and twisted fanaticism of the Puritans. America's greatest living playwright, Arthur Miller, in the 1950s used the trials as the basis of a play, The Crucible *(1953).*

Clearly, many people of that era believed in witchcraft. President Increase Mather of Harvard in 1684 had written a book against the practice of witchcraft and the need to cope with it. He described a test for identifying witches and using "spector evidence" in court. His son Cotton Mather, although a sophisticated and learned individual, was much taken with the subject and cited his father's writings approvingly in a book of his own, The Wonders of the Invisible World *(1693).*

Below are a variety of documents: an excerpt from the trial record of Susanna Martin, June 29, 1692; speculations by the Mathers; and a dissent by Thomas Brattle, who opposed the hysteria, doubted the evidence, and feared the consequences of witchcraft trials.

Questions

Do you think that fear, or the pressure to conform, in a small, strict community may have motivated some people?

How did the laws of evidence used in the trials compare with today's laws of evidence? What would prevent "spectral evidence" from being used currently?

Why would some people—up to 50 of them—admit to witchcraft? Are there modern examples of hysteria comparable to the Salem witch trials? How can they be explained?

The Salem witch trials have been compared with McCarthyism during the Red Scare of the 1950s. Is there validity to this comparison?

Susanna Martin Trial—

Susanna Martin, pleading *Not Guilty* to the Indictment of *Witchcraft,* brought in against her, there were produced the Evidences of many Persons very sensibly and grievously Bewitched; who all complained of the Prisoner at the Bar, as the Person whom they believed the cause of their Miseries. . . .

Magistrate. Pray, what ails these People?

Martin. I don't know.

Magistrate. But what do you think ails them?

Martin. I don't desire to spend my Judgment upon it.

Magistrate. Don't you think they are bewitch'd?

Martin No, I do not think they are. . . .

It was then also noted in her, as in others like her, that if the Afflicted went to approach her, they were flung down to the Ground. And, when she was asked the reason of it, she said, *I cannot tell; it may be, the Devil bears me more Malice than another.*

III. . . . *John Allen of Salisbury,* testify'd, That he refusing, because of the weakness of his Oxen, to Cart some Staves at the request of this *Martin,* she was displeased at it; and said, *It had been as good that he had; for his Oxen should never do him much more Service.* . . . In a few days, all the Oxen upon the Beach were found by their Tracks, to have run unto the Mouth of *Merrimack-River,* and not returned. . . . One of them then swam back again, with a swiftness, amazing to the Beholders. . . . So that, of fourteen good, Oxen, there was only this saved: The rest were all cast up, some in one place, and some in another, Drowned.

IV. *John Atkinson* testifi'd, That he exchanged a Cow with a Son of *Susanna Martin's,* whereat she muttered, and was unwilling he should have it. Going to receive this Cow, tho he Hamstring'd her, and Halter'd her, she, of a Tame Creature, grew so mad, that they could scarce get her along. She broke all the Ropes that were fastened unto her, and though she were ty'd fast unto a tree, yet she made her escape, and gave them such further trouble, as they ascribe to no cause but Witchcraft.

V. *Bernard Peache* testifi'd, That being in Bed, on the Lord's-day Night, he heard a

SOURCES: Increase Mather, *Cases of Conscience Concerning Evil Spirits Personating Men* (Boston, 1693), in Cotton Mather, *The Wonders of the Invisible World* (London, 1862), 221–4, 225, 229, 232, 233, 234, 247–8, 254, 255, 259–60, 262–3, 265, 269, 270, 273, 275, 276–7, 282, 283, 285–6; Thomas Brattle, "Letter, 1692," in G. L. Burr, ed., *Narratives of the Witchcraft Cases 1648–1706* (New York, 1914), 170–90.

scrabbling at the Window, whereat he then saw *Susanna Martin* come in, and jump down upon the Floor. She took hold of this Deponent's Feet, and drawing his Body up into an Heap, she lay upon him near Two Hours; in all which time he could neither speak nor stir. At length, when he could begin to move, he laid hold on her Hand, and pulling it up to his Mouth, he bit three of her Fingers, as he judged, unto the Bone. Whereupon she went from the Chamber, down the Stairs, out at the Door. . . .

VI. *Robert Downer* testified, That this Prisoner being some Years ago prosecuted at Court for a Witch, he then said unto her, "He believed she was a witch. Whereat she being dissatisfied, said, *That some She-Devil would shortly fetch him away!* Which words were heard by others, as well as himself. The Night following, as he lay in his Bed, there came in at the Window, the likeness of a *Cat*, which flew upon him, took fast hold of his Throat, lay on him a considerable while, and almost killed him. At length he remembered what *Susanna Martin* had threatened the Day before; and with much striving he cried out, *Avoid, thou She-Devil! In the Name of God the Father, the Son, and the Holy Ghost, Avoid!* Whereupon it left him, leap'd on the Floor, and flew out at the Window. . . .

VII. *John Kembal* testified, that *Susanna Martin*, upon a Causeless Disgust, had threatened him, about a certain Cow of his, *That she should never do him any more Good:* and it came to pass accordingly. For soon after the Cow was found stark dead on the dry Ground, without any Distemper to be discerned upon her. Upon which he was followed with a strange Death upon more of his Cattle, whereof he lost in one Spring to the value of Thirty Pounds. . . .

VIII. *William Brown* testifi'd, That Heaven having blessed him with a most Pious and Prudent Wife, this Wife of his, one day met with *Susanna Martin;* but when she approach'd just unto her, *Martin* vanished out of sight, and left her extreamly affrighted. After which time, the said *Martin* often appear'd unto her, giving her no little trouble; and when she did come, she was visited with Birds, that sorely peck'd and prick'd her; and sometimes, a Bunch, like a Pullet's Egg, would rise in her Throat, ready to choke her, till she cry'd out, *Witch, you shan't choak me!* While this good Woman was in this extremity, the Church appointed a Day of Prayer, on her behalf; whereupon her Trouble ceas'd; she saw not *Martin* as formerly; and the Church, instead of their Fast, gave Thanks for her Deliverance. . . .

IX. *Sarah Atkinson* testify'd, That *Susanna Martin* came from *Amesbury* to their House at *Newbury*, in an extraordinary Season, when it was not fit for any to Travel. She came (as she said, unto *Atkinson*) all that long way on Foot. She brag'd and shew'd how dry she was; nor could it be perceived that so much as the Soles of her Shoes were wet. . . .

X. *John Pressy* testify'd, . . . That after he had given in some Evidence against *Susanna Martin*, many years ago, she gave him foul words about it; and said, *He should never prosper more;* particularly, *That he should never have more than two Cows; that tho' he was never so likely to have more, yet he should never have them.* And that from that very day to this, namely for twenty years together, he could never exceed that number; but some strange thing or other still prevented his having any more.

XI. *Jervis Ring* testify'd, That about seven years ago, he was oftentimes and grievously oppressed in the Night, but saw not who troubled him; until at last he Lying perfectly Awake, plainly saw *Susanna Martin* approach him. She came to him, and forceably bit him by the Finger; so that the

Print of the bite is now, so long after, to be seen upon him.

XII. But besides all of these Evidences, there was a most wonderful Account of one *Joseph Ring,* produced on this occasion.

This Man has been strangely carried about by *Daemons,* from one *Witch-meeting* to another, for near two years together; and for one quarter of this time, they have made him, and keep him Dumb, tho' he is now again able to speak. There was one *T. H.* who having, as 'tis judged, a design of engaging this *Joseph Ring* in a snare of Devillism, contrived a while, to bring this *Ring* two Shillings in Debt unto him.

Afterwards, this poor Man would be visited with unknown shapes, and this *T. H.* sometimes among them; which would force him away with them, unto unknown Places, where he saw Meetings, Feastings, Dancings; and after his return, wherein they hurried him along through the Air . . . the business would end with dreadful Shapes, Noises and Screeches, which almost scared him out of his Wits. Once with the Book, there was a Pen offered him, and an Ink-horn with Liquor in it, that seemed like Blood: But he never toucht it.

This Man did now affirm, That he saw the Prisoner at several of those hellish Randezvouzes.

Note, this Woman was one of the most important, scurrilous, wicked Creatures in the World; and she did now throughout her whole Tryal, discover her self to be such an one. Yet when she was asked, what she had to say for her self? Her chief Plea was, *That she had lead a most virtuous and holy Life.*

Increase and Cotton Mather—

So odious and abominable is the name of a witch . . . that it is apt to grow up into a scandal for any, so much as to enter some sober cautious against the over hasty suspecting, or too precipitant judging of persons on this account. But certainly, the more execrable the crime is, the more critical care is to be used in the exposing of the names, liberties and lives of men . . . to the imputation of it. . . .

That there are devils and witches, the Scripture asserts, and experience confirms. That they are common enemies of mankind, and set upon mischief, is not to be doubted. That the Devil . . . delights to have the concurrence of witches, and their consent in harming men, is consonant to his native malice to man. . . . That witches, when detected and convinced, ought to be exterminated and cut off, we have God's warrant for. . . .

Only the same God who hath said, thou shalt not suffer a witch to live; hath also said, at the mouth of two witnesses, or three witnesses shall he that is worthy of death, be put to death: but at the mouth of one witness, he shall not be put to death. . . .

It is therefore exceeding necessary that in such a day as this, men be informed what is evidence and what is not. It concerns men in point of charity; . . . And it is of no less necessity in point of justice. . . . Evidence supposed to be in the testimony . . . is thoroughly to be weighed, and if it do not infallibly prove the crime against the person accused, it ought not to determine him guilty of it; for so a righteous man may be condemned unjustly. . . .

Among many arguments to evince this, that which is most under present debate, is that which refers to something vulgarly called Specter Evidence, and a certain sort of Ordeal or trial by the sight and touch. The principal plea to justify the convictive evidence in these, is fetched from the consideration of the wisdom and righteousness of God in governing the world, which they suppose would fail, if such things were permitted to befall an innocent person. But it is certain, that . . . God doth sometimes suffer such things to evene [happen] that we may thereby know how much we are beholden to Him, for that restraint which he lays upon the Infernal Spirits, who would else reduce a world into a chaos. That the resolutions of such cases as these is proper for the servants of Christ in the ministry cannot be denied; the seasonablness of doing it now, will be justified by the consideration of the necessity there is at this time of a right information of men's judgments about these things, and the danger of their being misinformed. . . .

The first case that I am desired to express my judgment in, is this: Whether it is not possible for the Devil to impose on the imaginations of persons bewitched, and to cause them to believe that an innocent, yea that a pious person does torment them, when the Devil himself doth it. . . ? The answer to the question must be affirmative. . . .

From hence we infer, that there is no outward affliction whatsoever but may befall a good man. Now to be represented by Satan as a tormentor of bewitched or possessed persons, is a sore affliction to a good man. . . .

This then I declare and testify, that to take away the life of anyone, merely because a specter or devil, in a bewitched or possessed person does accuse them, will bring the guilt of innocent blood on the land. . . .

These things being premised, I answer the question affirmatively. There are proofs for the conviction of witches which jurors may with a safe conscience proceed upon, so as to bring them in guilty. . . . But then the inquiry is, what is sufficient proof? . . .

A free and voluntary confession of the crime made by the person suspected and accused after examination, is a sufficient ground of conviction. Indeed, if persons are distracted, or under the power of phrenetic melancholy, that alters the case. . . .

If two credible persons shall affirm upon oath that they have seen the party accused speaking such words, or doing things which none but such as have familiarity with the Devil ever did or can do, that's a sufficient ground for conviction. . . . The Devil never assists men to do supernatural things undesired. . . . This notwithstanding I will add. It were better that ten suspected witches should escape, than that one innocent person should be condemned. . . . I had rather judge a witch to be an honest woman, than judge an honest woman as a witch.

Thomas Brattle—

As to the method which the Salem justices do take in their examinations, it is truly this. A warrant being issued out to apprehend the persons that are charged and complained of by the afflicted children, . . . said persons are brought before the justices (the afflicted being present). The justices ask the apprehended why they afflict those poor children; to which the apprehended answer, they do not afflict them. The justices order the apprehended to look upon the said children, which accordingly they do; and at the time of that look . . . the afflicted are cast into a fit. The apprehended are then blinded, and ordered to touch the afflicted; and at that touch, . . . the afflicted ordinarily do come out of their fits. The afflicted persons then declare and affirm, that the apprehended have afflicted them. Upon which the apprehended persons, though of never so good repute, are forthwith committed to prison, or suspicion for witchcraft. . . .

. . . I would fain know of these Salem gentlemen . . . how it comes about, I say, that, by a look of their eye, they do not cast others into fits, and poison others by their looks; and in particular, tender, fearful women, who often are beheld by them, and as likely as any in the whole world to receive an ill impression from them. This Salem philosophy, some men may call the new philosophy; but I think it rather deserves the name of Salem superstition and sorcery, and it is not fit to be named in the land of such light as New England is. . . .

. . . Yet certain is it, that the reasonable part of the world, when acquainted herewith, all laugh at the demonstration, and conclude that the said Salem gentlemen are actually possessed, at least, with ignorance and folly. . . .

With respect to . . . such as confess themselves to be witches . . . there are now about fifty of them in prison; many of which I have again and again seen and heard; and I cannot but tell you, that my faith is strong concerning them, that they are deluded, imposed upon, and under the influence of some evil spirit; and therefore unfit to be evidences either against themselves, or anyone else. . . .

These confessors . . . do very often contradict themselves. . . . But instead . . . the judges vindicate these confessors, and salve their contradictions, by proclaiming, that the Devil takes away their memory, and imposes on their brain. . . .

In the next place, I proceed to the form of their indictments, and the trials thereupon.

The indictment runs for sorcery and witchcraft. . . .

1. The afflicted persons are brought into court; and after much patience and pains taken with them, do take their oaths, that the prisoner at the bar did afflict them. . . . Often, when the afflicted do mean and intend only the appearance and shape of such an one. . . .

2. The confessors do declare what they know of the said prisoner; and some of the confessors are allowed to give their oaths; a thing which I believe was never heard of in this world; that such as confess themselves to be witches, to have renounced God and Christ, and all that is sacred, should yet be allowed and ordered to swear by the name of the great God! . . .

4. They [the accused] are searched by a jury; and as to some of them, the jury brought in, that [on] such or such a place there was a preternatural excrescence. . . .

It is true, that over and above the evidences of the afflicted persons, there are many evidences brought in, against the prisoner at the bar: either that he was at a witch meeting, or that he performed things which could not be done by an ordinary natural power; or that she sold butter to a sailor, which proving bad at sea, and the seamen exclaiming against her, she appeared, and soon after there was a storm; or the like. But what if there were ten thousand evidences of this nature; how do they prove the matter of indictment! And if they do not reach the matter of indictment, then I think it is clear, that the prisoner at the bar is brought in guilty and condemned, merely from the evidences of the afflicted persons. . . .

As to the late executions, I shall only tell you, that in the opinion of many unprejudiced, considerate and considerable spectators, some of the condemned went out of the world not only with as great protestations, but also with as good shows of innocency, as men could do.

They protested their innocency as in the presence of the great God whom forthwith they were to appear before . . . they forgave their accusers; they spoke without reflection on jury and judges, for bringing them in guilty, and condemning them. They prayed earnestly for pardon for all other sins. . . .

But although the chief judge, and some of the other judges, be very zealous in these proceedings, yet this you may take for a truth, that there are several about the Bay, men for understanding, judgment, and piety, inferior to few, (if any), in New England that do utterly condemn the said proceedings, and do freely deliver their judgment in the case to be . . . that these methods will utterly ruin and undo poor New England. . . . Several of the late justices, viz. Thomas Graves, Esq., N. Byfield, Esq., Francis Foxcroft, Esq., are much dissatisfied; also several of the present justices; and in particular, some of the Boston justices, were resolved rather to throw up their commissions than be active in disturbing the liberty of Their Majesties' subjects, merely on the accusations of these afflicted, possessed children.

Finally; the principal gentlemen in Boston, and thereabout, are generally agreed that irregular and dangerous methods have been taken as to these matters. . . . Nineteen persons have now been executed, and one pressed to death for a mute; seven more are condemned; two of which are reprieved, because they pretend their being with child; one, viz. Mrs. Bradbury of Salisbury, from the intercession of some friends; and two or three more, because they are confessors.

. . . I am very sensible, that it is irksome and disagreeable to go back, when a man's doing so is an implication that he has been walking in a wrong path. However, nothing is more honorable than, upon due conviction, to retract and undo, so far as may be, what has been amiss and irregular. . . .

. . . I am very apt to think, that, did you know the circumstances of the said confessors, you would not be swayed thereby, any otherwise than to be confirmed, that all is perfect devilism, and an hellish design to ruin and destroy this poor land. For whereas there are of the said confessors fifty-five in number, some of them are known to be distracted, crazed women; . . . Others of them denied their guilt, and maintained their innocency for above eighteen hours, after most violent, distracting and dragooning methods had been used with them, to make them confess. . . . They soon recanted their confessions, acknowledging, with sorrow and grief, that it was an hour of great temptation with them. . . .

But, finally, as to about thirty of these fifty-five confessors, they are possessed (I reckon) with the Devil, and afflicted as the children are, and therefore not fit to be regarded as to anything they say of themselves or others. . . .

What will be the issue of these troubles, God only knows; I am afraid that ages will not wear off that reproach and those stains which these things will leave behind them upon our land. I pray God pity us, humble us, forgive us, and appear mercifully for us in this our mount of distress.

7.5 Municipal Controls in New York City

Cities need more social controls than towns, and the bigger they get the more controls they need. Below are selected ordinances for New York CIty in 1731. They relate to government regulation of commerce, fire protection, traffic, welfare, waste disposal, taxes, trash collection, recreational customs, etc. They were published at the city hall "after the Ringing of three Bells and Proclamation made for silence."

Questions

If these were the only ordinances you were aware of, what conclusions would you draw about life in New York City—its racial composition, commerce, quality of life, etc.? In particular, what do these laws reveal about the government's relationship to the private sector? In the past, New Yorkers were forced to participate personally and directly in the keeping of good civic order. Do you think it improved their sense of community? Would this be a practical alternative today?

Laws Orders and Ordinances. Established by the Mayor Recorder Aldermen and Assistants of the City of New York Convened in Common Council for the good Rule and Government of the Inhabitants. . . .

A Law for the Observation of the Lords Day Called Sunday. . . . No Children to play on the sabbath. Penalty one Shilling or House of Correction. . . . No Publick Housekeepers to Sell Strong Liquors on Sundays. . . . Slaves not above three to meet together . . . on the Lords Day . . . penalty of being Whip'd at the publick Whipping Post fifteen Lashes, unless the Master or Owner of such slave will pay Six shillings to Excuse the Same. . . .

A Law to Prevent Strangers from Being a Charge to This Corporation. Masters of Vessells and Boats to give Account of their Passengers. . . . Constables to make A Strict Search and Enquiry after Strangers. . . . Fine on Housekeepers who Entertain Strangers [more than two days] without giving Notice. . . .

A Law for the Better Preventing of Fire. Viewers of Chimneys and Hearths . . . Shall View the same once in Every Month, and where they find any defective . . . give Notice, that the same may be Swept or mended. . . . Fire Engines Hooks and Ladders . . . to be kept in Convenient

SOURCE: *Minutes of the Common Council of the City of New York: 1675–1776* (New York: Dodd, Mead, 1905), IV, 77–86, 90–97, 101–105, 107–109, 122–127.

places within this City for Avoiding the Peril of fire. . . . Leather Bucketts to be in Every House. . . .

A Law for Marking of Bread. . . . Every Baker within this City shall put a Mark with the two letters of his Name plainly to be Seen, upon all the Loaf Bread he Shall Expose to sale within the said City. . . . Assize of Bread to be sett Every Three Months or oftner and Viewers of Bread . . . to Inspect the goodness thereof, and see that the same be of full and due Assize.

A Law for Regulating Negroes and Slaves in the Night time. Slaves above fourteen years Old not to Appear an hour after Sunsett without A Lanthorn and lighted Candle unless in Company with Some White Person. . . .

A Law for Regulating of Carts and Carmen. . . . That there be so many Carmen Lycenced . . . (not Exceeding One hundred) and that no Person do serve in that Capacity for hire or Wages but who shall be . . . Lycenced. . . . Carmen to Mend the Streets & Highways Gratis . . . each Cart imployed for the Carrying of any goods. Merchandise, Fire Wood or Other things, within this City, shall be two foot Eight Inches wide, and three foot high. . . . No Carmen [to] . . . drive his Cart a Trot in the Street, but Patiently. . . . Number of his Licence [to be] fairly Painted upon each side of his Cart with Red Paint. . . . Penalty on Carmen who Refuse to . . . Employ his Horse and Cart for any Person when Required. . . . Carmen are to Cart goods Subject to damage before any Other. . . . Prices and Rates to be taken by Carmen . . . [to] be According to the Rates and Prices hereafter mentioned. . . .

A Law for Regulating the Office of Gugers Packers and Cullers . . . that they will not put the Packers Mark to any Cask of Beef or Pork but to Such as Shall be good and wholsome Meat, fit for Transportation, and in Cask according to Law. . . .

A Law Relating to Making Freemen . . . no Person or Persons whomsoever, within this City and Liberties thereof, do Keep shop, or sell or Expose to Sale any Goods or Wares by Retail, or Exercise any Handy Craft Trade or Occupation, but such as are Freemen thereof, or so Admitted by the Mayor Recorder and Aldermen . . . and all Persons . . . made Free of this Corporation shall pay for the Freedom thereof . . . Every merchant Trader or shopkeeper the sum of three pounds of Current Money of this Colony, and Every Handy Craft Tradesman the sum of twenty shillings. . . .

A Law for Cleaning the Streets Lanes and Alleys of the Said City . . . all . . . Citizens, Freeholders, Housekeepers and Inhabitants . . . shall on Every Friday, Weekly, Either by themselves or servants Rake and sweep together all the Dirt, Filth and soil lying in the Streets before their Respective dwelling Houses upon heaps and on the same day or on the saturday following shall Cause the same to be Carried away and thrown into the River, or some Other Convenient place under the Penalty of six shillings for each Neglect Refusal or Default. . . . No Carrion Guts Garbige &c: to be Cast in the Streets. . . . Streets not to be Encumbed with Beams Timber &c or any Other Lumber without leave of the Mayor. . . . No Tubs of Dung, Close Stools &c: to be Emptied in the Streets. . . . Ordures to be Emptied in the River [but not] to be Emptied or Carried through any Street, till after Eleven of the Clock at Night from the twenty fifth day of March to the twenty Ninth day of September and till after Ten A Clock at Night from the twenty Ninth day of September to the twenty fifth day of March. . . .

A Law for Paving the Streets Lanes & Alleys Within the City of New York . . . all . . . Citizens, Freeholders and Inhabitants . . . shall . . . Well and sufficiently Pave or Cause to be well and sufficiently Paved with good and sufficient Pibble Stones Suitable for Paving, all, or so much of the Streets Lanes and Alleys, within the . . . City as shall Front the Respective Buildings and Lots of Ground that belong to them Respectively . . . and keep and Maintain the same in good Repair. . . .

A Law for Preventing Frauds in Firewood. . . .

A Law for Regulating the Publick Marketts Within the City of New York. Forasmuch as the Marketts of this City of New York are Chiefly Supplyed by the Country People with Provisions and Victuals by Water Carriage from the Neighbouring Counties and Colonies at Different times and seasons, as the Tides, Winds and Weather will permit, by Reason whereof no Certain Times or Days Can Conveniently be appointed for holding the said Marketts, without Manifest Hurt and prejudice as well to the Inhabitants of the said City as to the Country People who frequent and supply the said Marketts. . . . Every day in the Week (Sundays Excepted) . . . are hereby Appointed Publick Market Days . . . from sun Rising to sun Setting, where the Country People, and Others Resorting to the said Markets may stand or Sitt, and Vend their Flesh, Fish, Poultry Herbs, Fruit, Eggs Butter Bacon and Other such like Provisions and Commodities. . . . No unholsome Victualls Blown Meat or Leprous Swine to be Exposed to Sale. . . . Butter to be Marked & if wanting weight to be forfeited to the Poor. . . .

A Law for Establishing and Better ordering the Night Watches in the City of New York . . . all . . . Persons able and fitt to Watch or to find an Able and fit Person to Watch . . . in . . . their Stead, do and Ought, by Reason of their Habitation Occupation and dwelling, to keep Watch within the said City, for the Preservation of the Kings Peace and for the Arresting and Apprehending of all Night Walkers Malefactors and suspected Persons which shall be found Passing Wandering and Misbehaving themselves. . . . A Constable & Eight Watchmen to Watch Every Night. . . . Equal Duty to be done by Every Ward. . . . Constables to Warn [notify] the Inhabitants to Watch the day before the Watch Night. . . . And deliver A List of the Names of those who are to Watch and when to the Constables of the Watch and to the Supervisor. . . . Persons Appointed & Warned to Watch Making Default to forfeit Eight Shillings. . . . Supervisor [of the Watch] to be appointed . . . by the Common Council . . . to take Care . . . that the Watch and Watches . . . be . . . duely kept, and that the Constables and Watchmen do their Duties and services therein or Otherwise pay their Forfeitures . . . for their Defaults. . . . *And* that no Boys Apprentices or servants be Admitted to be Watchmen, and None but able and sober Men of good Reputation be Received as such.

7.6 An American Utopia

In the early nineteenth century most social reformers believed that the best way to improve American society was to engage in direct political action. A few, however, were convinced that a better method was to form collective communities based on utopian principles. They thought that like-minded individuals should establish small, voluntary, experimental communities based on spiritual, ethical or educational goals. Their objectives would be to reform the participants and, indirectly, society at large.

Scores of communes based on such beliefs actually came into existence. Some were religious, while others were secular—although even the secular ones often drew on religious beliefs. A famous early secular commune was Brook Farm, established in 1841 at West Roxbury, Massachusetts (about eight miles from Boston).

Brook Farm was founded by George Ripley (1807–1880), a Unitarian preacher and literary editor. At first, he accepted the philosophical principles of Transcendentalism, a belief system stressing individualism, and the unity of all humans with nature and God. But in 1843 he adopted the theories of a French social philosopher, Charles Fourier. Brook Farm achieved economic stability until a fire ravaged a main building in 1846, forcing permanent closure the following year. Before it folded, prominent literary figures dropped in to visit or stay for a while. Several published their impressions. The best-known resident was the novelist Nathaniel Hawthorne, who worked there for a time as a specialist in the care of pigs. When the farm collapsed and he lost all his savings, he expressed his personal bitterness in a famous short story, "The Blithedale Romance."

Would-be utopias faced many obstacles. Economic survival was not usually the main one, for the residents often found ways to make a living. A bigger problem was that the general public seemed to thrive on individualism and competition. And since the nation appeared to offer limitless economic opportunity and natural abundance, as well as institutions that favored personal freedom, the majority of Americans found little appeal in retreating to small, separate and relatively static communities. Beyond that lay the problem of commitment: how to retain the allegiance of worthy participants once they had made the decision to give up their wordly goods and work for the common good. Although commune builders experimented with various forms of persuasion—instilling a sense of sacrifice, renouncing the material world, communal sharing, and almost church-like confessional—these did not always work against the hardships and tensions of daily life.

The documents presented below reflect some of the pros and cons of Brook Farm. The articles of agreement (constitution) of 1841 reveal the objectives and governing mechanisms. The statement by George Ripley represents a favorable commentary. Finally Ralph Waldo Emerson, a distinguished essayist and philosopher, explains his position. Though not completely hostile to the ends of the utopians, in the end he comes down on the side of individualism.

Questions

Obviously, Brook Farm drew on the Puritan experience. How do the goals and structure of Brook Farm compare with those of the Puritans presented in Documents 7.1 and 7.2? Compare specific objectives and governmental provisions to learn what is common to all documents, and what is different.

What do the supporters think are the benefits of communal life? How will profits and property be shared at Brook Farm?

What problems do the critics see in Brook Farm—or in all such communes?

Communes made a major comeback a century later, in the 1960s. What role have they played in society in recent decades? How do modern communes compare with communes of the past? Which are now the most successful and long-lasting ones? Why is the public so suspicious and resentful of communes?

Articles of Agreement—

In order more effectually to promote the great purposes of human culture; to establish the external relations of life on a basis of wisdom and purity; to apply the principles of justice and love to our social organization in accordance with the laws of Divine Providence; to substitute a system of brotherly coöperation for one of selfish competition; to secure to our children, and to those who may be entrusted to our care, the benefits of the highest physical, intellectual and moral education in the present state of human knowledge, the resources at our command will permit; to institute an attractive, efficient and productive system of industry; to prevent the exercise of worldly anxiety by the competent supply of our necessary wants; to diminish the desire of excessive accumulation by making the acquisition of individual property subservient to upright and disinterested uses; to guarantee to each other the means of physical support and of spiritual progress, and thus to impart a greater freedom, simplicity, truthfulness, refinement and moral dignity to our mode of life,—

We, the undersigned, do unite in a Voluntary Association, to wit:—

ARTICLE 1. The name and style of the Association shall be "(The Brook Farm) Institute of Agriculture and Education." All persons who shall hold one or more shares in the stock of the Association, and shall sign the articles of agreement, or who shall hereafter be admitted by the pleasure of the Association, shall be members thereof.

ART. 2. No religious test shall ever be required of any member of the Association; no authority assumed over individual

SOURCES: The constitution is from John T. Codman, *Brook Farm: Historic and Personal Memoirs* (Boston: Arena Publishing Co., 1894), 11–15. The Ripley item is from *The Harbinger* (1845–46), II, 32. The comments by Emerson items are from C. W. Emerson and W. E. Forbes, eds., *Journals of Ralph Waldo Emerson*, (Boston, 1911), V, 473–74, and from R. W. Emerson's essay, "Self-Reliance," in *Essays and English Traits* (New York: P. F. Collier & Sons, 1909).

freedom of opinion by the Association, nor by any member over another; nor shall anyone be held accountable to the Association except for such acts as violate rights of the members, and the essential principles on which the Association is founded; and in such cases the relation of any member may be suspended, or discontinued, at the pleasure of the Association.

ART. 3. The members of this Association shall own and manage such real and personal estate, in joint stock proprietorship, as may, from time to time, be agreed on, and establish such branches of industry as may be deemed expedient and desirable.

ART. 4. The Association shall provide such employment for all of its members as shall be adapted to their capacities, habits and tastes, and each member shall select and perform such operation of labor, whether corporal or mental, as he shall deem best suited to his own endowments, and the benefit of the Association.

ART. 5. The members of this Association shall be paid for all labor performed under its direction and for its advantage, at a fixed and equal rate, both for men and women. This rate shall not exceed one dollar per day, nor shall more than ten hours in the day be paid for as a day's labor.

ART. 6. The Association shall furnish to all its members, their children and family dependents, houserent, fuel, food and clothing, and all other comforts and advantages possible, at the actual cost, as nearly as the same can be ascertained; but no charge shall be made for education, medical or nursing attendance, or the use of the library, public rooms or baths to the members; nor shall any change be paid for food, rent or fuel by those deprived of labor by sickness, nor for food of children under ten years of age, nor for anything on members over seventy years of age, unless at the special request of the individual by whom the charges are paid, or unless the credits in his favor exceed, or equal, the amount of such charges.

ART. 7. All labor performed for the Association shall be duly credited, and all articles furnished shall be charged, and a full settlement made with every member once every year.

ART. 8. Every child over ten years of age shall be charged for food, clothing, and articles furnished at cost, and shall be credited for his labor, not exceeding fifty cents per day, and on the completion of his education in the Association at the age of twenty, shall be entitled to a certificate of stock, to the amount of credits in his favor, and may be admitted a member of the Association.

ART 9. Every share-holder in the joint-stock proprietorship of the Association, shall be paid on such stock, at the rate of five per cent, annually.

ART. 10. The net profits of the Association remaining in the treasury after the payments of all demands for interests on stock, labor performed, and necessary repairs, and improvements, shall be divided into a number of shares corresponding with the number of days' labor, and every member shall be entitled to one share for every day's labor performed by him.

ART. 11. All payments may be made in certificates of stock at the option of the Association; but in any case of need, to be decided by himself, every member may be permitted to draw on the funds of the treasury of an amount not exceeding the credits in his favor.

ART. 12. The Association shall hold an annual meeting for the choice of officers, and such other necessary business as shall come before them.

ART. 13. The officers of the Association shall be twelve directors, divided into four departments, as follows: first, General Direction; second, Direction of Agriculture; third, Direction of Education; fourth, Direction of Finance; consisting of three persons each, provided that the same persons may be a member of each Direction at the pleasure of the Association.

ART. 14. The Chairman of the General Direction shall be presiding officer in the Association, and together with the Direction of Finance, shall constitute a Board of Trustees, by whom the property of the Association shall be managed.

ART. 15. The General Direction shall oversee and manage the affairs of the Association so that every department shall be carried on in an orderly and efficient manner. Each department shall be under the general supervision of its own Direction, which shall select, and, in accordance with the General Direction, shall appoint, all such overseers, directors and agents, as shall be necessary to the complete and systematic organization of the department, and shall have full authority to appoint such persons to these stations as they shall judge best qualified for the same.

ART. 16. No Directors shall be deemed to possess any rank superior to the other members of the Association, nor shall be chosen in reference to any other consideration than their capacity to serve the Association; nor shall they be paid for their official service except at the rate of one dollar for ten hours in a day, actually employed in official duties.

ART. 17. The Association may, from time to time, adopt such rules and regulations, not inconsistent with the spirit and purpose of the Articles of Agreement, as shall be found expedient and necessary.

George Ripley—

The highest life, of which the nature of man is capable, is rarely witnessed, and then forms a signal exception to the general rule.

It is no wonder that theologians have so generally maintained the doctrine of innate, hereditary depravity. This was the only way, by which they could account for the universal prevalence of limited, distorted, noxious forms of character. The idea, on which their dogma was based sprung from experience, from observation, from a correct knowledge of human action. For what is every man soon taught by the intercourse of life? Certainly, the subjection of the world to the dominion of evil. He learns to calculate on selfishness [and] falsehood. . . .

It is an easy inference, that these monstrous evils are the true growth of human nature, that they belong to man as man. . . . A more profound view, however, shows us that the fault is not in the intrinsic elements of human nature, but in the imperfect institutions under which that nature is trained and developed.

The savage is not guilty of the frightful acts of cruelty . . . because there is a necessary tendency to brutal ferocity in human nature, but because all the influences that have acted on him, all the excitements that have been applied to his passions, have been adapted to cherish the warlike spirit. . . . Place the savage in a different

[*This was signed by*]

GEO. RIPLEY,	WARREN BURTON,	SOPHIA W. RIPLEY,
MINOT PRATT,	SAML. D. ROBBINS,	MARIA J. PRATT,
D. MACK,	GEO. C. LEACH,	NATH. HAWTHORNE,
MARIANNE RIPLEY,	LEML. CAPEN,	MARY ROBBINS.

situation; let the first words that fall upon his ear be those of Christian gentleness and peace; let him be surrounded by generous and loving hearts; another spirit will be manifested; and you would almost say that he had been endowed with another nature.

The man who is so devoted to gaining wealth, that he appears on 'Change like a walking money-bag, . . . with no hope but that of becoming a millionaire, and no fear but that of being surpassed in property by his more lucky neighbor, was not born to be a muck-worm; if he has not the faculties of an archangel, . . . he has the elements of goodness, disinterestedness, a sincere devotion to the common weal, and under more favorable influences, might have been a worthy, useful, and happy man, instead of being a little above the vilest reptile.

We cannot believe that the selfishness, the cold-heartedness, the indifference to truth, the insane devotion to wealth, the fierce antagonisms, the painted hypocrisies, the inward weariness, discontent, apathy, which are everywhere characteristic of the present order of society, have any permanent basis in the nature of man; they are the poisonous weeds that a false system of culture has produced; change the system and you will see the riches of the soil; a golden fruitage will rejoice your eye; but persist in the mode, which the experience of a thousand years has proved defective, and you can anticipate no better results. . . .

The influences of modern society . . . do not give fit nutriment to the noblest forms of character. They do not make man what he is intended to be by the constitution of his nature. They help him not to fulfil the destiny which is assigned to him by the Creator. It is because we are convinced that the Associative Order is the Divine Order, that life in Association is the only true life of the soul, just as harmony with outward nature is essential to the true life of the body, that we are unwilling to give sleep to our eyes or slumber to our eyelids till we witness the commencement of the great and solemn work, which is to emancipate man from the terrible scourges of a false order of society, and reinstate him in the glorious life for which a benignant Providence has adapted his nature.

Emerson's, *Journal* –

Yesterday George and Sophia Ripley, Margaret Fuller and Alcott discussed here the Social Plans [for the Brook Farm community]. I wished to be convinced, to be thawed, to be made nobly mad by the kindlings before my eye of a new dawn of human piety. . . . And not once could I be inflamed, but sat aloof and thoughtless; my voice faltered and fell. It was not the case of persecution which is the palace of spiritual power, but only a room in the Astor House hired for the Transcentalists. I do not wish to remove from my present prison to a prison a little larger. I wish to break all prisons. . . .

Emerson's "Self-Reliance" –

Trust thyself: every heart vibrates to that iron string. Accept the place the divine providence has found for you, the society of your contemporaries, the connection of events. Great men have always done so, and confided themselves childlike to the genius of their age, betraying their perception that the absolutely trustworthy was seated at their heart, working through their hands, predominating in all their being. And we are now men, and must accept— in the highest mind the same transcendent destiny; and not minors and invalids in a protected corner, not cowards fleeing before a revolution, but guides, redeemers and benefactors, obeying the Almighty effort and advancing on Chaos and the Dark. . . . Society everywhere is in conspiracy against the manhood of every one of its members. Society is a joint-stock company, in which the members agree, for the better securing of his bread to each shareholder, to surrender the liberty and culture of the eater. The virtue in most request is conformity. Self-reliance is its aversion. It loves not realities and creators, but names and customs.

Whoso would be a man must be a nonconformist. He who would gather immortal palms must not be hindered by the name of goodness, but must explore if it be goodness. Nothing is at last sacred but the integrity of your own mind. Absolve you to yourself, and you shall have the suffrage of the world. I remember an answer which when quite young I was prompted to make to a valued adviser who was wont to importune me with the dear old doctrines of the church. On my saying, "What have I to do with the sacredness of traditions, if I live wholly from within?" my friend suggested—"But these impulses may be from below, not from above." I replied, "They do not seem to me to be such; but if I am the Devil's child, I will live then from the Devil." No law can be sacred to me but that of my nature. Good and bad are names very readily transferable to that or this; the only right is what is after my constitution; the only wrong what is against it. . . . Expect me not to show cause why I exclude company. Then again, do not tell me, as a good man did to-day, of my obligation to put all poor men in good situations. Are they my poor? I tell thee, thou foolish philanthropist, that I grudge the dollar, the dime, the cent I give to such men as do not belong to men and to whom I do not belong. There is a class of persons to whom by all spiritual affinity I am bought and sold; for them I will go to prison if need be; but your miscellaneous popular charities; the education at college of fools; the building of meeting-houses to the vain end to which many now stand; alms to sots, and the thousand-fold Relief Societies; though I confess with shame I sometimes succumb and give the dollar, it is a wicked dollar, which by and by I shall have the manhood to withhold. . . .

7.7 City versus Country

Though Americans are now mostly urbanized, they have always had an inherent distrust of cities and an attraction for rural values. This can be traced back to our frontier agricultural beginnings. From the historic perspective of the pioneer family farm, the plantation or the small town, cities are always too confining and complex, and too corrupting. This hostility toward urban life, with its corresponding romantic attraction for rural life, is expressed vividly in the works of American intellectuals from Thomas Jefferson in the eighteenth century to the twentieth century architect Frank Lloyd Wright (who wanted to demolish all metropolises). It also shows up in the attitudes of plain citizens.

Occasionally, a debate over the virtues of the city and the country erupts in a popular journal. Such was the case in the columns of The Prairie Farmer, *a mid-Western newspaper, in 1849–1850, when a lover of the city exchanged words with a lover of the country. These letters, from Illinois and Wisconsin, are reprinted below.*

Questions

What, according to these writers, are the virtues of country and of city living? Which one seems to have the better argument?

What are the advantages or disadvantages of city life and country life today? If you could live anywhere in the United States, where would it be?

In Defence of the City—

The powers of language have been completely exhausted in eulogy of country life. The poets have found it a neverfailing theme of song, and have portrayed its beauties in the brightest colors, calculated to captivate every individual possessing the least spark of enthusiasm or romance. Politicians too, prate about the importance of agriculture, the dependence of the other branches upon it, the dignity of labor &c.—claiming the command to "earn our bread by the sweat of our brow," to be one of the greatest blessings ever conferred upon our race. But, notwithstanding the vehemence with which they preach, they are extremely cautious, not to fret their maiden palms by too close familiarity with any implement of labor, preferring that others should practice what they preach. The true statesman, however, regards the uncorrupted morals, unvitiated intelligence and sterling integrity of the country population, as the only hope and salvation of the nation, the chief conservators of the government. The merchant and mechanic also, look forward to a residence in the country, as an elysian to their wearied and jaded spirits. All alike sigh for that independence and freedom from care supposed to exist in the country. Alas! how many foolish, absurd, and erroneous notions have been imbibed? how many individuals and families have been deceived and disappointed? having found, by sad experience, country life, instead of a bed of roses to be one of thorns. That boasted independence to consist in an absolute denial of most of the comforts and refinements of life, indispensably necessary to maintain a creditable station in society. That much desired freedom from anxiety to consist in perplexing care, a thousand unpropitious influences to be guarded against, the best

SOURCES: "A Practical Farmer," Batavia, Kane Co., Illinois, August, 1849, in, *The Prairie Farmer* (November, 1849), IX, pp. 348–349; and "A Lover of the Country," Walworth, Wisconsin, November, 1849, ibid., (January, 1850), X, 18–19.

skill and utmost exertion frequently proving unavailing—vexatious disappointment—unrequitted labor—loss of crops—necessity compelling the reduction of the expense of living to the lowest common denomination, obliged to practice the most rigid parsimony—thus eking out a miserable existence, the slave of toil. Is not this a true story? founded upon observation, and the experience of a large majority of the operative agriculturists. . . .

The opinion of Gov. Briggs and W. C. Calhoun that "ninety out of one hundred young men who emigate from the country to the city fail of success," is now making its second or third tour through the press, and meets with universal approbation—an assertion of this kind needs to be well supported by facts, although emanating from such high authority. For my part I am inclined to withhold my assent until better informed in regard to the premises upon which said assumption is founded. If I mistake not when I first had the pleasure of seeing this statement it referred to mercantile pursuits alone, but as usual in such cases it has taken a wider latitude and now embraces all who emigrate. I cannot conceive any good reason why the young man reared in the country, in industrious, frugal and economical habits should fail of success. My own observation convinces me that a large majority of the young men who abandon agricultural life and engage in other avocations are eminently successful; from the fact that labor is better compensate in the mechanical, mercantile, or manufacturing branches, to say nothing of the professions, than in agricultural pursuits. . . .

I think, Messrs Editors, you much underrate the intelligence of the young men and women of the country, in supposing that the "smooth garb, white hands, and pale countenances of their city cousins," should "warm their imaginations" for city life! Had you said they look upon the tattered garments of the farmer—his hard, careworn and wrinkled visage, marked by exposure to summer's heat and winter's cold—his frame bent and stooping by hard and incessant labor—his hopes blasted by loss of crops from various and unavoidable causes—his over exertion in the most enervating season of the year, frequently necessary in order to secure his crops, the final issue of his toil—a bare pittance, insufficient for a decent support, grudgingly meted out to him by the concentrated capital and combined action of those classes above him, who are supported by his labor. Had you assigned these as reasons to account for the desire which you speak, you certainly would have guessed nearer the truth, and have paid a greater compliment to the sound common sense of our young men and ladies; perhaps too, the young man has not the capital necessary to conduct farming operations profitably; his health may require a less laborious occupation, the monotony of country life may not be congenial to his taste or suit his temperament, or the success of his former associates may "warm his imagination" and prompt him to flee from the hard and uncertain life of the farmer—expecially so here at the present time—and seek a life of comparative ease in the city. And as far as the accumulation of wealth—the pleasures of social intercourse—the amenities of polished society are concerned, his success is equally if not more certain. Let him but practice the same restraining caution, the same rigid economy, and use the same exertion, physical and mental, absolutely necessary to gain wealth or even competence on the farm. . . .

. . . It is for the especial benefit of those who have not been victimized, but liable so to be, in the absence of the knowledge of the hardship and disappointment appertaining to the farmer's life, that I have written this lengthy epistle; perhaps unadvisedly, but nevertheless in earnesty and sincerity.

In Defense of the Country –

In your number for November . . . the public have been enlightened by a communication under the head of "The Poetry and Profit of Country Life." . . . I have too much regard myself for truth on subjects intended more particularly for the young—too much love for the pursuits of agriculture, and too high a regard for this favored country of my adoption, to allow such a tissue of spleen and misrepresentation, to find currency in your journal, without some animadversion.

He must be a bold writer at least, who, at the present day, would say any thing to depreciate the *pursuits of agriculture;* they are so connected with every thing around us which tends to enlighten and enoble the mind, improve the condition of society, and promote the common welfare—and its influences have so direct a bearing in all its ramifications, upon individual and national felicity, that it would seem as if a man must come from some other planet, who could find any thing to say in its disparagement. This writer, however, had made the discovery, in a section of country depending almost exclusively upon agriculture for support, that a city life is far preferable to that of the country. The "luxuries" and "polished society" and "city investments," which are indeed the *"poetry of city life,"* and which will truly prove so, neither more or less, to the young man from the country, seem to outweigh, in his judgment, all the charms of a country life. I would as soon undertake to demonstrate, what is conceived by all at the present day, that a Republican system of Government in this happy country, is more congenial with the spirit of the age, and more conducive to public prosperity and happiness, than any other, as to enter into an argument to prove what is universally admitted, that the pursuits of agriculture are subordinate to no other calling. I have had too much experience with city life, and have too well learned in schools of earlier days the salutary influence of agricultural pursuits upon every thing worthy of being cherished, to dwell a moment in replying to this position of your correspodent; besides, one who has no respect to the opinion of *public writers from the earliest ages,* to the *statesmen, politicians, poets, merchants, mechanics,* and *manufacturers,* all of whom he seems to quote with derision—and who doubt the facts to which he refers, as having been stated by such men as Governor Briggs, and Wm. B. Calhoun of Massachusetts, in reference to the ill success of most of the young who leave the country for the city, will not likely be enlightened by any arguments of mine.

Your correspondent professes to be a *practical farmer,* and yet there is hardly a line in what he calls his "lengthy epistle," but what betrays his *ignorance* or *disgust* with agricultural pursuits, as well also of his ignorance of city life, that he seems so much to admire. He complains of want of fairness in public writers, in speaking of the pursuits of agriculture; that they present the *bright side* of the picture, and leave the *dark side* untouched. Has your corresponent done any better? Has he shown any of the rocks upon which the young men of the city are shipwrecked and lost, and their characters utterly ruined? Has he ever manifested the least sympathy with those who follow the plow? Does he not rather resemble the Eastern dandy, who pays us an occasional visit, and who by the pressure of circumstances, is glad to escape from the "poetry" of "city life" to take breadth for a while, and swell and strut about, with all the aristocracy and pomp of city gentility, and then return to his mother, with his hands browned by the sun, to detail his adventures among the *barbarians of the West?* . . .

We hear of no mourning or complaint, no sighing for the "luxuries" of the East, or for "city investment"—no troubles, real or imaginary, that continually disturb your correspondent, but a steady and cheerful application of the powers of body and mind in improving the beautiful fields provided for the farmer's hand, and a ready and cheerful contribution of his mite, in co-operating with those around, for building up the institutions of our new country, and laying the foundations of its private and public welfare.

Your correspondent has yet many things to learn before he can finish his picture, either of country life, or city life. He must not only be able in some degree to appreciate the privileges and blessings of a country life, of which, as yet, he appears to be insensible—and he should, by a short experience in a city residence, learn something more of the "poetry" of "city life" that *crushes, enslaves,* and *ruins so many thousands of our young men,* who are insensibly made the victims of *dissipation,* of *reckless speculation,* and of *ultimate crime*—but he must also learn something more to be properly qualified for instructing the young on subjects of some importance to them as the one he has so confidently undertaken to discuss—*and that* is to learn the true source of happiness, (which is the great end of life) and not murmur and repine because to this day the smiles of Providence are not as bright as he could wish—and that a *contented mind* is worth more than *gold* or *silver,* to lay the foundations of *successful enterprise,* of *real independence, respectability* and honor.

7.8 The Greening of the City

Frederick Law Olmsted (1822—1903) is the father or urban design and landscape architecture in America. He was among the very first to propose basic solutions to major urban ills. To the growing problems of urban life—crowded tenement living, noise, traffic congestion, air pollution and shattered nerves—his proposed cure was to bring nature back to the city. He would construct tree-lined parks and parkways in as many places as possible.

Olmsted was born in Connecticut and educated at Yale University. He farmed for a while, and travelled widely throughout the country. In 1858 he won a contest to design a park for New York City—Central Park, the first great city park in the United States. Because he fought pitched battles against local politicians, private land developers, race track promoters and amusement park owners who had their own schemes for the Park, he became a controversial figure. Olmsted was later hired to apply his design concepts for other projects, including suburban communities and college campuses. The grounds of the University of California, Berkeley, and of Stanford University were laid out by him.

In 1870 Olmsted presented a comprehensive plan for the redesign of Boston, and gave a public address there on the work he had been doing to improve urban life. Excerpts from the speech follow.

Questions

Who is Olmsted trying to serve and what is he trying to achieve? Is he an avowed enemy of private enterprises? Was he right about the way to solve urban ills? Were his ideas practical?

Do city parks still seem to work as a buffer against the evils of the city? Explain. What amount of city land should be given over to parks and parkways? How should college campuses—yours in particular—be designed to better serve the people who use them daily?

There can be no doubt . . . that, in all our modern civilization, . . . there is a strong drift townward. . . . It also appears to be nearly certain that the recent rapid enlargement of towns and withdrawal of people from rural conditions of living is the result mainly of circumstances of a permanent character. . . . Now, knowing that the average length of . . . life . . . in towns has been much less than in the country, and that the average amount of disease and misery and of vice and crime has been much greater in towns, this would be a very dark prospect for civilization, if it were not that modern Science has beyond all question determined many of the causes of the special evils by which men are afflicted in towns. . . . It has shown . . . that . . . in the interior parts of large and closely built towns, a given quantity of air contains considerably less of the elements which we require to receive through the lungs than the air of the country . . . and that . . . it carries into the lungs highly corrupt and irritating matters, the action of which tends strongly to vitiate all our sources of vigor . . . and very seriously affect the mind and the moral strength. . . . People from the country are even conscious of the effect on their nerves and minds of the street contact—often complaining that they feel confused by it; and if we had no relief from it at all during our waking hours, we should all be conscious of suffering from it. It is upon our opportunities of relief from it, therefore, that not only our comfort in town life, but our ability to main-

SOURCE: F. L. Olmsted, *Public Parks and the Enlargement of Towns* (Cambridge, Mass.: Riverside Press, 1870), 4, 10–11, 15–18, 21–25.

tain a temperate, good-natured, and healthy state of mind, depends. . . .

Air is disinfected by sunlight and foliage. Foliage also acts mechanically to purify the air by screening it. Opportunity and inducement to escape at frequent intervals from the confined and vitiated air of the commercial quarter, and to supply the lungs with air screened and purified by trees, and recently acted upon by sunlight, together with opportunity and inducement to escape from conditions requiring vigilance, wariness, and activity toward other men—if these could be supplied economically, our problem would be solved. . . .

What I would ask is, whether we might not with economy make special provision in some of our streets—in a twentieth or a fiftieth part, if you please, of all—for trees to remain as a permanent furniture of the city? . . . If such [tree-lined] streets were made still broader in some parts, with spacious malls, the advantage would be increased. If each of them were . . . laid out with laterals and connections . . . to serve as a convenient trunkline of communication between two large districts of the town or the business centre and the suburbs, a very great number of people might thus be placed every day under influences counteracting those with which we desire to contend. . . .

We come then to the question: what accommodations for recreation can we provide which shall be so agreeable and so accessible as to be efficiently attractive to the great body of citizens, and . . . also cause those who resort to them for pleasure to subject themselves . . . to conditions strongly counteractive to the special enervating conditions of the town? . . . If I ask myself where I have experienced the most complete gratification of [the gregarious and neighborly instinct] in public and out of doors, among trees, I find that it has been in the promenade of the Champs Élysées. As closely following it I should name other promenades of Europe, and our own . . . New York parks. . . . I have several times seen fifty thousand people participating in them; and the more I have seen of them, the more highly [do] I . . . estimate their values as means of counteracting the evils of town life. . . .

If the great city . . . is to be laid out little by little, and chiefly to suit the views of land-owners, acting only individually, and thinking only of how what they do is to affect the value in the next week or the next year of the few lots that each may hold at the time, the opportunities of so obeying this inclination as at the same time to give the lungs a pure sunny air, to give the mind a suggestion of rest from the devouring eagerness and intellectual strife of town life, will always be few to any, to many will amount to nothing. . . . We want a ground to which people may easily go after their day's work is done, and where they may stroll for an hour, seeing, hearing, and feeling nothing of the bustle and jar of the streets. . . . Practically, what we most want is a simple, broad, open space of clean greensward . . . as a central feature. We want depth of wood enough about it . . . to completely shut out the city from our landscapes. The word *park,* in town nomenclature, should, I think, be reserved for grounds of the character and purpose thus described.

A park fairly well managed near a large town, will surely become a new centre of that town. With the determination of location, size, and boundaries should therefore be associated with duty of arranging new trunk routes of communication between it and the distant parts of the town existing and forecasted. . . . I hope you will agree with me that . . . reserves of ground for the purposes I have referred to should be fixed upon as soon as possible, before the difficulty of arranging them, which arises from private building, shall be greatly more formidable than now . . . for want of a little comprehensive and business-like foresight and study.

Chapter Eight: Environment

8.1 First Impressions
George Percy, 1607

8.2 The Colonial Environment
Virginia Colony Regulations, 1610; Francis Higginson, 1630; Peter Kalm, 1770, Benjamin Franklin

8.3 Creatures Great and Small
Thomas Jefferson, 1785

8.4 Population and Resources
Thomas R. Malthus, 1798

8.5 The Mountain Men
George F. Ruxton, 1849

8.6 Mothering Nature
George Catlin, ca. 1830

8.7 Divinity in Wilderness
Henry David Thoreau, 1851

8.1 First Impressions

"I was almost ravished at the first sight thereof," wrote George Percy of the moment when he first landed in Chesapeake Bay in 1607 and looked at the world about him. The first impressions of Europeans upon setting foot on American soil are captivating, even though the authors usually printed their accounts with an eye to capturing the interest of future backers. The diary of George Percy on the expedition that founded Jamestown is such an account. But from it one gets a lively sense of the trees, flowers, shrubs, animals, fish, rivers, and human inhabitants seen by these first English adventurers.

Questions

How much validity can we give to these observations? What appeals to Percy; what does he fear? Does his account give you a sense of what it must have been like in Virginia almost 400 years ago? How does he compare the new land with the old?

The six and twentieth day of Aprill [1607], about foure a clocke in the morning, wee descried the Land of *Virginia*.

The same day, wee entred into the Bay of *Chesupioc* directly, without any let or hindrance.

There wee landed and discouered a little way: but wee could find nothing worth the speaking of, but faire meddowes and goodly tall Trees; with such Fresh-waters running through the woods, as I was almost rauished at the first sight thereof.

At night, when wee were going aboard, there came the Sauages creeping vpon all foure, from the Hills, like Beares; with their Bowes in their mouthes: [who] charged vs very desperately in the faces, [and] hurt Captaine *Gabri*[*e*]*ll Archer* in both his hands, and a sayler in two places of the body very dangerous[ly]. After they had spent their Arrowes, and felt the sharpnesse of our shot; they retired into the Woods with a great noise, and so left vs. . . .

The eighteenth [or rather 28th] day [of April], we la[u]nched our Shallop. The Captaine and some Gentlemen went in her, and discouered vp the Bay . . . We past through excellent ground full of Flowers of diuers kinds and colours, and as goodly trees as I haue seene, as Cedar, Cipresse, and other kindes. Going a little further, we came into a little plat of ground full of fine and beautifull Strawberries, foure times bigger and better then ours in *England*. . . .

Wee rowed ouer to a point of Land, where wee found a channell; and sounded

SOURCE: George Percy, in Edward Arber, ed., *Travels and Works of John Smith* (Edinburgh: John Grant, 1910), pp. lvii–lxiii.

six, eight, ten, or twelue fathom: which put vs in good comfort. Therefore wee named that point of Land, Cape Comfort. . . . where we saw fiue Sauages running on the shoare.

Presently the Captaine caused the shallop to be manned; so rowing to the shoare, the Captaine called to them in signe of friendship: but they were at first very timersome, vntil they saw the Captain lay his hand on his heart. Vpon that, they laid downe their Bowes and Arrowes, and came very boldly to vs: making signes to come a shoare to their Towne, which is called by the Sauages, *Kecoughtan.*

Wee coasted to their Towne, rowing ouer a Riuer running into the Maine, where these Sauages swam ouer with their Bowes and Arrowes in their mouthes.

When we came ouer to the other side, there was a many of other Sauages, which directed vs to their Towne, where we were entertained by them very kindly. . . .

The thirteenth day [of May], we came to our seating place in *Paspihas* Countrey, some eight miles from the point of Land [of] which I made mention before: where our shippes doe lie so neere the shoare that they are moored to the Trees in six fathom water.

The fourteenth day [of May, 1607], we landed all our men; which were set to worke about the fortification, and others some to watch and ward as it was conuenient.

The eighteenth day, the *Werowance* of *Paspihae* came himselfe to our quarter, with one hundred Sauages armed, which garded him in a very warlike manner with Bowes and Arrowes: thinking at that time to execute their villany. *Paspihae* made great signes to vs to lay our Armes away: but we would not trust him so far. He seeing he could not haue conuenient time to worke his will, at length made signes that he would giue vs as much land as we would desire to take.

As the Sauages were in a throng in the Fort, one of them stole a Hatchet from one of our company; which spied him doing the deed: whereupon he tooke it from him by force, and also strooke him ouer the arme. Presently another Sauage seeing that, came fiercely at our man, with a wooden sword, thinking to beat out his braines. The *Werowance* of *Paspiha* saw vs take to our Armes, [and] went suddenly away with all his company, in great anger. . . .

The nineteenth day, my selfe and three or foure more walking into the Woods, by chance wee espied a pathway like to an *Irish* pace: wee were desirous to knowe whither it would bring vs. Wee traced along some foure miles, all the way as wee went, hauing the pleasantest Suckles, the ground all flowering ouer with faire flowers of sundry colours and kindes, as though it had beene in any Garden or Orchard in *England.* There be many Strawberries, and other fruits vnknowne. Wee saw the Woods full of Cedar and Cypresse trees, with other trees [out of] which issues our sweet Gummes like to Balsam. Wee kept on our way in this Paradise. At length, wee came to a Sauage Towne, where wee found but few people. They told vs the rest were gone a hunting with the *Werowance* of *Paspiha.* We stayed there a while, and had of them Strawberries and other things. . . . One of the Sauages brought vs on the way to the Wood side, where there was a Garden of Tobacco and other fruits and herbes. He gathered Tobacco, and distributed to euery one of vs; [and] so wee departed. . . .

At Port *Cotage* in our Voyage vp the Riuer, we saw a Sauage Boy about the age of ten yeeres, which had a head of haire of a perfect yellow, and a resonable white skinne; which is a Miracle amongst all Sauages.

This Riuer which wee haue discouered is one of the famousest Riuers that euer was found by any Christian. It ebbes and flowes a hundred and threescore miles, where ships of great burthen may harbour in safetie. Wheresoeuer we landed vpon this Riuer, wee saw the goodliest Woods as Beech, Oke, Cedar, Cypresse, Wal-nuts, Sassafras, and Vines in great abundance which hang in great clusters on many Trees, and other Trees vnknowne; and all the grounds bespred with many sweet and delicate flowres of diuers colours and kindes. There are also many fruites as Strawberries, Mulberries, Rasberries, and Fruites vnknown. There are many branches of this Riuer, which runne flowing through the Woods with great plentie of fish of all kindes; as for Sturgeon, all the World cannot be compared to it. In this Countrey I haue seene many great and large Medowes hauing excellent good pasture for many Cattle. There is also great store of Deere both Red and Fallow. There are Beares, Foxes, Otters, Beuers, Muskats, and wild beasts vnknown.

The foure and twentieth day, wee set vp a Crosse at the head of this Riuer, naming it *Kings Riuer,* where we proclaimed *Iames* King of *England* to haue the most right vnto it. When wee had finished and set vp our Crosse, we shipt our men and made for *Iames* Fort. . . .

The fifteenth of June [1607], we had built and finished our Fort, which was triangle wise: hauing three Bulwarkes, [one] at euery corneer, like a halfe Moone, and foure or fiue pieces of Artillerie mounted in them; [thus] we had made our selues sufficiently strong for these Sauages. We had also sowne most of our Corne on two Mountaines. It sprang [had sprung] a mans height from the ground. . . .

Munday the two and twentieth of June 1607, in the morning, Captaine *Newport* in the admirall departed from *Iames* Port for *England.*

8.2 The Colonial Environment

Environmental problems are part of the human condition everywhere. It should come as no surprise, then, that even in the colonial era people expressed concern about them.

The following quotes from original sources provide glimpses of some environmental questions that arose among the English colonists. In 1610, only three years after the founding of Jamestown, the Virginia colony passed a law that clearly reveals an awareness of the problem of water pollution in and around the colonists' living quarters.

But the quality of the air was greatly appreciated, at least by the Puritan clergyman, Francis Higginson. Harassed and driven from England, he came to Salem in 1629 a very sick man. In a book he published in 1630, Higginson compares the air favorably to that of England's. Although he rallied briefly, he died the year his book was published.

Farming created particular environmental issues. European visitors often noticed them more readily than the colonists themselves. The Swedish botanist, Peter Kalm, after closely studying the colonies over a four-year period, wrote very critically about the wastefulness of American farmers. But even the colonists were not totally blind to these matters. Benjamin Franklin, for example, mentioned the negative impact of getting rid of certain birds.

Questions

What ecological problems were created in and around towns and villages? How did farming create problems, especially close to wilderness areas? What incentives did colonial farmers have for conserving their land?

Is there a scientific basis for Higginson's observations?

Should we judge the colonials harshly for their wasteful attitudes toward the environment? Did they lack the right information to act more wisely, or did they simply ignore the knowledge available to them?

Jamestown water law—

There shall no man or woman, Launderer or Launderesse, dare to wash any unclean Linnen, drive bucks [wash clothes], or throw out the water or suds of fowle cloathes, in the open streete, within the Pallizadoes, or within forty foote of the same, nor rench, and make cleane, any kettle, pot, or pan, or such like vessell within twenty foote of the olde well, or new Pumpe: nor shall any one aforesaid, within lesse then a quarter of one mile from the Pallizadoes, dare to doe the necessities of nature, since by these unmanly, slothfull, and loathsome immodesties, the whole Fort may bee choaked, and poisoned, with ill aires, and so corrupt (as in all reason cannot but much infect the same) and this shall they take notice of, and avoide, upon paine of whipping and further punishment, as shall be thought meete, by the censure of a martiall Court.

SOURCES: *For the Colony in Virginia Britannia. Lawes Divine, Morall and Martiall, &tc., 1612,* in Susan Myra Kingsbury, ed. (Washington, D.C.: Government Printing Office, 1933); Francis Higginson, *New England's Plantation* (London, 1630); Peter Kalm, *Travels in North America* (1770); Benjamin Franklin, *Familiar Letters and Miscellaneous Papers,* Jared Sparks, ed. (London, 1833).

Francis Higgison—

THE Temper of the Aire of *New-England* is one speciall thing that commends this place. Experience doth manifest that there is hardly a more healthful place to be found in the World that agreeth better with our English Bodyes. Many that haue beene weake and sickly in old *England*, by comming hither haue beene thoroughly healed and growne healthful and strong. For here is an extraordinarie cleere and dry Aire that is of a most healing nature to all such as of a Cold, Melancholy, Flegmatick, Reumaticke temper of Body. None can more truly speake hereof by their owne experience then my selfe. My Friends that knew me can well tell how verie sickly I haue been and continually in Physick, being much troubled with a tormenting paine through an extraordinarie weaknesse of my Stomacke, and aboundance of Melancholicke humors; but since I came hither on this Voyage, I thanke God I haue had perfect health, and freed from paine and vomitings, hauing a Stomacke to digest the hardest and coursest fare who before could not eat finest meat; and whereas my Stomacke could onely digest and did require such drinke as was both strong and stale, now I can and doe oftentimes drink *New England* water verie well; and I that haue not gone without a Cap for many yeeres together, neither durst leaue off the same, haue now cast away my Cap, and doe weare none at all in the day time: and whereas beforetime I cloathed my selfe with double cloathes and thicke Wastcoats to keepe me warme, euen in the Summer time, I doe now goe as thin clad as any, onely wearing a light Stuffe Cassocke vpon my Shirt and Stuffe Breeches of one thicknesse without Linings. Besides, I haue one of my Children that was formerly most lamentably handled with sore breaking out of both his hands and feet of the Kings-Euill, but since he came hither he is verie well ouer hee was, and there is hope of perfect recouerie shortly, euen by the verie wholesomnesse of the Aire, altering, digesting and drying vp the cold and crude humors of the Body: and therefore I thinke it is a wise course for all cold complections to come to take Physicke in *New-England*: for a sup of *New-Englands* Aire is better then a whole draft of old *Englands* Ale.

Peter Kalm—

The rye grows very poorly in most of the fields, chiefly because of careless agriculture practices and the poor soil, which is seldom or never manured. After the inhabitants have converted into a tillable field a tract of land which was forest for many centuries, and which consequently had a very fine soil, they use it as long as it will bear any crops. When it ceases to bear any they turn it into pastures for the cattle, and take new grain fields in another place, where a rich black soil can be found that has never been used. This kind of agriculture will do for a time; but it will afterwards have bad consequences. A few of the inhabitants, however, treat their fields a little better.

Their eyes are fixed upon the present gain, and they are blind to the future. Their cattle grow poorer daily in quality and size because of hunger. On my travels I observed several wild plants which horses and cows preferred to others, and which grew well on the driest and poorest ground where no others would thrive. But the inhabitants did not know how to turn this to their advantage, owing to the *slight respect for natural history,* that science being here, as in other parts of the world, looked upon as a mere trifle and the pastime of fools. . . . I found everywhere the wisdom and the goodness of the Creator; but too seldom saw any inclination among men to make use of them.

Benajmin Franklin—

In New England they once thought Black-birds useless and mischievous to their corn, they made [laws] to destroy them, the consequence was, the Black-birds were diminished but a kind of worms which devoured their Grass, and which the Black-birds had been used to feed on encreased prodigiously; Their finding their Loss in Grass much greater than their savings in corn they wished again for their Black-birds.

8.3 All Creatures Great and Small

Thomas Jefferson, as we saw in Chapter 4, bristled at the way Count de Buffon characterized the Native Americans. It seemed as if the French naturalist, like most leading European intellectuals, belittled everything about the New World. He demeaned not only the "savages," but also the colonial literary output, the wildlife, and even the domesticated animals. He claimed that North American animals were puny compared to those of Europe. In the following excerpt from Notes on the State of Virginia, *the only full-length book he ever wrote, Jefferson adopts a cool and scientific approach to set the record straight regarding the animals of America.*

Questions

What did most Europeans think of America and the American frontier? Wasn't Buffon something of an exception in his negativism?

How did Jefferson try to refute Buffon's ideas regarding animal life? Which man seems more accurate? Why did Jefferson care so much about Buffon's insults?

What do naturalists say about these matters today?

The opinion advanced by the Count de Buffon, is 1. That the animals common both to the old and new world, are smaller in the latter. 2. That those peculiar to the new, are on a smaller scale. 3. That those which have been domesticated in both, have degenerated in America: and 4. That on the whole it exhibits fewer species. And the reason he thinks is, that the heats of America are less; that more waters are spread over its surface by nature, and fewer of these drained off by the hand of man. In other words, that *heat* is friendly, and *moisture* adverse to the production and development of large quadrupeds. I will not meet this hypothesis on its first doubtful ground, whether the climate of America be comparatively more humid? Because we are not furnished with observations sufficient to decide this question. And though, till it be decided, we are as free to deny, as others are to affirm the fact, yet for a moment let it be supposed. The hypothesis, after this supposition, proceeds to another; that *moisture* is unfriendly to animal growth. The truth of this is inscrutable to us by reasonings a priori. Nature has hidden from us her modus agendi. Our only appeal on such questions is to experience; and I think that experience is against the supposition. It is by the assistance of *heat* and *moisture* that vegetables are elaborated from the elements of earth, air, water, and fire. We accordingly see the more humid climates

SOURCE: Thomas Jefferson, *Notes on the State of Virginia* (1785).

produce the greater quantity of vegetables. Vegetables are mediately or immediately the food of every animal: and in proportion to the quantity of food, we see animals not only multiplied in their numbers, but improved in their bulk, as far as the laws of their nature will admit. . . . Let us take two portions of the earth, Europe and America for instance, sufficiently extensive to give operation to general causes; let us consider the circumstances peculiar to each, and observe their effect on animal nature. America, running through the torrid as well as temperate zone, has more *heat*, collectively taken, than Europe. But Europe, according to our hypothesis, is the *dryest*. They are equally adapted then to animal productions; each being endowed with one of those causes which befriend animal growth, and with one which opposes it. If it be thought unequal to compare Europe with America, which is so much larger, I answer, not more so than to compare America with the whole world. Besides, the purpose of the comparison is to try an hypothesis, which makes the size of animals depend on the *heat* and *moisture* of climate. If therefore we take a region, so extensive as to comprehend a sensible distinction of climate, and so extensive too as that local accidents, or the intercourse of animals on its borders, may not materially affect the size of those in its interior parts, we shall comply with those conditions which the hypothesis may reasonably demand. The objection would be the weaker in the present case, because any intercourse of animals which may take place on the confines of Europe and Asia, is to the advantage of the former, Asia producing certainly larger animals than Europe. . . .

He tells us too that on examining a bear from America, he remarked no difference "in the *shape* of this American bear compared with that of Europe." But adds from Bartram's journal, that an American bear weighed 400 lb. English, equal to 367 lb. French: whereas we find the European bear examined by Mons. D'Aubenton weighed but 141 lb. French. Kalm tells us that the Moose, (Orignal) or (palmated Elk) of America, is as high as a tall horse; and Catesby, that it is about the bigness of a middle sized ox. (I have seen a skeleton 7 feet high, and from good information believe they are often considerably higher. The Elk of Europe is not two-thirds of his height). The wesel is larger in America than in Europe, as may be seen by comparing its dimensions as reported by Mons. D'Aubenton and Kalm. The latter tells us, that the lynx, badger, red fox, and flying squirrel, are the *same* in America as in Europe: by which expression I understand, they are the same in all material circumstances, in size as well as others: for if they were smaller, they would differ from the European. Our grey fox is, by Catesby's account, little different in size and shape from the European fox. . . . The white bear of America is as large as that of Europe. . . .

. . . There remain then the buffalo, red deer, fallow deer, wolf, (the renne), glutton, wild cat, monax, vison, hedgehog, martin, and water rat, of the comparative sizes of which we have not sufficient testimony. It does not appear that Messrs. de Buffon and D'Aubenton have measured, weighed, or seen those of America. It is said of some of them, by some travellers, that they are smaller than the European. But who were these travellers? Have they not been men of a very different description from those who have laid open to us the three quarters of the world? Was natural history the object of their travels? Did they measure or weigh the animals they speak of? or did they not judge of them by sight, or perhaps even from report only? Were they acquainted with the animals of their own country, with which they undertake to compare them? Have they not been so ignorant as often to mistake the species? A true answer to these questions would probably lighten their authority, so as to render it insufficient for the foundation of an hypothesis. How unripe we yet are, for an accurate comparison of the animals of the two countries, will appear from the work on Mons. de Buffon. The ideas we should have formed of the sizes of some animals, from the information he had received at his first publications concerning them, are very different from what his subsequent communications give us. And indeed his candour in this can never be too much praised. One sentence of his book must do him immortal honour. "I love as much a person who corrects me in an error as another who teaches me a truth, because in effect an error corrected is a truth." He seems to have thought the Cabiai he first examined wanted little of its full growth. "It was not yet full grown." Yet he weighed but 46½ lb. and he found afterwards, that these animals, when full grown, weigh 100 lb. He had supposed, from the examination of a jaguar, said to be two years old, which weighed but 16 lb. 12 oz. that, when he should have acquired his full growth, he would not be larger than a middle sized dog. But a subsequent account raises his weight to 200 lb. Further information will, doubtless, produce further corrections. The wonder is, not that there is yet something in this great work to correct, but that there is so little. The result of this view then is, that of 26 quadrupeds common to both countries, 7 are said to be larger in America, 7 of equal size, and 12 not sufficienly examined. So that the first table impeaches the first member of the assertion, that of the animals common to both countries, the American are smallest, "and that without any exception." It shews it not just, in all the latitude in which its author has advanced it, and probably not to such a degree as to found a distinction between the two countries. . . . [of] quadrupeds . . . which are domestic in both countries. That some of these, in some parts of America, have become less than their original stock, is doubtless true; and the reason is very obvious. In a thinly peopled country, the spontaneous productions of the forests and waste fields are sufficient to support indifferently the domestic animals of the farmer, with a very little aid from him in the severest and scarcest season. He therefore finds it more convenient to receive them from the hand of nature in that indifferent state, than to keep up their size by a care and nourishment which would cost him much labour. If, on this low fare, these animals dwindle, it is no more than they do in those parts of Europe where the poverty of the soil, or poverty of the owner, reduces them to the same scanty subsistance. It is the uniform effect of one and the same cause, whether acting on this or that side of the globe . It would be erring therefore against that rule of philosophy, which teaches us to ascribe like effects to like causes, should we impute this diminution in size in America to any imbecility or want of uniformity in the operations of nature. It may be affirmed with truth that, in those countries, and with those individuals of America, where necessity or curiosity has produced equal attention as in Europe to the nourishment of animals, the horses, cattle, sheep, and hogs of the one continent are as large as those of the other. There are particular instances, well attested, where individuals of this country have imported good breeders from England, and have improved their size by care in the course of some years. To make a fair comparison between the two countries, it will not answer to bring together animals of what might be deemed the middle or ordinary size of their species; because an error in judging of that middle or ordinary size would vary the result of the comparison. . . . In Connecticut and Rhode-Island, where the climate is favorable to the production of grass, bullocks have been slaughtered which weighed 2500, 2200, and 2100 lb. nett; and those of 1800 lb. have been frequent. I have seen a hog weigh 1050 lb. after the blood, bowels, and hair had been taken from him. Before he was killed an attempt was made to weigh him with a pair of steel-yards, graduated to 1200 lb. but he weighed more. Yet this hog was probably not within fifty generations of the European stock. I am well informed of another which weighed 1100 lb. gross. Asses have been still more neglected than any other domestic animal in America. They are neither fed nor housed in the most rigorous season of the year. Yet they are larger than those measured by Mons. D'Aubenton, of 3 feet 7¼ inches, 3 feet 4 inches, and 3 feet 2½ inches, the latter weighing only 215.8 lb. These sizes, I suppose have been produced by the same negligence in Europe, which has produced a like diminution here. Where care has been taken of them on that side of the water, they have been raised to a size bordering on that of the horse; not by the *heat* and *dryness* of the climate, but by good food and shelter. Goats have been also much neglected in America. Yet they are very prolific here, bearing twice or three times a year, and from one to five kids at a birth. Mons. de Buffon has been sensible of a difference in this circumstance in favour of America. But what are their greatest weights I cannot say. A large sheep here weights 100 lb. I observe Mons. D'Aubenton calls a ram of 62 lb. one of the middle size. But to say what are the extremes of growth in these and the other domestic animals of America, would require information of which no one individual is possessed. The weights actually known and stated in the third table preceeding will suffice to shew, that we may conclude, on probable grounds, that, with equal food and care, the climate of America will preserve the races of domestic animals as large as the European stock from which they are derived; and consequently that the third member of Mons. de Buffon's assertion, that the domestic animals are subject to degeneration from the climate of America, is as probably wrong as the first and second were certainly so. . . .

8.4 Population and Resources

Thomas Robert Malthus, an English preacher, was the first writer to examine the relationship between population and natural resources. In his "First Essay on Population," published in 1798, he presented a pessimistic assessment and a dismal prophesy for the future. It was more in keeping with European perspectives than American. America's population doubled every few decades, but, then again, it also had vast resources and "empty" spaces, so that it seemed senseless to give much thought to this alleged problem of crowding or the exhaustion of resources. America was perceived as immune to the problem, an exception to the rule.

Questions

What did Malthus predict? Even if Americans had taken Malthus's warning to heart, what could they have done about it?

If population growth is a problem now, what are the alternatives for dealing with it? Are restrictions on the birth rate, on immigration, or on the use of resources warranted at this time? If so, how can such restrictions be instituted fairly and democratically so as not to interfere with personal liberty, normal market forces or private business initiative?

I think I may fairly make two postulata.

First, That food is necessary to the existence of man.

Secondly, That the passion between the sexes is necessary, and will remain nearly in its present state. . . .

Assuming then, my postulata, as granted, I say, that the power of population is indefinitely greater than the power in the earth to produce subsistence for man.

Population, when unchecked, increases in a geometrical ration. Subsistence increases only in an arithmetical ratio. A slight acquaintance with numbers will shew the immensity of the first power in comparison of the second.

By that law of our nature which makes food necessary to the life of man, the effects of these two unequal powers must be kept equal.

This implies a strong and constantly operating check on population from the difficulty of subsistence. This difficulty must fall some where; and must necessarily be severely felt by a large portion of mankind.

Through the animal and vegetable kingdoms, nature has scattered the seeds of life abroad with the most profuse and liberal hand. She had been comparatively sparing in the room, and the nourishment necessary to rear them. The germs of existence contained in this spot of earth, with ample food, and ample room to expand in, would fill millions of worlds in the course of a few thousand years. Necessity, that imperious all pervading law of nature, restrains them within the prescribed bounds. The race of plants, and the race of animals shrink under this great restrictive law. And the race of man cannot, by any effort of reason, escape from it. Among plants and animals its effect are waste of seed, sickness, and premature death. Among mankind, misery and vice. The former, misery, is an absolutely necessary consequence of it. Vice is a highly probable consequence, and we therefore see it abundantly pre-

SOURCE: Thomas Robert Malthus, *First Essay on Population* (1798).

vail; but it ought not, perhaps, to be called an absolutely necessary consequence. The ordeal of virtue is to resist all temptation to evil.

This natural inequality of the two powers of population, and of production in the earth, and that great law of our nature which must constantly keep their effects equal, form the great difficulty that to me appears insurmountable in the way to the perfectibility of society. All other arguments are of slight and subordinate consideration in comparison of this. I see no way by which man can escape from the weight of this law which pervades all animated nature. No fancied equality, no agrarian regulations in their utmost extent, could remove the pressure of it even for a single century. And it appears, therefore, to be decisive against the possible existence of a society, all the members of which, should live in ease, happiness, and comparative leisure; and feel no anxiety about providing the means of subsistence for themselves and families.

Consequently, if the premises are just, the argument is conclusive against the perfectibility of the mass of mankind.

8.5 The Mountain Men

From the first colonial adventures to the end of the 1840s fur trading was a principle source of frontier activity in America. There were probably never more than a thousand mountain men tracking beaver in the mountain passes from Mexico to Canada, but their exploits were legendary and their adventures read like fiction. The biographies of Kit Carson, Jim Bridger, and Jedediah Smith are the stuff of heroes. As they left beaver trapping they usually went on to become traders, buffalo hunters, army scouts, or guides for pioneer wagon trains. An Englishman, George F. Ruxton, spend some months living among them in 1847, just the time that the beaver was beginning to fade commercially. He wrote of his adventurers. A brief section from his account follows.

Questions

From this excerpt what can you assume about the mountain man's overall perception of wild nature—the animals, forests, other humans, etc.? Did they have any concept of living with nature on its own terms? How damaging were they and their tools to the environment? This is not a particularly attractive view of the fur men as human beings, and yet they become heroic figures. Can you explain why?

How have Americans been affected by the presence of the western frontier? Would we not be a very different nation if it had not existed?

The trappers of the Rocky Mountains belong to a "genus" more approximating to the primitive savage than perhaps any other class of civilized man. Their lives being spent in the remote wilderness of the mountains, with no other companion than Nature herself, their habits and character assume a most singular cast of simplicity mingled with ferocity, appearing to take their colouring from the scenes and objects which surround them. Knowing no wants save those of nature, their sole care is to procure sufficient food to support life, and the necessary clothing to protect them from the rigorous climate. This, with the assistance of their trusty rifles, they are generally able to effect, but sometimes at the expense of great peril and hardship. When engaged in their avocation, the natural instinct of primitive man is ever alive, for the purpose of guarding against danger and the provision of necessary food.

Keen observers of nature, they rival the beasts of prey in discovering the haunts and habits of game, and in their skill and cunning in capturing it. Constantly exposed to perils of all kinds, they become callous to any feeling of danger, and destroy humans as well as animal life with as little scruple and as freely as they expose their own. Of laws, human or divine, they neither know nor care to know. Their wish is their law, and to attain it they do not scruple as to ways and means. Firm friends and bitter enemies, with them it is "a word and a blow," and the blow often first. They may have good qualities, but they are those of the animal; and people fond of giving hard names call them revengeful, bloodthirsty, drunkards (when the wherewithal is to be had), gamblers, regardless of the laws of *meum* and *tuum*—in fact, "White Indians." However, there are exceptions, and I *have* met honest mountain-men. Their animal qualities, however, are undeniable. Strong, active, hardy as bears, daring, expert in the use of their weapons, they are just what uncivilised white man might be supposed to be in a brute state, depending upon his instinct for the support of life. Not a hole or corner in the vast wilderness of the "Far West" but has been ransacked by these hardy men. From the Mississippi to the mouth of the Colorado of the West, from the frozen regions of the North to the Gila in Mexico, the beaver-hunter has set his traps in every creek and stream. All this vast country, but for the daring enterprise of these men, would be even now a *terra incognita* to geographers, as indeed a great portion still is; but there is not an acre that has not been passed and repassed by the trappers in their perilous excursions. The mountains and streams still retain the names assigned to them by the rude hunters; and these alone are the hardy pioneers who have paved the way for the settlement of the western country.

Trappers are of two kinds, the "hired hand" and the "free trapper:" the former hired for the hunt by the fur companies; the latter, supplied with animals and traps by the company, is paid a certain price for his furs and peltries.

There is also the trapper "on his own hook;" but this class is very small. He has his own animals and traps, hunts where he chooses, and sells his peltries to whom he pleases.

On starting for a hunt, the trapper fits himself out with the necessary equipment, either from the Indian trading-forts, or from some of the petty traders—coureurs des bois—who frequent the western country. This equipment consists usually of two or three horses or mules—one for saddle, the others for packs—and six traps, which are carried in a bag of leather

SOURCE: George F. Ruxton, *Adventures in Mexico and the Rocky Mountains* (London, 1849), 241–246.

called a *trap-sack.* Ammunition, a few pounds of tobacco, dressed deer-skins for mocassins, &c., are carried in a wallet of dressed buffalo-skin, called a possible-sack. His "possibles" and "trap-sack" are generally carried on the saddle-mule when hunting, the others being packed with the furs. . . .

Thus provided, and having determined the locality of his trapping-ground, he starts to the mountains, sometimes alone, sometimes with three or four in company, as soon as the breaking up of the ice allows him to commence operations. Arrived on his hunting-grounds, he follows the creeks and streams, keeping a sharp look-out for "sign." If he sees a prostrate cotton-wood tree, he examines it to discover if it be the work of beaver—whether "thrown" for the purpose of food, or to dam the stream. The track of the beaver on the mud or sand under the bank is also examined; and if the "sign" be fresh, he sets his trap in the run of the animal, hiding it under water, and attaching it by a stout chain to a picket driven in the bank, or to a bush or tree. A "float-stick" is made fast to the trap by a cord a few feet long, which, if the animal carry away the trap, floats on the water and points out its position. The trap is baited with the "medicine," an oily substance obtained from a gland in the scrotum of the beaver, but distinct from the testes. A stick is dipped into this and planted over the trap; and the beaver, attracted by the smell, and wishing a close inspection, very foolishly puts his leg into the trap, and is a "gone beaver."

When a lodge is discovered, the trap is set at the edge of the dam, at the point where the animal passes from deep to shoal water, and always under water. Early in the morning the hunter mounts his mule and examines the traps. The captured animals are skinned, and the tails, which are a great dainty, carefully packed into camp. The skin is then stretched over a hoop or framework of osier-twigs, and is allowed to dry, the flesh and fatty substance being carefully scraped (grained). When dry, it is folded into a square sheet, the fur turned inwards, and the bundle, containing about ten to twenty skins, tightly pressed and corded, and is ready for transportation. . . .

. . . All the wits of the subtle savage are called into play to gain an advantage over the wily woodsman; but with the natural instinct of primitive man, the white hunter has the advantages of a civilised mind, and, thus provided, seldom fails to outwit, under equal advantages, the cunning savage.

Sometimes, following on his trail, the Indian watches him set up traps on a shrubbelted stream, and, passing up the bed, like Bruce of old, so that he may leave no track, he lies in wait in the bushes until the hunter comes to examine his carefully-set traps. Then, waiting until he approaches his ambushment within a few feet, whiz flies the home-drawn arrow, never failing at such close quarters to bring the victim to the ground. For one white scalp, however, that dangles in the smoke of an Indian's lodge, a dozen black ones, at the end of the hunt, ornament the camp-fires of the rendezvous.

At a certain time, when the hunt is over, or they have loaded their pack-animals, the trappers proceed to the "rendezvous," the locality of which has been previously agreed upon; and here the traders and agents of the fur companies await them, with such assortment of goods as their hardy customers may require, including generally a fair supply of alcohol. The trappers drop in singly and in small bands, bring their packs of beaver to this mountain market, not unfrequently to the value of a thousand dollars each, the produce of one hunt. The dissipation of the "rendezvous," however, soon turns the trapper's pocket inside out. The goods brought by the traders, although of the most inferior quality, are sold at enormous prices:—Coffee, twenty and thirty shillings a pint-cup, which is the usual measure; tobacco fetches ten and fifteen shillings a plug; alcohol, from twenty to fifty shillings a pint; gunpowder, sixteen shillings a pint-cup; and all other articles at proportionably exorbitant prices.

The "beaver" is purchased at from two to eight dollars per pound; the Hudson's Bay Company alone buying it by the pluie, or "plew," that is, the whole skin, giving a certain price for skins, whether of old beaver or "kittens."

The rendezvous is one continued scene of drunkenness, gambling, and brawling and fighting, as long as the money and credit of the trappers last. Seated, Indian fashion, round the fires, with a blanket spread before them, groups are seen with their "decks" of cards, playing at "euker," "poker," and "seven-up," the regular mountain-games. The stakes are "beaver," which here is current coin; and when the fur is gone, their horses, mules, rifles, and shirts, hunting-packs, and *breeches*, are staked. Daring gamblers make the rounds of the camp, challenging each other to play for the trapper's highest stake,—his horse, his squaw (if he have one), and, as once happened, his scalp. There goes "hos and beaver!" is the mountain expression when any great loss is sustained; and, sooner or later, "hos and beaver" invariably find their way into the insatiable pockets of the traders. A trapper often squanders the produce of his hunt, amounting to hundreds of dollars, in a couple of hours; and supplied on credit with another equipment, leaves the rendezvous for another expedition, which has the same result time after time; although one tolerably successful hunt would enable him to return to the settlements and civilised life, with an ample sum to purchase and stock a farm, and enjoy himself in ease and comfort the remainder of his days.

An old trapper, a French Canadian, assured me that he had received fifteen thousand dollars for beaver during a sojourn of twenty years in the mountains. Every year he resolved in his mind to return to Canada, and, with this object, always converted his fur into cash; but a fortnight at the "rendezvous" always cleaned him out, and, at the end of twenty years, he had not even credit sufficient to buy a pound of powder.

These annual gatherings are often the scene of bloody duels, for over their cups and cards no men are more quarrelsome than your mountaineers. Rifles, at twenty paces, settle all differences, and, as may be imagined, the fall of one or other of the combatants is certain, or, as sometimes happens, both fall to the word "fire."

8.6 Mothering Nature

Before the Civil War, the Great Plains and Rockies were off-limits to all but the heartiest of adventurers. Americans who came there to carve out new farms, or to hunt and buy furs, cared little or nothing about the destruction of the beaver or the buffalo. They regarded the Indians as their mortal enemies George Catlin (1796–1872), who devoted his life mainly to studying and painting Indians—his Indian portraits now grace the Smithsonian Institution—had a different view. He became alarmed at the dangers inherent in annihilating the native peoples and decimating the wildlife. In the excerpt from his writings reprinted here, Catlin introduces the germ of an idea about preservation that would take shape a generation later.

Questions

What did Catlin fear, if the losses continued? What did he propose should be done about the problem?

If more of the public domain had been reserved for parks in the early years of the republic, would the nation be better or worse off today? In what way?

How much wilderness land should be preserved? Should it be preserved in a natural state, or "improved"—"restocked" with wildlife, and plant life?

The basic federal laws for preserving wild nature also now encourages the preservation of historic buildings. How many old structures—say, pre-Civil War homes, battlegrounds, cemeteries, etc.—would you preserve? How would you decide which to keep and which to destroy?

When I first arrived at this place, on my way up the river, which was in the month of May, in 1832, and had taken up my lodgings in the Fur Company's Fort, . . . [I was told] that only a few days before I arrived (when an immense herd of buffaloes had showed themselves on the opposite side of the river, almost blackening the plains for a great distance), a party of five or six hundred Sioux Indians on horseback, forded the river about mid-day, and spending a few hours amongst them, recrossed the river at sun-down and came into the Fort with *fourteen hundred fresh buffalo tongues*, which were thrown down in a mass, and for which they required but a

SOURCE: George Catlin, *North American Indians: Being Letters and Notes on their Manners, Customs, and Conditions, Writeen during Eight Years' Travel Amongst the Wildest Tribes in North America, 1832–1839* (2 vol.; London, 1880), I, 288–295. Some obvious errors in spelling and punctuation have been corrected.

few gallons of whiskey, which was soon demolished, indulging them in a little, and harmless carouse.

This profligate waste of the lives of these noble and useful animals, when, from all that I could learn, not a skin or a pound of the meat (except tongues), was brought in, fully supports me in the seemingly extravagant predictions that I have made as to their extinction, which I am certain is near at hand. . . .

From the above remarks it will be seen, that not only the red men, but red men and white, have aimed destruction at the race of these animals. . . .

Thus much I wrote of the buffaloes, and . . . of the fate that awaits them; and before I closed my book [i.e., diary or journal], I strolled out one day to the shade of a plum-tree, where I lay in the grass on a favourite bluff, and wrote thus:—

It is generally supposed, and familiarly said that a man '*falls*' into a reverie; but I seated myself in the shade a few minutes since, resolved to *force* myself into one; and for this purpose I laid open a small pocket-map of North America. . . .

The world turned gently around, and I examined its surface; continent after continent passed under my eye, and yet amidst them all, I saw not the vast and vivid green, that is spread like a carpet over the Western wilds of my own country. I saw not elsewhere in the world, the myriad herds of buffaloes—my eyes scanned in vain for they were not. And when I turned again to the wilds of my native land, I beheld them all in motion! For the distance of several hundreds of miles from North to South, they were wheeling about in vast columns and herds—some were scattered, and ran with furious wildness—some lay dead, and others were pawing the earth for a hiding-place—some were were sinking down and dying, gushing out their life's blood in deep-drawn sighs—and others were contending in furious battle for the life they possessed, and the ground that they stood upon. They had long since assembled from the thickets, and secret haunts of the deep forest, into the midst of the treeless and bushless plains, as the place for their safety. I could see in an hundred places, amid the wheeling bands, and on their skirts and flanks, the leaping wild horse darting among them. I saw not the arrows, nor heard the twang of the sinewy bows that sent them; but I saw their victims fall!—on other steeds that rushed along their sides, I saw the glistening lances, which seemed to lay across them; their blades were blazing in the sun, till dipped in blood, and then I lost them! In other parts (and there were many), the vivid flash of *fire-arms* was seen—*their* victims fell too, and over their dead bodies hung suspended in air, little clouds of whitened smoke, from under which the flying horsemen had darted forward to mingle again with, and deal death to, the trampling throng.

. . . Hundreds and thousands were strewed upon the plains—they were flayed, and their reddened carcasses left; and about them bands of wolves, and dogs, and buzzards were seen devouring them. Contiguous, and in sight, were the distant and feeble smokes of wigwams and villages, where the skins were dragged, and dressed for white man's luxury! where they were all sold for *whiskey*, and the poor Indians lay drunk, and were crying. I cast my eyes into the towns and cities of the East, and there I beheld buffalo robes hanging at almost every door for traffic; and I saw also the curling smokes of a thousand *Stills*—and I said, "Oh insatiable man, is thy avarice such! wouldst thou tear the skin from the back of the last animal of this noble race, *and rob thy fellow-man of his meat, and for it give him poison!'*

Many are the rudenesses and wilds in Nature's works, which are destined to fall before the deadly axe and desolating hands of cultivating man: and so amongst her ranks of *living,* of beast and human, we often find noble stamps, or beautiful colours, to which our admiration clings; and even in the overwhelming march of civilised improvements and refinements do we love to cherish their existence, and lend our efforts to preserve them in their primitive rudeness. Such of Nature's works are always worthy of our preservation and protection: and the further we become separated (and the face of the country) from that pristine wildness and beauty, the more pleasure does the mind of enlightened man feel in recurring to those scenes, when he can have them preserved for his eyes and his mind to dwell upon.

Of such "rudenesses and wilds," Nature has nowhere presented more beautiful and lovely scenes, than those of the vast prairies of the West; and of *man* and *beast,* no nobler specimens than those who inhabit them—the *Indian* and the *buffalo*—joint and original tenants of the soil, and fugitives together from the approach of civilised man; they have fled to the great plains of the West, and there, under an equal doom, they have taken up their *last abode,* where their race will expire, and their bones will bleach together. . . .

Reader! Listen to the following calculations, and forget them not. The buffaloes (the quadrupeds from whose backs your beautiful robes were taken, and whose myriads were once spread over the whole country, from the Rocky Mountains to the Atlantic Ocean) have recently fled before the appalling appearance of civilised man, and taken up their abode and pasturage amid the almost boundless prairies of the West. An instinctive dread of their deadly foes, who made an easy prey of them whilst grazing in the forest, has led them to seek the midst of the vast and treeless plains of grass, as the spot where they would be least exposed to the assaults of their enemies; and it is exclusively in those desolate fields of silence (yet of beauty) that they are to be found—and over these vast steppes, or prairies, have they fled, like the Indian, towards the "setting sun;" until their bands have been crowded together, and their limits confined to a narrow strip of country on this side of the Rocky Mountains.

This strip of country, which extends from the province of Mexico to Lake Winnipeg on the North, is almost one entire plain of grass, which is, and ever must be, useless to cultivating man. It is here, and here chiefly, that the buffaloes dwell; and with, and hovering about them, live and flourish the tribes of Indians, whom God made for the enjoyment of that fair land and its luxuries.

It is melancholy contemplation for one who has travelled as I have, through these realms, and seen this noble animal in all its pride and glory, to contemplate it so rapidly wasting from the world, drawing the irresistible conclusion too, which one must do, that its species is soon to be extinguished, and with it the peace and happiness (if not the actual existence) of the tribes of Indians who are joint tenants with them, in the occupancy of these vast and idle plains.

And what a splendid contemplation too, when one (who has travelled these realms, and can duly appreciate them) imagines them as they *might* in future be seen (by some great protecting policy of government) preserved in their pristine beauty and wildness, in a *magnificent park,* where the world could see for ages to come, the native Indian in his classic attire, galloping his wild horse, with sinewy bow, and shield and lance, amid the fleeting herds of elks buffaloes. What a beautiful and thrilling specimen for America to preserve and hold up to the view of her refined citizens and the world, in future ages! A *nation's Park*, containing man and beast, in all the wild and freshness of their nature's beauty!

I would ask no other monument to my memory, nor any enrolment of my name amongst the famous dead, than the reputation of having been the founder of such an institution. . . .

8.7 Divinity in Wilderness

Henry David Thoreau, whose classic essay "On Civil Disobedience" was presented earlier (Chapter 2), is renowned for his writings on nature. He studied the rural parts of his native Concord, Massachusetts and he roamed the wilds endlessly, keeping extensive journals. He did not seek grandeur in nature, but simplicity. The mutilation of nature saddened him. He valued nature for its beauty and recreational benefits, as well as for its religious implications; the natural world provides a window for glimpsing divinity. His most famous work, Walden *(1854), summarizes many of his views about nature, individualism, and religion. It is a critical commentary on the spread of the industrial-urban order.*

In 1851 he presented a lecture in his home town on the theme of "Walking" (excerpted below) that embodies many of his views, including his belief in the West as a symbol of free and unspoiled nature. Philosophically he is a Transcendentalist. Wilderness enthusiasts consider him a hero, a man before his time.

Questions

What does Thoreau see in wild nature? How does it affect his daily life? If his ideas about preserving wilderness had prevailed, would the nation be better or worse off today? How would it be different?

He has gained stature and popularity as a nature advocate in the last generation. Does this reflect a genuine revolution in sentiment, or are people merely giving lip service to his "quaint" beliefs?

I wish to speak a word for Nature, for absolute freedom and wildness, as contrasted with a freedom and culture merely civil. . . .

When we walk, we naturally go to the fields and woods: what would become of us, if we walked only in a garden or a mall? . . . Of course it is of no use to direct our steps to the woods, if they do not carry us thither. I am alarmed when it happens that I have walked a mile into the woods bodily, without getting there in spirit. In my afternoon walk I would fain forget all my morning occupations and my obligations to society. But it sometimes happens that I cannot easily shake off the village. . . .

Nowadays almost all man's improvements, so called, as the building of houses, and the cutting down of the forest and of all large trees, simply deform the landscape, and make it more and more tame and cheap. A people who would begin by burning the fences and let the forest stand! . . .

I can easily walk ten, fifteen, twenty, any number of miles, commencing at my own door, without going by any house, without crossing a road except where the fox and the mink do: first along by the river, and then the brook, and then the meadow and the woodside. There are square miles in my vicinity which have no inhabitant. From many a hill I can see civilization and the abodes of man afar. The farmers and their works are scarcely more obvious than woodchucks and their burrows. Man and his affairs, church and state and school, trade and commerce, and manufacturers and agriculture, even politics, the most alarming of them all,—I am pleased to see how little space they occupy in the landscape.

At present, in this vicinity, the best part of the land is not private property; the landscape is not owned, and the walker enjoys comparative freedom. But possibly the day will come when it will be partitioned off into so-called pleasure-grounds, in which a few will take a narrow and exclusive pleasure only,—when fences shall be multiplied, and man-traps and other engines invented to confine men to the *public* road, and walking over the surface of God's earth shall be construed to mean trespassing on some gentlemen's grounds. . . .

What is it that makes it so hard sometimes to determine whither we will walk? I believe that there is a subtle magnetism in Nature, which, if we unconsciously yield to it, will direct us aright. It is not indifferent to us which way we walk. There is a right way; but we are very liable from heedlessness and stupidity to take the wrong one. . . .

When I go out of the house for a walk, uncertain as yet whither I will blend my steps, and submit myself to my instinct to decide for me. I find strange and whimsical as it may seem, that I finally and inevitably settle southwest, toward some particular wood or meadow or deserted pasture or hill in that direction. My needle is slow to settle,—varies a few degrees, and does not always point due southwest, it is true, and it has good authority for this variation, but it always settles between west and south-southwest. The future lies that way to me, and the earth seems more unexhausted and richer on that side. . . . Eastward I go only by force; but westward I go free. Thither no business leads me. It is hard for me to believe that I shall find fair landscapes or sufficient wildness and freedom behind the eastern horizon. I am not excited by the prospect of a walk thither; but I believe that the forest which I see in the western horizon stretches uninterruptedly toward the setting sun, and

SOURCE: Henry David Thoreau, "Walking," *The Writings of Henry David Thoreau* (11 vols.; Boston, 1893), IX, 251, 258–260, 254–267, 275, 277–280, 292.

there are no towns nor cities in it of enough consequence to disturb me. Let me live where I will, on this side is the city, on that the wilderness, and ever I am leaving the city more and more, and withdrawing into the wilderness. I should not lay so much stress on this fact, if I did not believe that something like this is the prevailing tendency of my countrymen. I must walk toward Oregon, and not toward Europe. And that way the nation is moving, and I may say that mankind progress from east to west. . . .

We go eastward to realize history and study the works of art and literature, retracing the steps of the race; we go westward as into the future, with a spirit of enterprise and adventure. The Atlantic is a Lethean stream, in our passage over which we have had an opportunity to forget the Old World and its institutions. . . .

The West of which I speak is but another name for the Wild; and what I have been preparing to say is, that in Wildness is the preservation of the World. Every tree sends its fibres forth in search of the Wild. The cities import it at any price. Men plough and sail for it. From the forest and wilderness come the tonics and barks which brace mankind. Our ancestors were savages. The story of Romulus and Remus being suckled by a wolf is not a meaningless fable. The founders of every state which has risen to eminence have drawn their nourishment and vigor from a similar wild source. It was because the children of the Empire were not suckled by the wolf that they were conquered and displaced by the children of the northern forests who were.

I believe in the forest, and in the meadow, and in the night in which the corn grows. We require an infusion of hemlock-spruce or arbor vitae in our tea. . . .

I would not have every man nor every part of a man cultivated, any more than I would have every acre of earth cultivated; part will be tillage, but the greater part will be meadow and forest, not only serving an immediate use, but preparing a mould against a distant future, by the annual decay of the vegetation which it supports. . . .

Ben Jonson exclaims,—

How near to good is what is fair!

So I would say,—

How near to good is what is wild!

Life consists with wildness. The most alive is the wildest. Not yet subdued to man, its presence refreshes him. One who pressed forward incessantly and never rested from his labors, who grew fast and made infinite demands on life, would always find himself in a new country or wilderness, and surrounded by the raw material of life. He would be climbing over the prostrate stems of primitive forest-trees.

Hope and the future for me are not in lawns and cultivated fields, not in towns and cities, but in the impervious and quaking swamps. . . . I derive more of my subsistence from the swamps which surround my native town than from the cultivated gardens in the village. . . .

My spirits infallibly rise in proportion to the outward dreariness. Give me the ocean, the desert, or the wilderness! . . . A town is saved, not more by the righteous men in it than by the woods and swamps that surround it. A township where one primitive forest waves above while another primitive forest rots below,—such a town is fitted to raise not only corn and potatoes, but poets and philosophers for the coming ages. In such a soil grew Homer and Confucius and the rest, and out of such a wilderness comes the Reformer eating locusts and wild honey.